The Peace In Between

This volume examines the causes and purposes of 'post-conflict' violence.

The end of a war is generally expected to be followed by an end to collective violence, as the term 'post-conflict' that came into general usage in the 1990s signifies. In reality, however, various forms of deadly violence continue and sometimes even increase after the big guns have been silenced and a peace agreement signed. Explanations for this and other kinds of violence fall roughly into two broad categories – those that stress the legacies of the war and those that focus on the conditions of the peace. There are significant gaps in the literature, most importantly arising from the common premise that there is one, predominant type of post-war situation. This 'post-war state' is often endowed with certain generic features that predispose it towards violence, such as a weak state, criminal elements generated by the war-time economy, demobilized but not demilitarized or reintegrated ex-combatants, impunity and rapid liberalization.

The premise of this volume differs. It argues that features which constrain or encourage violence stack up in ways to create distinct and different types of post-war environments. Critical factors that shape the post-war environment in this respect lie in the war-to-peace transition itself, above all the outcome of the war in terms of military and political power and its relationship to social hierarchies of power, normative understandings of the post-war order and the international context.

This book will be of much interest to students of war and conflict studies, peacebuilding and IR/Security Studies in general.

Astri Suhrke is a Senior Researcher at the Chr. Michelsen Institute, Bergen, Norway.

Mats Berdal is Professor in the Department of War Studies, King's College London.

Series: Studies in Conflict, Development and Peacebuilding
Series editors: Keith Krause, Thomas J. Biersteker and
Riccardo Bocco
Graduate Institute of International and Development Studies, Geneva

This series publishes innovative research into the connections between
insecurity and under-development in fragile states and into situations of
violence and insecurity more generally. It adopts a multidisciplinary
approach to the study of a variety of issues, including the changing nature
of contemporary armed violence (*conflict*), efforts to foster the conditions
that prevent the outbreak or recurrence of such violence (*development*),
and strategies to promote peaceful relations on the communal, societal
and international level (*peacebuilding*).

The Political Economy of Peacemaking
Achim Wennmann

The Peace In Between
Post-war violence and peacebuilding
Edited by Astri Suhrke and Mats Berdal

The Peace In Between

Post-war violence and peacebuilding

Edited by Astri Suhrke and Mats Berdal

Routledge
Taylor & Francis Group

LONDON AND NEW YORK

First published 2012
by Routledge
2 Park Square, Milton Park, Abingdon, Oxon OX14 4RN

Simultaneously published in the USA and Canada
by Routledge
711 Third Avenue, New York, NY 10017

Routledge is an imprint of the Taylor & Francis Group, an informa business

British Library Cataloguing in Publication Data
A catalogue record for this book is available from the British Library

Library of Congress Cataloging-in-Publication Data
The peace in between: post-war violence and peacebuilding/edited
by Astri Suhrke and Mats Berdal.
    p. cm.
    1. Peace-building. 2. Conflict management. I. Berdal, Mats R.,
1965– II. Suhrke, Astri.
    JZ5538.P435 2011
    303.6–dc22

                                                  2011000947

ISBN: 978-0-415-60932-6 (hbk)
ISBN: 978-0-415-68059-2 (pbk)
ISBN: 978-0-203-80892-4 (ebk)

Typeset in Baskerville
by Wearset Ltd, Boldon, Tyne and Wear

Contents

Contributors

Dionísio Babo-Soares has a PhD from the Australian National University. He co-chaired the joint Timor-Leste and Indonesian Truth and Friendship Commission. His publications include *Out of the Ashes: Destruction and Reconstruction of East Timor*, co-edited with James Fox (Canberra, 2003).

Michael Beaton has a BA in Modern History from Oxford and an MA from the Johns Hopkins School of Advanced International Studies. He has worked for NATO and the Kosovo International Civilian Office.

Mats Berdal is Professor in the Department of War Studies, King's College London. He was formerly Director of Studies at the International Institute for Strategic Studies (IISS) in London and is the author of *Building Peace After War* (Routledge/IISS, 2009).

Michael J. Boyle is an Assistant Professor of Political Science at La Salle University. His research work focuses on political violence, terrorism, insurgencies and American foreign policy. He has published articles in a range of scholarly journals and popular outlets and is currently finishing a book manuscript on violence in post-conflict states.

Merima Zupcevic Buzadzic holds a BA from the Faculty of Philosophy, University of Sarajevo, an MA from La Sapienza University in Rome and University of Sarajevo and an MA from King's College London. She now works for the International Finance Corporation.

Torunn Wimpelmann Chaudhary is a Researcher at the Chr. Michelsen Institute and a PhD candidate at the School of Oriental and African Studies. Her current work focuses on intersections of gender, violence and political orders in Afghanistan.

Gemma Collantes-Celador is a Lecturer in International Security at the Department of International Politics, City University London. She specializes on the security dimensions of post-conflict peacebuilding.

Toby Dodge is Reader in International Relations in the Department of International Relations, London School of Economics and Politics Science. He is also the Senior Consulting Fellow for the Middle East at the IISS. His publications include *Iraq's Future; the Aftermath of Regime Change*, (London: IISS and Routledge, 2005).

Trine Eide is a PhD candidate in social anthropology at the University of Tromsø.

Antonio Giustozzi is research fellow at the LSE. He is the author of several articles and papers on Afghanistan, as well as of three books, including *Koran, Kalashnikov and Laptop: The Neo-Taliban Insurgency* (Columbia University Press, 2007) and *Empires of Mud: War and Warlords in Afghanistan* (Hurst, 2009). He also edited *Decoding the New Taliban* (Hurst, 2009).

Kristian Berg Harpviken is Director of the International Peace Research Institute Oslo (PRIO). He is the author of *Social Networks and Migration in Wartime Afghanistan* (Palgrave Macmillan, 2009).

Are Knudsen is a Senior Researcher at the Chr. Michelsen Institute and has done fieldwork in Lebanon, Pakistan and Palestine. He is the author of *Violence and Belonging: Land, Love and Lethal in the North-West Frontier Province of Pakistan* (NIAS Press, 2009).

John-Andrew McNeish is an Associate Professor at the Norwegian University of Life Sciences (UMB) and a senior researcher at the Chr. Michelsen Institute.

Sorpong Peou is Chair of the Politics Department and Professor, University of Winnipeg, Canada. He was formerly Professor of International Security at Sophia University, Tokyo. His publications include *Peace and Security in the Asia-Pacific* (Praeger, 2010), *Human Security in East Asia: Challenges for Collaborative Action*, ed. (Routledge, 2008) and *International Democracy Assistance for Peacebuilding: Cambodia and Beyond* (Palgrave Macmillan, 2007).

Michael Richards is Reader in Spanish History at the University of the West of England and author of *A Time of Silence: Civil War and the Culture of Repression in Franco's Spain, 1936–1945* (Cambridge University Press, 1998) and *The Splintering of Spain* (Cambridge University Press, 2005).

Oscar López Rivera is a Senior Researcher and Head of the Poverty Studies Research Group at the Faculty of Latin American Social Sciences (FLACSO) in Guatemala.

Ingrid Samset is a Researcher at the Chr. Michelsen Institute and a PhD candidate at the University of Bergen, working on peacebuilding, natural resources and conflict and transitional justice.

Astri Suhrke is a Senior Researcher at the Chr. Michelsen Institute. She is currently completing a book on the international engagement in Afghanistan, which will be published in 2011.

Nasser Yassin holds a PhD from University College London. He is currently an Assistant Professor at the American University of Beirut, Lebanon where he teaches population studies.

Acknowledgements

This book is the result of a research project launched at the Chr. Michelsen Institute in 2006 with generous financial assistance from the Research Council of Norway. Special thanks are due to many persons involved in the project – to the contributing authors, some of whom have patiently revised their chapters more than once; to Kristine Höglund of Uppsala University and Muhammed Suleman of the Cooperation for Peace and Unity in Kabul, who enriched our deliberations with valuable insights from the field as well as the academic literature; and to Torunn Wimpelmann Chaudhary, who has been involved in the entire project cycle: drafting the original proposal, coordinating the work, managing the workshops, authoring a case study and providing critical but always constructive comments on the overall structure of the project.

Bergen and London, April 2011
Astri Suhrke and Mats Berdal

Abbreviations

AFDL	*Alliance des forces démocratiques pour la libération du Congo*
AFL	Armed Forces of Liberia
AI	Amnesty International
AMF	Afghan Military Force
AMS	Association of Muslim Scholars (*Hayat al-Ulama al-Muslimin*)
ANBP	Afghanistan New Beginnings Program
ANPPCAN	African Network for the Prevention and Protection against Child Abuse and Neglect
APODETI	Timorese Popular Democratic Association, East Timor (*Asso-ciacão Popular Democratica Timorense*)
APREDE	Association for Crime Prevention
AQIM	Al Qaeda in the Islamic Maghreb
ARBiH	Bosniak Army
ASDT	*Associação Social Democrática de Timor*
ASEAN	Association of Southeast Asian Nations
BiH	Bosnia and Herzegovina
BLDP	Buddhist Liberal Democratic Party
CAVR	Commission for Reception, Truth and Reconciliation
CEH	Commission for Historic Clarification (*Comisión para el Esclarecimiento Histórico*)
CFF	Cambodian Freedom Fighters
CGDK	Coalition Government of Democratic Kampuchea
CIA	Central Intelligence Agency
CIVPOL	Civilian police
CNDP	National Congress for the Defence of the People
CNRM	*Conselho Nacional da Resistência Maubere*
CNRT	*Conselho Nacional da Resistência Timorense*
CPA	Coalition Provisional Authority
CPD-RDTL	*Conselho Popular pela Defesa da República Democrática de Timor Leste*
CPP	Cambodian People's Party
CUC	Committee for Peasant Unity
DDR	Disarmament, demobilization and reintegration
DDRR	Disarmament, demobilization, rehabilitation and reintegration

DIAG	Disarmament of illegal armed groups
DRC	Democratic Republic of the Congo
ECOWAS	Economic Community of West African States
EPG	Guerrilla Army of the Poor
EUPM	European Union Police Mission
Ex-FAR	Former Armed Forces of Rwanda (*Forces Armées Rwandaises*)
FALINTIL	*Forças Armadas da Libertação Nacional de Timor-Leste*
FAR	Rebel Armed Forces (*Fuerzas Armadas Rebeldes*)
FARDC	Armed Forces of the Democratic Republic of the Congo
FDD	Forces for the Defence of Democracy
FDLR	Democratic Forces for the Liberation of Rwanda (*Forces démocratiques pour la libération du Rwanda*)
FECLETI	*Frente Clandestina Estudantil de Timor-Leste*
F-FDTL	*Força de Defesa de Timor-Leste*
FNL	Forces for National Liberation
FRETILIN	*Frente Revolucionária de Timor-Leste Independente*
FUNCINPEC	National United Front for an Independent, Neutral, Peaceful and Cooperative Cambodia
GEMAP	Governance and Economic Management Assistance Program
GNI	Gross national income
HDI	Human Development Index
HDK	*Hizb-i Demokratik-i Khalq*
HRW	Human Rights Watch
HVO	Bosnian-Croat Army
ICC	International Criminal Court
ICTR	International Criminal Tribunal for Rwanda
ICTY	International Criminal Tribunal for the former Yugoslavia
IDP	Internally displaced persons
IEBL	Inter-Entity Boundary Line
IFOR	Implementation Force
IGC	Iraqi Governing Council
INA	Iraqi National Alliance
INC	Iraqi National Congress
INE	National Institute of Statistics
IPTF	International Police Task Force
ISCI	Islamic Supreme Council of Iraq
ISF	International stabilization force
ISI	Inter-Services Intelligence
JAM	*Jaish al-Mahdi*
JEMB	Joint Electoral Management Board
KDP	Kurdistan Democratic Party
KFOR	Kosovo Force
KLA	Kosovo Liberation Army
KPNLF	Khmer People's National Liberation Front
LEP	*Liga dos Estudantes Patriotas*
LF	Lebanese Forces

LNP	Liberian National Police
LRA	Lord's Resistance Army
LURD	Liberians United for Reconciliation and Democracy
MIF	Multinational Intervention Force
MINUGUA	United Nations Verification Mission to Guatemala
MINUSTAH	United Nations Stabilization Mission in Haiti
MODEL	Movement for Democracy in Liberia
MONUC	United Nations Mission in the Democratic Republic of the Congo
MONUSCO	United Nations Organization Stabilization Mission in the Democratic Republic of the Congo
NAC	Norwegian Afghanistan Committee
NKVD	People's Commissariat of Internal Affairs (*Narodnyy komissariat vnutrennikh del*)
NPFL	National Patriotic Front of Liberia
NSD	National Security Directorate
NTGL	National Transitional Government of Liberia
OHR	Office of the High Representative
ORPA	Organization of People in Arms
OSCE	Organization for Security and Cooperation in Europe
PAC	Paramilitary patrol groups (*patrullas de auto-defensa civil*)
PCE	Spanish Communist Party (*Partido Comunista de España*)
PDH	Human Rights Ombudsman's Office (*Procuradoría de Derechos Humanos*)
PDK	Democratic Party of Kosovo (*Partia Demokratike e Kosovës*)
PDPA	People's Democratic Party of Afghanistan
PfP	Programme for peace
PGT	Guatemala Workers' Party
PKK	Communist Party of Kampuchea
PNC	National Civil Police
PNT	*Partido Nacionalista Timorense*
PNTL	*Polícia Nacional de Timor-Leste*
PRK	People's Republic of Kampuchea
PRPK	People's Revolutionary Party of Kampuchea
PST	*Partido Socialista Timor*
PUK	Patriotic Union of Kurdistan
RCD	Congolese Rally for Democracy
RDC	Research and Documentation Centre
REMHI	*Proyecto Interdiocesano de Recuperación de la Memoria Histórica*
RENETIL	*Resistencia Nacional dos Estudantes Timor-Leste*
RPA	Rwandan Patriotic Army
RPF	Rwandan Patriotic Front
RPG	Rocket propelled grenade
RS	*Republika Srpska*
RUF	Revolutionary United Front
SBiH	Party for Bosnia and Herzegovina

SDA	Bosniak Party for Democratic Action
SFOR	Stabilization Force
SLA	South Lebanese Army
SOC	State of Cambodia
SRSG	Special Representative of the Secretary-General
SSR	Security sector reform
STL	Special Tribunal for Lebanon
UCK	Kosovo Liberation Army (*Ushtria Çlirimtare e Kosovës*)
UDT	*União Democrática Timorense*
UNAMIR	United Nations Assistance Mission for Rwanda
UNDP	United Nations Development Programme
UNHCR	United Nations High Commissioner for Refugees, also known as the United Nations Refugee Agency
UNICRI	United Nations Interregional Crime and Justice Research Institute
UNIFIL	United Nations Interim Force in Lebanon
UNIIIC	United Nations International Independent Investigation Commission
UNMIBH	United Nations Mission in Bosnia and Herzegovina
UNMIEST	United Nations Mission of Support in East Timor
UNMIK	United Nations Mission in Kosovo
UNMIL	United Nations Mission in Liberia
UNMIT	United Nations Mission in Timor-Leste
UNODC	United Nations Office on Drugs and Crime
UNPOL	United Nations police
UNSC	United Nations Security Council
UNTAET	United Nations Transitional Administration in East Timor
URNG	Guatemalan National Guerrilla Unity

1   The peace in between[1]

Astri Suhrke

Framing the issues

The end of a war is generally expected to be followed by an end to collective violence, as the term 'post-conflict' that came into general usage in the 1990s signifies. In reality, however, various forms of deadly violence continue and sometimes even increase after the big guns have been silenced and a peace agreement signed. Why is this so? What form does such violence take? What purposes – and whose purposes – does it serve? The present book is framed around these questions as they relate to contemporary, internal wars.

The idea that wars affect the level of violence in post-war societies goes back centuries, long before the more recent interest in 'post-conflict' societies. The phenomenon of post-war violence has been explored by philosophers (Erasmus), statesmen (Sir Thomas More) and sociologists (Emile Durkheim), and was methodically examined by social scientists in the early twentieth century. But while the idea has 'a rich history', as Archer and Gartner (1976) note in their seminal work in criminology, systematic studies are rare. The Archer and Gartner study is the most comprehensive and methodologically rigorous comparative analysis in recent years. Analysing the aftermath of international wars in the period 1900–76, they found that, as a rule, post-war societies are considerably more violent than they were before the war. In some cases, the homicide rate doubled; in Italy, the murder rate in a five-year period after the Second World War increased 133 per cent compared to a similar period before the war (p. 948). A similar study looking at homicide rates after internal wars came to a similar result (Collier and Hoeffler 2004)

In light of this, it is unsurprising that the aftermath of the civil wars in Central America in the late twentieth century was marked by extraordinarily high levels of violent crime. In El Salvador, homicides peaked four years after the war at an amazing rate of around 150 per 100,000 inhabitants, which was about five times higher than the pre-war rate and the highest in all of Central America (Call 2007: 41; Savenije and van der Borgh 2004: 156). In Guatemala, violence increased to the point where 40 per cent of the population of Guatemala City in 2006–7 expected to be a victim of violent crime within the following six months (Torres 2008: 1).

This is not the only kind of post-war violence reported. Ethnically-directed violence erupted in Kosovo after the 1999 NATO intervention dismantled Serb rule. The same happened in northern Afghanistan after the US-led military intervention in 2001. In Liberia, ex-combatants forcibly seized rubber plantations. In East Timor, factions of the police and the army battled each other and triggered a major conflagration in 2006, seven years after the violent secession from Indonesia. In Rwanda, the post-genocide government methodically hunted down the *genocidaires* as well as tens of thousands of civilians who had fled across the border to Zaire. The list goes on. Are there some commonalities to these disparate events that reflect their proximity to war?

The literature

'Violence and war', Christopher Cramer reminds us, 'have been common experiences of [societal] transition since the very early origins and spread of capitalism' (Cramer 2006: 288), and civil war is often a key element in such transitions. War-to-peace transitions may be particularly vulnerable to social violence for reasons that are generally seen to fall into two categories: legacies of the war and conditions of the peace.

One approach emphasizes socio-cultural factors. Wars create social disorganization and a general legitimation of violence stemming from wartime reversal of customary prohibitions on killings. The violent consequences in peacetime are sometimes ascribed to a 'culture of violence'. Societies can develop the collective equivalent of post-traumatic stress disorder, leading to a loss of basic trust in the order of things and sowing the seeds of new violence such as domestic violence, rape, kidnapping, gang violence and organized crime (USIP 2001). Both gang violence and peasant lynching in Guatemala have been related to the trauma of large-scale atrocities inflicted by the state's 'security forces' during the war, or a 'democratization' of such terror (Godoy 2002; Prophette *et al.* 2003). While fairly common in one form or another, 'culture of violence' explanations are also criticized on empirical and normative grounds (Steenkamp 2005).

An institutional approach situates problems of post-war violence in a different context. Continued or renewed violence is attributed to faltering institutions, above all a weak state, which fails to constrain unruly agents left over from the war (such as warlords, ex-combatants that are not reintegrated, or mafia groups empowered by the war economy) and creates widespread impunity for crimes. In this perspective, peasant lynching in Guatemala does not reflect 'a culture of violence' but expresses the community's need to establish justice given the failure of the state to do so (Fernández García 2004). Institutional approaches have informed much of the policy-oriented literature on 'peacebuilding' which emphasizes institution-building in public administration and the security sector (Cousens and Kumar 2001; Milliken and Krause 2003; Rotberg 2004; Junne and Verkoren 2005; Call 2007; Nilsson 2008; Toft 2009). Until such institutions are in place, an international presence is necessary to stabilize the peace, especially in the form of security guarantees (Walter 2002). This literature has significantly influenced needs assessments and policy development in the UN peacebuilding regime that has developed since the early 1990s. An increasingly standardized understanding of peacebuilding emphasizes security sector reform (SSR), the rule of law, good governance, rapid economic reconstruction and timely humanitarian assistance; the implication is that failure in these areas may lead to renewed violence (UN 2009).

In a political economy perspective, the problem is more fundamental. The starting point here lies in the understanding of war itself. Rather than a fight over political goals that can be settled by a compromise or outright military victory, war, and the violence it entails, serves a variety of economic, political and social functions. The political economy of violence literature emphasizes violence as a tool of accumulation and domination rather than as a means of political transformation (Duffield 1998; Berdal and Malone 2000; Keen 2000). This applies not only to entrepreneurs in the wartime economy but more broadly to a range of military and political actors. The prototype within this logic is the so-called warlord – a self-appointed military leader with armed followers and a more or less willing constituency – for whom the war is not only a source of enrichment but also a basis of political power (Giustozzi 2003). In addition, some analysts argue that violence meets a number of immediate psychological and security needs of the belligerents, particularly otherwise disempowered youths (Keen 2002; Utas 2003). The implications for peace are clear: if the violence of war serves a multiplicity of social, economic and political functions, we cannot expect it to disappear once a peace agreement is signed. When these functions are tied to distinct social and economic structures, they produce vested interests in the means of violence as a source of power and determinant of social relations. For example, warlordism and 'warlord politics' appear in this light as inherently violent structures that are inimical to state-building in a framework of accountability (Reno 1998), or at least rather resistant to conversion to suit a non-violent peace (Goodhand and Cramer 2002).

In a different perspective, some explanations for post-war violence focus on the nature of the peace settlement and the associated assistance and reforms to peacebuilding known as 'the liberal peace'. Widely promoted as a model for post-war reconstruction since the end of the Cold War, 'the liberal peace' is based on market forces and political democracy operating within a neoliberal international economic system. Reforms of this kind are associated with systematic inequalities, marginalization and exclusion of weaker groups (Robinson 2003; Stewart 2001), which are potential sources of violence, particularly in the form of state repression and crime. In societies emerging from civil war, institutions and the national consensus are often weak and the negative consequences of liberalization and competition are likely to be especially marked (Paris 2004; Richmond 2005). National elites become increasingly oriented towards international sources of power available through international peacebuilding and less attuned to the demands of post-war development and social integration (Pearce 1999). Post-war democratization is a similarly double-edged sword. While in the long run associated with non-violent conflict resolution, in times when rules of the new order are being defined in the aftermath of war the stakes are high and the democratization process has historically been punctured by violence (Tilly 2003). Early elections in post-war societies carry a particular risk of reinforcing divisions and courting violence according to some analysts, although others consider it overstated (Sisk 2009).

Varieties of post-war states

The premise of general studies such as those cited above is that post-war environments have significant common features. That may be so, but should not obscure regional variations in post-war environments that are particularly relevant to understanding forces of conflict and violence. Studies of post-war societies in Central America typically emphasize a constellation of factors: entrenched and highly unequal socio-economic hierarchies, weak or partisan institutions of state and justice, and the negative socio-economic effects of integration into a regional international economy dominated by the United States (Hume 2009; Zinecker 2006). Studies of conflict in the post-war Balkans, by contrast, emphasize the transformation of wartime economies into post-war compacts between organized crime and political elites to establish 'shadow economies' of exploitation (Pugh *et al.* 2004). In parts of Africa, similar alignments developed after Cold War patronage disappeared, and rebels and governments alike had to finance themselves by opportunistic and often violent exploitation of local natural resources in war as well as peacetime. Some scholars have noted a fluid line between war and peace in Africa more generally. While the purpose of violence is in both cases to accumulate resources and suppress the opposition, behaviour becomes similar as belligerents fraternize during war and fight each other afterwards (Keen 2000; Nordstrom 2004).

This literature takes us some way towards understanding the dynamic of post-war violence. Puzzles remain, however. In Central America, for instance, a striking but unexplored piece of data is the very low crime rate in post-war Nicaragua, which otherwise has many features in common with El Salvador and Guatemala. Some countries have not experienced high levels of post-war violence even though the war was enormously destructive and peace initially seemed fragile. 'There were good grounds for expecting a "violent peace" in Bosnia, the most diverse and delicately balanced of the former Yugoslav republics in terms of ethnicity', Berdal, Celador and Zupcevic write in chapter 4 of this volume. Yet, as they go on to show, apart from immediate 'aftershocks' of ethnically directed violence and incidents associated with minority refugee returns, Bosnia has had relatively little overt post-war violence. As for elections, the literature is inconclusive and the debate goes on. Violent elections have taken place in countries without a recent civil war (Kenya in 2007 and recent elections in Zimbabwe), while the 1994 elections in Mozambique immediately after the peace agreement proceeded calmly and served as an essential transition mechanism from war to peace. Other war-torn countries (Iraq and Afghanistan) have had violent elections, however.

The variations are important. First, they point to a question that has so far been ignored. What is the most significant puzzle to be addressed – that societies which have descended into brutal civil war experience continuous and heavy violence afterwards, or that they experience only limited violence? Why would a brutal war in Bosnia and Liberia suggest a particularly violent peace? Put differently, what are the underlying assumptions here about 'normal' levels of violence in a society and particularly a post-war society? For social scientists, the question can only be addressed historically and empirically. In the absence of empirically-based, aggregate data analysis of post-war violence except for homicide (Archer and Gartner 1976; Collier and Hoeffler 2004), a case study approach that places individual country experiences in their historical context is a methodologically reasonable way to go. Second, the variations in post-war violence suggest that there is no such thing as one generic post-war environment, but rather many types. The singular term 'the post-war state' masks this kind of variation and inhibits a nuanced understanding.

One main purpose of this book is to start sorting out these different types of post-war environment, or what we will call difference kinds of post-war peace. The variations, as we shall see, include some of the kinds of factors that determine whether peace agreements are implemented or collapse (Hampson 1996; Stedman *et al.* 2002; Doyle and Sambanis 2006). More specifically, we shall look at the nature of the war, the way it ended in terms of the political bargain and balance of power on the ground, the political-normative framework for the new post-war order, and the presence and absence of institutions for managing violence, including, importantly, international forces and agencies. Four main post-war 'peaces' can be identified, based on empirical cases that lend themselves to the construction of 'ideal types'. The first, which we have called the *Victor's Peace*, is based on an older historical case – the Spanish Civil War. Its counterpart, the *Loser's Peace*, is also based on an older case, namely the post-bellum ex-Confederacy states in the United States. The two remaining types are derived from contemporary situations. The *Divided Peace* is constructed around the relatively short post-war situation in Afghanistan after the fall of the Taliban (2001–4/5), while post-war Liberia is the model for what we have called the *Pacified Peace*. The four types, their determinants and their susceptibility to post-war violence are discussed in later sections of this chapter.

The second main purpose of the book is to present in-depth analysis of different types or dynamics of violence in various post-war environments. Recognizing the importance of regional variations, we selected contemporary cases from different geographical areas – two from Europe, two from the Middle East, three from sub-Saharan Africa (West and Central), three from Asia and one from Latin America. Two much older cases were added to provide historical depth and invite reflections on the importance of changes in the global context for post-war environments. These 'historical cases' are the aftermath of the Spanish Civil war in the mid-twentieth century and of the American Civil War in the mid-nineteenth century. The cases reflect the diversity of contemporary post-war environments and post-war violence. Some chapters have overall country reviews of levels and types of post-war violence; others focus on particular conflict dynamics. Individually these chapters provide insight into particular cases; collectively they offer material for identifying commonalities and variations in both the dynamics of post-war violence and the types of post-war situation where they occur.

But first, a note on concepts.

A note on concepts: violence, post-war violence and violence in the post-war state

The term 'post-conflict' that came into widespread use in the 1990s is somewhat awkward in an analysis that examines violence in the aftermath of war and similar kinds of armed conflict. Taken literally, 'post-conflict violence' is an oxymoron and we shall therefore use the term 'post-war violence'.

Violence has many meanings (Scheper-Hughes and Bourgois 2002). This book mainly discusses what Charles Tilly (2003) calls 'collective violence', that is, physical violence undertaken by a collectivity or involving some degree of coordination. This may include 'ordinary' crime such as robberies and murders, which are often associated with gangs, as well as violence by organized non-state groups such as 'warlords', associations of ex-combatants, 'spontaneous' mobs (that in reality are rarely spontaneous) and community structures (e.g. village lynchings of thieves). In addition, a whole range of extrajudicial violence is associated with the state and its agents or ex-agents, often so-called 'security forces'. Threats of violence that operate as a deterrent are only one step removed from its overt use and are examined in some of the case studies.

At a certain level, violence short of war in countries that are formally at peace can create insecurity and impose costs, including violent death, that resemble war-time conditions. How, then, does a situation of 'post-war violence' differ from a state of 'war', or a state of 'peace'? The boundary lines between war and peace are fluid, as both the qualitative and quantitative literature recognize (Keen 2000; Sambanis 2004). But if we accept that 'war' is distinguished by a certain level of violence, organization and collective purpose – the standard criteria used in widely referenced data sets on internal wars (Gleditsch *et al.* 2001) – then a situation of 'post-war violence' would conceptually speaking be located somewhere in between 'war' and 'peace – the more precise location depending upon whether the 'post' or the 'war' part is the more prominent. It is a violent peace, bracketed by peace' and war, a 'peace in between'.

As for the question of when a post-war period ends, the answer is essentially a matter of judgement, although informed by qualitative and quantitative markers. In qualitative analysis, 'post-war' usually means a phase that is extraordinary in some sense, a transition from war to more 'normal' conditions. The time element embedded in the term *post* suggests that period cannot last too long, but how long is another matter. In the classic cases of Germany and Japan after the Second World War, the end of allied occupation, membership in international organizations and rapid economic growth during the early 1950s are commonly used markers. Since contemporary war-torn countries are rarely occupied, other markers of economic progress and political stability are often used (Berdal 2009: 20–4).

The case-study approach used in this volume does not require a definition with common cut-off points, and trying to construct a general definition of 'the post-war period' serves no purpose. Rather, the question of defining post-war violence becomes a matter of analytical perspective and methodology. One approach is simply to define a certain time period as 'post-war'; all violence within this period then becomes *violence in the post-war state*. In quantitative studies, a common cut-off point is typically one five-year period (Archer and Gartner 1976) or two five-year periods (Collier and Hoeffler 2004). This methodology records rape as 'post-war rape' if it occurred in, say, the Democratic Republic of the Congo (DRC) within five or ten years of the last war, but 'just' rape if it occurred 20 years after the last war (or in Tanzania, which has never had a civil war).

An explicitly causal approach, by contrast, seeks to trace the lineages of violence evident in the legacy of the war and the conditions of peace. Violence in this sense can linger, reproduce or transform itself long after the country has passed other milestones on the road to recovery and is no longer viewed as a post-war state. Contemporary racial violence in the United States, for instance, has roots in the civil war that ended more than 150 years ago and to that extent is *post-war violence*, even though the United States is no longer a post-war society in any meaningful sense of the word (at least in relation to that war).

Both the causal and the temporal approaches assume that post-war societies have particular features that may make them particularly vulnerable to violence as compared to the time before the war, or compared to states that have not experienced such wars.

Post-war environments I: Victor's Peace and Loser's Peace

As noted above, there is a tendency in the policy discussion as well as the academic literature to assume that there is one, predominant type of post-war situation, which has certain generic features that predispose it towards violence. Problems associated with a weak state, criminal elements generated by the war-time economy, demobilized but not demilitarized or reintegrated ex-combatants often feature in this discussion, as do frustrated expectations of rapid reconstruction and large-scale unemployment. These features are associated with some violence in some post-war situations, as the case studies in this volume show. More importantly, a main argument of this book is that features which constrain or encourage violence stack up in ways that create distinct types of post-war environment. Critical factors that shape the post-war environment in this respect lie in the war-to-peace transition itself, above all the outcome of the war in terms of military and political power and its relationship to social hierarchies of power, normative understandings of the post-war order and the international context. Two strikingly different types of post-war environment in these respects are suggested by the two historical cases considered in this book – the Spanish Civil War and the American Civil War. The cases, analysed by Michael Richards and Michael Beaton in Chapters 2 and 3 respectively, form the basis for the construction of two 'ideal types' of violent post-war environment. Both differ from contemporary notions of post-war violence arising from weak states unable to confront criminals, warlords and apolitical armed gangs. Rather, violence in these post-war environments is dominated by a political logic and purpose. We have called the two types 'Victor's Peace' and 'Loser's Peace'.

Victor's Peace

In Spain, the Nationalist forces under General Franco had systematically repressed or eliminated Republican forces and supporters as they advanced during the civil war (1936–9). After the Republican forces were decisively defeated, the Franco regime launched systematic purges – significantly called *limpieza* (cleansing) – to rid society of threats to the new order and its foundational principles. Violence became an integral part of the post-war order, in effect creating a 'victor's peace' where – as in 'victor's justice' – the reality is the opposite of the literal meaning of the last, defining term.

The violence orchestrated by the Francoist state, with the support of the army, the clergy and the landed propertied class, was directed against particular civilian segments such as trade unions, 'reds' and professionals. The terminology and practice of violence reflected a view of social conflict as absolute. The we/they distinction was laced with normative connotations of good and evil, permitting no compromise. Violence was most intense in the post-war decade examined by Richards, when it took the form of systematic purges, mass imprisonment and executions, but continued until Franco's death in 1974. It was a case where post-war violence can be said to have outlasted the post-war period as defined by conventional markers. The regime also used indirect violence by regulating access to basic necessities (ration cards, employment, medical care and food in detention centres) so as to weaken 'the enemy' and reward regime supporters. Importantly, the violence proceeded without attracting much international concern, let alone effective restraint. With attention focusing on the escalating confrontation with Germany, other Western governments overlooked the excesses or considered the Franco regime a bulwark against Soviet-led communism. The Second World War soon overshadowed events in Spain and Franco's anti-communist stance later played to his advantage in Western liberal democracies.

The case lends itself to the construction of an ideal type. In schematic form, the preconditions for a Victor's Peace and the nature of violence associated with it are as follows.

Enabling conditions

- Nature of the conflict – perceived as total in an ideological and/or social sense;
- Outcome of the war – total victory/total defeat;
- State power when war ends – unified: the victorious party has a monopoly of violence; supported by major social segments;
- Sovereignty – unconstrained by international law or international sanctions.

Nature of violence

- Purpose – consolidate victory and the new political order, prevent future opposition and 'cleanse' society to secure the new order;
- Target – social and political segments associated with 'the enemy' which threaten the new order by their very existence;
- Agent – the state and its apparatus of physical coercion (armed forces, police, prisons, court system), aided by individual denunciations for opportunistic and private purposes;
- Means – economic and physical (purges, executions, imprisonment).

Contemporary shades

There are few contemporary cases of a 'Victor's Peace'. Elements are recognizable in the Cambodian case study, presented by Sorpong Peou in Chapter 10 below. But even though the Hun Sen faction utilized the power advantages confirmed by the 1991 Paris peace agreement to suppress the internal political opposition ruthlessly, this was violence as commonly practised in conventional political autocracies. The government did not seek to eliminate, terrorize or disenfranchise an entire social segment in the name of a new order. Government involvement in later, spectacular cases of land-grabbing to promote international capital ventures in property development was part of a general, rent-seeking strategy.

Perhaps the clearest contemporary version of a Victor's Peace after internal war is Rwanda after the genocide in 1994. As Trine Eide discusses in Chapter 14 below, post-genocide Rwanda has all the parameters of the Spanish classic case. The Rwandan case also has two unique features that set it apart from other contemporary post-war environments. First of all is the enormity of the genocide itself and the logic of total social conflict that it expressed. The victim-turned-victor (the Rwandan Patriotic Front, RPF) subsequently resorted to targeted violence, followed by more subtle means of control to instil fear and silence among the ethnic 'other'. The second distinguishing feature is the passivity in the international community towards the violence committed by the new Rwandan government. Although international human rights organizations reported violence within Rwanda and the UN issued investigative reports on the killings in neighbouring DRC, governments were mostly silent. As in post-war Spain, Rwandan sovereignty was in effect unconstrained. International passivity reflected general reluctance to sanction a government that represented genocide victims as well as the paralysing memory of UN failure to prevent the massacres despite having been present on the ground with a peace-keeping force when the killings started.

Loser's Peace

The Loser's Peace is in important respects the mirror image of the Victor's Peace. While the latter signifies a violent consolidation of the post-war order, the former denotes violence unleashed to sabotage the new order. In this case, the party that lost the war retains the power to obstruct and sabotage and, if successful, can block the implementation of the post-war order in territory under its control. This happened in the ex-Confederate states of the United States during the post-civil war period known as Reconstruction (1865–77).

In Chapter 3 below, Michael Beaton discusses the origins, structure and purposes of the post-war violence in the states of the ex-Confederacy. As in the Victor's Peace, the purpose of the violence – in this case unleashed by 'the losers' in the civil war – was primarily political (to influence the post-war political order), but there were other important dimensions as well. Violent constraints on the mobility of blacks served to keep the cost of labour down, and violence along racial lines reinforced identity boundaries that were particularly important for poor whites, as Beaton notes. As in Franco's Spain, violence was targeted against particular social segments and political groups, often couched in the language of 'cleansing'.

While the state is the major agent of violence in the Victor's Peace, the Loser by necessity relies more on vigilante-type violence – or asymmetrical warfare in contemporary terminology. In the post-bellum Southern states, vigilante and paramilitary violence was tacitly backed by the local elites and by local political and law enforcement authorities as the 'redeemers' increasingly won political office.

In the absence of any international restraints, the only external limitation on violence came from the federal authorities. Yet federal troops stationed in the South during the period under consideration were far too few to prevent violence in a far-flung territory. Moreover, vigilante groups were careful not to attack the troops or other symbols of federal power directly and thereby provide a pretext for more direct intervention. The other federal agency with a specific justice-related mandate in the South was the Federal Freedman's Bureau, originally established by President Abraham Lincoln to help refugees from the civil war and freed slaves. The bureau maintained a record of human rights abuses, murders and lynchings, but, however admirable, did not prevent massive and sustained human rights abuse against blacks and their white sympathizers. Arguably, the minimal presence and de facto permissiveness of the federal state was a significant enabling condition of the violence characteristic of the Loser's Peace; 100 years later, it will be recalled, the deployment of federal troops to the South dramatically demonstrated the federal government's commitment to enforcing civil rights and helped change the situation.

Contemporary shades

A full-blown case of the Loser's Peace is difficult to find in contemporary post-war environments, but some elements are recognizable. The pattern of violence in post-war Guatemala – as outlined by John McNeish and Oscar López Rivera in Chapter 15 – suggests powerful forces at work to obstruct the sweeping reforms envisaged in the 1996 peace agreement. Yet it was a distinctly contemporary form of Loser's Peace in that it was based on a compromise settlement and showed the imprint of international constraints.

The Guatemalan war ended with no clear winners or losers. The armed forces, however, were set to lose in institutional and ideological terms. The peace agreement called for drastic cuts in the numbers and budgets for the military. Paramilitary forces would be disbanded and military intelligence services closed down. Politically, the peace accords were framed in terms of principles that the military had fought against during the long war as representing threats to the integrity of the state and the very fabric of the nation – social justice, indigenous rights, human rights and democratic participation. As a result, elements of the military used threats, political manipulation and violence in order to prevent the implementation of the peace agreement. Most famously, ex-military formed the core of the 'hidden powers' – an amorphous structure of networks with links deep into organized crime as well the state administration, the economic elite and the political establishment. Organized into groups with names such as *The Syndicate*, the 'hidden powers' resembled a conventional mafia operation, using violence to maximize profits and working with organized crime in a wide range of illegal operations (Peacock and Beltran 2003).

'The hidden powers' became a synonym for an invisible hand that appeared to facilitate the staggering level and variety of violence in post-war Guatemala. One study identified 70 different types in urban areas alone (Moser and McIlwaine 2001). The 'hidden powers' also had vested interests in a dysfunctional police and court system. Only some 2 per cent of the approximately 5,000 murders annually in the immediate post-war years were investigated by police, fewer arrests were made and the judiciary was impotent (Torres 2008). With general impunity for crimes of all kinds, violence seemed to have developed into a social norm.

The fact that the key structures behind this violence were hidden, operating outside the formal political process and not seeking to 'redeem' the past by challenging the principles of the peace agreement sets the post-war environment of Guatemala apart from the Loser's Peace modelled on the American Civil War. The forces that allowed the 'hidden powers' to stay hidden were mostly international in nature. The military had since the end of the Cold War gradually lost favour with its powerful North American patron and its appalling human rights record was internationally condemned. The peace agreement principles for a new and better post-war order were endorsed by the United Nations, which also established a sizable human rights verification mission on the ground two years before the final peace agreement and maintained it for a decade.

Towards the end of the first post-war decade, overtly political violence was a small category compared to other types of violence, which continued to make Guatemala one of the most violent societies in Latin America. Killings of women, adolescents and youth predominated, some of it associated with domestic violence and much of it attributed to Guatemala's infamous gangs – the *maras*. Apart from the *maras*, which had their own peculiar links to war-time migration, the violence seemed to reflect less the legacy of war than the pathologies of a development trajectory and a drug economy that continued to underwrite poverty, inequality and impunity, as McNeish and López discuss below.

The international context

As the Guatemalan case suggests, there are two main reasons why political violence characteristic of the Victor's Peace and the Loser's Peace modelled on the earlier historical cases rarely occurs in contemporary post-war environments. Most civil wars in recent years have ended in compromises, thus nullifying a critical enabling condition for both a Victor's Peace and a Loser's Peace.[2] Moreover, negotiation and implementation of peace agreements have taken place in an international context of UN-authorized peace operations designed to prevent renewed war and collective violence.

The growth of the international peacebuilding regime in the past two decades has been remarkable by any standard. By 2008, the UN had more than 50 active peace operations around the world; other operations were coalitions of the willing authorized by the UN. Peace operations had become multidimensional, with economic, political human rights and military functions designed to secure a sustainable peace. As a result, international agencies and organizations moved in visibly and sometimes massively to help with economic, social and political reconstruction, spinning a dense web of monitoring, assistance and intervention in post-war environments.

The effects of this web on post-war violence are hard to assess. International peace operations can have unintended and counterproductive consequences. In general, there is a built-in contradiction between long-term development and short-term control. Large, international peace operations tend to undermine the development of effective and legitimate state power and institutions of justice that can defuse tension, address sources of conflict and restrain violence. On the other hand, the pervasive international presence in post-war environments has increased the awareness and monitoring of violence and thereby exposed those responsible to potential counter-intervention. The rapid expansion of the human rights regimes during the past two decades in particular has enormously increased the capacity to monitor violations, advocate political, legal or educational intervention and support local human rights organizations. Since the Rwandan genocide – where the UN system failed spectacularly – human rights field missions under the High Commissioner for Human Rights are routinely included in all UN peace operations.

International peacekeeping operations have made the use of collective violence to challenge or consolidate the post-war political order more risky and costly. Statistically speaking, the presence of international peacekeepers is likely to reduce the chances of renewed war as defined by battle-related deaths (Doyle and Sambanis 2006). The role of military peacekeepers or observers in preventing or reducing other forms of post-war violence is more uncertain. Peacekeepers can be in a situation resembling the federal troops in the post-bellum Southern states some 150 years ago – few in number, thinly stretched, and without a clear authorization to stop mob violence, riots or violence against civilians carried out by men armed with guns and political connections. In the DRC a UN peacekeeping force of almost 20,000 (United Nations Mission in the Democratic Republic of the Congo peace operation, MONUC/ United Nations Stabilization Mission in the Democratic Republic of the Congo MONUSCO) was unable to prevent widespread attacks on civilians and systematic violence associated with the illegal exploitation of natural resources in the country's eastern provinces.

On the other hand, some peace operations take on unconventional tasks to reduce post-war violence. In Haiti, MINUSTAH cleaned out armed gangs in Port-au-Prince, with savoury effects that lasted for at least a couple of years until the massive earthquake of 2010 (Berdal 2009). In Liberia, United Nations Mission in Liberia (UNMIL) troops defused tension and probably prevented violence when ex-combatants occupied rubber plantations. In the DRC, UN troops helped local police stop street fights during the 2006 elections that left more than a dozen dead in Kinshasa. In East Timor, it is often noted that violent street riots and fighting between factions of the police and army occurred after the UN peacekeepers had left and stopped when an international stabilization force was reintroduced.

While the international capacity to constrain those who control the means of violence in post-war environments has increased as a result of historical changes in the international system, other international developments tend to have the opposite effect. Unequal integration of post-war economies into the international economy has been associated with poverty, inequality and crime. Neoliberal economic reforms and political democratization in post-war societies can create a different set of tensions, as critics of 'the liberal peace' argue. More generally, some analysts note that some of the conditions that generate conflict and violence in post-war environments are in important respects related to the contemporary forces of globalization – an open international economic system permits easy flows of illegal transactions to sustain violent groups in post-war environments and migration flows reproduce social patterns associated with violent urban gangs (Duffield 2001; Zinecker 2006). In this perspective, the international context appears as a bundle of fundamental, internal contradictions where the right hand is trying to constrain the effects of what the left hand is doing. The situation resembles the analogy famously used by Alvaro de Soto and Graciana del Castillo to describe the lack of coordination between the UN and the Bretton Woods institutions in constructing the international parameters for post-war El Salvador – 'as if a patient lay on the operating table with the left and right sides of his body separated by a curtain and unrelated surgery being performed on each side' (1994: 74) In the radical critique, however, this situation is a result of structural contradictions that better coordination alone cannot resolve.

The contradictory effects of the international context on contemporary post-war environments are evident in many of the case studies included below. So are signs that the way these processes work themselves out depends heavily on the local context. In what follows we will consider two contemporary post-war environments that were both heavily circumscribed and influenced by an international presence, but differed in other important respects.

Post-war environments II: divided peace and pacified peace

The remaining contemporary cases included in this volume are diverse in terms of conflicts, war-to-peace transitions and post-war violence. Sorted according to a rough scale of post-war violence, Bosnia and Liberia appear overall towards the relatively peaceful end of the scale, while Kosovo and Timor Leste have both had violent episodes. Post-war Lebanon has seen continuing political assassinations and attack. Large parts of the DRC have been in a state of 'no war – no peace', despite a 2003 peace agreement. The short period in Afghanistan that can be called 'post-war' was marred by diverse and pervasive violence quite apart from the renewed fighting between the militant Islamists and the international forces. In this rough scale, Afghanistan and Liberia appear at different ends and thus as promising subjects for further examination.

Afghanistan may be a prototype of a violent post-war state in the period that arguably qualifies as 'post-war', that is, from late 2001, when the US-led intervention removed the Taliban regime, until early 2005 when mounting clashes between US-led forces and a revived insurgency had produced a de facto state of renewed war in much of the country. In Liberia, on the other hand, the post-war environment was relatively peaceful, despite a long and extremely brutal war. In both cases, the nature of the political transition and the role of the international presence help explain the patterns of post-war violence. We have called them respectively 'divided peace' and 'pacified peace'.

Divided peace in post-war Afghanistan (2001–5)

An underlying source of continuous conflict in Afghanistan's short post-war period was the sudden regime change, brought about primarily by US airpower, without any prior agreement on the basis for the post-war order. The main partner of the United States on the ground consisted of ethnic minorities (Tajik, Uzbek, Hazara) that before the US intervention controlled only about 10 per cent of the territory. The rest of the country had been controlled by the Taliban, mostly in alliance with local Pashtun leaders. The latter were not invited to the international conference in Bonn in December 2001 that adopted a transitional framework, and the Afghan factions that were invited were not in agreement either. Lasting only about a week, the conference approved a two-and-a-half-year framework for transition drafted mainly by the UN Special Representative to Afghanistan, Lakhdar Brahimi.

The post-war period thus opened without an agreement among even the nominal victors on the substantive provisions for the new order or an authoritative distribution of power, only a schedule for a competitive process to settle these matters. The result was a ferocious stampede for power among the victors to determine what North *et al.* (2009) call a balance between the 'violence potential' of the elite and the distribution of rents between them. The struggle divided the participants according to clan, religious and political affiliation, with an overarching distinction between the Pashtun, who had traditionally ruled Afghanistan but were now politically weakened with the main factions in exile or associated with Taliban and the ethnic minorities who had partnered with the United States to defeat the Taliban. On the local level, new strongmen supported by Kabul and the international forces moved in to displace, harass and kill factions that had been aligned with the Taliban, adding another level of violence and laying the foundation for a revived insurgency.

The power struggle among the anti-Taliban factions – or what we elsewhere have called 'conflictual peacebuilding' – was fought in many arenas, sometimes with overt violence and almost always against the backdrop of threats of violence (Suhrke *et al.* 2004; Barnett and Zürcher 2009). The central government and the local strongmen struggled for control over revenue, territory and formal state power. Sometimes local rivals fought pitched battles (in the North), at other times US military force was used in support of the government to settle the score (in Herat). Military strongmen organized or facilitated violent riots to demonstrate their power vis-à-vis competing factions (in Kabul in and the provinces). By the time of the parliamentary elections in 2005, some types of 'armed politics' had become less visible due to co-optation, the UN disarmament programme, diversification of rent-seeking opportunities and political alignments, as Antonio Giustozzi discusses in Chapter 8 below. Meanwhile, the Taliban was recovering and regrouping to fight the new government and the international forces. Despite the targeted nature of the violence, the mounting warfare caused significant death and damage among civilians.

The intense, post-war struggle for power among the anti-Taliban factions made it difficult to recreate a central state that had been practically demolished over the past almost 25 years of revolutionary strife, foreign invasion, civil war and deliberate neglect. Attempts to reform the sub-national administration, the justice sector and the police – areas of critical importance for constraining violence – were opposed by entrenched and mostly armed Afghan leaders. Many had political backing from the internationals. While the major Western states and the UN were committed in principle to helping establish an effective and representative Afghan state, the parallel 'war on terror' fought by US-led forces on Afghan soil had profoundly distorting effects. The international community represented in Afghanistan was divided over whether to prioritize fighting the war or consolidating the peace, consequently also in their willingness to pressure Afghan parties to disarm and reform. Governments that prioritized the war had no obvious interest in promoting an effective and accountable Afghan state that might be a less willing client rather than a highly dependent one. More directly, the United States and some of its allies armed and paid Afghan commanders to participate in the war, thereby strengthening armed factions and their reliance on violence to maintain themselves. The UN disarmament programme, as a result, was slow and incomplete.

The post-war Afghan government, then, was a loose coalition of armed, or partially disarmed, competing factions and foreign-supported technocrats. Collectively they lacked both capacity and incentives to create an effective and accountable state that could have constrained violence. Removing a local strongman who abused his power, for instance, or prosecuting an official involved in land-grabbing at gunpoint, was very difficult; a person with the capacity to inflict serious harm on others usually also had political protection higher up, often because he was useful in the war. Except for the poor and the powerless, impunity prevailed.

A small international 'security assistance' force (ISAF) was deployed to the capital, Kabul, where it helped deter open fighting and at least one planned military coup. However, the mission lacked the political support even to start addressing the security and order problems that plagued the immediate post-war period, including violence associated with the factional struggles for power and the drug economy, illegal confiscation of land, harassment and forced displacement of ethnic minorities, and the everyday human rights violations committed by local strongmen and government officials against the population. The UN Special Representative to Afghanistan described the situation in July 2003:

> We continue to receive daily reports of abuses by gunmen against the population – armed gangs who establish illegal checkpoints, tax farmers and traders, intimidate, rob, rape and do so – all too often – while wielding the formal title of military commander, police or security chief.
>
> (Cited in Suhrke *et al.* 2004: 45)

The political transition also encouraged opportunistic violence of a different kind. In the north, for instance, the fall of the Taliban encouraged opportunistic violence for economic gain against local Pashtun who in the late nineteenth century had been given government land grants in areas primarily settled by Uzbek, Tajik and Hazara. When the latter emerged as victors after the defeat of the Taliban, a forced reversal of landownership took place. Northern Pashtun were systematically harassed by armed gangs operating under the protective wing of local warlords. Land was seized, people killed and families threatened. With no national or international agency to protect them, northern Pashtun fled to the mainly Pashtun-populated south, most ending up in huge IDP camps supported by international aid agencies (Mundt and Schmeidl 2009).

In sum, the key factors that structured the 'divided peace' of the immediate post-Taliban order were defined by the contradictions of the transition. The political bargain reached in Bonn was inconclusive and did not reflect the balance of power on the ground, the parties to the bargain retained a capacity for armed action, the central state was weak yet strongly contested and the international intervention that had brought about the post-war state was inextricably linked to continued warfare in ways that that sharpened political conflict and encouraged impunity for everyday violence. Even discounting the legacy of nearly 25 years of violent strife and displacement, these conditions formed an environment ripe for multifaceted and multidirectional violence. The potential for violence was not only embedded in the unresolved struggle among the victors. Local points of tension, such as disputes over land that in more benign environments could have been defused or restrained by relevant authorities, were joined to the broader conflict of the transition and allowed to run a violent course.

Pacified peace in Liberia

In Liberia's case, two important factors helped to define a very different post-war trajectory. First, peace negotiations involved all the relevant Liberian parties and in important respects reflected the military balance on the ground. Second, the UN and the major regional organization, the Economic Community of West African States (ECOWAS), established an international presence in the country that was massive relative to Liberia's small size and population and had three main foci – the need to end the violence, implement the peace agreement and establish at least a minimally effective and accountable state.

When the final Comprehensive Peace Agreement was signed in 2003, the Liberian civil war had lasted for more than a decade, interspersed with short periods of relative calm and had been marked by several abortive ceasefires and previous negotiations. The protagonists were largely mobilized on ethnic/tribal grounds, with a changing list of rebel groups fighting the government forces, as Torunn Wimpelmann Chaudhary discusses in Chapter 13 below. The decisive break in the war came when the United States and neighbouring Guinea shifted their support from the government forces of Charles Taylor to rebel groups, enabling the main rebel group (Liberians United for Reconciliation and Democracy, LURD) to gain control of about 80 per cent of the country in 2002. Pressured by international forces, Taylor sued for peace in an agreement that led to his exile (and later arraignment before the International Criminal Court (ICC) in The Hague), but included other members of the government as well as the principal rebel groups in a transitional administration. The transitional administration established by the peace agreement was extraordinarily inclusive, with the factional distribution of 21 government departments, 22 public corporations and 22 autonomous agencies specified in the agreement. The transitional bargain held until the 2005 elections, when several former rebel commanders and faction leaders transited into the political arena through election or appointment by the new president, an internationally supported technocrat.

The political transition was supported by a huge international presence. The UN had authorized advance deployment of 3,500 ECOWAS troops to constrain the parties shortly before the peace agreement was signed. It was followed by a UN peacekeeping force of 15,000 troops, around 1,100 police (including armed police) and 250 military observers. For a country the size of Portugal, with a population just over 3 million, it meant a dense presence of soldiers with a broad mandate to maintain order and security, including providing security at government installations, ensuring freedom of movement, supporting the safe return of refugees and IDPs and 'protect[ing] civilians under imminent threat of physical violence' in areas around UN troops (Res. 1509/2003). UNMIL also supervised the disarmament and demobilization of rebel forces. The disarmament, demobilization, rehabilitation and reintegration (DDRR) programme started immediately and, despite some snags, had by early 2005 completed the process for around 100,000 soldiers – just in time for the elections. Meanwhile, the army was restructured under the auspices of the United States.

The political bargain and UN-supervised disarmament of the rebels provided a reasonably stable framework for the post-war environment that helps explain why politically oriented and other forms of collective violence were quite limited, as Chaudhary discusses. This was so even in the absence of an effective and accountable Liberian state, which was much more difficult to establish and was not immediately in evidence. Institutions of justice and order, in particular the police, remained weak, creating concern about crime, gangs and vigilante justice, such as lynching. On the other hand, it is not clear against what standards to judge this level of post-war violence. There are no readily available records of pre-war crime and data from comparable post-war or no-war environments are non-existent or highly uncertain.[3]

Liberia, then, was demilitarized and to that extent 'pacified' by international forces in a way that Afghanistan obviously was not. This does not mean that a 'Liberian solution' in terms of a heavier international presence from the outset would have reduced post-war violence in Afghanistan. The international presence helped constrain post-war violence in Liberia for several reasons: the internationals had one common objective – making and consolidating peace; the local parties were amenable to negotiations; and Liberia was a small country where a favourable ratio of peacekeepers to population and territory was within the financial reach of the UN. None of these conditions applied in Afghanistan.

Points of vulnerability

Transitions from war to peace raise basic issues about access to political power in the post-war society. These are inherently conflictual and contested questions, particularly so in societies emerging from violent strife fought over the legitimacy or control of the state. Attempts to influence the political transition may in some cases lead to pervasive and politically-oriented post-war violence, as exemplified in the Victor's Peace; elsewhere, the transition may be contested with less violence, as in the Pacified Peace.

A war-to-peace transition involves many other changes and adjustments as well on both collective and individual levels. We can think of these as points of vulnerability that, as in all cases of social change, carry the potential for violence.

At least six such points of vulnerability can be readily identified; all are recognized in international peacebuilding programmes as areas requiring attention and assistance. They are:

1 *Demobilization and demilitarization; integration/restructuring of rebel and government armed forces.* Inadequate DDR (disarmament, demobilization and reintegration) programmes risk creating a recruiting pool for armed gangs, criminal elements and political conflict entrepreneurs. Short-term risks include violent protests and direct action by ex-combatants to press their demands.

2 *The illegal or 'shadow' economy* developed during the war. Profit-seeking structures may develop into organized crime and seek protection through political alliances. While not always overtly violent, illegal economic structures of this kind have historically used at least the threat of violence to maintain themselves.

3 *Property disputes.* Wars create forced population displacement and often conflicting property claims when displaced persons return. Incomplete administrative records and competing legal traditions typically complicate settlements.

4 *Justice sector.* Lack of accountability mechanisms for war-time criminal violence and human rights violations is often assumed to encourage continued impunity and post-war violence, but the empirical evidence overall is weak and inconclusive (Thoms *et al.* 2008). Ongoing and continuing impunity, however, clearly encourages vigilante justice, whether used politically to reverse the new order or to assert a community sense of justice (which happens in countries that have not experienced internal war as well).

5 *'Aftershocks'.* The end of the war can be followed by targeted violence that follows the war-time divisions but on a smaller scale, such as revenge or reprisal killings and social or ethnic cleansing.

6 *The peace dividend.* The end of a war encourages expectations of peace and prosperity. Contemporary post-war expectations are inflated by high-profile international pledging conferences and aid agencies arriving with ambitious reconstruction agendas. High post-war unemployment is particularly likely to create tension and a pool of potential recruits for conflict entrepreneurs and street politics.

Types of violence. Post-war environments also seem vulnerable to particular forms of violence. A spike in homicides is one. Although variations in crime rates are notoriously difficult to explain the much-cited case of El Salvador prominently reflects the virtual absence of a national police for almost the entire first two years of the post-war period. The 1992 peace agreement stipulated the dissolution of the previous police forces (three different branches) and the constitution of a new force. The first unit of the new police (PNC) was deployed in March 1993 and national deployment was not completed until 1994 (Call 2007: 37–8). The reintroduction of police clearly helped to bring crime down to 'normal' levels. The subsequent rise has been attributed to broader social dysfunctional developments of inequality, poverty and social exclusion, combined with repressive policing (*mano duro*) that backfired.

Violence against women can also be understood at least in part as a direct legacy of the war in cases where sexual violence has been widespread or used instrumentally during the conflict, as in Guatemala. The extremely high murder rate of women in post-war Guatemala – around 4,000 were killed in the period 2000–8 alone – is often interpreted this way (GHRC 2008). But the extreme violence against women a decade after the war reflected other factors as well. Human rights activists pointed to the near total impunity for such crimes. Intense lobbying by rights activists led to the recognition of murder of women as a special category under the law – *femicide* – which obligated the state to follow special procedures of investigation and impose severe punishment. The conditions were incorporated in the Law against Femicide and other Forms of Violence against Women passed by the Guatemalan Parliament in April 2008.

How these conflict dynamics develop will depend on the capacities of a given post-war environment to constrain or manage the potential for violence. Institutions that can address claims of injustice and grievances and defuse tension are central to this process, but so, as *ultima ratio*, is the coercive capacity of the state. The conflict dynamics are heavily context-dependent but some general features can be suggested.

The role of the state or an equivalent agent is critically important in constraining or managing the potential for social violence and post-war environments can here differ markedly. A post-war situation structured in the logic of the Victor's Peace is marked by a strong but deeply partisan state. This state is able to deal decisively with a range of post-war vulnerabilities, but in a post-war and still divided society this is likely to entail a great deal of state violence and state-directed deprivation, and to encourage private violence under cover of political denunciations. In a Loser's Peace, certain kinds of bottom-up violence are welcomed and used strategically by local elites to capture or control the state; issues of justice, the peace dividend and property claims will depend heavily upon the relationship to the dominant power structure. In the Divided Peace, the state remains strongly contested yet weak and the protagonists have few incentives to disarm. Contentious issues relating to post-war transitions are settled in the context of a privatization of security and violence, and a state captured by factions. International peace operations can to some extent modify the use of violence to assert claims or resolve disputes associated with the transition in all these cases. In certain situations, a unified and coherent international peace operation can virtually substitute for a weak or dysfunctional state, at least in the short run, as in the Pacified Peace.

The case study chapters that follow explore a range of conflict dynamics in post-war environments. They are selected to demonstrate the range and variety – tragically, the richness – of the phenomenon. After the two 'classic' cases of 'Victor's Peace' and 'Loser's Peace' in an earlier historical period, the current cases are grouped according to geographical region where contemporary versions of all four sociological types are found.

Notes

1 I wish to thank Torunn Wimpelmann Chaudhary and Ingrid Samset at the Chr. Michelsen Institute for contributions and comments to this chapter.
2 Note that compromise peace settlements are more prone to collapse in renewed war than conflicts which end in total victory/defeat; this has been an argument for letting wars be fought out to the bitter end. If the purpose is to reduce violence, however, the possibility of massive post-war violence after total victory must be included in the calculus.
3 The closest is probably a study by the United Nations Interregional Crime and Justice Research Institute (UNICRI) of victimization surveys in 13 African nations (not including Liberia) for the period 1992–2002 (Naude *et al.*, 2006.

Bibliography

Archer, D. and Gartner, R. (1976) 'Violent acts and violent times', *American Sociological Review*, 41(6): 937–63.

Barnett, M. and Zürcher, C. (2009) 'The peacebuilder's contract: why peacebuilding recreates weak states', in R. Paris and T.D. Sisk, *The Dilemmas of Statebuilding*, New York: Routledge.

Berdal, M. (2009) *Building Peace after War*, London: The International Institute for Strategic Studies.

Berdal, M. and Malone, D. (eds) (2000) *Greed and Grievance: Economic Agendas in Civil War*, Boulder, CO: Lynne Rienner.

Call, C.T. (2007) 'The mugging of a success story: justice and security sector reform in El Salvador', in Charles T. Call (ed.) *Constructing Justice and Security After War*, Washington, DC: US Institute of Peace.

Collier, P. and Hoeffler, A. (2004) 'Murder by numbers: comparisons and interrelationships between homicide and civil war', *CSAE, Working Paper Series*, 2004–10.

Collier, P., Elliott, V.L., Hegre, H. and Hoeffler, A. (2003) *Breaking the Conflict Trap*, Washington, DC: World Bank.

Cousens, E. and Kumar, C. (2001) *Peacebuilding as Politics*, Boulder, CO: Lynne Rienner.

Cramer, C. (2006) *Civil War is Not a Stupid Thing: Accounting for Violence in Developing Countries*, London: Hurst & Co.

Doyle, M.W. and Sambanis, N. (2006) *Making War and Building Peace: United Nations Peace Operations*, Princeton: Princeton University Press.

Duffield, M. (1998) 'Post-modern conflict: warlords, post-adjustment states and private protection', *Civil Wars*, 1(1): 65–102.

Duffield, M. (2001) *Global Governance and the New Wars: The Merging of Development and Security*, London: Zed Books.

Fernández García, M.C. (2004) *Lynching in Guatemala: Legacy of War and Impunity*,

Center for International Affairs, Harvard University. Online, available at: www. wcfia.harvard.edu/fellows/papers/2003–04/fernandez.pdf.

Giustozzi, A. (2003) *Respectable Warlords? The Transition from War of All Against All to Peaceful Competition in Afghanistan*, Crisis States Research Center. Online, available at: www.crisisstates.com/download/others/SeminarAG29012003.pdf.

Gleditsch, N.P., Eriksson, M., Sollenberg, M. and Strand, H. (2001) 'Armed conflict 1946–2001: a new dataset', *Journal of Peace Research*, 39(5): 615–37.

Godoy, A.S. (2002) 'Lynchings and the democratization of terror in postwar Guatemala: implications for human rights', *Human Rights Quarterly*, 24(3): 640–61.

Goodhand, J. and Cramer, C. (2002) 'Try again, fail again, fail better? War, the state and the "post-conflict" challenge in Afghanistan', *Development and Change*, 33(5): 885–910.

Guatemala Human Rights Commission/USA (2008) *Guatemala's Femicide Law: Progress against Impunity*. Online, available at: www.ghrc-usa.org/Publications/Femicide_Law_ProgressAgainstImpunity.pdf.

Hampson, F.O. (1996) *Why Peace Settlements Succeed or Fail*, Washington, DC: US Institute of Peace.

Hume, M. (2009) 'El Salvador: the limits of a violent peace', in M. Pugh, N. Cooper and M. Turner (eds), *Critical Perspectives on the Political Economy of Peacebuilding*, London: Palgrave Press.

Junne, G. and Verkoren, W. (eds) (2005) *Postconflict Development: Meeting New Challenges*, Boulder, CO: Lynne Rienner.

Keen, D. (2000) 'War and peace: what's the difference?', *International Peacekeeping*, 7(4): 1–22.

Keen, D. (2002) '"Since I am a dog, beware my fangs": beyond a "rational violence" framework in the Sierra Leonean war', *LSE Crisis States Programme Working Paper 14*.

Milliken, J. and Krause, K. (eds) (2003) *State Failure Collapse and Reconstruction*, Oxford: Blackwell.

Moser, C. and McIlwaine, C. (2001) *Violence in a Post-Conflict Context: Urban Poor Perceptions from Guatemala*, Washington, DC: World Bank.

Mundt, A. and Schmeidl, S. (2009) 'Between a rock and a hard place: the return of internally displaced persons to Northern Afghanistan', Brookings Project on Internal Displacement. Online, available at: www.brookings.edu/opinions/2009/0601_afghanistan_mundt.aspx.

Naudé, C.M.B., Prinsloo, J.H. and Ladikos, A. (2006) *Experiences of Crime in Thirteen African Countries: Results from the International Crime Victim Survey*. Online, available at: www.rechten.uvt.nl/icvs/pdffiles/ICVS%2013%20African%20countries.pdf.

Nilsson, R.A. (2008) *Dangerous Liaisons: Why Ex-combatants Return to Violence. Cases from the Republic of Congo and Sierra Leone*, Uppsala: Uppsala University Press.

Nordstrom, C. (2004) *Shadows of War: Violence, Power, and International Profiteering in the Twenty-First Century*, Berkeley, CA: University of California Press.

North, D.C., Wallis, J.J. and Weingast, B.R. (2009) *Violence and Social Orders*, New York: Cambridge University Press.

Paris, R. (2004) *At War's End*, New York: Cambridge University Press.

Peacock, S.C. and Beltran, A. (2003) *Hidden Powers in Post-Conflict Guatemala: Illegal Armed Groups and the Forces Behind Them*, Washington, DC: Washington Office on Latin America.

Pearce, J. (1999) 'Peace-building on the periphery: lessons from Central America', *Third World Quarterly*, 20(1): 51–68.

Prophette, A., Paz, C., Noval, J.G. and Gomez, N. (2003) *Guatemala: Violence in the Guatemalan Post Conflict Society – Manifestations and Ways of Resolution*, CERI-IPA-UNUPG Project 2002–3.

Pugh, M., Cooper, N. and Goodhand, J. (2004) *War Economies in a Regional Context*, Boulder, CO: Lynne Rienner.

Reagan, A. (2008) 'The Bougainville intervention: political legitimacy and sustainable peace-building', in G. Fry and T. Tara Kabutaulaka, *Intervention and Statebuilding in the Pacific*, Manchester: Manchester University Press, 184–208.

Reno, W. (1998) *Warlord Politics and African States*, Boulder, CO and London: Lynne Rienner.

Richmond, O. (2005) *The Transformation of Peace*, Basingstoke: Palgrave.

Robinson, W.I. (2003) *Transnational Conflicts: Central America, Social Change and Globalization*, London: Verso.

Rotberg, R.I. (2004) *When States Fail: Causes and Consequences*. Princeton: Princeton University Press.

Sambanis, N. (2004) 'Using case studies to expand economic models of civil war', *Perspectives on Politics*, 2(2): 259–79.

Savenije, M. and van der Borgh, C. (2004) 'Youth gangs, social exclusion and the transformation of violence in El Salvador', in K. Koonings and D. Krujit, *Armed Actors: Organised Violence and State Failure in Latin America*, London: Zed Books, 155–71.

Scheper-Hughes, N. and Bourgois, P. (2002) 'Introduction: making sense of violence', in N. Scheper-Hughes and P. Bourgois, *Violence in War and Peace*, London: Blackwell Publishing, 1–33.

Sisk, T.D. (2009) 'Pathways of the political: election processes after civil war', in R. Paris and T.D. Sisk, *The Dilemmas of Statebuilding*, New York: Routledge, 196–224.

Soto, A. de and del Castillo, G. (1994) 'Obstacles to peace-building', *Foreign Policy*, 94 (Spring).

Stedman, S.J., Rothchild, D. and Cousens, E.N. (eds) (2002) *Ending Civil Wars: The Implementation of Peace Agreements*, Boulder, CO: Lynne Rienner.

Steenkamp, C. (2005) 'The legacy of war: conceptualizing a "culture of violence" to explain violence after peace accords', *Round Table*, 94(379): 253–67.

Stewart, F. (2001) *Horizontal Inequalities: A Neglected Dimension of Development*, Helsinki: UN/WIDER.

Suhrke, A., Berg Harpviken, K. and Strand, A. (2004) *Conflictual Peacebuilding: Afghanistan Two Years after Bonn*, Bergen: Chr. Michelsen Institute. Online, available at: www.cmi.no/publications/publication/?1763=conflictual-peacebuilding.

Thoms, O.N.T., Ron, J. and Paris, R. (2008) *The Effects of Transitional Justice Mechanisms: A Summary of Empirical Research Findings and Implications for Analysts and Practitioners*, Centre for International Policy Studies, University of Ottawa. Online, available at: www.gsdrc.org/go/display&type=Document&id=3090.

Tilly, C. (2003) *The Politics of Collective Violence*, Cambridge: Cambridge University Press.

Toft, M.D. (2009) *Securing the Peace: The Durable Settlement of Civil Wars*, Princeton: Princeton University Press.

Torres, G.M. (2008) 'Social justice amidst Guatemala's post-conflict violence', *Studies in Social Justice*, 2(1).

United Nations (2009) *Report of the Secretary-General on Peacebuilding in the Immediate Aftermath of Conflict*, 11 June. A/63/881–S/2009/304.

USIP (2001) *Training to Help Traumatized Populations*, Washington, DC: United States Institute of Peace. Online, available at: www.usip.org.

Utas, M. (2003) *Sweet Battlefields: Youth and the Liberian Civil War*, Uppsala University: Dissertations in Cultural Anthropology.

Walter, Barbara F. (2002) *Committing to Peace: The Successful Settlement of Civil Wars*, Princeton and Oxford: Princeton University Press.

Zinecker, H. (2006) *Violence in Peace: Forms and Causes of Postwar Violence in Guatemala*, Frankfurt: Peace Research Institute of Frankfurt, PRIF Report no. 76.

Part I
Echoes from history

2   Violence and the post-conflict state in historical perspective

Spain, 1936–48

Michael Richards

In the rebel zone during the Spanish Civil War repression and death were closely related to the construction of a new power which claimed to be coherent; in the government or loyalist zone, as the authorities recognized, repression and death had to do with the collapse of power (Juliá *et al.* 1999: 25).[1] Notwithstanding the several similarities between the repressive processes in both zones, this essential difference in relation to power is important. In the rebel zone, a state of war was declared immediately in July 1936.[2] Ultimate power passed to the military and was based on a rigorous system of authority enshrining codes of honour, order and discipline. The most coherent and effective element of Franco's nascent 'New State' was therefore precisely its coercive apparatus. By contrast, access to the Republican state's coercive instruments had been undermined by the military rebellion on 18 July. Its institutions were in disarray and had lost public credibility. In Republican Spain, the state of war was not declared until January 1939, only months prior to General Franco's final victory. Virtually from the beginning of the conflict the rebel system of authority was therefore more secure, solid and stable than that of the government. Based on the evidence of his own eyes as he prepared to flee from Republican Spain as the popular revolution burgeoned in response to the military coup, the English writer Gerald Brenan argued in August 1936[3] that

> Those who point to atrocities … on the Government side often forget the provocation and the circumstances. When soldiers and police have to go to the front because other soldiers and police have rebelled, who is left to keep order among an enraged population?

As the republic clawed back control of its coercive forces from trade union militias and revolutionary committees, particularly from May 1937, the level of violence against 'enemies of the revolution' declined dramatically. The war was thereby prolonged by organized resistance, but by then the rebel state had established itself militarily, domestically and internationally.

Spain's war did not arise, therefore, from a mere outbreak of troublesome insurgency, but from an efficient coalition force (soon to be called 'the Nationalists') which was well aided from the beginning and benefited

from considerable social support. Since this chapter is primarily concerned with *post*-civil war violence, it will be focusing particularly on the
repression carried out by these Nationalist forces, which would gradually
become the basis of the victorious Francoist state. Thus, the state-building
process ran along a continuum, from 18 July 1936 (the date of the military
rising) and beyond the formal end of the war (1 April 1939) into the
1940s. We therefore need to talk at some length about the civil war years
and to have a sense of the scale of the Nationalist violence.

In the northeastern region of Aragón, to take one instance, around
8,500 men and women were killed by rebel forces during the period
1936–46. Some 940 of them – a very substantial number – were to be
executed after the formal end of the civil war in April 1939. The vast
majority of the total died in the first months of the war and, importantly,
in areas where there had been no real fighting. This was a purge of
enemies and potential enemies. Those executed can be categorized fairly
accurately into social groups. Overwhelmingly they were industrial and
urban manual workers, rural proletarians, peasants, middle-class Republicans, liberals, left-of-centre political functionaries, trade union organizers
and professionals (Casanova *et al.* 1992: 221). Elsewhere, during the first
days of the rebellion in Logroño, La Rioja, there were 30 executions on
average per day. Some 2,000 were to be executed in total although, again,
there had been no war. Navarra was another rural northern province
which had fallen straight away to the rebels in July 1936 with very little
fighting. The repression was extremely bloody, resulting in more than
2,700 killings. In the south, in Huelva, there were more than 3,000
recorded killings and the word *guerra* there has long referred to political
repression rather than a military clash. The minimum number of deaths
in western Badajoz, according to an exhaustive study, was 6,610; the real
number could easily be doubled in calculating the number killed throughout the province (Espinosa Maestre 2003).

Overall, across both competing zones, there were some 350,000 deaths
during the period 1936–9, over and above the predictable rate based on
pre-war statistics. The pre-war norm was 380,000 deaths annually whereas
413,000 mortalities were recorded officially for 1936, 472,000 in 1937,
485,000 in 1938, and 470,000 in 1939, roughly a 20 per cent rise in the
1935 rate each year during the period 1937–9. In terms of the two competing zones, it is generally accepted by historians that some 100,000 'Reds'
were executed by the Nationalists during the war years and probably a
further 50,000 in the post-war purge (Juliá *et al.* 1999: 410–12). Fewer,
approximately 38,000, were killed in the Republican zone, mostly during
the first three months, from July to September 1936, in the revolutionary
violence and murderous anticlerical purge which followed the military
rebellion. Almost 50 per cent of killings in the Republican zone took place
in Madrid and Catalonia. In sum, therefore, throughout Spain, about half
of the total wartime deaths recorded in one way or another occurred
through non-battle front violence. The vast majority of these, on both
sides, were not prisoners who had been captured at the front but individuals rounded up in communities, or taken from city and provincial

prison cells, because of alleged political affiliations and allegiances, often resulting from a denunciation from within the community to the authorities. The nature of political control in a given locality was affected by the level of popular support and collaboration offered in exchange for protection provided to the population by the 'liberators' from the 'enemy' and from the human effects of the war.

The post-war death toll resulting from repression, hunger, disease and imprisonment was almost as high as wartime. Mortality did not return to pre-war levels until 1943. Deaths through war-related violence continued significantly until 1948. With an official figure of 484,000, there were as many deaths recorded in 1941 as there were at the height of the war. In some instances this was because of delays in registering the wartime dead (for fear of association with 'the defeated'), but in the main death resulted from political repression and a continuation of wartime political and social conditions – the failure of reconciliation – leading to widespread epidemic disease and post-war hunger. To take one example, in Catalonia, one of the country's most developed regions, the infant mortality rate was on average 40 per cent higher throughout the 1940s than in 1935, reaching levels unheard of since the influenza epidemic of 1918–19, and only beginning to decline during the second half of the decade. Average general life expectancy in Catalonia in 1941–5 was lowered by four years from that of 1935; the number of widows under 30 multiplied by five times that of 1930 (Riquer and Culla 1989: 27, 42). Adding the post-war recorded figures of deaths above the pre-war norm (215,000 during 1940–2) to the wartime figure, we can therefore estimate the total human losses on both sides attributable directly or indirectly to the civil war as 565,000. Some three-quarters of the total war-related deaths in the period 1936–44 were non-battle fatalities.

Although there are important, relatively conventional, battle fronts, the territorial boundaries in intra-state or irregular wars are put in place provisionally, as a result of contingent factors, through social interaction as well as state power, the latter being debilitated and fluctuating as a result of the conflict. Civil war boundaries are therefore highly fluid and more often than not run through localities and communities rather than around them. Crossing or transgressing such sinuous lines, or finding oneself on the wrong side, is easily done and potentially fatal. In rural peasant communities in Spain, victims and perpetrators often knew one another personally. But also in urban situations it is in the nature of civil wars that loss is intimate and very few families in Spain remained unaffected by the trauma of this intimacy. In many communities, those who had access to weapons and were able to use them with impunity, effectively *became* the state.[4] Those who were the targets of the violence were forcibly placed 'beyond the state', in a precarious condition of legal limbo. If they survived, the later ostracism suffered depended on the manner of the post-war reconstruction of authority as exercised in each locality.

Departing from much of the historiography on Spain's conflict, which has mainly focused on politics understood narrowly, the intention here is to employ explicitly a *generic* understanding of civil war as 'armed combat within the boundaries of a recognized sovereign entity between parties subject to a common authority at the outset of the hostilities' (Kalyvas 2006: 5). In what is nothing less than a struggle for the nation, the irreconcilability of the goals of the belligerents in civil wars can be assumed. In the case of Spain, the social and geographic salience of the fighting and the reach and depth of the issues of contention, were important factors in accounting for the scale of the violence, whether as direct justifications of terror or in creating indirect political pressures and fears which produced opportunities and actions, such as denunciation, ultimately leading to violence. This may not be quite the case in strict terms in other sub-state wars involving relatively reduced numbers of insurgents, covering a relatively contained geographic area and representing a relatively mild threat to the state.

There are international and domestic ramifications of placing sovereignty at the heart of our analysis of Spain's war. This chapter has to do with the latter – civil conflict and its aftermath as a state-building process – though the international aspects are not insignificant. Since it was not immediately suppressed by forces at the disposal of the government, the military rebellion on 18 July 1936 had the effect of de-legitimating existing the state's sovereignty and disabling coercive apparatus. The rebels' declaration of a state of war profoundly challenged the state's monopoly of legitimate force and was thus a claim to sovereignty. In the process, the distinction between war and crime was also confused.

Internationally, it should be remembered that although the established state and the elected government of the Second Republic enjoyed international legal recognition at the time of the military rebellion – and a substantial degree of popular legitimacy (though this had come under severe pressure, especially since 1931) – in pursuance of the policy of appeasement adopted by Britain, France and the United States the incumbent government was denied access to foreign allies and trade relationships with all other governments (through the August 1936 'non-intervention' agreement), apart from the highly uneven relationship resorted to with Stalin's Soviet Union. On the other side, with substantial aid from Hitler and Mussolini more or less from the first moment in July 1936 and widespread, though not unanimous, support from the middle classes and from within the Spanish state's apparatus of coercion (particularly policing forces of various kinds), the military rebellion cannot be seen as mere insurgency. Common authority was rent asunder immediately and (unusually in civil wars) the incumbent power was placed in a situation of inferiority almost from the beginning.

Both sides became locked in battle to reconstruct the state and its legitimacy. The relevant criteria were: the effectiveness or otherwise of existing legal institutions and instruments and the nature of their wartime reformation; their own respective ideologies; the human and material resources marshalled; the harnessing of reserves of coercive force; the level and nature of social support enjoyed; and the aforementioned international attitudes. After a civil war situation, such as that in Spain in 1939, legitimacy *across society* is unlikely, but the post-war aim, for whoever wins, is bound to be a gradual expansion of social consent. For various reasons reconciliation in Spain took many years. Alongside these criteria of legitimation, the internal dynamics of civil war – its irregular nature – suggest several further areas which affect the nature of violence during and after the conflict: varying levels of organization; access to information and means of communication; the ability to employ these effectively; clear structures of command; and ideological unity (King 1997: 44). Ultimately, the struggle for sovereignty revolves around the collaboration of individuals and groups with political actors locally who possess such resources and have access to the resurgent or embryonic state forces on each side.

Charles Tilly has defined collective violence as 'episodic social interaction' that results at least in part from coordination among the perpetrators (Tilly 2003: 3). This coordination is often achieved ideologically. The nature of collective violence in civil wars is affected by the balance between coercion and legitimation already mentioned and the dynamics of (*a*) military conquest and resistance and (*b*) social revolution and counter-revolution. Violence as social interaction in the Spanish case was thus inflicted not only physically through arms but through economic relations – against property, for example – and psychologically, culturally and ideologically. Violence encompasses non-consensually imposed resolutions to conflicts, through other means than physical force, including economic strategies of resource hoarding imposed through the outcome of internal war, although the opportunity for material and political advantage is always accompanied by the threat of physical force.

From war to post-war: processes of violence

To summarize, the processes and mechanisms through which violence occurred in the Spanish war can be explained by reference to (*a*) sovereignty, legitimacy and the state and (*b*) contingent political, doctrinal and cultural dynamics. In the Spanish case, considerations relating to the state and the nature of power have generally been applied to the violence of the Republican or government zone, whereas ideological considerations have been applied to analysis of rebel violence. In the Republican zone, the use of collective violence was not always well controlled and for a substantial period, in many areas, there was no unitary political authority. Revolutionary measures aimed at property and against religion were popularly adopted as a response to the military rebellion. The incumbents occupied the largest cities – Madrid and Barcelona – but this advantage was only relative because Republican divisions made protection of the citizenry extremely difficult. The government left the besieged capital for Valencia in November 1936 leaving Madrid in the hands of the remnants of the army and the political militias. The defence turned out to be successful and prolonged, but, paradoxically, the large cities were also strongholds of the republic's main ideological opponents – middle-class Catholics – whose underground activities threatened to undermine the war effort. The defenders were therefore drawn towards bloody purges, only partially rational as a war strategy. Almost as soon as the military coup took place and the revolution surged in response, legal judges in Republican areas came under suspicion and many were arrested, were killed, or fled in fear. People's Tribunals, headed by local leaders of workers' parties, took their place. The influence of the Spanish Communist Party (*Partido Comunista de España*, PCE) and its Soviet advisers, owing to the republic's dependency on Stalin's military aid, led to the importation of the chillingly rational liquidating methods of the People's Commissariat of Internal Affairs (*Narodnyy komissariat vnutrennikh del*, NKVD), witnessed notoriously in the mass killings of Nationalist prisoners at Paracuellos del Jarama, outside Madrid, in November and December 1936 (Viñas 2007: 35–87).

Given the outcome of the war, this chapter examines the violence of the Francoist (or 'Nationalist') forces (those who became the victors), as the foundation of what followed the war. An important continuity between war and post-war related to the magnitude and geographic extension of the conflict. Although the war was formally declared by General Franco to have ended on 1 April 1939, if we look at the regional and local dimensions, in practice it 'ended' at various moments throughout the almost three years of warfare. This has a direct bearing on what we call 'post-war violence'. Territory fell and authority was re-established continuously throughout the period from July 1936 to April 1939. The conditions of the military rebellion against the government in the summer of 1936 were re-created as Spain was conquered. In many areas, such as Cádiz, Seville, Huelva, Aragón or parts of Córdoba or Badajoz, there had been no war at all, as we have seen, but an organized process of killing of certain identifiable sections of society.

The rebels' ideological imperative, stated often enough before the rebellion took place and which informed the military modus operandi, cannot be doubted. General Mola's secret instruction to rebels issued in May 1936 is notorious: 'it is necessary to propagate an atmosphere of terror ... Anybody who openly or secretly defends the Popular Front must be shot'. When approached by the Socialist leader Indalecio Prieto, shortly after the war had begun, to open negotiations for peace, Mola replied that 'this war has to end with the extermination of the enemies of Spain' (Iribarren 1937: 169). Once the conflict was raging, however, the objectives tended to be restated in precise and rational politico-military strategic terms: the short-term aim of securing territory and pacifying a potentially hostile rear-guard and the longer-term aim of purging the working class and its allies, leaders and activists 'to exorcise the threat, once and for all, of proletarian disturbances, risings and revolutions' (Fraser 1979: 170). Not forgetting the constant presence of the ideological framework which demonized the 'other', 'selective violence' was used in two ways: in the form of mass violence, as witnessed in the massacre of Republican supporters in the bull ring of Badajoz in August 1936, as an *example* to cause the occupied population to cower; and as a rationalized strategy, based on private information through denunciation, to deter defections to the other side. 'Information', as used in the latter formulation, has no necessary connotation of accuracy, of course, but is instead dependent on individuals' positioning for power in a threatening situation. Information *across* the divide played a different role to that exchanged *within* the zones, but is also relevant to generating violence. The newspapers of both zones offered sensational accounts of repression in the opposite camp and little about violence in their own localities. Atrocity stories were filtered in from the opposing side, by radio for example, and were often disseminated by political newspapers, fuelling calls for revenge. State authorities sought 'information' knowing that what came back was partly based on rumours and ideological propaganda and social and political pathological perceptions, which had often been constructed originally by the very same authorities. Private information included not only personal denunciation, but also more codified intelligence such as blacklists drawn up by employers and the ubiquitous index cards of opposition political groups, often drawing on official records.

The post-war state-building process can therefore be traced to the civil war itself and indeed to its beginning on 18 July 1936 rather than its formal end on 1 April 1939. In some instances – Navarra, Zaragoza and Burgos, for example, in northern and central Spain and large parts of the south – the conflict ended within weeks or even days of the initiating rebellion, almost three years before April 1939, and the 'purge' of society began instantly as a central element in the construction of the new authority.

Typically, conquest and occupation entailed the collaboration of units of the rebel army with insurgent militia groups. Posts in the local government were named by the 'liberating' forces and conquered regions were referred to as though they were colonies and their populations, more or less, as 'natives'. The military regions were ruled by high-profile military officers who frequently in the 1940s would combine the roles of civil governor, provincial head of the party and chief of the military region.

The Nationalist militias were raised from the civilian population and were closely associated with the political organizations which had been at the heart of opposition in the pre-war years to the Republican reformist and democratizing programme. These fighting bands were principally composed of the fascist Falange and the Requeté, the militia of the monarchist, Catholic and traditionalist Carlist movement. With the rebellion in July 1936 there was intense mobilization for the cause in Castile and Navarra, where large numbers of rural tenant farmers and smallholders could be called upon, and in more socially mixed regions such as Granada. Militiamen were active in the repression in two distinct situations: first, in taking the lead in military combat units; and second, in staying behind in the rear-guard. Both groups were involved in the 'purges', but while those who fought were 'idealists', those who stayed behind (in both zones) were often seen, at the time and long afterwards, as 'criminals' because of their role in political killing.

Though officially volunteers, these uniformed groups had a more or less paramilitary background and functioned according to significant warrior myths. Exaltation of violence was an element of the ideology which fuelled the killing accompanying the rebellion and subsequent occupation of territory. Violence behind the lines was depicted as a necessary sacrifice. There were many volunteers ready to join in Falangist sorties – effectively death squads – into the countryside in search of 'Reds' to kill. Their brutal work was gradually incorporated into various ad hoc public order columns and forces of occupation and there was increasingly closer collaboration between the militia and military courts.

The violence associated with the activation of 'us-and-them' boundaries could potentially be avoided by political affiliation: party registration rose spectacularly in both zones during the war, in part because of commitment and effective mobilization but also because of the positive opportunity a membership card presented in the struggle to avoid suspicion or gain advantage. This led to post-war dangers if membership cards of left-wing organizations were discovered.

Established pre-war local elites, linked through networks of local economic and social power, collaborated in the elimination of Republican authorities, left-wing supporters, 'Marxists' and class enemies, liberal intellectuals, 'troublemakers', recalcitrant employees and those on landowners' 'blacklists'. The territoriality of sovereignty was expressed by the landed class in the violent reclaiming of property. Elites did not act alone, however. Through the issuing of certificates of good conduct, for example, relatively lowly individuals could become the arbiters of people's lives (e.g. Lazo 1998: 59). The division of those who were 'supporters' (*'adictos'*) and those who were 'suspect' was determined by such local, often private, initiatives and procedures, which were often disturbingly intimate.

Many victims of the wartime and post-war violence were denounced by a neighbour or a family member merely for their political beliefs. Denunciation in a political context has been defined as 'the volunteered provision of information by the population at large about instances of disapproved behaviour' (Gellately 1990: 130). In Spain, the voluntary element from society was essential to much of the repression. In extreme circumstances – totalitarian rule, occupation, revolution or civil war – voluntary acts of individuals can lead directly to violence; indeed, denunciation can be seen as a primary micro-level basis of intimate violence. The pressure to conform is considerable in this environment and can lead to complicity. In some cases, the closeness of the relationship between denouncer and denounced, potentially construed suspiciously by the new authorities, was part of the motivation because it seemed to be a way of distancing oneself from those who would inevitably be targets. This intimate violence was what was felt brutally and kept memories alive for decades. The 'midnight knock on the door' became part of post-war folklore. The effects on established social networks – family, friendship, employment, work and patronage and community and the neighbourhood – were also profound.

As has often been noted in such circumstances, barbarity, ultimately and paradoxically, contributed to a sense of normality. A liberal republican chemist commented on the situation in Falangist Castile shortly after the rebellion, when the wave of executions was at its height, that 'only by acting as though everything is perfectly normal can you show that you are above suspicion' (Fraser 1979: 168). In fact, many people went further and obeyed the instinct of self-preservation and the will to prove loyalty by denouncing others to the authorities. But denunciation was also actively solicited by authorities, which is not necessarily to say that people were reluctant. In any event, the informal social reinforcement of the terror system was important.

Denouncing 'enemies' was constructed by civil war authorities (on both sides) as a duty. On the Francoist side, denunciation was so common an occurrence that we can view it as part of the process of rebuilding the state. The head of public order in Lérida, Catalonia, published an order in July 1938, as the region was occupied, which succinctly reinforces this point: 'Whoever does not denounce those not worthy of forming part of the New State will be considered a poor citizen' (Barallat 2002: 69). The effect in such a deeply fragmented society was a virtual hysteria of suspicion and a wave of accusations which penetrated as far as private life and the family (e.g. Cobo Romero and Ortega López 2005: 124, 126). In the immediate aftermath of the war, an archive was established by the Francoist authorities to collect and collate 'evidence' of Republican wartime 'crimes against Spain' (Ministerio de Justicia 1943).

In Málaga, the calls for denunciations played on the emotions as well as familiar tropes of 'purification'. Appealing to instincts of revenge and fears of difference, in the daily newspapers the local Falange called for 'the criminal low-life' and the 'badly born' who had 'blooded the streets of the city' to be exposed and the civil governor threatened fines for anyone intervening on behalf of those detained. In an era of 'martyrdom' there was no place for 'sentimentalism' (Gómez Bajuelo 1937: 51). One young domestic servant in the city was reported by her employer because, though she had been of 'normal conduct and antecedents' before the war, later announced that she had 'joined the anarchists'. Afterwards, it was claimed in the denunciation, she had declared that her employers, the householders, would probably be killed like many others because 'if the situation had been the other way around, they would have been doing the killing'.[5] There was little need for any further evidence, although the case illustrates how the definition of 'crime' had been blurred by the fearful circumstances of war and the ideological pressure of the nascent Francoist state.

A 40-year-old working-class woman, also from Málaga, received a prison sentence of six years for 'excitation of revolution' after being denounced as a 'leftist' and for having supported anti-clerical incendiary assaults on her parish church in the Republican years prior to the civil war, later 'displaying happiness' at killings and, like other women, of 'celebrating' the expulsion of the religious from convents and ecclesiastical residences. Again, there was little evidence to support these accusations of 'crimes of thought'. She was also suspended from holding any public or private employment, any office or right to aid, assistance or suffrage and, for good measure, the court had noted that she ought to have dedicated herself to 'women's labours' rather than involving herself in political matters. Her case, as was automatic for political convicts until 1942, was referred to the Court of Political Responsibilities for the possible order of reparations and confiscation of her property and that of her family. Another woman, 30 years old with four children and married to a man at the front with government forces, was denounced for showing support for the Republican fighters as they passed through in lorries bound for the war. When the city fell, she left and did not return voluntarily thereafter. Her case typified the way an individual's unexplained absence sometimes presented somebody else with an opportunity to prove loyalty or gain economically by denouncing, with the assumption that the subject would not be located and therefore not suffer any penalty: a potentially 'victimless' act in order to gain benefit.

To summarize, the violence of occupation and its social reinforcement through denunciation, bound together the insurgents and their supporters during the civil war. The rebellion had not signalled a mere change of political regime, but the beginnings of a new correlation of social forces in which all who participated were, in theory, implicated. A framework of shared and largely anti-democratic ideas confirmed the sense of justification. Nationalist and socially conservative ideology ascribed particular meanings to the key political identities of the 1930s and this process was intensified during the war itself. Justification of the war as a religious crusade involved group activation of pre-existing social distinctions between believers and unbelievers, deserving and undeserving, and 'good' and 'evil'. The extensive and violent purge of liberal schoolteachers was a case in point. Rather than party political sympathies or even ideology, the political dynamics peculiar to civil war – the loss of state authority, fear of abandonment by law, the threat to property – shaped the violence with which the post-war era 'proper' (from 1 April 1939) would begin and hence determined the nature of the post-war state-building process.

This conclusion is borne out in the sentiments expressed by local representatives of the Francoist 'New State'. The Provincial head of the state party in Toledo, for example, outlining problems and aims to Madrid in October 1939:

> The first moral problem is to carry out rapid and energetic justice; the families of those killed [by the Republican side in the war], who are the most solid moral mainstay that the province and the Cause possesses, become demoralized if they see weakness. The province has approximately 20,000 killers who must urgently disappear; these people have never worked and they never will, they have never been grateful and they never will; assuming that each one costs only 2 pesetas daily, that is still 40,000 pesetas a day; 15 million a year! With that I could sort out this province economically.

And from the south of the country in June 1939: 'We lived before without justice, which is the greatest torment that a man can suffer. But now we have justice, rapid, pure, perfect. It is the bread of the soul.... Everything is going well. The criminals are falling'.[6]

Post-war state-building and the economy of repression, 1939–48

With Axis aid, substantial technological advantage and few if any military setbacks, wartime factionalism within the Nationalist side was insignificant.

Moreover, there would be no peace-keeping force and no neutralized zone as refugees fled through Catalonia towards France. Few limitations were imposed on the actions of the victors. The prolonged intensity of the fighting and of the violence, its viciousness and extensiveness, particularly against non-combatants, and the intractability of the war and the seeming impossibility of negotiation were all significant as sources of post-war violence. State-building and stability were bound up with total victory and therefore with a continuation of extreme violence (King 1997: 35–6). Franco described the purpose of the post-war purge as 'cleaning the site ready for our structure'.[7]

Considerable political capital, as well as economic wealth, had been accumulated during the war itself. In the propaganda no real distinction was to be drawn between war aims and public perceptions of the leader and Franco's personal commitment to retaining power was an important factor. There was a providential note to Franco's 'charismatic leadership' (in Weberian terms) and socially the Crusade narrative plausibly encapsulated the defence of religion, the successful crushing of social revolution and the liquidation of thousands of both real and imagined 'Marxists' and other revolutionaries.

The process of demobilization and social integration of Republican soldiers, many of them conscripts, would begin with holding camps. Official reckoning suggested that more than 430,000 prisoners had been captured by the Nationalists during the fighting (over and above those disposed of summarily by firing squad). By mid-March 1939, some 180,000 of these were 'awaiting classification'.[8] In addition, there were thousands of political detainees: by the end of 1939, according to regime figures, some 270,000.[9] Prisoners had few formal rights. An elevated number of post-war deaths occurred in prison as a result of the overcrowding and malnutrition which was a corollary of the exhaustive process of classification and purging set in train since July 1936. By the end of the civil war in April 1939 it has been estimated that around 600,000 individuals had become subject to penal discipline of some kind during the conflict. Of these, some 300,000 were recorded as being in a state of 'conditional liberty' in the early 1940s, requiring vigilance by the military police.

Post-war state-building therefore began with the marginalization of 'the defeated'. The rupture of the civil war was the political point of departure of the post-war era. The democratic Constitution of the republic of the 1930s was permanently suspended and the Francoist state of war prevailed until 1948. In judicial terms, defence of the previous legal constitutional and democratic order became 'military rebellion'. 'Franco's Justice' was a clear reflection of the prevailing political, social and military order. Constitutional guarantees were replaced by a new moralism and military justice applied to a broad range of activities, including the expression of opinions inimical to the new power. Formal post-war legal process can be divided into two broad periods: first, continuation of what was termed 'military jurisdiction', the application of the wartime Military Code, from February to the end of June 1939; and, second, 'ordinary jurisdiction', marking an alleged 'return to normality', as provided in a law of February 1942 which reserved all acts related to questions of order and disorder – including strikes – for the authority of military justice. In fact, several other legal measures were introduced which conflicted with the notion of 'normality', in effect formalizing exceptional armed force: the so-called Law for the Repression of Freemasonry and Communism (March 1940) remained in force; a Law of the Security of the State (29 March 1941), and the Law against Banditry and Terrorism (18 July 1947), introduced at the high point of guerrilla resistance to the regime.

The promulgation of legal instruments was symbolic of the state-building project which placed violent behaviour by official representatives of the state beneath the cover of law. Franco declined to pursue reconciliation or mediation and declared that no general amnesty would be granted until the wartime revolutionary killings had been 'expiated' (Richards 1998: 152–6). Enemies were hunted down, denunciations were followed up and executions continued, though not quite in the extraordinary numbers of wartime. In Zaragoza, 447 prisoners were executed in the period from the formal end of the war in April 1939 until 1946. In Badajoz, the majority killed by the Nationalists died in 1936 (4,661) but 565 were killed in 1940 (3.5 times more than in 1937), 232 in 1941, more than in any of the years 1937, 1938 or 1939, and 122 in 1942 (more than the 112 in 1939). The killing of a 32-year-old land worker on 19 January 1945 signalled the end of a cycle of executions in Badajoz which had begun in July 1936.

Málaga presents another example. The city had been a revolutionary and bloody place during the seven-month period of formal Republican wartime 'authority'. The revolutionary killings in the city were related, in fact, to the deficiencies of governmental control and internecine political conflict. Nonetheless, when the city was 'liberated' in early February 1937, although thousands of people had fled, the number of those remaining who were to be killed by the occupiers was much higher than the total of those killed in the revolution. The purge was protracted and thorough, almost rhythmical, and was fuelled by revenge and a desire to be 'exemplary': more than 80 documented victims fell to the firing squads on 16 February 1937, the first anniversary of the Popular Front election which had brought the last democratic pre-war government to power. The executions would continue in regular batches until 1940. There were some 4,700 recorded killings during the city's first two 'post-war' years (1937–9), though it has been estimated that as many as 7,000 died (Juliá *et al.* 1999: 411). The repression did not cease on 1 April 1939. There was no reason why it should since April 1939 represented merely a continuation of the situation in Málaga prevailing since February 1937. A further 710 recorded executions took place between April 1939 and December 1942. The number of 'enemies' left to eliminate was clearly reducing and international pressures would also become significant as the repression tailed off, although a further 35 victims were to fall in Málaga in 1943 and 1944 and the last recorded execution took place in May 1948 (Eiroa 1995).

Requiring a notoriously low standard of evidence and based on an extreme broadening of the definition of 'crime', to cover political affiliations which pre-dated the war and were legal before July 1936, the Franco state project represented only an embryonic 'rule of law'. Judicial procedures in the wake of the civil war were poorly legitimated. Measures were applied arbitrarily, personal issues rather than general principles had undue influence and there continued to be great confusion between *de jure* and de facto legality.

Military justice was at the heart of a strongly militarized society epitomized by a greatly increased military and public order budget and manpower through military service and a swollen officer corps. Partly in response to the European war, national service lasting 24 months was introduced by decree in August 1940. In the period 1940–2 some 100,000 young men from Catalonia alone were conscripted into Franco's army, in which daily conditions were dreadful and morale exceedingly low. Conscripts were badly treated and even resorted to begging for food in city streets. Most were stationed outside their home regions and many lost whatever civilian employment they had secured. This forced movement was to become a significant element in post-war migration. Military spending in 1935 represented 22 per cent of public expenditure, while from 1940–5 it was usually above 50 per cent. This order of priorities was at the expense of initiatives in state social provision. The military budget in 1949 (32.74 per cent of total expenditure) can be compared to the 0.85 per cent proposed for agriculture while Spain was still suffering serious and widespread hunger. Regardless of economic rationale, regime rhetoric claimed that the military would play a direct role in national reconstruction. Rationality came second to the financial deals which leading army officers could strike with landowners and industrialists in the aftermath of the civil war. The army could not successfully stand in for the state in rebuilding the economy and infrastructure but it did become a highly significant actor with others, forming a pattern of social and political relationships which would gradually and fitfully, at national, regional and local levels, re-establish state authority.

Local economic networks, linking sources of wealth with the military, and war and post-war political dynamics, were fundamental to the incorporation of the local *arriviste* caste of Falangists who had come to the fore during the conflict. These connections and exchanges were possible partly through agencies of repression and law enforcement: the Local Commissions of Conditional Liberty, for example, to enforce the conditions on which civil war prisoners were released, and the local commissions for the Nationalist ex-combatants' benefits in pay and employment. Other localities set up their own commissions to take evidence and inform the authorities about civil war violence such as church burning and collectivization. A civil law of 'Political Responsibilities', announced in early February 1939, had the function of imposing primarily economic sanctions against Republicans whose political support for the former government (or, in fact, lack of active support for the rebels) was seen as encouraging the social revolution and the material damage it had caused. Local Political Responsibilities tribunals were composed of a high-ranking army officer, a Francoist member of the judiciary and a local Falangist. By the end of 1941 some 100,000 cases had been heard specifically under this legislation.

As a counterpart to this institutionalized favouring of Nationalist ex-combatants, there was a thorough purge of those deemed to be Republican sympathisers from public employment. A minimum of 25,000 were dismissed from the public administration in Catalonia, for example, a measure which was effected by newly-installed municipal and provincial authorities who would oversee the forced reincorporation of the region into the Spanish state (Riquer and Culla 1989: 26, 55). There were many thousands of dismissals of employees from private companies, although re-employment could theoretically be gained with a certificate of good conduct signed and issued by a regime insider. Again, the link between the institutions and social groups was reinforced.

Spain's immediate post-war years were lived amid a climate of general discontent, as we can see in analysing the daily economy of repression and resistance in the period 1939–48. In rural areas, particularly, the daily life of much of the population was shaped by fear and hunger. Basic freedoms were extraordinarily constrained. Movement was controlled for all in the countryside, at least in theory: in certain areas rural labouring families required a pass in order to reach the fields they worked or rented for production or the small plots they owned, making daily productive work problematic to such an extent that they abandoned the exercise, contributing to the concentration of rural wealth in the hands of those with a link to the authorities and pushing country dwellers towards migration. The social fracturing created by revolution, war and the process of collaboration and denunciation in the aftermath was often impossible to heal. Political, legal and mental boundaries were rarely completely de-activated. Long-standing pre-war social or personal issues of contention, usually to do with land ownership or tenancies, were reinvigorated by war divisions and post-war pressures, often associated with profiteering, opportunism and the general complex of politico-economic relations.

Immediate post-war memories of the 'people of order' (the middle classes; those with property) were dominated by the wartime period of Republican control and the social convulsion, including the burning of churches and killing of priests, which accompanied the authority of 'the Reds'. Memories of physical violence intermingled with experiences of revolution as they affected property so that when people spoke in the aftermath of war in terms of the most extreme violence they conflated this with the loss of property in order to legitimate their claims in relation to the latter. In many rural areas, such as the countryside of Aragón, this threat revolved around the collectivization of land. The wartime violence accompanying the process seemed to justify, in turn, the violence of the Francoists. Many collaborated with the authorities and, as historians of comparable situations have found, the often hard-pressed authorities required this involvement if they were to carry out a 'purge' in line with the policy of 'justice' declared from the highest reaches of the regime (e.g. Gellately 1990). People remember that many were imprisoned for their involvement (however tangentially) with wartime 'excesses' and that many of them never returned to the village.

One justification used by wartime Francoist forces was that the thorough purge of 'Reds', especially through sorties into the countryside, was necessary to avoid a future guerrilla (or 'underground') war. The harshness of the wartime violence, however, gave many leftists and supporters of the Republican government little option but to flee into the hills, woods and mountains as villages, towns and cities were captured. Thus, the end of formal hostilities merged with the onset of sporadic underground wars, which lasted throughout the 1940s. This signalled a return of the harshest repression seen since the immediate aftermath of the civil war, particularly in areas where Republican ideas had held sway and reforms, revolutionary violence and the collectivization of land and property had been introduced during the civil war. Survival was the key, both in the sense of maintaining the Republican faith (in the hope that allied victory over Hitler would also mean the end of Franco), on the one hand, and, on the other, the physical survival of the marginalized *guerrilleros* and their communities of support, especially in villages and small towns. The endogenous population suffered the worst because it was dependent on locally-generated resources, which could be controlled relatively easily by the authorities and their brokers.

The anti-Francoist *guerrilleros* were not principally demobilized Republican soldiers but largely, at first, politicized left-wingers who had fled into the hills and the countryside as towns were 'liberated', a process beginning as early as the summer of 1936. Later the guerrilla forces were supplemented by those escaping Francoist prisons and concentration camps and those avoiding military service. Republican exiles, organized by the PCE, who by the time of the liberation of much of France in 1944 were veterans of the French resistance movement, brought greater discipline and politicization to the Spanish resistance. There were thus two overlapping phases to the guerrilla struggle, those who had fled being supplemented at the end of 1944 by the more uniformly political *maquisard* movement from France. The generalized use of coercive force in response to the guerrilla campaigns was very publicly justified by the authorities through the need to suppress the subterranean struggle and also symbolized reclamation of the monopoly of legal coercive force by the nascent Francoist state.

As in the civil war ten years earlier, Falangists and the Guardia Civil (the Spanish civil guard) co-operated closely in the renewed repression. Meanwhile, the relationship between the guerrilla effort and communities was underlined by the role that denunciations played. The populace in general was made to suffer. As 'war zones' were decreed by the regime, the so-called 'pact of hunger', ensuring that the families of *guerrilleros* had no employment and, therefore, no means of making a living, was widely enforced by the authorities. The tactic of starving out the 'Reds' and the forced clearance of cultivated land and crop burning were used, subjecting entire villages to martial law and curfew regimes and even alienating some conservative peasant farmers who had previously supported the wartime 'Crusade'. The sense of continuity with the war was palpable in many locations. Giving shelter to the *maquis* could be punishable by death and women were sometimes imprisoned as 'bait' for *guerrilla* fighters on the run.

Villagers or townsfolk were caught in a dilemma: if they failed to tell what they knew they risked violence (including beatings and other forms of torture) from the authorities, but if they succumbed and provided information, they were also in real danger from the resisters. 'Denouncers' could pay the ultimate price as an example, according to the quasi-judicial pronouncements of the *guerrilleros*. The PCE leadership also feared that the 'purity' of the movement might be infiltrated and was consequently ready to be brutal. There was a general sense of fear in rural society, which may be related to a significant increase in suicide rates in the early 1940s.

The social dimensions of the guerrilla struggle underline how economic exchange became a key area for the daily imposition of non-consensual social relations in the decade following the civil war. Exploitative and punitive control of food supplies gradually became a popular rationale for a shift from mere passive opposition or relative indifference towards a more active stance of resistance on the part of the economically humble rural classes. This resource-related political activity is not only true of intra-state war in regions where there is a struggle to control exportable raw materials. Popular resistance was indeed mounted in Spain as it became known that large quantities of agricultural produce were being dispatched to Germany and Italy in the early 1940s to help pay off civil war debts. Economic repression also arose, however, in the generalized manipulation of wartime and post-war *domestic* food resources in favour of those with connections to the victors. A classic example from Spain, on both a small and large scale, was the forced depositing of grain and olive oil with local state authorities in exchange for a certificate of political reliability (e.g. Lazo 1998: 60). With official acquiescence, the process became a form of repression of 'the defeated', although the economic losers tend to be distributed widely across the social spectrum. Tilly sees this 'opportunity hoarding' operating 'when members of a categorically-bounded network acquire access to a resource that is valuable, renewable, subject to monopoly, supportive of network activities, and enhanced by the network's modus operandi' (Tilly 2003: 10). In the immediate aftermath of Spain's civil war, considerable extra value was extracted from basic necessities, such as wheat and other primary food products, through the manipulation of scarcity by those who became known as 'the food-controllers', at the expense of those distanced from political power.

It was a two-way process between state officials, on the one hand, and opportunistic individuals and influential landowning families and groups, forming a network of advantage and privatizing power, on the other. The operation of social relations and categorical boundaries resulting from the conflict reinforced this process. The essential 'us and them' boundary, that between Republicans and rebels, was reinforced by the experience of war since wartime violence threw into relief other boundaries based on rural and urban mentalities and antagonisms, party political identification, ideology and religion, all corresponding more or less precisely with the essential originating division (between 'us' and 'the others'). Supporting beliefs legitimated this control of vital resources, reinforcing networks which had already functioned during the war years, not least in the practices of violence already discussed (Richards 1998).

This network activity was fuelled by finance and war connections which flowed in many forms and in several directions: in the form, for example, of publicizing personal or group wartime adherence to the 'Glorioso Movimiento Nacional'; war heroism; of donations to the organizations of the Falange, establishing unimpeachable political credentials and also securing future deals; in the relationship between denunciations and financial reward; the lucrative and arbitrary use of official standing, in imposing economic penalties for such petty infringements as using irreverent language, defying the curfew, and most commonly, of buying small items of basic foodstuffs, such as bread, from a black market supplier (of which more below). Deadly informal 'justice' was employed by landowners and their agents in punishing 'economic crimes', such as petty theft of food or poaching.

The role of the black market requires further explanation. As a continuation of wartime economic nationalism (aiming for autarky) and of official controls, the Francoist state in embryo designed a programme of intervention in food production, harvesting, sale, distribution and consumption. There would be state-regulated rationing and controlled prices, administered with the assistance of the forces of public order. The national wheat programme was thus from the beginning shaped by wartime ideology. Prices were to be 'guaranteed' for peasant growers and other, grander, producer-landowners, who had been respectively the fighting and financial basis of the wartime 'Crusade'. The official price was set low and production was slow to get going, the result being great shortage, hunger, a rampant black market, increased social marginalization and extraordinary material and political benefits for those connected to the regime.

The reach and efficiency of state institutions was insufficient for the task assigned, but the monopolization of resources by the victors was also informally encouraged. A substantial proportion of production was explicitly reserved for disposal by the local authorities, ministers and high government officials and a further amount was earmarked for the usc of the armed services and police. This was virtually an invitation for a great deal of hoarding to take place. State pricing officials forcibly requisitioned produce from small producers and in collusion with local power brokers, such as Falangist civil governors, the Guardia Civil and leading party officials, had the authority to impose sanctions without any legal process. Nepotism followed and the black market, which soon dominated the economy at all levels, became a form of economic repression which was looked on by the population as an element of the post-war terror.

Peasants were reminded of their duty to repay the state for the creation of the pricing system, 'born in the hard years of our war', by declaring their whole harvest, but supplies were hoarded and the official price was largely ignored. The same applied to many other crops and staple food products, such as bread and olive oil. While large landowners had storage capacity to hold back supplies and direct them to the most lucrative market at the right moment, small producers could not. This further concentrated landholding and accelerated capital accumulation.

With labour cowed by war and dictatorship the purchasing power of the peseta had declined by 1946 to one-third of what it had been in 1936, though internal state documents show that the real situation was worse still. In the 1940s, an illicit kilogram of poor quality bread, if it could be found at all, cost about 12 pesetas, the daily wage of the highest paid worker, although rural labourers were paid considerably less. The olive oil ration was a paltry 100–50 grams per month; a litre of black market oil could be bought by those with 60 pesetas to spare. Small-time black market activities were often sanctioned but the authorities repeatedly failed to act on reports of major illegal dealings by those with real power. Franco justified economic benefits through the black market by reference to the custom in the Middle Ages

> Of sharing out titles, lands, goods and even the hand of some maiden among the combatants who had excelled in battle ... In our days there is no way of rewarding properly those who we think have efficiently contributed to the triumph of the Movement.
>
> (Garriga 1986: 178)

Reporting racketeers who were part of the local network of power had obvious risks. At a time when many people were aiming for anonymity because of their own political pasts, denunciation inevitably entailed an investigation into the background of the denouncer. Meanwhile, hunger forced people to resort in droves to the feeding stations of the Falange, allowing positive propagandistic opportunities for officials but also reinforcing control over the populace. Such agencies were frequently also fronts for further illicit profiteering.

Food scarcity was at least as calamitous in the overcrowded cities. Supplies were again often controlled by 'insiders' who had a hand in post-war local power. It was reported, for example, that in the industrial Basque province of Vizcaya the food black market was operated by the head of the Civil Guard. In the populous city of Málaga, in the south of the country, the civil governor was transferred to Galicia in August 1939 on account of his 'shady transactions with foodstuffs'. His successor was to resign a few months later because he could not break out of the deplorable food situation and because he was 'too energetic' in his efforts to stamp out abuses among local tradesmen known to be supporters of the Movement. In other places the civil governor controlled illegal economic relations. The balance between profiteering, maintaining power and social cohesion was certainly a fine one. Networks of advantage, dependency and provision came together in an internal report in Madrid in 1942 stating that food supplies were to be halted temporarily, for a week or so, in order to strengthen the link between each family and its particular illegal provider. The civil governor of Córdoba, who had managed to quadruple the size of the paltry bread ration by seizing the stores hitherto disposed of by the Falangist syndicates on the black market, was 'got rid of' as a result of this attempt to break out of the party's grip on the starving population (Brenan 1965: 48).

Such was the importance of localized power in some cases that supplementary rations of bread were controlled by a political board comprising the mayor, the parish priest and the head of the local Falangist organization, which made a judgement based on the acceptability of the moral and political behaviour of those who were hungry. Certificates of good conduct were issued by priests in the process of distributing rations and purging the labour force. To receive a ration or employment card it was necessary to have an identity card, having gone through a rigorous process of investigation. A black market in these identity cards was soon flourishing, run by officials of the local party. Republicans in hiding could therefore not feed themselves 'officially'.

Since it functioned at many levels and tended to discriminate against those with political pasts, the black market constituted not only a channel for repression, however, but also for resistance, particularly as part of the struggle for survival in rural areas. The guerrilla struggle interacted with this broader struggle for survival. The *guerrilleros* were usually supplied with food, often by female relatives, through small-scale black market dealing which, of course, was illegal. To be successful, women needed to move from place to place with the paltry goods they had to sell; but in the process of this daily itinerant lifestyle they could also aid the guerrilla campaign by, for example, carrying information. The winter of 1941 saw the very worst of the hunger and it is not coincidental that there was a great surge of peasant and working-class women into prison during this period as a result of sentences for small-scale illegal buying and selling (Barranquero Texeira *et al.* 1994: 39–42).

Conclusions

Violence during the Spanish Civil War followed the logic of civil wars as struggles to achieve a coherent and effective basis of political power and the exercise of sovereignty, resting on both coercion and collusion. State formation began, therefore, during the war and with great violence. The use of physical force to achieve order suited the rebels more than the incumbent government: armed coercion, after all, was the basis of the rebellion. The identities and threat ascribed to liberals, proletarians, intellectuals, teachers and freemasons, amongst others, by Catholic, counter-revolutionary ideology and wartime propaganda constructed such groups as 'criminals' and contributed to extracting denunciations. As the Nationalist General Mola put it, the war 'had to end with the elimination of the enemies of Spain' and the reactionary army was an appropriate agent of this 'purification'. Remaking the state began not only with executions, however, but with social relationships, which became the conduits of collaboration and persuasion. The formation of local networks of power was achieved as rebel 'liberators' promised the 'return of law' and could act as protectors of pre-war elites and potential social support from lower down the social structure (especially property owners), partly by exterminating other groups inimical to conservative interests. Opportunities for accruing power arose as substantial numbers of civilians were able to gain advantage by allying with 'the liberation', directly or indirectly participating in the violence and enjoying the economic advantages on offer, even to the extreme detriment of neighbours and family. Jan Gross's proposal about the nature of the power of the totalitarian state during the Soviet conquest of Eastern Poland in 1939 has some bearing on the nature of power and violence in civil wars:

> The absence of the rule of law in a totalitarian regime finds its concrete and most characteristic expression in the fact that every citizen has direct access to the coercive apparatus of the state, unmediated by lengthy and complicated judicial procedures. Everybody can use the political police against everybody else – quickly, without delays or undue formalities.
>
> (Gross 1988: 120–1)

A simple application, wholesale, of Gross's claim to Spain's civil war suggests, however, that the ideological divide counted virtually for nothing. It was not quite true that everybody in Spain could 'use the political police against everybody else'. Neither, however, did ideology explain everything and there was an important level of 'privatization' of violence in Spain.

The point at which *post-war* violence began in Spain has been shown here as difficult to pin down, since the war – and its violence – took on many different forms from 18 July 1936 through to 1 April 1939 and beyond into the 1940s. This suggests some considerable level of continuity of violence, not least in its intimate nature. This problem underlines the sense in which military, social, economic, cultural and psychological demobilization is intractable after civil wars. Militarism, purging, purification, categorization – all of these prior processes made any degree of reconciliation barely thinkable. Memories of republican revolution kept 'atrocities' alive and were used to justify the considerable violence of the early 1940s. Sometimes the evidence for revolutionary 'crimes' was insubstantial, though the Republican collectivization of property may have been extensive: 'crimes' could 'stand in' for the expropriation of the wealthy in many middle class minds since its justificatory power was considerably greater in fuelling revenge. In the aftermath of war, networks of advantage continued to incorporate 'old' and 'new' power groups, their composition based on the dynamics of the war, the post-war and the accompanying violence and the economic opportunities thrown up. The black market was highly significant in this process, as was the guerrilla struggle which briefly turned the calendar back to 1936, to popular struggle and to fierce repression, in the second half of the 1940s. This continuity, the main feature which has been stressed in the present chapter, rested on a wartime/post-war perpetuation of the relationship between military-ideological state-builders and dominant social groups. Subordinate social groups were discriminated against and excluded as they were associated with wartime enemies.

Because in many ways the civil war made living together in communities impossible, the extended period of violent conflict in Spain, from 1936 until around 1948, set in motion the great post-war drama of mass migration towards the relative anonymity of the larger cities. Unintentionally, the constellation of forces produced by the civil war, which saw the victors take control of state-building activities, led ultimately, after several painful decades, to the creation of a modernized society. The civil war and the first post-war decade not only constituted the founding 'moment' of General Franco's dictatorship but also, partly because of the extraordinary intimacy of its violence, represented the major social watershed of contemporary Spain.

Notes

1 On the wartime construction of the rebels' state, see Serrano Suñer 1963: 33–70.
2 In Seville the state of war was declared in Article 1 of a decree of 18 July 1936. The priorities were clear: Article 2 decreed that strikers would be shot.
3 *Manchester Guardian*, 31 August 1936.
4 For a wartime example comparable to rural Spain, see Gross 1988 (specifically: 119).
5 Archivo de la Prisión Provincial de Málaga, Expedientes Personales, no. 259, C3, L2.
6 *ABC*, 1 June 1939.
7 Speech in Barcelona, 24 January 1942, *ABC*, 29 January 1942: 1.
8 Inspección de Campos de Concentración de Prisioneros, report: 15 March 1939. Archive of Ministerio de Asuntos Exteriores, Madrid, Archivo de Burgos, R1067, exp. 6.
9 The official average for the period 1930–4 was 9,403. By the end of 1942 the official prison population was still almost 125,000 and at least 38,000 by 1948.

Bibliography

Barallat, Mercè (2002) 'La repressió en la postguerra civil a Lleida', in *El primer franquisme a les terres de Lleida (1938–1950)*, Lérida: Institut d'Estudis Ilerdencs.

Barranquero Texeira, Encarnación, Eiroa, Matilde and Navarro Jiménez, Paloma (1994) *Mujer, cárcel, franquismo: La prisión provincial de Málaga (1937–1945)*, Málaga: Junta de Andalucía.

Brenan, Gerald (1965 [1950]), *Face of Spain*, Harmondsworth: Penguin.

Casanova, Julián, *et al.* (1992) *El pasado oculto: Fascismo y violencia en Aragón (1936–1939)*, Madrid: Siglo XXI.

Cobo Romero, Francisco and Ortega López, Teresa María (2005) *Franquismo y posguerra en Andalucía oriental*, Granada: Universidad de Granada.

Eiroa, Matilde (1995) *Viva Franco: hambre, racionamiento, falangismo (1939–1942)*, Málaga: Junta de Andalucía.

Espinosa Maestre, Francisco (2003) *Columna de la muerte: el avance del ejército franquista de Sevilla a Badajoz*, Barcelona: Crítica.

Fraser, Ronald (1979) *Blood of Spain*, Harmondsworth: Penguin.

Garriga, Ramón (1986) *Franco-Serrano Suñer: un drama político*, Barcelona: Planeta.

Gellately, Robert (1990) *The Gestapo and German Society: Enforcing Racial Policy, 1933–1945*, Oxford: Oxford University Press.

Gómez Bajuelo, Gil (1937) *Málaga bajo el dominio rojo*, Cádiz: np.

Gross, Jan T. (1988) *Revolution from Abroad: the Soviet Conquest of Poland's Western Ukraine and Western Belorussia*, Princeton, NJ: Princeton University Press.

Iribarren, José María (1937) *Con el general Mola*, Zaragoza: Librería General.

Juliá, Santos (ed.) (1999) *Víctimas de la guerra*, Madrid: Temas de Hoy.

Kalyvas, Stathis (2006) *The Logic of Violence in Civil Wars*, Cambridge: Cambridge University Press.

King, Charles (1997) *Ending Civil Wars*, Adelphi Paper 308, Oxford: International Institute for Strategic Studies.

Lazo, Alfonso (1998) *Retrato de fascismo rural en Sevilla*, Seville: Universidad de Sevilla.

Martín Jiménez, Ignacio (2003) *La posguerra en Valladolid (1939–1950)*, Valladolid: Ámbito.

Ministerio de Justicia (1943) *Causa General: La dominación roja en españa. Avance de la Información Instruída por el Ministerio Público*, Madrid: Ministerio de Justicia.

Richards, Michael (1998) *A Time of Silence: Civil War and the Culture of Repression in Franco's Spain, 1936–1945*, Cambridge: Cambridge University Press.

Riquer, Borja de and Culla, Joan (1989) *El Franquisme i la Transició Democràtica (1939–1988)*, Barcelona: Edicions 62.

Serrano Suñer, Ramón (1963) *Entre Hendaya y Gibraltar*, sixth edition, Madrid: Ediciones y Publicaciones Españolas.

Tilly, Charles (2003) *The Politics of Collective Violence*, Cambridge: Cambridge University Press.

Viñas, Ángel (2007) *El escudo de la República*, Barcelona: Crítica.

3 Reconstruction and violence in the post-bellum American South 1865–77

Michael Beaton

Introduction

Scallawags, bushwhackers and freedmen: the world the war made

On 9 April 1865, the Confederacy's General Robert E. Lee surrendered to the Union General Ulysses S. Grant in an Appomattox court house deep in the Virginia countryside. With him surrendered the Army of Northern Virginia, the strongest of all the Confederate armies and the last hurdle standing between Grant and the Confederate capital of Richmond. Over the following days, the Confederacy's other generals surrendered their swords in Alabama, Georgia and North Carolina and the American Civil War came to an end. Jefferson Davis, the Confederacy's strident president, fled to Georgia on horseback, carrying with him the remnants of the South's fire-eaters and politicians. For the brief few weeks before his capture, Davis dreamed of carrying with him the seeds of guerrilla war and continuing to fight for the so-called 'Lost Cause' of Confederate nationalism even as the would-be nation collapsed around him.

That would-be nation that Davis left behind emerged devastated from the American Civil War: 600,000 men had died on both sides, more than the sum of all America's casualties from all her subsequent wars combined. The US Army under General Sherman had burnt a strip through the Confederacy from Atlanta to the sea, operating under the total war maxim that it was better to make war hell than let the Confederacy's battered population grow any fonder of it. The Northern strategy to demolish the sources of Confederate power – cotton, slavery and the plantation order – created four million freedmen (former slaves) by war and proclamation, leaving the institution of slavery in tatters. Meanwhile, the sudden demobilization of the Confederate army had released hundreds of thousands of frustrated casualties of Jefferson's 'Lost Cause' ideology across the South. In the divided border states, bitterness still burned brightly between Union and Confederate bushwhacker *banditti* (wartime guerrillas), as many bands turned to revenge and criminality overnight to settle wartime scores. In the lawless river towns such as Vicksburg, New Orleans and Memphis, poor whites jostled with freed blacks, sparking violence and riots between Southern white supremacists and their former slaves. The South's great land- and labour-lords, furiously lobbying for the restoration of their political power, looked with anger towards the US army of occupation. Meanwhile, Northern 'carpetbaggers' – those who came south to help engineer and profit from the post-war peace – and 'scallawags' – Southern Unionists committed to the Northern cause – multiplied, expecting to share in the spoils of the inevitable 'reconstruction' of the South (Foner 1988: 1–35, 176–228).[1]

The Radical Republicans who had swept Congress in 1864 saw a great opportunity in this victory. The Radical Republican movement – an alliance of churchmen, political radicals, business interests and anti-slavery Northerners – was determined to bring their revolution to the South and refashion it in the 'free land, free labour, free men' tradition of the industrial North. Republican President Abraham Lincoln, by contrast, was more magnanimous in victory. 'With malice toward none, and charity for all', he declared at his Second Inaugural in March 1865, 'let us bind up the nation's wounds … and do all which may achieve and cherish a just and lasting peace'. Bolstered by the respect of the Radical Republican majority in Congress and a conservative, Southern vice-president in Tennessee's Andrew Johnson, Lincoln was hopeful that he could steer the course between radical and moderate and do what was necessary to rebind the republic back into a single nation (Schultz *et al.* 1999: 296).

Lincoln, of course, never got that chance. By April 1865, he was dead – shot and killed by actor and former Confederate agent John Wilkes Booth in Ford's theatre on a balmy Washington night. When his conservative Southern vice-president, Andrew Johnson, was sworn in on the steps of the Capitol the following morning, the political storm was already brewing. Johnson, a Southerner by birth and a conservative by instinct, had no intention of imposing a radical victor's peace on the defeated South. The 'dark stain on the Republican robe' (as Lincoln had described slavery in 1854) was abolished by the Constitution's Thirteenth Amendment, which states had to ratify before re-entry into the Union. That done, Johnson ruled that the governments of the Southern states were to be reconstituted as swiftly as possible, their representatives readmitted to Congress and the US Army withdrawn. The Confederate stars were to be rewoven into the American flag – and there, according to Johnson, the revolution was to end.

Johnson's programme of reconciliation towards the defeated South (since labelled 'Presidential Reconstruction') created bitter divisions in both North and South. The reconstituted Southern governments, in many cases old conservative and Confederate elites, saw the limited ambition of Presidential Reconstruction as a green light to delegislate the Thirteenth Amendment and return to business as usual. Those elites shared Johnson's belief that the Confederacy's military surrender was an honourable restoration of the status quo, a bid to save the remnants of Southern society from total collapse (Rable 1984: 1–15). To them, the abolition of slavery was a symbolic concession, not a blueprint for social and political revolution (Rable 1984: 18–29). Through a series of legislative enactments called the Black Codes, one by one the South's conservative and Democrat state governments tried to reverse emancipation, forcing millions of freed blacks to sign annual labour contracts with their former masters. Those who resisted faced arrest and prosecution for vagrancy, accompanied by lengthy spells of hard labour which, more often than not, returned them to the plantations. Meanwhile, in the turbulent, lawless post-war South, African-Americans and freedmen faced violent attacks, race riots and killings on an almost daily basis. The perpetrators of this violence were frequently protected by the agents and officials of the Southern state. The Freedmen's Bureau, a small federal organization sent to assist with the birth of a free labour society, sent a constant stream of telegrams and letters to Washington requesting federal military assistance to curb the violence. The US Army demobilized at breathtaking rate, shrinking from more than a million men under arms to 50,000 in the space of a year (Scheips 1989: 282). Meanwhile, Southern Republicans – known as 'scallawags' – and returning US Army veterans, particularly in Texas and the divided border states such as Missouri, faced fierce reprisals from their embittered neighbours (Foner 1988: 176–204).

These events created a storm in the victorious North. While Northern opinion was also deeply divided over the rights and responsibilities a black freedman should have in comparison to the white, most Northerners were nonetheless outraged that the South could so blatantly abrogate the emancipation they had won at such a high cost. Radical Republicans stormed the congressional elections in 1866, winning the congressional supermajority required to override Johnson's presidential power of veto. The Radical Congress refused to seat the representatives of the Southern governments, effectively forcing Johnson to abandon his programme of Presidential Reconstruction. In 1866, Congress passed the United States' first Civil Rights Act, designed to give black freedmen federal protection where the states could not (or would not) provide it. Congress initiated impeachment proceedings against Johnson in 1866, and although they failed to remove him from office they continued to use their own super-majority to force through Radical legislation over his veto. From 1867 through to 1877, congressional Radicals such as Thaddeus Stevens and Charles Sumner were the main drivers of the North's reconstruction policy and the period known as Radical Reconstruction was born.

The victor's peace and the gospel of prosperity: the world the peace made

The congressional architects of Radical Reconstruction saw measures such as the Civil Rights Act as necessary parts of the victor's peace, to export the fruits of the Republican national ideology and rebuild ('Reconstruct') what they saw as a repressive, feudal and belligerent South from the ground up. The ease with which the Black Codes reappeared on the statute books all across the South between 1865 and 1866 had reinforced the Radical sense that the war, to all intents and purposes, had not ended. Nothing less than a second revolution, it was said, could break the back of the feudal 'slave power' and usher in the Republican 'gospel of prosperity'. This 'gospel', a loose amalgamation of Northern pro-business, anti-slave ideology, was best captured by the pre-war Republican slogan of 'Free Soil; Free Labor; Free Men'. Put another way, the gospel meant breaking up the South's great plantations; cementing the economic freedom of the freed slaves and their poor white counterparts (although often this freedom was little more than the opportunity to toil for low wages in the factories or on the railroads); and guaranteeing the freedmen's political freedom through civil rights legislation. Girded by thousands of miles of railroads, the gospel would free the blacks from the plantations, industrialize and modernize the South and bring the fruits of so-called Northern 'progress' to its backward neighbour (Summers 1984: 1–27). The political foundations of the so-called gospel would be anchored by the Constitution's Fourteenth and Fifteenth Amendments, which extended full citizenship, federal civil rights and suffrage to all black men born in the United States. To protect these newfound rights, the 1867 Reconstruction Acts placed the former Confederacy under martial law, which would last until the Southern states had ratified the Fourteenth and Fifteenth Amendments and a new Constitution and registered its black voters. To further tip the balance in favour of the freedmen, Congress also instituted the Ironclad Oath, designed to disenfranchise former Confederate elites for taking up arms against the Union.

The gospel, as with other gospels at other times, was seen as a silver bullet that would finally transform the South into a land of free soil, free labour and free men. For die-hard abolitionists, the gospel would for evermore destroy the foundations of the slave system and usher in a new era of black advancement under the paternalist eye of the federal government. For bankers and railroad magnates, it was a means of driving the capitalist revolution deep into the Southern heartlands, ushering in a new age of mechanization, industrialization and free labour. For eager Republican politicians, the gospel promised a prosperous – and grateful – labouring class of black and white Southerners, who would reject the machinations of the old conservative-Democrat landowning masters and foster a generation of Republican politicians in their stead. For congressional whips, this would crush the Democratic Party and its conservative successors under the weight of the black vote and prevent for evermore the resurgence of a secessionist tendency. For African-Americans themselves, the gospel meant, if nothing more, the promise of sustained federal civil rights protection – at least for so long as the African-American vote was needed to support the aims of its disciples.

Radical Reconstruction, however, was everything the defeated South feared of the victor's peace. In many ways, the American Civil War had broken out over the South's God-given right to resist the spread of Republican 'Free Soil, Free Labor, Free Men' ideology across the Mason–Dixon line and into its own society. The Confederacy went to war in 1860 for the South's right to defend its own institutions (which included slavery) against the perceived designs of the Northern Radicals to remake the fabric of Southern society through the power of the federal government. Those fears now seemed closer than ever to being realized. Black emancipation would elevate African-Americans to the political and social equality of citizenship, destabilizing the existing social and economic order in almost every corner of the old Confederacy. The Freedmen's Bureau, backed by the US Army – which also had several all-black battalions – was mandated to use martial law to enforce federal civil rights legislation, which would end the South's own monopoly on force. Finally, the Radical Republican alliance promised high redistributive taxation to fund the transition to emancipation, from black schooling to expensive railroad projects. Many Southerners perceived this new form of Republican statism to be a stalking horse for massive corruption (Les Benedict 1984: 507–14).

Together with the Radical Republican carpetbaggers – Northerners who came south, lured by humanitarian concerns, the aggrandizing opportunities of the gospel of prosperity or the prospect of office – Radical Reconstruction now seemed to threaten a revolution in politics and race relations. The electoral mathematics was clear. Two Southern states – Mississippi and South Carolina – were majority black. Georgia, Florida, Alabama and Louisiana had razor-thin white majorities. Most African-Americans could be expected to vote for Radical Republicans, or for their fellow freedmen, over any ticket supported by their old white conservative or Democratic masters. And so it proved: over the course of Radical Reconstruction, 650 African-Americans were elected to state office, including 15 US Congressmen and two US Senators – positions slaves could not even vote for before the war. Thousands more served as sheriffs, taxmen and other local elected positions across the South (Foner 1988: 102–10). By 1870, by which time all 11 former Confederate states had been readmitted to the Union, only one of them – Virginia – was not governed by the Radical Republicans. With blacks in positions of authority all across the South and white conservatives and Democrats frustrated at every turn, the scene was now set for a bitter and violent counter-revolution against this new Radical order.

A history of violence: reconstruction and redemption 1865–77

Most Republican Southern governments, elected with a strong African-American vote, were built on shaky political foundations. Most Southern whites, either disenfranchised by the Ironclad Oaths or solidly allied to the conservative-Democrat camp, gave only limited consent to be governed by them and in many cases openly rebelled against them. As early as the passage of the Reconstruction Acts of 1867, patterns of violence in the South had begun to migrate from local attempts to retain the white monopoly on force to a more organized, sub-state counter-revolution against all representatives of the new Radical order. While spontaneous, populist violence against African-Americans continued on the sidewalks of Southern towns, the breakdown of white supremacy in the face of Radical Republican government inspired new, competitive monopolies on force to rise across the Southern countryside. The 'Union' or 'Loyal Leagues' – organizations that mobilized blacks and whites to support the Radical Republican agenda – were a particular challenge to the white supremacist resurgence. The essence of sub-state resistance was to destroy representatives and allies of the Radical state, not to rebel against the Federal Union. Blacks, Radicals, scallawags and Loyal Leagues were thus the most common targets of counter-revolutionary violence: federal forces, carpetbaggers and Northern Democrats, for the most part, were not.

The precise scale of the violence remains contentious. No author has been able to compile a definitive list of battle deaths across the period that could be measured against the threshold for other civil wars and post-war reconstructions. From the records that survive – often reports from lonely Freedmen's Bureau outputs and beleaguered state Capitols – violence against African-Americans across many counties of the Reconstruction South was clearly widespread and pervasive. Where numbers do exist from congressional reports, Freedmen's Bureau estimates or elsewhere, they have been used. But as this chapter hopes to demonstrate, violence – while also spontaneous – was often planned along clear and distinct lines with distinct objectives. Outbursts of violence and blood-letting – for example, at Republican rallies or black political events – would then be followed by a period of relative calm, as the violence achieved its stated aim and the black population failed to vote, march or retaliate. This chapter aims to demonstrate not just the scale and depth but also the purposes of that violence, which often achieved its objectives through brutality and intimidation rather than mass blood-letting or open warfare. Given the paucity of the records, one must always bear in mind that in many states and counties such violence was the exception rather than the norm; but, as we shall see, in many cases it was the horrors of violence in isolated pockets that helped achieve the perpetrators' objectives elsewhere.

Organized violence began with the Ku Klux Klan, which was founded in Tennessee in 1868 as a mass-membership paramilitary force dedicated to reimposing law and order as the freed blacks supposedly ran amok under federal protection. The Klan, which claimed to have 550,000 members by the end of 1868, spawned dozens of violent franchises in every Southern state under the guise of 'nightriders' or 'regulators'. Most Klan operations were organized at least at county level, with a reasonable level of coordination between counties to frustrate state or federal enforcement. In many counties, the local authorities – postmasters, sheriffs, judges and juries – were in full collusion with the Klan, while the newly-elected Radical Republican state governments could do little to stem the tide of violence. Without federal troops – and there were generally far too few to go around – state governments had to rely on the state militia, which was formed either of local whites or freed blacks and which could rarely be deployed without fear of a race riot.

Social, economic and political violence, which was directed against freedmen and women and their white allies, was particularly fierce in states such as Louisiana, Mississippi, South Carolina and Florida, where the racial – and thus political – balance was tight. Political 'vote regulation', an infant science designed to attack black political mobilization root and branch and gut the Southern Republican vote, became a prominent feature of Klan campaigning. Meanwhile, armed gangs – successors to

Confederate 'bushwhackers' – rode across the border states and Midwest, attacking facets of the Republican 'gospel', including railroads, banks, Unionists and blacks, with the tacit encouragement of busy conflict entrepreneurs among the Democratic press.

In 1872, however, the Klan overreached. Responding to a mounting level of domestic terror, President Ulysses S. Grant passed the Enforcement Acts, which allowed federal forces to flood back into the South to shore up the beleaguered Republican governments and combat the Klan. In the aftermath, much of the Southern neo-paternalist landholding class – who had an increasing economic interest in limiting anti-black violence – turned against the Klan as a violent and counter-productive agent of political restoration. However, the neo-paternalists, who branded themselves the New Departure, proved unable to build a centrist alternative to Republican Reconstruction that could woo sufficient numbers of African-Americans at the ballot box. A putative centrist coalition of Liberal Republicans and Southern Democrats failed spectacularly during the presidential election of 1872, wrecking the Southern elites' hopes of a political alliance with African-Americans. Faced with a solid black Republican vote, most conservative-Democrat elites settled on a political convergence with the inheritors of the Klan tradition as the fastest way to demolish Southern Republicanism. Although rarely committed to paper, the understanding was clear. Conservative-Democrat elites would defend bottom-up violence from the publishing houses, bully-pulpits and state legislatures and in turn the white population would use violence and intimidation to destroy the black vote and mobilize behind the conservative-Democratic ticket. Conservative-Democrats could then destroy Radical Reconstruction with the statute book, taking care to follow the letter of the Thirteenth Amendment while nonetheless subverting the spirit of federal civil rights protection and, in many cases, reversing emancipation in all but name.

This convergence, also known as the Redemption movement, revolved around mobilizing the white constituency against the black in order to recapture ('Redeem') Southern state houses and destroy Radical Reconstruction. The colour line became stark and emotive and mass political terror grew to proportions that dwarfed even Klan activity. White supremacist organizations such as the White Leagues, Red Shirts, Rifle Clubs and White Liners – the successors to the Ku Klux Klan – delivered systematic and instrumental political terror, aimed at eliminating black political activists and office-holders and intimidating African-Americans away from the polls. Meanwhile, the US Army continued to disband at a rate of knots, from a million men in 1865 to 45,000 in 1869: a mere 20,000 of whom were stationed in the South to guard the peace (Scheips 1989: 282–3). By 1876, the year the Redemption peaked, there were only 6,000 US soldiers in the southern states, the majority of them guarding the border between Texas and Mexico (Trelease 1971: 34–5).

With the federal government's refusal to bolster Reconstruction governments with the bayonet, the Redeemers were able to seize whole counties of Mississippi, South Carolina and Louisiana, and challenge the besieged Republican state governments that opposed them. Republican state governments could not raise sufficient numbers of loyal militiamen to exercise their writ or enforce civil rights protections. A broken or at best partial monopoly on force in many states exacerbated lawlessness, social violence and criminality on all sides. Riots, rallies and political murder, often sponsored by or with the active collusion of Democrat or Redeemer political elites, enabled local forces to carry election after election at the barrel of a gun. By 1877, every Southern state had been 'Redeemed' at the polls, often at the cost of a huge proportion of its black votes and Radical Reconstruction was pronounced dead.

Elections carried by storm: the political functions of violence

Reconstructions, as Cramer has noted, are often erroneously viewed as mainly technical rather than political feats of post-war engineering (Cramer 2006: 245–79). In the post-bellum United States, the technical objective of Radical Reconstruction – the birth of a sustainable free soil, free labour, free enterprise society – was conditional on the continued political dominance of the Radical Southern Republican Party over its conservative-Democrat opponents. African-American voters, backed by old Union scallawags and carpetbagger allies of the gospel of prosperity, formed the building blocks of this political alliance. By contract, many Southerners considered Republican government to be an imposed despotism and pointed to its carpetbagger element as proof that it was nothing but a stalking horse for corrupt Northern commercial and railroad interests (Summers 1984: 8–14). The Ironclad disenfranchisement of as many as 10,000 Confederate elites also contributed to a crisis of legitimacy for Republican state governments, damaging their capacity to incorporate conservative-Democrat challengers peacefully through existing democratic power mechanisms. Moreover, for the New South economic elite, Republican government and black political mobilization were direct threats to their coercive reordering of the Southern agrarian economy and their own restoration to state government.

Meanwhile, it became quickly apparent that Republican political domination was not matched by a corresponding monopoly on force. By 1870, with few federal garrisons available to quell outbreaks of electoral violence, most new Southern Republican governments had become dependent on a predominantly white state militia of questionable loyalty and a local judicial system thoroughly compromised either by their conservative-Democrat political opponents or even Ku Klux Klansmen and their sympathizers (Trelease 1971: 1–36). In many states, what sustained protections the authorities could offer Republicans (of both races) were limited to the state Capitol and those few counties where the rule of law could be enforced by detachments of the US Army, pockets of white Republicans or a black state militia. In more modern terms, many Republican state governments could be characterized as low capacity, undemocratic regimes insofar as they were largely unable to mobilize violence specialists to suppress violence, while at the same time were unwilling or unable effectively to manage or incorporate political actors considered to be legitimate by the white population (Tilly 2003: 65–71).

The dual political domination and military weakness of Republican government did much to allow political terror to evolve from a position espoused by the Ku Klux Klan and its allies – and opposed by the neo-paternalist Democratic elite – into a successful political joint venture by the 1870s. As Redeemer elites in state after state failed to mobilize the black vote, their hopes of luring African-Americans to the flag through economic and neo-paternalist incentives gave way to more direct methods. With the failure of a centrist, conservative presidential platform to win over African-American allegiance in 1872, a new 'expressive' political strategy – designed to mobilize the white vote fully while eliminating the black – became the political model of Redemption. Under the burgeoning alliance between white paramilitary organizations and the conservative, Democratic elites, the most important common target that emerged was the 'root and branch' dismantling of Radical Republican government, which, peacefully or otherwise, meant above all the destruction of the African-American vote (MacPherson 1985: 545–50).[2] As the White Liner slogan ran in Mississippi in 1875, one way or another Redeemers were going to carry the election: 'peaceably if we can – forcibly if we must' (MacPherson 1985: 549).

Political violence was not just a racial enterprise. The earliest political violence began in Missouri and the predominantly white badlands of the border states even as the American Civil War drew to a close. Kansas and Missouri had already been torn apart before the war by battles between pro- and anti-slavery forces, known at the time as the 'Bleeding Kansas' conflict. During the Civil War, both states again suffered the bitterest political violence between pro-slaver bands – known as bushwhackers – and their increasingly ruthless pro-Union militia opponents. Fierce guerrilla battles both before and during the war had blurred the line between civilian and soldier to the point where it became almost meaningless. By 1865, the two sides had created swathes of dead country across Kansas and Missouri. The logic on both sides was political terror, which transcended the colour line and, indeed, the formal declaration of peace. As early as 1863, prominent bushwhacker warlords such as 'Bloody Bill' Anderson (who commanded the young outlaws Frank and Jesse James) had been determined to wage a war of political and ideological cleansing against Missouri's white Radical and Union civilians. As Anderson declared before massacring a group of captured Union prisoners in 1864, this political war was an all-or-nothing enterprise. Victory against Radicals, Republicans and Unionists had but one object: '[that] you are all killed and sent to hell' (Stiles 2003: 119–21). Nowhere was political terror against Radical civilians and white Republican 'scallawags' as systematic as in the border states, the Midwest (where few African-Americans lived) and in the bushwhackers' old wartime safe haven of Texas. For all they suffered at the hands of the bushwhackers, however, scallawag whites were rarely numerous enough to be singlehandedly in a position to change the political map of the South. Although many whites were killed by bushwhackers who sought to use the contested peace to settle the scores of war, the true target of anti-Reconstruction political violence was never so much Republican whites as the black majority that mobilized behind them.

The earliest organized anti-black political violence instead began in Tennessee, where the state's fast-track readmittance to the Union had been made conditional on an accelerated programme of civil rights, black suffrage and (by extension) the election of the state's first Radical Republican government. In the first post-Reconstruction Act election of 1867, the old conservative order was confident that slavery would continue at the ballot box. The neo-paternalist belief continued to hold that the master knew what was best for the slave, and that the black freedman – with the added encouragement of losing his tenancy if he voted Republican – would always fall into line. The assistance of the Klan and other organized, 'blunt instrument' forms of political coercion were rejected with disdain by the Democratic planter elites. However, in 1867 Tennessee paternalism was delivered a shocking blow. The black Republican vote was overwhelming, the conservative order humiliated and embittered, and the Ku Klux Klan – which had been up until that time a weak force in much of Tennessee – greatly emboldened (Trelease 1971: 22–36, 114–38). With the Tennessee State House in Republican hands and the conservative-Democratic elite in disarray, it was now the Klan that took the initiative to turn back Southern Republicanism at the root. By the end of 1868, highly mobile armed Klansmen – usually in disguise – were engaged in raiding, abusing and murdering black Union veterans, schoolteachers and Republican voters in nearly every county of rural Tennessee (Trelease 1971: 138–54). The violence was unmistakably political, illustrated as it was by promises to execute freedmen caught voting Republican and bitter threats against Republican (white) sheriffs, office-holders and Freedmen's Bureau agents (Lemann 2006: 120–54, 173–8).

The first organized political terror began with the Presidential election of 1868, which pitted former US General Ulysses S. Grant (a strong supporter of Radical Reconstruction) against Horatio Seymour of the conservative, anti-Reconstruction Democrats. The white South was galvanized by Seymour and as a consequence the line between the local Democratic political establishment and white paramilitary organizations became repeatedly blurred. Rifles were distributed to 'Seymour Clubs' in North Carolina. Black Republican organizers were targeted for assassination in South Carolina, where the Klan was widely considered to be an extension of the vocal and ferocious local Democratic establishment. The Freedmen's Bureau recorded 142 'outrages', including 31 killings, in the build-up to the elections in Georgia; in one incident, an armed posse broke up a black Republican rally in south Georgia and then spent the rest of the day methodically hunting down and killing freedmen. A '*nameless terror*' spread across Alabama, where the Klan waited armed and in full regalia outside black political meetings. Blacks in every state were whipped, assaulted, terrorized and threatened with death if they voted Republican. White Republican leaders and government officials, including a sheriff, a judge, a Freedmen's Bureau agent and an Arkansas congressman were murdered; Republican presses were destroyed; and vote registrars in Arkansas were menaced into withholding Republican ballots. White 'vote regulators' issued 'protection papers' to African-Americans promising to vote for the Democratic ticket, some signed by the chairman of the Louisiana Democratic Central Committee – a practice that was also widespread in Texas (Trelease 1971: 137–8). In Louisiana, the Knights of the White Camellia, the Seymour Knights and the local Klan dominated the state, counting among their membership many of the leading citizens and local Democratic officeholders of the Louisiana parishes.

Where blacks attempted to defend themselves, retribution was swift. Led by members of the Seymour Knights, whites in Louisiana's St. Landry Parish combed the countryside for armed blacks, killing 200 in the space of three days without reporting a shot fired in return. Organized black militiamen were ordered to surrender and then massacred in Little River, Arkansas. New Orleans – where almost half of the white population were members of the Knights of the White Camellia – was also the scene of significant electoral bloodshed in 1868. After a Republican procession was ambushed, Republican clubs were sacked and the police headquarters besieged in October, after which white paramilitaries and Democratic clubs ruled the streets until the election in November. Overstretched and outnumbered, the US Army could do little to prevent the riots, looting and political violence that followed, in which 63 blacks were killed and hundreds more driven out of the city. A congressional committee later found that over 1,000 persons had been killed and countless more terrorized in Louisiana between April 1868 and the elections in November. In the three months before November 1868, 200 murders were reported to the governor of Arkansas. In almost every county and parish where significant electoral violence was reported, the Republican vote plummeted (MacPherson 1985: 550).

Even after the Klan was destroyed as an organization by federal intervention in 1872, the electoral terror it had inspired lived on. Before its destruction as a recognizable movement, and at the peak of its terror, the Klan had decimated the Republican political establishment and its black supporters in North Carolina and Georgia, allowing Redeemers to sweep the vote and capture their respective state houses in 1870 and 1871. Moreover, Klan violence had carried a wave of local conservative or Democrat officeholders into power and so comprehensively broken the back of the Union Leagues that terror was increasingly held up as the fastest route to political Redemption. In Mississippi, South Carolina and Louisiana – all still 'un-Redeemed' by 1872 – the federal government's cautious prosecutions against the Ku Klux Klan and other organizations emboldened agents of political violence and disheartened the besieged Southern Republicans.

In Louisiana in particular, Grant's re-election in 1872 had not been a tidy affair. By the following year the parishes were approaching a state of low-intensity civil war between black Republicans and white Democrats. On Easter Sunday 1873, a white posse of 300 attacked the county government at Colfax, drove out the Republican sheriff's 70-strong black militia and massacred them. As with other attempts at federal enforcement against paramilitary violence, the arrest of the culprits by the US Army proved short-lived. The trial of the Colfax ringleaders ended in acquittal in a federal courthouse, emboldening the agents of political and racial violence once more. In place of the now-outlawed Klan, the White League of Louisiana – dedicated to removing the Republicans from power and disenfranchising the black population by extra-judicial means – flourished in its place. Later described as 'the military arm of the Democratic Party' in the South, the political ties of the White League to Southern Democrats were much more overt than those of the Klan (Rable 1984: 131–2). In a matter of months, the movement surged across the border into Mississippi and Arkansas, forming what became known as the White Liner clubs, who shared similar aims of driving Republican government from the state by fair means or foul. Terror not only spread around the countryside, as it had during the Klan years, but now into the county seats and even major towns.

In December 1874 the White Liners captured the former Confederate stronghold of Vicksburg, evicted the black sheriff and opened fire on the black militia detachment raised by the governor to recapture it. In neighbouring Louisiana, the White League kidnapped a Republican senator in order to give the Democrats a majority in the New Orleans legislature, obliging federal forces to enter to the state house and forcibly unseat them. As Mississippi prepared for state-wide elections in 1875, a familiar pattern of electoral violence began to unfold. White Liners began breaking up Republican rallies and events and shooting their speakers; at one political rally in Clinton, Mississippi, a Democrat speaker turned up to debate with his Republican opponent accompanied by several companies of White Line infantry. After shots were fired into the crowd, the paramilitaries went on a manhunt for the county's Republican leaders that left 50 blacks dead. Such actions soon became commonplace in Mississippi: Democrats would disrupt Republican political gatherings, force them to disperse and then request the assistance of the White Liners to put down the dispersed black 'mob'. Inevitably, this culminated in the decimation of a predominantly Republican crowd and – under the pretext of restoring order – provided an excuse to find and execute most politically active African-Americans in the county (Lemann 2006: 170–209).

The exuberant and thoroughly politicized conflict entrepreneurs of the Democrat press would provide vital propaganda support for this effort, consistently casting these incidents as black riots put down by brave white defenders – a version of events which soon became gospel. Always with an eye to the federal government, White Liner paramilitaries had a vested interest in propagating a narrative that cast blacks as the aggressors and white violence as a spontaneous, law-abiding and justifiable reaction to it. In reality, White Liner electoral violence was anything but spontaneous. Over the course of the 1875 elections, the White Liners laid their hands on several cannon and towed them round the country as a show of force. County seats – where balloting would take place – were captured by force and held in defiance of state government. Some more persistent Republican voters were simply shot at the polls; many more, intimidated by the White Liners' utility of violence, were induced to disperse or even vote Democratic. Paramilitaries estimated that 'one smart nigger [would] control the votes of two or three hundred niggers'. As such, pre-electoral violence was thus also predicated on bribing, hanging or murdering these key political activists, which would avoid attracting the kind of federal attention that would come from targeting a white carpetbagger. Against the backdrop of this violence, in 1875 the Democrats swept the black-majority state of Mississippi, forcing the Republican governor to resign. In some black-dominated counties, Republican majorities more than 10,000 strong literally disappeared.

The so-called 'Mississippi Plan', as it became known, soon spread to the other un-Redeemed states of the South. Vote regulators began riding in Florida and South Carolina and several prominent local Republicans were assassinated as the 1876 presidential campaign heated up. Along the lines of the Mississippi experience, the Democrat–White Liner alliance began exploiting its new-found monopoly on violence (in the absence of substantive federal intervention) to engage in selective terror rather than mass violence, a nod to the old white supremacist monopoly on violence in ante-bellum days. Nonetheless, an estimated 150 blacks were murdered in South Carolina during the 1876 campaign. Although figures are hard to come by, the campaign in Louisiana was thought to be similarly brutal.

In many ways, the political violence of Redemption was a harbinger of the classic modern pattern of a revolutionary insurgency. At Vicksburg and elsewhere, White Liners drove out or eliminated representatives of state authority through terrorist action, and then expanded their own parallel rule of law into the vacuum. Without the robust or sustained intervention of central and state government, agents of the state and their allies – often African-Americans – conceded more and more ground until the conservative-Democrat alliance was in a position to seize the organs of government for themselves. The White Liners, however, consistently avoided federal intervention by targeting facets of the Radical Republican state, rather than rebelling against instruments of the Federal Union.

There were many agents of political violence during the Redemption period. In some cases, the ties between the White Liner paramilitaries and their Conservative-Democrat political allies were strong. In Mississippi, the chairman of the Democratic Party – former Confederate General Zachariah George – was later found by federal investigators to be running an extensive telegraph network with White Liners all over the state, receiving information and giving out instructions – including advice on when (and when not) to 'resist' black mobilization violently. More starkly, in 1875 a White Line mob under the shotgun-wielding command of Mississippi's own Senator James L. Alcorn drove the elected Republican sheriff out of the Mississippi town of Friar's Point and then began hunting and shooting an African-American militia as they tried to re-enter the town. The Democratic press immediately wired nationwide news of Alcorn's 'heroic defence' of the town against the 'negro mob', bolstering the narrative of heroic white (Democrat) resistance to murderous African-American militia running amok under a carpetbagger (Republican) government.

The press provided a vital conduit between the political and military arms of Redemption, performing a crucial 'brokerage' function between violence specialists, conflict entrepreneurs and political actors (Tilly 2003: 21–2). Virulent scientific racism and incendiary op-eds on the part of staunch conservative-Democratic editors did much to create an atmosphere in which political atrocities could be committed. As demonstrated by Pillay in his study of political death squads in Apartheid South Africa, the creation of a grand lie – a mythical 'good society' to contrast with the evil – can serve a critical function in legitimizing violence against the 'evil' political other (Pillay 2005: 417–29). The supposed illegitimacy of Republican rule and black enfranchisement played into this narrative. As in Apartheid South Africa and elsewhere, the sense (propagated by the Democrat press) that the state was under an existential threat authorized actions outside of the law precisely because they were perceived to be operating in defence of it. Jesse James, whose legendary criminal exploits were rebranded as the glorious actions of a 'Lost Cause' Robin Hood by alcohol-fuelled Democrat newspaper editor John Newman Edwards, believed to the end his own propaganda that every bank robbed and train derailed was part of a political struggle to oust the Radical despotism of Republican government (Stiles 2003: 128–30). The Lost Cause of Southern Redemption thus provided a coherent ideological cover for a series of arguably very mundane motives, which allowed many to conceal their violent acts under the banner of Redemption.

Nonetheless, the conservative-Democrat Redemption enjoyed the support of a clear majority of Southern whites along the existing identity/ antagonist boundary. Redeemers posited themselves as the *solution* to ethnic, social and political violence, at the cost of returning political control to conservative-Democrat whites and their allies. Redemption, they claimed, meant the restoration of good governance and (by implication) the management and suppression of violent actors that would limit the necessity for the federal government to become involved once more in the South. The subtle logic of this violence was that by attacking local political facets of Radical Republicanism rather than the federal state itself, it allowed the Redeemers ultimately to disavow ownership of the violence and marginalize its symbolism in the post-civil war context. The price of this Redemption, although unspoken in Washington, was the demolition of the African-American vote and the restoration of a system of white supremacy that would allow the New South state to institutionalize and regulate its agents of violence. Once this was done, the Redeemers' argument ran, and the aberration of black political power swept away, the South would finally be at peace and the unhealed wounds of the civil war could be forgotten.

Killing the mockingbird: the social functions of violence

The violence of political Redemption in many ways represented the resurrection of the South's social and racial constructs in new guises. For many, the very existence of four million freed blacks was a harbinger of the end of civilization. Popular ante-bellum writers such as Dr Samuel Cartwright and Thomas Dew had done much to popularize the 'scientific' theory that the black was a rampaging savage when freed from the 'civilizing' influence of slavery (Fredrickson 1987: 51–5). Pre-war slave revolts in Virginia, San Domingo (Haiti) and Latin America had cemented the idea that institutionalized violence – expressed through violent collective rituals, such as the lynch law – were the only way to order the relationship between society and the slave. As Cartwright wrote in 1861, the fate of the American black was, of necessity, to be either 'the slave of man or the slave of Satan' (Fredrickson 1987: 43–71).

The gospel of prosperity, bringing with it black infantry battalions, political mobilization and organized Loyal Leagues imperilled this unquestioned racial monopoly on violence. With conservative-Democratic movements in disarray and US Army-backed Republican governments in power, it was clear to many southern whites that the invisible ordering violence on which southern society was premised needed to become visible again (Pillay 2005: 425–6). Many of the ferocious newspaper columns that cast White Liner political vigilantism in a good light were self-conscious propagators of the ante-bellum narrative that black organizations posed an existential security threat to Southern whites. Dark rumours abounded, and were believed, that the Loyal Leagues were sworn by blood oath to partake of the mass slaughter of the white population (Lemann 2006: 80).

The logic of Klan terror, in this context, was clear. In many states it was the 'best men' of the county – judges, sheriffs, lawyers, doctors and the like – that ended up leading and directing Klan operations. In many counties the entire apparatus of local government, from postmasters to railway workers to elected officials, was subverted by Klan agents (Trelease 1971: 7–14, 20–2). Many of these agents believed that they were providing justice and order in a new and lawless world (Trelease 1971: 1–22). Freedmen's Bureau records for 1865 and 1866 reported scores of attempted and actual murders in Georgia, Louisiana, Tennessee and other states by white posses seeking to forcibly disarm Southern freedmen (Freedmen's Bureau 1869a, 1869b, 1869c). To many Klansmen, night-riding – and the attendant beatings, whippings, garrottings and murder that accompanied them – were defensive acts, designed to serve the wider social function of protecting white supremacy and dissuading blacks from mobilizing under the shield of federal civil rights protection. The maintenance of law and order also meant engaging in disproportionate shows of collective violence, as in ante-bellum days, to serve as a deterrent to the black population. In April 1866 (a month before Tennessee's formal re-accession to the Union) a confrontation between the Memphis city police and a group of black infantrymen spiralled into a mass race riot in which white police, firemen and ordinary citizens hunted freedmen through the streets for three days. At least 40 blacks were killed, hundreds more injured and many homes and businesses destroyed in an effort, according to the *Memphis City Recorder,* to 'clean out every damned son of a bitch of a nigger out of town' (Freedmen's Bureau 1868). Where White Liners and associated groups gained ground, as at Vicksburg, this supremacist system of parallel justice became re-institutionalized in defiance of the Republican state.

Violence as identity

As Aristotle first illustrated in *Politics*, new egalitarian democracies – in Athens, as 2,000 years later in South Africa, Australia and the young United States – can share a strong tendency to create and perpetuate a racial underclass against which the egalitarianism of their '*Herrenvolk*' master race can be defined (Mann 2004; Vickery 1974). Settler democracy's very egalitarianism can rest on creating an 'other' to give meaning to the rights and responsibilities shared by members of the master race citizenry – from the greatest Mississippi planter to the Kentucky mountain distillery owner to the lowliest bushwhacker horse thief. The fiercest racial animosity, therefore, is seen at the margins, where the poorest sections of the master race come to believing that their own rights, freedoms and status as citizens are conditional upon the continued suppression of that underclass. In the pre-war context, the ordering principle of slavery meant that even those on the very bottom rung of white society could take solace in the knowledge that they were more masters than slaves. In the post-emancipation 'victor's peace', where the foundations of this system came tumbling down, many poor whites saw their closely-guarded privileges disappearing. The advantages of policing the colour barrier thus accrued to Ku Klux Klansmen and White Liners on the bottom rung: those who wanted to protect their own social place in the 'Good Society' of the *Herrenvolk*, in which citizenship (symbolized by the attendant right to vote) was the most jealously guarded privilege. The ferocity of this social aversion to black suffrage was particularly evident in the failure of the New Departure political elites – who shared none of this status anxiety – to mobilize black voters in the neo-paternal mould, forcing the Redeemers to harness rather than look down upon the collective 'ethnic capital' they shared with the *Herrenvolk*. Black disenfranchisement, by fair means or foul, thus served a social function by restoring a two-tier sense of citizenship, which cemented the boundary between black and white and mobilized race prejudice (rather than class privilege) in the service of Redemption (Tilly 2003: 82–5; Vickery 1974: 309–28).

The defence of *Herrenvolk* superiority as a social identity also provided the justification for seemingly irrational acts of violence. Freedmen's Bureau records abounded with stories of summary killings for such offences as a freedman failing to remove his hat when passing a white man; a black man refusing to give up the sidewalk; refusing to hand over a whisky flask; just 'to see a damn nigger kick'; and, in one case, simply to test a revolver (Crouch and Madaras 2003: 108–9). In all these cases, whites sought to assert their God-given power of life-and-death over their black neighbours. Those who tasked themselves with policing the racial barrier also resorted readily to violence as an instrument for defending white sanctity and identity in all its forms. One Georgia freedman accused of raping a white woman was kidnapped and tortured to death in front of a crowd of citizenry; another was shot by vigilantes outside a North Carolina courthouse; yet another forcibly castrated by a doctor and attendant mob in Texas (Freedmen's Bureau 1867a, 1867b, 1867c). Interracial couples were strictly punished by Klan agents, and the merest suspicion of 'miscegenation' was punished by whipping, assault and even murder (Cardyn 2002: 770). At the same time, rape was a major weapon in the Klan arsenal, designed to reinforce poor whites' dominant position in the hierarchy and to expand the political battle space through 'sexual terror' (Cardyn 2002: 754–60).

Free only to labour: the economic functions of violence

War in the New South was more than simply a continuation of social conflict by other means. Many whites had direct economic motives for seeking the violent end of Radical Reconstruction. With the confiscation of millions of dollars' worth of human property from the South's most powerful plantation owners, the sons of the Old South economic elite were forced to embark upon an ambitious economic reordering of labour relations. As the plantations disappeared, tens of thousands of black freedmen aspired to tenant farms and smallholdings that could guarantee a level of economic independence. This was a direct challenge both to the economic dominance of the old planter elites and to the poor white tenant farmers that already farmed the South. As such, it had to be controlled: while planters could not force freedmen to be slaves, they could restrict their options until they were free to do nothing but labour. The new economic system – a revolution, in some senses, in Southern agriculture – nonetheless rested on the fruits of political coercion, designed to ensure that African-Americans remained legally landless and unable to mobilize against the stacked deck that was the economic order of the New South (Weiner 1978; Foner 1988).

As neither side dominated the labour equation, violence greased the wheels of the new economic order in a number of ways. Freedmen's Bureau reports in almost every state of the South recorded the murder or beating of a freedman between 1865 and 1866 for requesting fair or overdue wages, refusing to sign share contracts with a plantation owner, or for 'unauthorized' movement off the land (Freedmen's Bureau 1868). As late as 1871, Mississippi and Alabama Klansmen were routinely invited onto the old plantations to whip, beat or even murder blacks who sought to exercise their constitutional freedoms of labour, movement and assembly (Trelease 1971: 288). One Freedmen's Bureau official in southwestern Alabama stated that white patrols routinely hung, shot or drowned blacks found on roads, rivers or boats in his district in order to enforce labour immobility. In his opinion, the explicit motivator of this violence was economic: to 'wring' the freedmen's labour from them 'by every device an inhuman ingenuity can devise', up to and including the death penalty for economic defection (Schurz 2004: 128). In many ways, the revolutionary transition to wage labour lowered the costs of violence: the pecuniary value of a freed black being almost nothing compared to that of the pre-war slave, planters and landowners could make violent examples of their workforce without themselves making a significant economic loss (Trelease 1971: 5–9). As became common parlance during and after Redemption, 'one dies, get another' became an increasingly accepted response to the changed circumstances of labour relations (Mancini 1996: 1–9).

If violent coercion, labour repression and worker intimidation all cemented unfavourable economic relations in favour of the master, blocking black landownership was another important means of consolidating economic power (Burton 1988: 233–40). Many of the paternalist, planter classes had a vested interest in perpetuating white terror outside the gates of the sharecropping plantations in order to drive labourers back through them. FitzGerald demonstrated that in the case of Alabama (where only one in ten Alabama Nightriders had a connection to planter families), savage violence by white subsistence farmers against prospective black migrants in the up-country Piedmont was largely responsible for the flight of thousands of African-American labourers back to the state's planter-dominated cotton belt (FitzGerald 1997: 197–8). Meanwhile violence and targeted assassination against black political activists, Union veterans and white carpetbaggers severely constrained African-Americans' organizational capacity and their ability to organize themselves into viable economic groups (Trelease 1971: 8–14). With the dispersal of black families into isolated tenant farms, violence helped sever the organizational bonds formed by the Loyal Leagues and political blocs, and so forced many African-Americans to accept the sharecropping system for want of an alternative. Meanwhile, political terror was also necessary to prevent black political majorities from raising taxes or legislating against the planter interest, as well as to block the election of African-American sheriffs and officeholders who might interfere with their new economic drive (FitzGerald 1997: 193–4).

Meanwhile, the Malthusian competition between poor blacks and whites meant that the comparative advantage of violence accrued disproportionately to the bottom economic rung of white rather than black society (Cramer and Goodhand 2003: 124–5; Hirschleifer 1993). While many poor whites faced a relative decline in their fortunes, the freedmen themselves – who had begun life with nothing – suddenly faced greater economic opportunity than ever, and thus greater and greater potential costs for resorting to violence (Ransom and Sutch 1977: 19–22). Racial competition over grazing space, theft and tenant rights in heavily mixed states such as North Carolina, Mississippi and Alabama was fierce and violent. Even where African-Americans remained on the plantations, the obligations of share-cropping (through which most of their crop went straight back to the planter elite) meant that they still faced a bitter Malthusian struggle with their neighbours to survive. This economic competition was at its most intense where both sizeable black and white communities existed: it was probably no coincidence that the Appalachian counties and Ozark mountains, where few blacks lived, also saw the least violence, and in fact became the major strongholds of white 'scallawag' Republicanism (Trelease 1971: 22–4). By contrast, freedmen in North Carolina, Florida and Mississippi were terrorized off their homesteads by Klansmen who simply wanted to farm the land themselves (Trelease 1971: 202, 242). In the few industrializing areas of the South, such as the Atlanta-to-Richmond corridor, Klansmen terrorized semi-skilled black railroad workers by night so as to take their jobs by day (Reynolds 1999: 9–16). The Republican gospel of prosperity was unable to provide palliatives to the violent struggle that dominated the countryside. With the failure of land distribution and of expensive railroad projects to usher in industrialization, no Republican government seemed capable of building an institution better able to appeal to the economic interests of Southern whites than the old race-based ordering principle of conservative-Democrat white supremacy (Les Benedict 1984: 507–09).

Many Redeemer elites profited enormously from this violent reordering of the Southern economy. By 1877 one of the major features of Redemption governments (alongside sharecropping) was convict leasing, a resurrected form of Black Code slavery in modernizing garb. As Republican governments fell and the black vote shrank amidst political violence, Southern states such as Alabama, Louisiana, Georgia and Mississippi legislated so that vast armies of penal workers – almost all of them landless blacks – could be swept up under vagrancy laws and sold to the highest bidder. In most cases, these bidders represented the wealthy conservative-Democrat political classes: in Mississippi, most were leased straight back to the state's new commercial plantations, while in Alabama they formed the majority of the iron and steel workers at Birmingham, the engine of New South industrialization. This new form of state economic coercion, which has since been described as 'more crucial than share-cropping' in paving the Southern path to modern capitalism, was a result of the economic fruits of violence (Glickstein 1997; Worger 2004).

The commercialization of agriculture was made possible by the reordering of the freedmen into share-cropping tenancies and the violent suppression of a potentially non-market-oriented black subsistence class by their Malthusian competitors. The imperfect free market of the post-emancipation South thus stacked the deck against African-Americans, enforcing class and labour immobility as rigorously as Klan regulators and their nightrider allies. It is instructive that, by the 1890s, white Southern industrial workers in Tennessee were protesting against the political elites' use of black convict labour, which had become a tool of strike-breaking and wage suppression. In many ways, the future of Southern modernization – which had been wrested from the Radical Republicans at such cost – saw the erection of a series of flawed economic institutions that used racial inequality to mask a deeper, more fundamental system of durable inequality that bolstered the Southern elite classes against the rest of society (Weiner 1978).

Conclusions: revolutions can go backwards

Redemption was the triumph of a 'Loser's Peace'. The battered and bowed states of the old Confederacy were able over 12 years to mount a sufficient counter-revolution against the Radical Republicans' 'victor's peace' that the major revolution of Reconstruction was effectively turned backwards. The litany of violence that accompanied the Redemption was at every turn a political one: coloured by bitter economic competition, and fuelled by social constructs and racial animosity, but one that first and foremost served the political interests of its Redeemer architects.

The main driver of Redemption was to destroy the pillars of what the South perceived to be an unjust 'victor's peace' imposed at gunpoint by the Radical Republicans. Of these pillars, the greatest 'original sin' was considered by the Redeemers to be the political enfranchisement of the freedmen, which opened a Pandora's box of social and economic consequences that threatened to revolutionize Southern society. The politics of the 'victors peace' thus became inextricably linked to Reconstruction's social and economic outcomes. As such, Redemption was a broad rallying cry for tens of thousands of southerners against the peace: from paternalist conservative-Democratic political elites outraged at the rebellion of African-Americans at the ballot box; to *Herrenvolk* townsfolk, who formed rifle clubs and meted out their own brand of 'justice' to preserve their God-given places on the social and economic ladder; to solitary Bushwhackers, such as the James Gang, who aimed to keep Missouri burning long after the Lost Cause had died in order to enrich themselves; to hard-bitten Southern yeomen, determined by fair means or foul to force their African-American competitors out of the already crowded marketplace (Stiles 2003).

The collapse came when the Southern Republican centre could not hold. Black suffrage was an inherent structural weakness in the system, which many (North and South) found instinctively unpalatable, and which the federal government after 1872 had neither the resources nor the will to defend. Many former scallawags changed sides, like Senator Alcorn, who began his post-war career as a scallawag Republican politician only to end it wielding a shotgun at the head of a conservative-Democratic mob at Friar's Point in 1875. As new doctrines of scientific racism gathered momentum into the 1870s and 1880s, many – both North and South – embraced Redemption's 'expressive' political strategy of disenfranchising blacks as a means of securing Southern 'progress'. It is illustrative of how comprehensively the Redeemers won the argument at the time that the greatest Southern 'progressives' at the turn of the century were also virulent racists, who believed that the main lesson of Reconstruction was that the African-American vote was a commodity on the market, which threatened to forever stall the rise of a modern, politically developed South (Fredrickson 1987: 314–30).

In fact, Redemption in many ways took the South down its troubled 'Prussian Road' towards modernization. By 1900, the social and economic trajectory of the New South had cemented an underdeveloped, unsustainable agrarian system in which violence bubbled beneath the surface even as the industrial houses and plantations enriched a generation of white elites with the fruits of African-American labour. Moreover, as one South African writer put it in 1915, the 'Solid South' resembled 'a block of ice, inert, immovable, without thought or life' except on the question of race, which 'saturated' the minds of whites 'with fear and hatred' (Worger 2004: 65). The triumph of the 'Loser's Peace' was in many ways a failure for the South as a whole: by allowing the violent subjugation of a racial underclass for the better part of a century, the Southern *Herrenvolk* created a system by which economic development was the fruit of African-American forced labour rather than the key to one's own advancement, and violence was the ordering principle by which it was guaranteed.

The Northerner Carl Schurz, touring the Reconstruction South in 1865, argued that emancipation had done little to undermine the fundamental nature of Southern society: the African-American was still 'the slave of society' and all southern states would 'share the tendency to [keep] him such' (Schurz 2004: 68–9). Redemption, and the violent end to Reconstruction, was more than anything else the bitter triumph of this mantra.

Notes

1 For an overview of the situation in the immediate post-bellum period, see Foner, E. (1988) *Reconstruction: America's Unfinished Revolution*, New York: Harper & Row (particularly chapters I, pp. 1–35 and V, pp. 176–228).
2 For further discussion of the politicization of violence, see the review essay by McPherson, James (1985) 'Redemption or counterrevolution? The South in the 1870s', *Reviews in American History*, 13(4), December.

Bibliography

Anonymous (1901) *History of the Original Ku Klux Klan*. Online, available at: http://ia350624.us.archive.org/2/items/HistoryOfTheOriginalKuKluxKlan/oK.pdf (accessed 25 July 2010).

Burton, V. (1988) 'Economics as postbellum Southern history', *Reviews in American History*, 16(2).

Cardyn, L. (2002) 'Sexualised racism/gendered violence: outraging the body politic in the Reconstruction South', *Michigan Law Review*, 100(4).

Cramer, C. (2006) *Civil War is Not a Stupid Thing: Accounting for Violence in Developing Countries*, London: Hurst and Company.

Cramer, C. and Goodhand, J. (2003) 'Try again. Fail again. Fail better?', Milliken, J. (ed.) *State Failure, Collapse and Reconstruction: Issues and Responses*, London: Blackwell.

Crouch, B. and Madaras, L. (2003) *The Dance of Freedom: Texas African Americans during Reconstruction*, Austin: University of Texas Press.

Federal Bureau of Refugees, Freedmen and Abandoned Lands (1867a) *Records of the Assistant Commissioner for the State of Georgia: Reports of Murders and Assaults in Thomasville Sub District from January 1st to October 1st 1868*, US National Archives Microfilm Publication M798 Roll 32.

Federal Bureau of Refugees, Freedmen and Abandoned Lands (1867b) *Records of the Assistant Commissioner for the State of North Carolina: Semi-Monthly Report of Outrages by Whites Against Blacks in the State of North Carolina, for the Fifteen Days ending February 28 1867*, US National Archives Microfilm Publication M843 Roll 33.

Federal Bureau of Refugees, Freedmen and Abandoned Lands (1867c) *Records of the Assistant Commissioner for the State of Texas: Registered Reports of Murders and Outrages Sept. 1866–July 1867*, US National Archives Microfilm Publication M821 Roll 32.

Federal Bureau of Refugees, Freedmen and Abandoned Lands (1868) *Records of the Assistant Commissioner for the State of Texas: Miscellaneous Records Relating to Murders and Other Criminal Offenses Committed in Texas 1865–1868*, US National Archives Microfilm Publication M809 Roll 23.

Federal Bureau of Refugees, Freedmen and Abandoned Lands (1869a) *Records of the Assistant Commissioner for the State of Georgia 1865–1869*, US National Archives Microfilm Publication M798 Roll 32.

Federal Bureau of Refugees, Freedmen and Abandoned Lands (1869b) *Records of the Assistant Commissioner for the State of Louisiana: Miscellaneous Reports and Lists Relating to Murders and Outraged, Mar. 1867–Nov. 1868*, US National Archives Microfilm Publication M1027 Roll 34.

Federal Bureau of Refugees, Freedmen and Abandoned Lands (1869c) *Records of the Assistant Commissioner for the State of Tennessee. List of Outrages Perpetrated by the Whites Upon the Freedmen in the State of Tennessee from April 1865 to March 1866*, US National Archives Microfilm Publication M999 Roll 34.

FitzGerald, M. (1997) 'The Ku Klux Klan: property crime and the plantation system in Reconstruction Alabama', *Agricultural History*, 71(2).

Foner, E. (1988) *Reconstruction: America's Unfinished Revolution*, New York: Harper & Row.

Fredrickson, G.M. (1987) *The Black Image in the White Mind: The Debate on Afro-American Character and Destiny, 1817–1914*, Middletown, CT: Wesleyan University Press.

Giustozzi, A. (2005) 'The debate on warlordism: the importance of military legitimacy', *Crisis States Research Centre Discussion Papers*, 13.

Glickstein, A. (1997) 'Is it capitalism?', *Reviews in American History*, 25(2).

Hirschleifer, J. (2007) 'The dark side of the force: Western Economic Association International 1993 Presidential Address', *Economic Inquiry*, 32(1).

Kolchin, P. (1979) 'Race, class and poverty in the post-civil war South', *Reviews in American History*, 7(4).

Le Billon, P. (2003) 'Buying peace or fuelling war: the role of corruption in armed conflicts', *Journal of International Development*, 15.

Lemann, N. (2006) *Redemption: The Last Battle of the Civil War*, New York: Farrar, Straus and Giroux.

Les Benedict, M. (1984) 'The politics of prosperity in the Reconstruction South', *Reviews in American History*, 12(4).

MacPherson, J. (1985) 'Redemption or counterrevolution? The South in the 1870s', *Reviews in American History*, 13(4).

Mancini, M. (1996) *One Dies, Get Another: Convict Leasing in the American South, 1866–1928*, Columbia: University of South Carolina Press.

Mann, M. (2004) *The Dark Side of Democracy: Explaining Ethnic Cleansing*, Cambridge: Cambridge University Press.

Pillay, S. (2005) 'Locations of violence: political rationality and death squads in Apartheid South Africa', *Journal of Contemporary African Studies*, 23(3).

Rable, G.C. (1984) *But There Was No Peace: The Role of Violence in the Politics of Reconstruction*, Athens: University of Georgia Press.

Ransom, R.L. and Sutch, R. (1977) *One Kind of Freedom: The Economic Consequences of Emancipation*, New York: Cambridge University Press.

Reynolds, S. (1999) *Iron Confederacies: Southern Railways, Klan Violence and Reconstruction*, Chapel Hill: University of North Carolina Press.

Schultz, J., West J. and MacLean, I. (1999) *Encyclopaedia of Religion in American Politics Volume 2*, Phoenix: Oryx Press.

Schurz, C. (2004) *Report on the Condition of the South*, Kessinger Publishing.

Scheips, P. (1989) 'Darkness and light: the interwar years 1865–1898', *American Military History*, Washington, DC: US Army Center of Military History.

Seip, T. (1983) *The South Returns to Congress: Men, Economic Measures, and International Relationships 1868–1879*, Baton Rouge: Louisiana State University Press.

Stewart, F. (2000) 'Crisis prevention: tackling horizontal inequalities', *QEH Working Paper Series*, 33.

Stiles, T.J. (2003) *Jesse James: Last Rebel of the Civil War*, New York: Vintage.

Summers, M. (1984) *Railroads, Reconstruction and the Gospel of Prosperity: Aid Under the Radical Republicans, 1867–77*, Princeton, NJ: Princeton University Press.

Tilly, C. (2003) *The Politics of Collective Violence*, Cambridge: Cambridge University Press.

Trelease, A. (1971) *White Terror: The Ku Klux Klan Conspiracy and Southern Reconstruction*, New York: Harper and Row.

Vickery, K. (1974) 'Herrenvolk democracy and egalitarianism in South Africa and the US South', *Comparative Studies in Society and History*, 16(3).

Weiner, J.M. (1978) *Social Origins of the New South: Alabama, 1860–1885*, Baton Rouge, LA: Louisiana State University Press.

Worger, W. (2004) 'Conflict labour, industrialists and the state in the US South and South Africa, 1870–1930', *Journal of South African Studies*, 30(1).

Part II

Europe and the Middle East

4 Post-war violence in Bosnia and Herzegovina

Mats Berdal, Gemma Collantes-Celador and Merima Zupcevic Buzadzic

The levels and intensity of violence in Bosnia following the signing of the Dayton Peace Accords in December 1995 present an encouraging exception to the patterns of violence observed in many of the other post-conflict settings examined in this volume.[1] The suggestion here is emphatically not that post-war Bosnia has been spared 'post-conflict' violence. Indeed, violence was very much part of the early post-war landscape, especially so in the period between late 1995 and 1998. The overall picture nonetheless compares favourably to other cases of war-to-peace transitions where civil wars were also brought to a formal end through a negotiated settlement.

This requires explanation. After all, from the vantage point of late 1995 there were good grounds for expecting a 'violent peace' in Bosnia, the most diverse and delicately balanced of the former Yugoslav republics in terms of ethnicity. And there were certainly warnings to that effect from thoughtful and perceptive observers. Writing in May 1996 Susan Woodward concluded:

> The anarchy, chaos, and marauding by ex-soldiers and police that accompanied the transfer of Serb areas of Sarajevo [February–March 1996] will not be an isolated case. The conditions for a general breakdown in order as soldiers are sent home without jobs, politicians are preoccupied with elections, the trauma of war begins to be felt, and the resources for economic reconstruction are slow in coming will surely increase.
>
> (Woodward 1996: 89)

In the context of its time, such predictions were anything but far-fetched. The Dayton Peace Accords followed more than three years of brutal civil war among the country's Serb, Croat and Bosniak communities.[2] The war saw widespread physical destruction and the death of nearly 100,000 people. An estimated 40 per cent of those killed were civilians.[3] It was also a war that witnessed grave breaches of the Geneva Conventions, large-scale atrocities and countless crimes against humanity. Of special relevance to the prospect of post-settlement violence, it was an identity-driven conflict defined and fought in the name of ethnicity and religion. As ascriptive categories, these were far more malleable than nationalist politicians, determined to incite ethnic tensions and foment violence, made out. As in all civil wars, however, the experience of war itself, including in this case the heinous practice of 'ethnic cleansing', served to crystallize communal allegiances and radicalize identities. This development was bound to raise the spectre of continued ethnic violence, score-settling and revenge kill-ings after the formal end of hostilities.

There was yet another feature of the Bosnian war whose legacy it was thought, not unreasonably, would also be to stoke post-war violence. This was the large number of irregular and paramilitary formations involved in military operations during the war. Many of these had developed close ties to – and indeed were often indistinguishable from – organized criminal groups turned warlords. In the course of the war these had engaged in a range of illicit activities, from looting, theft and ransom to trafficking in contraband. Many of them were also deeply implicated in war crimes. The wartime alliances forged between criminal and political elites frequently survived into the post-war phase, contributing to the growth of organized crime in the country and the wider region (UNODC 2008; Andreas 2004). However, while organized crime remains an important challenge, the levels of overt violence associated with it have been low.

How, then, given these legacies of war should one account for the post-war level of violence in Bosnia?

Central argument

There are two basic reasons why post-war violence, using for now Charles Tilly's (2003) more restrictive focus on *physical* violence, has remained comparatively low. These are closely connected.

First, the early post-war years in Bosnia saw no sustained effort to reverse the facts created by war, that is, to undo the ethnic, territorial and political partition of the country. The official line at Dayton, it is true, called for post-war ethnic reintegration and gave refugees and displaced persons an unqualified right to return to their pre-war homes. In reality, as Marcus Cox has observed, the actual 'strategy implicit in the Dayton Accords was to allow the ethnically defined, wartime regimes to consoli-date their separate spheres of influence' (Cox 2008: 250–1). That strategy involved the creation of a very weak federal structure and saw no attempt to redraw de facto front lines at the end of hostilities. It also left the three wartime armies intact, even though it nominally merged the Bosnian Croat Army (HVO) and Bosniak Army (ARBiH). The result was to ensure that levels of 'minority' return remained low and thus, in effect, to remove or at least curtail an important source of violence in the early post-Dayton years. Since 2000, some localities, including areas that saw heavy fighting during the war, have experienced notable progress in minority returns and reintegration. Even so, wartime divisions still run deep and, as will be argued, official data (from both government sources and international agencies such as the UNHCR – United Nations High Commissioner for Refugees, also known as the UN Refugee Agency) tend to understate the country's persistent cleavages.

And yet, continued de facto ethnic segregation *alone* cannot explain the levels and patterns of post-war violence in Bosnia (Stroschein 2005). This brings us to the second reason why levels of violence have remained comparatively low: the violence-mitigating effect of the international military and civilian presence deployed to the country following the end of hostilities in 1995. The scale and the resources devoted by the international community to the stabilization of post-war Bosnia dwarf those of all other comparable cases. This extended international presence – 60,000 NATO troops and some 2,000 UN police following the peace agreement[4] – has generated its own problems, including a dependency relationship with the international community, which, some argue, has acted as a structural disincentive to meet post-conflict challenges, especially in the economic and political spheres. The quality of outside involvement and the strategic decisions taken on issues ranging from the organization of elections to the reform of the country's security sector have also been the subject of much debate and criticism. Even so, the sheer scale of the outside presence, along with the commitment to remain engaged for the 'long haul', has clearly had the effect of limiting levels of overt violence. Importantly, however, this effect was neither automatic nor immediate. It required – as will be argued more fully – an early readjustment of the force posture, some innovative action and the adoption of a less restrictive definition of the mandate on the part of the external actors – military and civilian – sent to implement the Dayton Agreement.

These considerations do raise a further question, one that goes beyond Tilly's (2003) definition but which the Bosnian case nonetheless prompts: has the unprecedented level of international involvement in post-war Bosnia adequately addressed the structural bases for renewed violence? Many feel that it has not. A detailed exploration of the structural bases of violence in Bosnia would require a more comprehensive analysis of the 'ethnification' of key institutions, which has done much to keep alive and harden ethnic positions in the media, education and within political parties. Such an analysis is outside the scope of the chapter, though we return briefly, towards the end, to the dilemma of how to balance short-term concerns about reducing violence with the long-term aims of stability and peacebuilding.

The chapter is divided into two necessarily overlapping parts. The first surveys the extent and forms of post-conflict violence in Bosnia. It also draws attention to some of the difficulties – practical and political – of categorizing violence, of arriving at reliable figures and of establishing clear-cut trends, including of nominal as opposed to 'true' refugee return. Even in the face of these difficulties, the data suggest that the wartime legacy of displacement and separation among communities has endured and shaped post-war patterns of violence.

The second part focuses on the 'nature of the post-war peace' and on the implementation of the Dayton Peace Accords. Specifically, this involves a closer look at the role played by the international presence in the mitigation and control of post-war violence.

Post-conflict violence in Bosnia: categories, trends, explanations

Presenting a picture of the extent and the types of post-war violence in Bosnia requires an initial and cautionary note about the problem of sources and data. Given the central role that control of populations played during the war, any discussion of numbers – whether of casualties or returned refugees – was bound to become, and has remained to this day, politically fraught and emotionally charged. The point is well illustrated by the long-running debate about, and the difficulties of organizing, a new population census. The last such census was held in 1991, that is, on the eve of the war. Although the need for a new census is therefore widely accepted in principle, the subject has proved too delicate for agreement to be reached (ICG 2009: 5; *Balkan Insight* 2010). The same holds true for discussion about the number of war deaths. Until 2007, when a newly created and independent research institute published its findings, the most widely cited casualty figures ranged from 250,000 to 300,000.[5] In contrast, the Research and Documentation Centre (RDC) in Sarajevo found that a total of 97,207 people were killed in the conflict, including 57,523 soldiers and 39,684 civilians. Of the soldiers killed or missing in action, the RDC concluded that 53.8 per cent were Bosniaks, 36.2 per cent Serbs and 9.8 per cent Croats. As for civilians, 83.3 per cent were said to be Bosniaks, 10.3 per cent Serbs and 5.4 per cent Croats.[6] While this research has generated much debate in Bosnia, the figures arrived at are now considered the most detailed and reliable to date. Indeed, the Demography Unit of the International Criminal Tribunal for the former Yugoslavia (ICTY) Office of the Prosecutor supports the RDC numbers, based on the results of their final estimate of death tolls.[7] Even so, the continuing debate on the subject and the passion it has generated within Bosnia shows just how deeply *political* the subject of population figures remains.

The fact is that political actors on all sides have manipulated figures, exploited the lack of reliable statistical information and made the most of anecdotal evidence to stoke ethnic tensions and promote partisan agendas. Most fundamentally, the absence of agreed-upon statistical data has complicated the task of establishing an accurate picture of refugee return (specifically 'minority' return), a critical shortcoming given that so much of the post-conflict violence in the country has been directly linked to this issue.

The politicization of data on violence is also evident in various attempts by societal actors to stir up nationalistic sentiment by deliberately mischaracterizing petty crime and 'conventional' criminal behaviour as ethnically motivated. Two incidents that shocked the citizens of Sarajevo in early 2008 are illustrative of this trend. In February 2008 a high school boy was stabbed to death by three juvenile delinquents. The subsequent investigation established that the assailants neither knew the victim, nor were they provoked by him into committing the crime. Yet, the fact that the boy was a Croat and the assailants Bosniak led sections of the Croatian media to portray Sarajevo as a 'dangerous city for Croats' (*Nova TV* 2008). In a second incident an elderly lady in a Sarajevan neighbourhood was brutally murdered. The victim was in this instance Serb and the assailants Roma juveniles, which prompted media in Republika Srpska (RS) to describe Sarajevo as a 'dangerous city for Serbs' (*Vecernje Novosti Daily* 2008), even though, again, the police had determined that the attack was not ethnically motivated.

These are but two illustrations of a broader trend. They also point to yet another deficiency in the source material: the paucity of micro-level studies of violence, that is, analysis of the role of 'local – village, town, community – and personal dynamics' in the generation and perpetuation of violence (Woodward 2007: 156). As Stathis Kalyvas's work on civil war violence makes clear, this problem is not unique to Bosnia and suggests, at the very least, that one should be cautious about 'meta' explanations for patterns of violence (Kalyvas and Sambanis 2005: 214–16).

Mindful of these caveats, it is nonetheless possible to construct an overall picture of post-conflict violence by drawing both on local sources (interviews and local media, down to the municipality level) and data collected by outside agencies and observers.

Ethnically motivated violence: a brief descriptive overview

Every year between 1995 and 2001 saw sporadic attacks on returnees, ethnically based violence and intimidation of journalists and international representatives. Following a period of escalated violence in the immediate post-war period, the scale and intensity of attacks has gradually declined, especially since 2001, though they have not ceased altogether. Attacks have ranged in gravity from murder and arson to the destruction (bombing or mining) of property, including mosques, churches, cemeteries and other sites of cultural significance. In general terms, it is possible to group the violence into three broad categories, which helps convey the evolution and pattern of attacks over time: unfinished ethnic cleansing; violence targeting refugee return; and intimidation and discrimination.

Unfinished ethnic cleansing

The first post-Dayton year, 1996, was also by far the most violent in Bosnia's post-war history, with tensions and violent incidents involving all three of Bosnia's main ethnic groups. Along with extensive human rights abuses, ethnically motivated killings and return prevention, violence also took the form of large-scale forced civilian displacement. The single largest case of such displacement was the exodus of approximately 60,000–70,000 Serb civilians in February and March 1996 from the Grbavica neighbourhood and the suburbs of Vogosca, Ilijas, Hadzici and Ilidza, areas of Sarajevo held by the Serbs during the war but which under the Dayton Peace Accords were to be transferred to Federation control.

Many of these Serbs were resettled in areas formerly inhabited mainly by Bosniaks. The goal was to prevent Bosniaks from returning and in doing so, consolidate Bosnian Serb control over those areas acquired during the war. The Bosniak authorities adopted a similar strategy, moving

Bosniak refugees from other parts of the country into newly acquired suburbs. All in all, an estimated 200,000 people were moved in this single episode (Sell 2000: 180; Human Rights Watch 1997).

Although Bosniak leaders did much to stoke the fears of local Serbs in the days before the transfer, the exodus from Sarajevo was initiated and encouraged by the Serb leadership in Republika Srpska (RS), who wanted the remaining Serbs to leave the city now that it was almost entirely in the hands of the Federation of Bosnia and Herzegovina. Many were forced to leave under threat of death and some were killed for disobeying orders (Sell 2000: 183, 193–7; Kinzer 1996).

This exodus, and the accompanying violence, is to date Bosnia's most concentrated burst of post-conflict violence. That this episode of widespread violence marked the first year of peace was, at one level, unsurprising, given the rawness of recent memories of war and its many horrors. But there is another, albeit related, reason for the scale of violence in early 1996. The immediate post-Dayton period saw the logic of wartime 'ethnic cleansing' play itself out in those few areas where it had yet to do so following the 1995 ceasefire, most notably in the Serb-controlled suburbs of Sarajevo. As Louis Sell put it (2000: 179–80), 'the emptying of the Serb-held suburbs locked into place the last piece of a jigsaw puzzle that completed the ethnic map of Bosnia'. A similar pattern of post-war cleansing also played itself out in Croat-dominated parts of Bosnia in the immediate aftermath of the war. Throughout 1995–6, in the words of Vesna Bojicic-Dzelilovic (2004), 'the mainstream strategy was to continue low-intensity ethnic cleansing by specifically forcing elderly residents out of their homes and later by attacking refugees returning to Croat dominated areas'. The international force deployed to implement Dayton was not prepared to prevent that from happening, ensuring that, as Woodward observed at the time (1996: 17), 'the outcome of the peace implementation process in its first three months has been further partition'. The fact that Bosnia's police forces at the time were still organized along ethnic lines, and 'were controlled by their respective political leaders', did much to fuel the violence (US General Accounting Office 1997: 40).

This trend continued into 1997, though at diminished intensity, no doubt in part because fear and intimidation now acted as a brake on attempts to return to pre-war localities. One of the year's most serious incidents was the re-expulsion by Croats of 400 Bosniaks from their homes around Jajce; a dozen houses were set on fire and one Bosniak returnee was killed (Human Rights Watch 1998). Also, in Mostar, Bosniaks from the western, Croat-controlled part of the city were forcibly evicted.[8]

Violence targeting refugee return

Each year between 1995 and 2001 saw both orchestrated and sporadic attacks on returnees, and weak responses by the competent police authorities in Bosnia. The violence was most pronounced in the immediate post-Dayton years and has diminished gradually since then without ever completely disappearing.[9]

In 1996, the return of 800 Bosniaks and Croats to their homes near Serb-controlled Doboj resulted in a major incident involving around 1,500 Serbs (Human Rights Watch 1997). Meanwhile, the return of displaced populations, particularly in RS, prompted arson attacks and the destruction of property which targeted the returnees either directly or indirectly. Other forms of attack included the looting of factories and of public utilities (Bildt 1998: 193–8). By one estimate, over 300 homes were destroyed in Bosnia in 'late 1996 and early 1997' alone in 'an effort to discourage cross-ethnic returns' (US General Accounting Office 1997: 67).

The violence against returnees carried over into 1997 and 1998. In 1997, 25 Serb houses in Croat-controlled Drvar were burned down as their pre-war occupiers attempted to return. In Bosniak-controlled Bugojno, Croats and their homes suffered a similar fate and in September two Croats were murdered in Travnik (Human Rights Watch 1998). The following year witnessed further violent incidents, from arson to assault and murder, targeting Serb returnees in the area of Drvar, Croat returnees in Travnik and Bosniak returnees in the Capljina and Stolac areas (Human Rights Watch 1999). Critically, local authorities rarely investigated cases of ethnic violence. Indeed, the local police, prosecutors and courts were often complicit in human rights abuses. This was especially the case in the eastern parts of the country, which were now part of RS but had prior to the war included municipalities with majority Bosniak populations (ICG 2002b: 18–19).

The year 2000 was presented as a 'breakthrough' for the return of refugees and displaced persons, this in spite of a major incident in Bratunac, in which Serbs attacked four buses carrying Bosniak returnees, and a number of similar assaults in Janja. The increase in returns witnessed during the year resulted from a combination of domestic and regional developments, including political changes in Croatia; advances in the property return process (for returnees); the international community's increasing readiness to use Office of the High Representative (OHR) powers and NATO forces to ensure returnees' freedom of movement and safety; and growing impatience on the part of refugees with the slow return process (ICG 2000: 5–6). Despite these factors, and a reduced rate of attacks, overall violence against formerly displaced populations continued. Such acts have occurred against a backdrop of more frequent, yet indirect, forms of intimidation, such as the disruption by a mob of the opening ceremony for the reconstruction of the Ferhadija Mosque in Banja Luka, an incident in which one person was killed and eight were wounded (Human Rights Watch 2001, 2002).

Intimidation and discrimination

The deliberate targeting of returnees occurred alongside a more general trend of ethnically based harassment, often conducted by members of the security forces. Until early 1998, police stationed at illegal checkpoints would single out travellers seeking to cross Bosnia's Inter-Entity Boundary Line (IEBL) and subject individuals to beatings, threats, arrest and even charges of war crimes, all to dissuade selected populations from travelling across Entity borders. This practice was significantly reduced with the unification of the vehicle licence-plate system in Bosnia in 1998. Described by Martin Barber, former senior official working for the UN mission in Bosnia and Herzegovina (UNMIBH), as 'the death knell of the check point system', it ensured that vehicles could no longer be identified by municipality of origin, which in addition to the ensuing increase in traffic at major crossing points, meant that the police found it more difficult to use illegal checkpoints to intimidate civilians. It is estimated that within the first month of the introduction of common licence plates there was a 50 per cent increase in crossings across Entities.[10] It was an ingenious and innovative response by UN and OHR (Office of the High Respresentative) officials on the ground to what had become a major obstacle to freedom of movement, and its immediate effect was to reduce the scope for violence and intimidation.

Even so, ethnically based intimidation has continued, but has tended to take less direct forms. Indeed, levels of outright physical violence have remained low since 2006; in a report released in 2008, the UN Office on Drugs and Crime (UNODC) went so far as to suggest that Balkan countries, including Bosnia, were, in many respects, safer than Western Europe (UNODC 2008: 9). And yet, violence directed against symbols of specific ethnic groups – churches, mosques, graveyards and cultural events – has continued. Examples of such ethnically motivated violence since 2006 have included the taking down of obituaries of 80 Bosniak war victims in Brcko before their funeral; the destruction of five tombstones in the graveyard of the Hadzi Omerova Mosque in Banja Luka; the provocation of Bosniaks in Trebinje at the beginning of a Ramadan prayer; the destruction of several tombstones in a Catholic cemetery near Bugojno; the attempt to set fire to the Serb Orthodox Church in Potocari, near Srebrenica; and the public turmoil over the illegal construction of religious monuments and buildings in various towns (US Embassy to Bosnia and Herzegovina 2008).

This all appears to confirm the finding of the United Nations Development Programme's (UNDP) 'ethnic stability index' for 2000–6, which concluded that ethnic relations did not improve over this period (UNDP 2006: 102–3). It also provides part of the background to more recent warnings of a further deterioration in inter-ethnic relations, leading to the question whether organized violence, if not war, can return.[11]

Nominal versus true refugee returns: the persistence of wartime divisions

As outlined above, most of post-conflict violence in Bosnia has been linked to the return of refugees, specifically to so-called 'minority returns'. Such violence can be seen as a continuation of wartime campaigns of ethnic cleansing, seeking both to create and to sustain ethnic demographic dominance in selected areas as a path toward broader, ultra-nationalistic, state-building projects (Mulaj 2008: chapter 3).

Such violence notwithstanding, the official statistics tend to paint a positive picture of refugee and internally displaced people (IDP) returns.

Of the 2.2 million people displaced during the war, 1.2 million of whom fled the country, it is estimated that by June 2010 approximately 579,600 IDP and 448,600 refugees had returned (UNHCR 2010).[12] Most of these returns occurred within the first few post-war years and with the help of various action plans issued both by domestic institutions (specifically the Ministry for Human Rights and Refugees BiH (Bosnia and Herzegovina)) and by international organizations (UNHCR, OHR, UNDP).

Still, these statistics only tell half the story. First, 'minority returns' – the return of a displaced or refugee person to the place of origin where s/he now represents a minority – accounts for approximately 468,800 returns (or 45 per cent of the total), of whom 275,200 (58 per cent) returned to the Federation, 171,500 (36 per cent) to RS and 22,000 (5 per cent) to Brcko District (UNHCR 2010).[13] These figures include some 'success stories', such as the return process in the Doboj area of RS, a centre of Serb nationalism during the war (ESI 2007). Nevertheless, the problem is that minority return figures cannot always be used as evidence of true and sustainable 'integration'.

Second, the conventional figures are largely based on the metric of *property return* or the right of would-be returnees to return to their pre-war flats or houses, taken away from them or abandoned in the flight from violence. Using this metric can be misleading, as 'no international organization or government agency has precise figures on how many Bosnians, after reclaiming their houses or flats – or receiving reconstruction assistance – then decide to sell or exchange them and relocate elsewhere', or simply never occupied them (ICG 2002b: 11). In Kupres Municipality, for example, an estimated 90 per cent of properties reclaimed were subsequently sold or exchanged. In Sarajevo Canton, half (around 10,000) of the apartments repossessed are thought to be uninhabited (ICG 2002b: 11; Prism Research Agency 2006: 20).

This situation can at least partly be explained in terms of the tendency, especially in the late 1990s, for cash-strapped homeowners to reclaim a returned property only to sell it on via intermediaries (family, friends and real estate agencies), albeit for extremely low prices. This desperate practice was encouraged by nationalist propaganda, as it helped prevent the re-establishment of ethnic minorities in these areas. It also created opportunities for self-enrichment for those people with liquid assets, who could purchase property cheaply and sell it at highly inflated prices within a few years. These buyers were often warlords and war profiteers, who unlike the vast majority of the population had neither lost their savings during the war nor spent them on outrageously overpriced commodities, but for whom, in many cases, conflict had been lucrative.[14]

Specific studies of individual towns add strength to these findings. Take the small eastern Bosnian town of Rogatica. Before the war, 13,029 of the town's citizens declared themselves as Muslims. Many of these Muslims were forced out of the town early in the war and some subsequently settled in and around Sarajevo. Return started soon after the war but in meagre numbers. As in other parts of the country, many returnees were elderly and had struggled to integrate in urban centres within or outside the country, or simply had no option but to return. As a result, it was not until 2005 that a returnee Bosniak baby was born in Rogatica (Boracic 2008; SIRLBIH 2008). Other small towns in rural BiH (of which there are many) have faced similar fates.

Going further, the 2008 municipal elections provide tentative evidence of initial returnees leaving their homes again. Over recent years, the number of Bosniak municipal councillors has declined in several municipalities of RS: in the 2004 municipal elections, the Party of Democratic Action (SDA) and the Party for Bosnia and Herzegovina (SBiH) – predominantly Bosniak parties – had four councillors in Rogatica, compared to only one in 2008; in Bratunac, the number went from ten councillors in 2004 to only five in 2008; in Srebrenica, it is 15 versus 11.[15] While this decline may also relate to a low electoral turnout, it may indicate that returnees prefer to leave areas where they constitute a minority.

The return rates in Bosnia must also be seen in the context of the country's precarious economic situation; indeed, the economic sustainability of return is often identified as a key factor in determining rates of 'true' return – without jobs, people cannot go back. Yet in Bosnia, the issue of the economy, further accentuated by the current global financial crisis, also has an ethnic slant, due to the 'ethnification' of institutions alluded to above. Entity employment laws and the nationalist manipulation of the privatization process to benefit one group or another have in the past contributed to 'institutionalized discrimination' against minority returnees seeking employment (ICG 2002b: 15). Returnees have also been subjected to discriminatory practices relating to access to pensions, social services, health care, education and public utilities (UNHCR 2001: 17–23). As summed up by one monitoring organization at the end of 2007, the overall picture was clear:

> The authorities have never made [a] distinction between returnees who only took repossession of their property and those who remained living in their property units. One of the primary goals in the implementation of Annex VII [of the Dayton Accords] is the restoration of the socio-demographic structure of the BiH society, which had been impaired by the war. Nothing has been done to that effect. BiH is today divided into almost ethnically pure territories, while consequences of war migrations have only deepened through long standing obstructions and administrative barriers of authorities at all levels.
>
> (Helsinki Committee for Human Rights in Bosnia-Herzegovina 2007)

In short, the limited number of 'true returns' – and the concomitant persistence of ethnic divisions created by war and enshrined in Dayton – provide part of the explanation for the comparative lack of large-scale post-conflict violence. As factors, low return rates, the fear of going back, and the subsequent tendency to sell former property rather than return to it created a situation where overt physical violence was only seldom needed to enforce and maintain the ethnic segregation vied for by some during the war. Even those who did return faced a tough choice: to live life under constant threat and usually in poverty and isolation or to attempt a new life elsewhere. Many opted for the second option. In a very powerful sense, therefore, the ethnic cleansing continued into the post-conflict environment, but by other means.

Dayton, the international presence and post-conflict violence

There is little doubt that the international security presence in Bosnia after 1995 played a key role in containing post-war violence. That role, however, has evolved over time. Indeed, there is a close correlation between the way in which the international military and police forces interpreted their mandate and the ambient levels of violence in Bosnia. This in turn suggests that the deployment of external military and police forces, even on the scale seen in Bosnia, is no guarantee *per se* of post-war stability; much depends on the intervening variables of mandate, mandate interpretation and of capabilities.

The Dayton Accords provided 'the first post-war set of benchmarks by which Bosnia-Herzegovina's contending factions were to govern themselves and be governed', including within the realm of security (Innes 2006: 2). The goal was to 'recreate as quickly as possible normal conditions of life in Bosnia and Herzegovina' (DPA 1995: Article 1(1), Annex 1A). Against this background, the activities of the international security forces can be divided into two main categories: (*a*) activities that aimed directly at stabilizing the country by preventing any further ethnic violence; and (*b*) those that sought to break the critical link between politics and the military and police forces. The latter task was deemed, rightly, to be the key to weakening the ethnic and nationalist manipulation of the security forces.

Military forces

Whereas the decision to maintain wartime ethnic cleavages in Bosnia in all likelihood prevented an immediate eruption of post-war violence, it also delayed the dismantling and professionalization of the various armed formations that had been active during the war. This prioritization of what *could* be done ahead of what *needed* to be done carried the risk of these forces being manipulated for ethnic purposes, this in a country awash with small arms and light weapons. The forces in question ranged from regular military forces to reservists, home guards, police officers, civilian militias, irregular and paramilitary formations and foreign fighters (UN 1994: 31–2).

Two annexes in the Dayton Peace Accords stipulated the measures the parties to the conflict had agreed to implement with the assistance and supervision of international military and police personnel. The NATO-led Implementation Force (IFOR) (succeeded by the Stabilisation Force (SFOR) from late 1996), was tasked with ensuring a definitive cessation of hostilities and the phased demobilization and disarmament of all military forces (including de-mining actions) along with the disarmament and disbanding of all armed civilian groups (except for the police) and foreign armies. However, more fundamental tasks, such as military restructuring and the creation of a national army, were postponed. Accordingly, the conditions to which the warring sides agreed through Annex 1A of the Dayton Peace Accords were largely concerned with consolidating the ceasefire rather than deep-rooted reform.

The ceasefire provisions seemed to have been fulfilled 'almost to the letter of Dayton's provisions' (Cousens and Cater 2001: 54). The separation, cantonment and progressive demobilization of all military forces got underway in 1996, followed in 1997 by arms and troop-reduction agreements. Despite these achievements, there was a limit to what IFOR/SFOR could accomplish in a country now divided along ethnic lines and with three ethnically defined wartime armies, whose outlook and, in many cases, personnel remained unchanged. It also meant that one of the mechanisms for the generation of violence (i.e. the manipulation of the armed forces) was still in place. In some ways this was of IFOR/SFOR's own making. As described by Elisabeth Cousens and Charles Cater in their 2001 assessment of the situation in Bosnia, IFOR/SFOR's initial reliance on a force separation strategy meant that they missed 'a critical opportunity [...] [B]oth implementation forces had the power to sever the link between military control of territory and political jurisdiction; but they have so far failed to do so' (2001: 65). This in turn adversely affected the capacity of the international security presence to control returnee-related violence and intimidation.

The 'Train and Equip' programme introduced by the United States at the time of the Dayton Peace Accords, but outside its framework, represents one of the first missed opportunities to weaken the nationalist hold on the armed forces. This programme was promised in exchange for reaching a peace agreement and it essentially re-armed Bosniak-Croat Federation forces in order to create an 'internal balance of forces' in Bosnia (Cousens and Cater 2001: 54; see also Pietz 2006: 161–2). The stabilization goal came at the price of only nominal integration of the wartime Bosnian Croat Army HVO and the Bosniak Army ARBiH, reaffirming the existence of three armies in Bosnia. Moreover, it increased the security dependence on NATO as – at the time – many considered that this programme gave 'an awful lot of men a lot of guns and taught them how to use them better' (senior SFOR officer quoted in Cousens and Cater 2001: 57).

What emerged as a particularly important turning-point, therefore, was the 2003 decision and subsequent efforts to merge the wartime military forces through the work of a Defence Reform Commission, created by former High Representative Paddy Ashdown in order to circumvent obstacles blocking this contentious reform.[16] It signalled a reversal of the policy adopted in the Dayton Accords, which accepted, and therefore reinforced, wartime ethnic cleavages as a means of avoiding violence. It essentially terminated the link between politics and the military forces, a link that nationalist parties had used to further their territorial agendas during the war. Effective from January 2006, this reform process created one common Ministry of Defence at the state level, integrating Bosniak, Croat and Serb professional forces under one operational command structure. Moreover, certain tasks that had been common in the early phases of the post-Dayton period were now prohibited or removed from military doctrine, including the use of military forces by the Entities for policing the entity boundaries and for internal security functions (Staples 2004: 35–6). Initiating defence reform – considered one of the most successful reforms in post-war Bosnia – had an 'ice-breaker effect' (Vetschera and Damian 2006: 39) on similar reforms, albeit with varying levels of success, in other areas of the security sector.

Police Forces

In the immediate post-Dayton phase, Bosnia's police forces – corrupt, unre-formed and organized along ethnic lines – were a major source of violence throughout the country, systematically obstructing minority returns and protecting war criminals.[17] The scale of the problem was noted in a UN report of December 1996, according to which 70 per cent of human rights violations were committed by police (US General Accounting Office 1997: 40). Through intimidation and harassment, often at mobile checkpoints set up illegally along the IEBL, as well as by direct physical violence, police forces of all three major ethnic groups (though especially Bosnian Croat and Bosnian Serb units), continued to pursue their wartime objectives of creating ethnically homogeneous territories. As late as 2002, the International Crisis Group observed that 'the role of the police is not seen as being to "serve and protect" everyone, but to serve and protect "one's own kind", whether they be co-nationals, colleagues or political masters' (ICG 2002a: i). Moreover, they continued to play a crucial role in nationalist patronage networks (Bechev 2007: 92). As late as 2000, nationalist parties in the Federation of BiH continued to exert control over the cantonal financial police, whose responsibilities included investigating corruption, money laundering and economic crimes. This control allowed nationalist parties to maintain a system of 'revenue-raising fines' from businesses and to audit opposition groups during election periods (Pugh 2002: 471).

Halting the police's involvement in ethnic violence required tackling the influence that nationalist and criminal networks had over them. Breaking this link has proved a major challenge. The UN Mission (UNMIBH) and the International Police Task Force (IPTF) worked on a number of initiatives aimed at terminating the politico-security nexus. An illustrative example of UNMIBH/IPTF efforts – continued and extended in many respects by the EU Police Mission[18] – is the Police Commissioner/Director of Police Project, introduced in 2000 with the aim of curtailing the wide powers vested in interior ministers by creating the position of 'Police Commissioner'/'Director of Police' and thereby separating policy making (ministers) from policy execution (civil servants) (ICG 2002a: 33). The latter was supposed to be an experienced police professional that would not serve a political agenda in the day-to-day management of police work. The implementation of this initiative was difficult, with nationalist forces either opposing the idea or introducing measures to weaken its impact (UN 2001: paragraph 16; ICG 2002a: 33–6). However, in many respects the nationalist grip on the police remains unchallenged to date, as exemplified by the 'failed' international attempt between 2004–8 to create a single police system and in doing so, reverse the fragmentation introduced at Dayton.[19]

Capabilities, mandates and post-war violence

So far we have analysed efforts by the international security presence to contain the political use of generalized violence in post-Dayton Bosnia. Equally important is the manner in which IFOR/SFOR and UNMIBH/ IPTF dealt with those situations where violence did occur. In this regard, the way in which they defined their mandate and went about implementing their responsibilities, particularly vis-à-vis the provision and guarantee of public security, was crucial.

In accordance with Annex 11 of the Dayton Peace Accords, the UN established a 2,000-strong IPTF with the mandate to assist, advise, monitor, train and inspect Bosnian civilian law enforcement personnel. It was the responsibility of the local police forces, not the UN international civilian police mission, to maintain a 'safe and secure environment for all persons in their respective jurisdictions' (DPA 1995 Article(1), Annex 1). In other words, IPTF had no mandate to carry out police actions or to sanction those law enforcement agents found to have contravened the Dayton Peace Accords; nor were IPTF officers armed. This outcome was the direct result of a difference of opinion during the negotiations that led to the Dayton Accords between the Holbrooke team – which pushed for a strong IPTF mandate and armed personnel – and NATO, the Pentagon and some Western European governments, who feared that the UN police, if provided with too ambitious a mandate, would get themselves into trouble and require NATO troops to intervene and protect them (ICG 2002a: 5; Holbrooke 1998: 251–2).[20] For US decision-makers for whom the images from previous interventions – during the Bosnian war but also in Somalia and Haiti – were still all too fresh, the preference was for a clear, simple mandate that would have American forces out of Bosnia within a year. A near obsession with force protection on the part of US forces in Bosnia severely restricted IFOR and initially SFOR's ability to limit and control post-war violence.

The limited powers given to IPTF in the peace agreement also prevented it from counteracting the violence witnessed in the first few years after Dayton. It also rendered its work and that of UNMIBH more dependent on NATO assistance, the very situation the Pentagon and NATO decision-makers had tried to avoid. Problematically, IFOR and initially SFOR were not keen, on grounds of 'mission creep', to engage in any activity that resembled law enforcement, despite the fact that, under the Dayton Accords, NATO forces were meant to participate actively in the creation of a secure environment for the implementation of the civilian aspects of the peace agreement. This backdrop helps explain the near total absence of an international response to the violence surrounding the transfer to the Federation of some Sarajevo suburbs, previously in Bosnian Serb hands. Similarly, it helps explain the virtual impunity enjoyed by paramilitary forces in the immediate post-Dayton phase, as these forces were considered outside IFOR/SFOR's realm of action, based again on a very restrictive reading of its powers as granted by the Dayton Accords.

The international military force's initial interpretation of its mandate did not help against the increase in inter-ethnic violence during the early post-Dayton period, something that became strikingly and embarrassingly apparent during the Bosnian Serb evacuation of Sarajevo. No effort was made to remove illegal checkpoints, nor was any serious effort made to apprehend war criminals or, more generally, to confront Bosnia's deeply factionalized police forces (Friesendorf 2010: 35–9). It is a paradox that the aforementioned licence-plate reform – initiated and implemented by UN and OHR officials on the ground – probably did more in the early post-war years to curtail violence than the actions by NATO-led forces.

The effect of this stance became clear when SFOR – following a May 1997 decision by Secretary of State Madeleine Albright – adopted a more proactive interpretation of its roles in supporting civilian implementation tasks, a decision that contributed directly to the decrease in ethnic-related violent incidents (Moodie 1998: 24–5). The change was, however, gradual and inconsistent. As a result, inter-ethnic violence frequently went unchecked in the years between 1997 and 2000. Still, SFOR's greater activity in protecting returning refugees from angry mobs was, for example, an important factor in the surge in returns in 2000 (Friesendorf and Penska 2008: 682). Similarly, its gradual, albeit reluctant, involvement in the apprehension of war criminals (although often with very restrictive rules of engagement) had a positive impact on the refugee return process.[21] So too did its efforts, tentative and half-hearted at first, to curtail the power of the Bosnian special police. The latter were suspected, and with good reason, of playing an important role in fomenting violence in the post-Dayton period, in protecting war criminals and in maintaining secret caches of heavy weapons (Moodie 1998: 28; Cousens and Cater 2001: 58).

Meanwhile, UNMIBH/IPTF's capacity to intervene in law enforcement also increased with time due, at least partly, to the restructuring and institution-building powers that it acquired from late 1996 onwards. For example, through Resolution 1088, UNMIBH/IPTF was given the capacity to investigate or assist in investigations of human rights abuses committed by law enforcement personnel (UN 1996: paragraph 28). This newly acquired prerogative was put to use during the certification (or vetting) process that sought – among other things – to remove all those police officers with war crime and other criminal records, whether those crimes were committed during the war or in the immediate aftermath, and those elements that contributed to the forces' continued militarization. Thus, although it was still not able to use force during episodes of violence or directly patrol the streets, these newly acquired powers made the UN into a more credible actor in the control of ethnic violence in post-Dayton Bosnia.[22]

Concluding thoughts

Levels of overt physical violence in post-war Bosnia were comparatively low for two main reasons. In the first instance, the undisputed control that each ethnic group had over its own territory contributed to a very slow and in some ways unsustainable return process, between Entities and between Croat and Bosniak areas in the Federation.[23] In turn, the sustained segregation rendered unnecessary the overt use of force as a means of entrenching wartime ethnic divisions. 'The Dayton formula', in the words of David Harland (1997: 13), was to 'freeze in place the situation as it was on the battlefield'. Second, the large-scale international military and police presence was unable to reverse this ethnic bifurcation and, if anything, in the immediate post-war period helped to consolidate it as an expedient means of maintaining stability (Cox 2008: 255). In the words of Cousens and Cater, 'preventing this violence was a task neither wanted by IFOR, which was permitted but not obliged to undertake it, nor suitable for IPTF' (2001: 65). This situation delayed the type of security sector reform (SSR) required for long-term post-war stability.

The international security presence has therefore helped to maintain a ceasefire in the country. Given the ferocity, the polarization and the open wounds left by the war of 1992–5, this achievement should not be under-valued. However, the decisions taken in terms of mandate design and interpretation – particularly in the early post-war period – have, arguably, failed to tackle structural bases of violence. Political turmoil in the last few years has been interpreted by some analysts as Bosnia being 'on the brink of collapse' with Bosnians 'once again talking about the potential for war' (McMahon and Western 2009: 69). Srecko Latal has argued that inter-ethnic incidents are on the rise, from a monthly average of seven in 2007, to nine in 2008 and almost 13 in 2009. He interprets this trend as meaning that 'local politicians could be losing their control over the masses' (Latal 2010). This view is not universally shared by those in the field, with questions being raised about the capacity today of local actors to generate large-scale organized violence faced with the international presence, the security and institutional measures brought in since Dayton, and the changed regional context. However, even those who question the likeli-hood of war or large-scale violence acknowledge the deteriorating climate of political dialogue and the dysfunctionality and lack of legitimacy of political institutions, leading – in the words of a long-standing interna-tional observer – to a 'complete lack of hope of any change for the better'.[24] It points to the dilemma of conducting operations that prioritize what *can* be done ahead of what *needs* to be done, in other words, short-term goals of violence reduction over longer-term aims of peacebuilding. In the words of a police expert, the political turmoil in the last few years shows an 'unresolved sense of trust massed over by the huge international presence that substituted for it'.[25] It also raises the question of whether Bosnia is today ready to stand on its own feet, or whether its stability remains a function of the ongoing international military, police and civil-ian presence still in the country.

Acknowledgements

The authors are particularly grateful to Martin Barber, Deputy Special Representative of the UN Secretary-General in UNMIBH from 1996 to 1998, for comments on various issues developed in the chapter. We are grateful to numerous interviewees in Bosnia who wished to remain anonymous.

Notes

1 Bosnia or BiH is used throughout the chapter to refer to Bosnia and Herzegovina.
2 According to the 1991 census, 'Muslim by nationality' accounted for 43.7 per cent of the population, Bosnian Serbs 31.4 per cent and Bosnian Croats 17.3 per cent with the remainder including various other ethnic groups and self-declared 'Yugoslavs' (Bieber 2006: 2).
3 See 'Human losses in Bosnia and Herzegovina 1991–1995' (also known as the 'Bosnian Book of the Dead'), RDC Sarajevo, online, available at: www.idc.org.ba.
4 The NATO presence was reduced to 32,000 in December 1996. The UN presence came closest to its authorized strength in November 1997.
5 See for example Holbrooke 1998: xv.
6 Information on the centre's website, online, available at: www.idc.org.ba/prezentacija/rezultati_istrazivanja.htm. For a detailed account of the politics and process of knowledge production in relation to this example see Nettlefield 2010.
7 The authors are grateful to Lara Nettlefield for her comments in relation to this point. For more information go to the ICTY website, online, available at: www.icty.org/sid/10591
8 For Mostar as a persistent site of violence and intimidation related to refugee return, see Bojicic-Dzelilovic 2004.
9 These abuses have been well documented by Human Rights Watch in its annual world reports (section on Bosnia). For more information see the reports from 1996 to 2001, online, available at: www.hrw.org/en/node/79288 (accessed 31 August 2010).
10 Interview with Martin Barber, Deputy Special Representative of the UN Secretary-General in UNMIBH from 1996 to 1998, London, January 2010.
11 See Ashdown and Holbrooke (2008).
12 The UNHCR statistics point out that since 2007 returnee numbers (including minority returns) are based on incomplete data submitted by local authorities. In December 2007 return data looked as follows: 578,400 IDPs and 446,600 refugees (UNHCR 2007).
13 The percentages are approximate figures based on the authors' calculation using the UNHCR 2010 data. The number of minority returns in 2007 stood at 465,700 (UNHCR 2007).
14 Confidential interviews with Bosnian citizens who lived in the country at the time in question, Sarajevo, August–September 2008.
15 This data is based on the authors' comparison of municipal council member lists for the municipalities in question on the basis of the local electoral results between 2004 and 2008. Data at the official site of the Central Election Commission of Bosnia and Herzegovina, online, available at: www.izbori.ba (accessed 10 May 2009).
16 A range of motivations were behind this strategy, from economic arguments to the exigencies of joining NATO's PfP (Partnership for Peace) programme. A number of breaches of Dayton's defence clauses by local authorities added impetus to the process (Pietz 2006: 163–4).
17 Interview with Martin Barber, former UNMIBH senior official, London, January 2010.
18 On 1 January 2003 the European Union Police Mission (EUPM) took over from the UN the responsibility for policing matters in Bosnia.
19 While progress has been made in terms of building citizen trust (ICG 2009: 2–3), the ongoing fragmentation of the current system, which included 15 operationally independent law enforcement agencies before 2008, works against the development of a robust police that is able to withstand political pressures.

20 Some also feared that arming the IPTF would slow down the police reform
    process by encouraging dependence on international security structures. Inter-
    view with Martin Barber, former UNMIBH senior official, London, January
    2010.
21 For a detailed study of the relationship between arrests of war criminals and
    refugee return patterns, see Orentlicher 2010: 28–9, 79–85.
22 At the 1997 Bonn Peace Implementation Council the OHR was given the
    power to take action against individuals holding office who were beyond
    UNMIBH's jurisdiction but were nevertheless working against the implementa-
    tion of Dayton. In those situations, UNMIBH could make recommendations to
    the OHR (UNMIBH Internal Memo, no date).
23 Interview with Martin Barber, former UNMIBH senior official, London,
    January 2010.
24 Confidential interview, Sarajevo, September 2009.
25 Confidential interview, Sarajevo, September 2009.

Bibliography

Andreas, Peter (2004) 'Criminalized legacies of war: the clandestine political
    economy of the Western Balkans', *Problems of Post-Communism*, 51(3): 3–9.
Ashdown, P. and Holbrooke, R. (2008) 'A Bosnian powder keg', *The Guardian*, 22
    October.
Balkan Insight (2010) 'Bosnia parliament fails to pass census law', Sarajevo, 30 July.
    Online, available at: www.balkaninsight.com/en/main/news/29782/.
Bechev, D. (2007) 'Whither Bosnia? Dilemmas of statebuilding in the Western
    Balkans', *Turkish Policy Quarterly*, 6(4): 87–95.
Bieber, F. (2006) *Post-War Bosnia: Ethnicity, Inequality and Public Sector Governance*,
    Basingstoke: Palgrave.
Bildt, C. (1998) *Peace Journey*, London: Weidenfeld and Nicolson.
Bojicic-Dzelilovic, V. (2004) 'Peace on whose terms? War veterans' associations in
    Bosnia', Paper for UNU Project on Spoilers for Peace Processes, December
    2004.
Boracic, S. (2008) 'Povratak spor i neodrziv [Return is slow and unsustainable]',
    Radio Free Europe, 15 December. Online, available at: www.slobodnaevropa.org/
    content/Article/1360086.html?spec=.
Cousens, E.M. and Cater, C.K. (2001) *Toward Peace in Bosnia: Implementing the
    Dayton Accords*, London: Lynne Rienner.
Cox, M. (2008) 'Bosnia and Herzegovina: the limits of liberal imperialism', in C.T.
    Call (ed.) *Building States to Build Peace*, Boulder: Lynne Rienner.
ESI (European Stability Initiative) (2007) *A Bosnian Fortress*, Berlin and Sarajevo,
    19 December.
Friesendorf, C. (2010) *The Military and Law Enforcement in Peace Operations: Lessons
    from Bosnia-Herzegovina and Kosovo*, Vienna: Lit Verlag/DECAF.
Friesendorf, C. and Penska, S. (2008) 'Militarized law enforcement in peace opera-
    tions: EUFOR in Bosnia and Herzegovina', *International Peacekeeping*, 15(5): 677–94.
Harland, D. (1997) 'Peace in Bosnia?', *New Zealand International Review*, 22(2).
Helsinki Committee for Human Rights in Bosnia-Herzegovina (2007) *Report on the
    Status of Human Rights in Bosnia and Herzegovina January–December 2007*, Sarajevo.
    Online, available at: www.bh-hchr.org/Reports/reportHR2007.htm.
Holbrooke, R. (1998) *To End a War*, New York: Random House.

Human Rights Watch (1997) *World Report 1997: Events of 1996*. Online, available at: www.hrw.org/reports/1997/WR97/.

Human Rights Watch (1998) *World Report 1998: Events of* 1997. Online, available at: www.hrw.org/legacy/worldreport/Table.htm0.

Human Rights Watch (1999) *World Report 1999: Events of 1998*. Online, available at: www.hrw.org/legacy/worldreport99/.

Human Rights Watch (2001) *World Report 2001: Events of 2000*. Online, available at: www.hrw.org/wr2k1/.

Human Rights Watch (2002) *World Report 2002: Events of 2001*. Online, available at: www.hrw.org/wr2k2/.

ICG (International Crisis Group) (1999) *Is Dayton Failing? Bosnia Four Years After the Peace Agreement*, Balkans Report no. 80, Sarajevo.

ICG (International Crisis Group) (2000) *Bosnia's Refugee Logjam Breaks: Is the International Community Ready?*, Europe Report no. 95, Sarajevo and Brussels.

ICG (International Crisis Group) (2002a) *Policing the Police in Bosnia: A Further Reform Agenda*, Balkans Report no. 130, Sarajevo and Brussels.

ICG (International Crisis Group) (2002b) *The Continuing Challenge of Refugee Return in Bosnia and Herzegovina*, Europe Report no. 137, Sarajevo and Brussels.

ICG (International Crisis Group) (2009) *Bosnia's Incomplete Transition*, Report no. 198, Sarajevo and Brussels.

Innes, M. (2006) 'Introduction: Security in between', in M. Innes (ed.) *Bosnian Security after Dayton: New Perspectives*, London: Routledge.

Kalyvas, S. and Sambanis, N. (2005) 'Bosnia's civil war: origins and violence dynamics', in P. Collier and N. Sambanis (eds) *Understanding Civil Wars: Evidence and Analysis – Europe, Central Asia, and Other Regions, vol. 2*, Washington, DC: World Bank.

Kinzer, S. (1996) 'Bosnian Serbs pressed to leave area near Sarajevo', *New York Times*, 21 February.

Latal, S. (2010) 'Bosnia faces critical challenges in 2010', *Balkan Insight*, Sarajevo, 21 January. Online, available at: www.balkaninsight.com/en/main/comment/25135/.

McMahon, P. and Western, J. (2009) 'The Death of Dayton', *Foreign Affairs*, 88(5):69–83.

Moodie, M. (1998) 'Tragedy in the Balkans: a conflict ended – or interrupted?', *Small Wars and Insurgencies*, 9(1): 12–31.

Mulaj, K. (2008) *Politics of Ethnic Cleansing*, Plymouth: Lexington Books.

Nettlefield, L. (2010) 'Research and repercussions of death tolls: the case of the Bosnian Book of Dead', in P. Andreas and K.M. Greenhill (eds) *Sex, Drugs and Body Counts: The Politics of Numbers in Global Crime and Conflict*, Ithaca, NY: Cornell University Press.

Nova TV (2008) 'Sarajevo: Ubojstvo 17-godisnjaka uznemirilo hrvatske duznosnike i crkvu [Sarajevo: The murder of a 17-year old distresses Croat politicians and the Catholic Church]', 8 February. Online, available at: www.dnevnik.hr.

Orentlicher, D. (2010) *That Someone Guilty Be Punished*, Report, New York: Open Society Institute.

Perdan, S. (2006) 'Security sector reform: the building of security in Bosnia and Herzegovina', *Conflict, Security and Development*, 6(2): 179–209.

Pietz, T. (2006) 'Overcoming the failings of Dayton: defence reform in Bosnia-Herzegovina', in M.A. Innes (ed.) *Bosnian Security after Dayton: New Perspectives*, London: Routledge.

Prism Research Agency (2006) *Istrazivanje o povratku izbjeglica i raseljenih lica* [Research on Return of Refugees and Displaced People], Report, Sarajevo.

Pugh, M. (2002) 'Postwar Political Economy in Bosnia and Herzegovina: The Spoils of Peace', *Global Governance*, 8(4): 467–82.

Saferworld (2010) *The Missing Peace: The Need for a Long Term Strategy in Bosnia and Herzegovina*, Sarajevo and London, August.

Sell, L. (2000) 'The Serb flight from Sarajevo: Dayton's first failure', *East European Politics and Societies*, 14(1): 179–202.

SIRLBIH (Union of Associations for Refugees, Displaced Persons and Returnees in Bosnia and Herzegovina) (2008) 'Jos oko 145 porodica bez krova nad glavom [Still around 145 homeless families]', 27 October. Online, available at: www.sirlbih.org.

Staples, J. (2004) 'Defence reform and PfP in Bosnia and Herzegovina', *RUSI Journal*, 149(4): 34–9.

Stroschein, S. (2005) 'Examining ethnic violence and partition in Bosnia-Herzegovina', *Ethnopolitics*, 4(1): 49–64.

Tilly, C. (2003) *The Politics of Collective Violence*, Cambridge: Cambridge University Press.

UN (1994) *Annexes to the Final Report of the Commission of Experts Established Pursuant to UN Security Council Resolution 780 (1992)*, vol. I – Annexes I to V, S/1994/674/Add.2 (vol. I).

UN (1996) UNSC *Resolution 1088*, S/RES/1088, 12 December.

UN (1999) *Report of the Secretary-General on UNMIBH*, S/1999/989, 17 September.

UN (2001) *Report of the Secretary-General on the United Nations Mission in Bosnia and Herzegovina (UNMIBH)*, S/2001/571, 7 June.

UNDP (2006) *Bosnia and Herzegovina Early Warning System Research 2000–2006*, Sarajevo, 18 October.

UNHCR (2001) *UNHCR's Position on Categories of Persons from Bosnia and Herzegovina in Continued Need of International Protection*, Sarajevo, 1 September.

UNHCR (2007) *Statistics Package*, Sarajevo, 30 December. Online, available at: www.unhcr.ba.

UNHCR (2010) *Statistics Package*, Sarajevo, 30 June. Online, available at: www.unhcr.ba.

UNODC (2008) *Crime and its Impact on the Balkans and Affected Countries*, Vienna International Centre.

US Embassy to Bosnia and Herzegovina (2008) *2007 Country Reports on Human Rights Practices: Bosnia and Herzegovina*, Sarajevo and Washington, DC, 11 March.

US General Accounting Office (1997) *Bosnia Peace Operation: Progress toward Achieving the Dayton Agreement's Goals*, GAO/NSIAD-97–132, May 1997.

Vecernje Novosti Daily (2008) 'Zapaljena starica [An old lady on fire]', 22 January. Online, available at: www.naslovi.net/2008–01–22/vecernje-novosti/zapaljena-starica/551372.

Vetschera, H. and Damian, M. (2006) 'Security sector reform in Bosnia and Herzegovina: the role of the international community', *International Peacekeeping*, 13(1): 28–42.

Woodward, S. (1996) *Implementing Peace in Bosnia and Herzegovina: a post-Dayton Primer and Memorandum of Warning*, Washington, DC: Brookings Institution.

Woodward, S. (2007) 'Do the root causes of civil war matter?', *Journal of Intervention and Statebuilding*, 1(2): 143–70.

5 Revenge and reprisal in Kosovo[1]

Michael J. Boyle

Introduction

Reprisal violence is one of the most common forms of violence in post-conflict states. As the tit-for-tat killings between Sunni and Shiites have demonstrated in post-war Iraq, high levels of inter-communal reprisal violence can imperil the prospects for peace and lead to a risk of renewed war.[2] The civil war which raged in Iraq from 2005–7 was in part driven by the reprisals between the communities, often following precipitant events like mass-casualty bombings.[3] Similarly, the extensive reprisals carried out by Rwandan Patriotic Front (RPF) army and locally organized Tutsi militias expelled nearly 800,000 Hutus into surrounding states and led to war in the Congo.[4] Yet despite clear evidence of its impact, reprisal violence remains an under-studied phenomenon. In the literature on peace building, for instance, reprisal violence is often portrayed as epiphenomenal to the central problem of restoring a liberal democratic order, as indicative of the extent to which culture matters in fuelling ethnic or sectarian violence, or evidence of the need for justice or reconciliation.[5] Within its own right, reprisal violence is rarely studied as a phenomenon with both theoretical importance and policy-relevance, especially in the context of intra-state conflict.[6]

One of the reasons that reprisal violence remains so widely acknowledged but so little studied is that it is difficult to detect conceptually and empirically. As a conceptual matter, reprisal violence is close to 'revenge' or 'retribution' killings, sharing characteristics of each while having a different, often more political, motive behind the act. The empirical problems with reprisal violence are substantial. By definition, a reprisal is tied to a prior act of violence, yet this relationship is not always clear or even reciprocal. Reprisals are sometimes conducted against those who had nothing to do with the prior act; in other instances, the attack is aimed indiscriminately at certain ethnic, religious or political groups. It is also difficult to connect a possible reprisal with its prior or precipitant act, in part because there is often a 'lull' in the ensuing violence and in part because the contextual details of the act are often lost to outside observers.[7] Data at the aggregate level can rarely capture the subtleties in intention and targeting behind these acts. Without detailed information about the victim's identity and the perpetrator's intent, parsing out reprisal violence from the rest of the undifferentiated violent transactions in the society often becomes a kind of guesswork, where the outside analyst must attempt to detect patterns of strategic targeting amidst considerable 'noise' in the data. Thick descriptions of violent events can provide glimpses of reprisal violence, but the universe of total reprisal acts is difficult to determine.[8]

While acknowledging these limitations, the purpose of this chapter is to develop the distinction between revenge and reprisal violence and to apply it to regional and event-level data on violence in post-conflict Kosovo. Reprisal violence is defined here as an act of strategic violence directed against a member of a targeted group in response to a prior or precipitant act. The theory developed in this chapter distinguishes reprisal violence from the expressive, and mostly uncoordinated, forms of violence that often fall under the category of 'revenge violence'. It argues that revenge and reprisal violence are mirror images of each other, sharing descriptive characteristics, yet they are distinct in their intention and the criteria for victim selection. The conceptual inter-relationship between revenge and reprisal violence confers a strategic advantage on actors who engage in carefully organized campaigns of reprisals after wars by allowing them to mask their actions as 'revenge' by individuals settling personal grievances. Further, it argues that the metaphor of 'revenge' lowers their costs and risks and enables perpetrators of violence to achieve goals they might not otherwise reach. As an illustrative case, it examines how reprisal attacks were used by the Kosovo Liberation Army (*Ushtria Çlirimtare e Kosovës*, UCK) following the Kosovo war to expel Serbs and Roma from Albanian majority regions, and how the metaphor of revenge was used to lower the costs that were paid for their campaign of reprisal violence.[9]

Defining revenge and reprisal violence

Revenge attacks are defined as acts of expressive violence against a member of a targeted group with the intention of punishing them for a previous act of violence.[10] As Jon Elster has described it, revenge is 'the attempt, at some risk of cost to oneself, to impose suffering on those who have made one suffer, because they have made one suffer'.[11] Revenge attacks are described as 'expressive' because they are motivated (at least in part) by emotions, such as sorrow, grief or anger.[12] Revenge violence is a search for emotional satisfaction after great suffering or loss. Yet while it is a product of emotion and passion, revenge is not by definition irrational, and can be consistent with, and even reinforce, social or cultural norms.[13] Those who seek revenge are not always motivated by blind fury and can act carefully, even opportunistically, to achieve satisfaction. Revenge attacks can be undertaken by individuals and by groups, that is, they can be loosely coordinated (i.e. a mob of returning refugees) or they can be entirely uncoordinated (i.e. isolated attacks). Victims of revenge violence are selected entirely on personal, discriminate grounds, generally in response to a previous action. Revenge violence is by definition reciprocal: the goal is to inflict harm on the agent of the prior harm, either by harming their person directly or by inflicting damage on his or her family or interests. Revenge attacks also can be mimetic, mirroring the violence done in the prior act.

The expressive motivation for revenge violence is essential but not exclusive. Revenge killings can sometimes be instrumental in achieving satisfaction for frustration or grief at a loss.[14] While they may be motivated in part by emotions and directed at those responsible for a prior act of violence, they can include an instrumental dimension, either by allowing the individual some degree of personal gain or by signalling communal strength and capacity to harm.[15] For instance, many returning refugees in Kosovo brutalized Serb and Roma civilians, who had in some cases confiscated their property or homes during the war itself. In these cases, the act was certainly an act of revenge (driven by anger at the perpetrator) but may have also had an instrumental dimension. This account of revenge violence, while highlighting its expressive and discriminate character, does not assume that it is non-instrumental or irrational, merely that the expressive motive carries primary causal weight in motivating the act.

In part because it is by definition reciprocal, revenge violence is usually proportionate to the prior act. The adage of an 'eye for an eye' often obligates perpetrators of revenge to ensure that their response matches in severity the original offence. Exceptions to this general rule of proportionality are often seen as dangerous in risking spirals of tit-for-tat violence. This is one of the reasons why revenge is so carefully regulated in codes of tribal or local justice. In states with underdeveloped law enforcement and judicial capacity, controlled amounts of revenge violence can be used to regulate the social order.[16] In Kosovo, for instance, the Kanun code was traditionally used to regulate relations between Albanian clans in the mountainous regions that lie outside the control of the central government.[17] By carefully specifying the penalties for certain kinds of actions, local authorities could deter would-be perpetrators and control escalatory spirals of violent activity. When revenge violence exceeds the original offence, it can trigger a chain of violent transactions which will be less connected (and thus less empirically traceable) to the original offending act. Tribal codes of honour are often designed to recognize the social function of revenge but to enforce a rough kind of proportionality which is designed to prevent the emergence of spirals of violence.[18]

Its mirror image, reprisal violence, is defined as an act of strategic violence directed against a member of a targeted group in response to a prior or precipitant act. It is strategic in that it is a deliberate attempt to change the balance of power or resources in a given territory; in this sense it is a particular kind (or subset) of instrumental action. Like revenge, it follows a precipitant event and is targeted at a group widely seen as responsible for a prior harm. However, with reprisal violence, an armed group is the source of the attack, not just a coordinator or facilitator of it, and as such the leadership selects the victim and orchestrates the strategy and tactics for the attack. While it may appear to the outside observer to be random, spasmodic or uncontrollable acts of revenge, reprisal violence is carefully organized by the political elites in pursuit of a strategic goal. Reprisal violence happens during windows of opportunity, is generally concentrated around strategically valuable or contested territory, and often includes violent acts (such as arson) with demonstration effects. Unlike revenge violence, reprisal violence is not caused by expressive motivations like fury or passion but instead reflects only a ruthless calculation of strategic advantage.

Unlike revenge violence, reprisal violence is neither reciprocal nor proportionate. Victims of reprisal violence are not chosen because they had any necessary connection to a previous act of political violence – that is, there are not elements of personal retribution involved – but rather are selected on strategic grounds. The victim will not be responsible for a prior act of violence, so the reciprocity which characterizes revenge violence is not present. This explains why reprisals are so often focused on vulnerable groups such as the elderly, poor, dispossessed and infirm. Reprisal violence is also not proportionate to an original offence. While reprisal attacks are often nominally linked by elites to prior acts of harm, the calculated violent response can exceed the original act of harm. In post-conflict states, disproportionate violence is often in evidence as noncombatants are killed, brutalized or expelled despite having remained uninvolved with the war itself.

One of the key distinctions between revenge and reprisal violence lies in the communicative aim of the violent act or, in other words, the scope of its audience. Revenge violence is essentially a private act that does not contain a message aimed at a public audience. Revenge killings, for example, are usually conducted covertly and only in rare cases does the perpetrator wish to send a message to other people in his or her immediate environment. The person who murders his business rival in the chaotic aftermath of a war might prefer that his competitors know what he did to intimidate them, but generally he would prefer that others, especially the police, know little about his act. Most ordinary revenge killings are intimate acts conducted between two people (or groups of people) with no message to the outside world.

By contrast, reprisal violence is a public act which has messages aimed at multiple audiences and conveys two very different messages. The first message is a threat directed at the target or victim group. A wide variety of demands can be conveyed with this message, ranging from convincing them to leave a contested territory or to adjust their political demands. Sometimes this message is conveyed directly through threats, warnings or letters. In Iraq, for instance, Sunni extremists would send Shi'a families DVDs with images of exploding houses as a warning to leave immediately.[19] But in other case the warning is implicit or subtle. For example, a coded message is sent to the Kosovo Serb community when a Serb farmer discovers his home in smouldering ruins and not a single Albanian witness willing to come forward with information. Not only is the victim aware of what the message behind the violent act is, but the surrounding Kosovo Serb community understands it as a signal to leave the territory or suffer the consequences.[20]

The second message is sent by the perpetrator to its self-ascribed constituency. This message holds that the constituency group is immune from similar attacks provided that they do not challenge the perpetrator. In the arson example, the Albanian neighbours of the Serb farmer do not worry that a similar attack will happen to them, provided that they do not cooperate with local or international law enforcement authorities. Even if they do not know who committed the attack, the selection of the victim and the contextual details of the crime send an implicit message to the constituency group that they will be protected by their own kind as long as they do not betray the perpetrator. This kind of polyvalent communication is often lost on outside observers, especially those unfamiliar with the communicative context of the country.[21] Implicit within this promise of protection lies a threat: that those acting violently are a powerful and attractive armed group who should command loyalty and cooperation. In this sense, reprisal violence is a kind of theatre for this constituency group, reminding them through scripted violence that the perpetrator has the capability of inflicting pain on the enemy and of protecting its chosen constituency. Table 5.1 summarizes the general characteristics of revenge and reprisal violence.

There are two important qualifiers to the distinction drawn here. First, it is important to stress that these are ideal types and that the distinction between the types remains permeable. Revenge violence can occur in contested areas and have a strategic impact. Reprisal attacks (for example, the mass arson of a settlement of a targeted group on strategically important territory) can involve the death of some responsible for previous atrocities, thus edging closer to revenge. Some violent acts will not correspond to either ideal type. The value of the distinction is heuristic: it allows for analytical differentiation between revenge and reprisal attacks among the patterns of inter-communal violence that often follows armed conflict. Second, revenge and reprisal violence are not mutually exclusive. Revenge and reprisal, for example, can (and often are) present in the same case. It is their inter-relationship which confers such an advantage to a strategy of reprisal.

The metaphor of revenge

Acts of revenge and reprisal violence share a number of common descriptive characteristics which make them hard to distinguish empirically. For example, both may be directed against vulnerable groups and be conducted immediately after a war ends. Moreover, in cases where a reversal

Table 5.1 Ideal-type differences between revenge and reprisal violence

	Revenge violence	*Reprisal violence*
Intention	Expressive	Strategic/instrumental
Victim selection	Individual	Categorical
Reciprocity	Yes	No
Proportionate	Yes	No
Audience	None	Multiple

of fortune transforms the relations of dominance between two groups, individuals and groups may act opportunistically to victimize the formerly dominant group for a variety of personal and political reasons.[22] How can one distinguish between the killing of a particularly targeted minority immediately following a war, which could equally be revenge for a personal grievance or reprisal for a strategic purpose? Both interpretations may be plausible given the descriptive characteristics of the act. The presence of strategic intent can only be deduced by examining anomalous patterns of violence (for example, the burning of dozens of homes at the same time) or by discovering telltale signs of advance planning or organization behind the attack. But in cases of limited information such details may be hard to detect from aggregate crime statistics. The fact that revenge and reprisal violence are mirror images of one another complicates efforts by outside observers to distinguish between what is truly revenge from what merely appears to be so.

The close empirical relationship between revenge and reprisal confers two advantages on those employing reprisal violence in post-conflict states because they are often able to mask highly forms of strategic violence as 'revenge' for wartime atrocities. First, it lowers the costs of opportunistic violence, allowing those seeking strategic advantage to assume lower risks for acting violently than they might otherwise. Amidst dozens of real revenge attacks, armed groups can use violence to clear territory of unwanted groups, to change their electoral fortunes in contested areas, or to claim important economic resources.[23] What allows these illicit goals to be achieved with relatively little notice is that they occur amidst waves of violence (and in some cases refugee movements) that provide them with political cover. Enveloped within the waves of violence by embittered victims or returning refugees, such strategic attacks are often described as 'revenge' in the media and elite portrayals of violence.[24] The presence of real revenge attacks provides an ideal cover for reprisal attacks because they are so similar in form, if not in function.

Such opportunism with reprisal violence is particularly cost-effective and attractive under conditions of widespread chaos and violence. In Iraq, for instance, insurgent groups manipulated civilian-on-civilian attacks and tried to encourage revenge and reprisal attacks.[25] For example, after the bombing of the mosque in Samarra in 2006, insurgents stoked public anger among the Shi'a community in order to generate more local violence and cleanse Sunnis from Shi'a dominated areas. Especially under the leadership of Abu Musab al-Zarqawi, Al-Qaida in Iraq (AQIM, Al Qaeda in the Islamic Maghreb) pursued a similar strategy, attacking Shia in the hopes of generating cycles of reprisal killings which would lead to civil war. Opportunistic reprisal violence can also be seen in inter-communal rioting, as the organizers of riots often 'ride the wave' of crowd anger to attack their enemies and achieve political advantage. Similarly, post-conflict environments rife with revenge killings and predatory crime provide excellent opportunities for armed groups to use reprisal violence to seize strategic advantage before the institutions of the state are functional. In some cases, the conditions of diminishing anarchy in a post-conflict state may have the perverse effect of making an armed group 'race against the clock' to achieve as much as possible through reprisal violence before the state is able to monitor and penalize such activity.

Second, the metaphor of revenge lowers the social penalty or sanction applied on those who act violently in post-conflict environments. Despite the social disapproval applied to it in legal and religious traditions, revenge remains a powerful motive for human action, as well as an intelligible explanation for explaining why people acted violently.[26] Revenge violence is seen as having a variety of functions, from the purely retributive justice to teaching a moral lesson to even placating a wider social need for justice.[27] Aside from its functional purposes, revenge is a deeply embedded social norm which is pervasive across human cultures. The widespread applicability of revenge and its innate intelligibility can explain – and often subtly justify – an act of harm. The notion that someone 'had it coming' or that it was 'just desserts' for a prior act of harm is a persuasive explanation for violent action, even to the extent to which it obscures other, perhaps conflicting motives for the action. Similarly the metaphor of revenge can justify actions that might otherwise be considered illegal or immoral because it is a natural human response or because the norm of reciprocity for harm demands it. The fact that revenge violence taps into deeply-held norms of reciprocity means that outsider observers may be more accepting and less inclined to oppose revenge violence than they might be for other forms of violent activity. The persuasiveness of the metaphor of revenge thus confers a powerful strategic advantage to groups employing reprisal violence, for it provides an exculpatory explanation which can obscure other, more strategic, motives for their actions. It also plays upon norms of reciprocity to generate tolerance for activities otherwise met by social disapprobation.

Revenge and reprisal violence are two distinct types of violent action. They share many descriptive characteristics, yet their conceptual differences render them fundamentally different forms of activity. Revenge violence is an intimate form of violence, often conducted between proximate individuals for a prior act of harm and driven by emotions such as grief or anger. Reprisal violence is a strategic form of violent action, where the brutality is conducted between strangers and disconnected from any prior act of harm. That revenge and reprisals are mirror images of one another makes them difficult to distinguish empirically; that the metaphor of revenge is so powerful confers a powerful strategic advantage on armed groups who use reprisal attacks to achieve illicit goals in post-conflict states. To illustrate this dynamic in practice, the rest of this chapter will examine the victimization of Serbs and Roma in post-conflict Kosovo (1999–2008) with particular reference to reprisal attacks allegedly conducted by the UCK to expel minorities from Albanian-majority regions. As evidence of reprisal violence, the following case study will examine (*a*) evidence that the targeted groups (Serbs and Roma) were singled out for attack; (*b*) the patterns of violence across the five regions; and (*c*) the qualitative or stylistic details of the attacks which are consistent with reprisal (but not revenge) violence.

Kosovo (1999–2001)

The post-conflict environment of Kosovo (1999–2001) was dominated by the interplay of revenge and reprisal attacks. There were two waves of violence during this period. The immediate post-war period (June 1999–June 2000) was dominated by revenge killings and population movements, with intermixed acts of reprisal violence by UCK operatives. The second wave of violence (June 2000–December 2001) featured relatively little revenge violence, yet regular but low intensity reprisal attacks by former UCK units against Serbs and Roma in Albanian-majority regions persisted. The rationale for this ongoing reprisal violence was clear: so long as Serbs remained in Kosovo after the war, Belgrade had a powerful argument to resist the full independence of the province. Under the terms of UNSCR 1244, the final status of Kosovo was left up as an issue to be negotiated with Belgrade at a later, still unspecified, point. The presence of Serbs in Kosovo provided a bargaining chip for Belgrade and a rationale for retaining Serbian control over the province; their very presence weakened the case for independence. The risk, in the eyes of those committed to an independent Kosovo, was that the presence of minorities in Kosovo would lead to a compromise solution which awarded less than full independence. Further, consistent with the argument above, reprisal violence during the second wave was regularly described (and excused) as 'revenge' for the murder and expulsion of the Kosovo Albanian population during the 1999 war. Employing the metaphor of revenge allowed the perpetrators of the violence – likely former UCK splinter groups and organized crime gangs – to shield themselves from moral blame and political responsibility for the attacks.

First wave (June 1999–June 2000)

After the withdrawal of Yugoslav forces from the province, Kosovo was struck by 'a rising tide of violence and crime' and a mass exodus of the Serb community.[28] As murders, kidnappings and arsons on Serbs and other minorities skyrocketed, it became increasingly clear to the NATO-led peacekeeping force (KFOR, Kosovo Force) and the nascent UN Mission in Kosovo (UNMIK) that the deaths and forced expulsions had created a ripe environment for revenge violence. Thousands of refugees flooded back in what was described as the 'biggest refugee return in modern history and also the quickest role reversal'.[29] This reversal of fortune – which left the long-repressed Kosovo Albanian population dominant in a province with a vulnerable Serb minority – brought about hundreds of small-scale revenge attacks. The OSCE (Organization for Security and Cooperation in Europe) reported 348 murders, 116 kidnappings, 1,070 lootings and 1,106 cases of arson within the first four months of their mission.[30] Within five months, KFOR had recorded over 400 murders, of which 33.8 per cent had Serb victims.[31] The pervasive insecurity of the Serbs and other minorities and a lack of job opportunities in an Albanian-dominated Kosovo encouraged thousands more to flee for Serbia and Montenegro. By early November, approximately 100,000 Serbs had left the province, reducing the pre-war population of Serbs by approximately 50 per cent.[32]

Especially in the immediate aftermath of the war, minorities were disproportionately victimized. The population of Kosovo was 89 per cent Albanian and 10 per cent Serb, with scattered populations of other minorities such as Roma, Slavs, Gorani, Turks and Egyptians (less than 1 per cent).[33] While there is only scattered data from UN CIVPOL (civilian police) on this period, the data clearly reveals that Serbs and minorities bore a higher share of the violence. In 1999, Serbs experienced 34 per cent of the murders and 23 per cent of the kidnappings. Other minorities – including the Roma, Gora, Bosniaks and Turkomen – experienced 26 per cent of the murders and 17.9 per cent of the kidnappings. By 2000, the rates of victimization had decreased, with Serbs facing 22.3 per cent of the murders and 10.5 per cent of the kidnappings and other minorities having 17.9 per cent of the murders and 22 per cent of the kidnappings.[34] Such disproportionate victimization is particularly striking given (*a*) the extent of the under-reporting of the data and (*b*) the fact that by 2000 thousands of Serbs had fled north to defensible pockets of control north of Mitrovica, where they were protected from attack after summer 1999. The Serbs, Roma and other minorities victimized during this period were predominantly located in small enclaves in Albanian-majority regions.

The first wave of revenge violence – comprising high levels of murder, arson, assault and property theft – provided incentives for ethnic groups to relocate and reinforced the ethnic partition of the province. According to the OSCE, in 1999, Serbs and other minorities constituted approximately 39 per cent of Pristina, 26 per cent of Gnjilane, 10 per cent of Pec, 15 per cent of Prizren and 37 per cent of Mitrovica. By 2000, despite the fact that the population had increased to approximately two million people, the numbers of Serbs and other minorities in most regions had decreased. By 2000, Serbs and other minorities constituted only 12 per cent of Pristina, 18 per cent of Gnjilane, 5 per cent of Pec, 10 per cent of Prizren and 54 per cent of Mitrovica.[35] This ethnic bifurcation into Albanian and Serbian zones of control was evidenced most clearly by the population transfers in Pristina and Mitrovica. By 2000, the Albanian population was 87.8 per cent of the Pristina region and nearly 100 per cent of the city itself. In the northernmost region of the country, Mitrovica, the reverse happened. In the period 1999–2000, the Serb population of Mitrovica jumped from 36.43 per cent to 53.68 per cent.

The movement of thousands of people in a chaotic environment where the institutions of the state had collapsed created a climate of impunity which facilitated brutality and violence. The following tables collected from unpublished data track the rates of violent crime on a regional basis for the period August–December 1999. Beyond the summary statistics from KFOR quoted earlier, no systematic data on the period where the worst revenge violence occurred (June–July 1999) is publicly available.

While these are aggregate crime statistics and reflect all recorded acts of violence, not just revenge attacks, they are nevertheless illustrative of the violence in Kosovo during this period. On a per capita basis, Kosovo

Table 5.2 August–December 1999 UNMIK data by region

Crime	Pristina	Gnjilane	Prizren	Pec	Mitrovica	Total
Murder	198	58	61	123	43	483
Attempted murder						
Kidnapping	55	33	48	27	15	178
Attempted kidnapping						
Aggravated assault						
Rape/attempted rape						
Arson	521	117	151	123	334	1,246
Looting	510	175	180	236	28	1,129
Total	1,284	383	440	509	420	3,036

Source: UNMIK SITREP records, obtained by author.[36]

featured a particularly high crime rate, particularly in murder and arson.[37] The violence statistics reflect the brutal ethnic partition of the province. In Pristina, murders and arsons were common, as Serbs and other minorities were expelled. Arsons were also high in Mitrovica, as Serbs targeted Albanian and Bosniak minorities in the north, while Albanians targeted Roma for allegedly being collaborators with the Serbs. In part due to the actions of extremists in both sides, Mitrovica was a particularly dangerous place to be if one were on the wrong side of the dividing line. Spasms of revenge violence were also present in regions like Pec and Prizren, which were directly in the path of refugee flows from Albania and Macedonia.

During this period there was growing evidence that the UCK was organizing reprisal attacks, often indiscriminately targeted at Serbs, during this period. There were numerous examples of the UCK organizing massacres to expel or intimidate Serbs. For example, in Belo Polje village, in Pec region, three ethnic Serb men were shot between the eyes at point-blank range on 19 July 1999. Witnesses said that ten uniformed UCK soldiers entered the village in broad daylight and executed the men on the street in front of their homes, in clear view of the rest of the population.[38] There was also significant evidence of coordinated grenade attacks. For example, the OSCE reported over 30 grenade attacks against Serbs and Roma homes in the Lipjan region by coordinated teams of Albanian couples, reflecting a level of premeditation which was far beyond uncontrollable spasms of revenge violence. A similar pattern was present elsewhere. In Oblic municipality, grenade attacks on Serb-owned cafes in the city centre occurred for two consecutive weeks in August 1999.[39] Four grenade attacks of Serb stores occurred, all in the space of one hour, each attack at a regular 15-minute interval. Those behind the grenade attacks knew that coordinated and timed attacks would send the limited KFOR forces scrambling back and forth across the town, in a clear demonstration of their inability to establish control over this contested space. Grenade attacks were also used on homes to signal capacity to KFOR. On 25 August 1999, there was a grenade attack on a Serb home in Gnjilane city just moments after a

KFOR foot patrol had passed by.[40] On 27 December 1999, a grenade attack occurred in Vitina, just as KFOR facilitated a visit to bring Kosovo Serbs to see their homes.[41] The types of weapons used – for example, mortars and rocket-propelled grenades are strongly suggestive of the extent of UCK coordination of the attacks. For example, in Klokat, mortars were fired into Serb village on 17 August 1999, killing two and wounding six.[42] On 19 October 1999, five rocket propelled grenades were simultaneously launched on the Serb houses in Mogila, in Vitina municipality.[43] Stylistic details of the attacks can also signal whether a network such as the UCK was involved. One of the most common themes in the reports on minority security is that attackers often had UCK insignias on the uniforms or identified themselves as ex-UCK.

Arsons were also employed to burn people out of their homes and force Serbs to flee. In Prizren, over 300 Serb homes burned immediately following the war, and KFOR recorded clear evidence of UCK involvement in at least 30 of them.[44] One tactic employed by the UCK was to burn multiple homes at the same time in one evening, thus making it difficult for KFOR or UNMIK CIVPOL to put out the fires. After tit-for-tat violence between Albanian and Serb civilians in Oblic municipality, the UCK launched highly coordinated arson attacks of a scale which could not be explained by revenge alone. In the period 5–10 July 1999, KFOR reported an upsurge in grenade attacks on Serb homes, 81 arson attacks, 36 lootings of homes, one kidnapping and four missing persons cases, most of which occurred in the mixed ethnicity villages.[45]

The targeted murder and assault of the elderly Serbs – especially those who could not or would not leave their homes – may have reflected a UCK-led effort to 'cleanse' Albanian majority regions of Serbs.[46] The murders of elderly women in strategically valuable territories also pointed to the degree to which the violence could not be explained with reference to wartime behaviour. Many of those killed were infirm and most likely incapable of victimizing Albanians during the forced expulsions in spring 1999. There was also evidence of UCK involvement in these attacks, as victims would be warned, threatened, and in some cases extorted for money before being killed.[47] Many of the perpetrators were often caught wearing UCK insignias and uniforms, as well as carrying ID cards which marked them as part of the UCK's illegal police service.

In 2000, the crime rates in Kosovo reflected the continuation of reprisal attacks against Serbs and other minorities. Arson remained a high percentage (28.5 per cent) of all violent crimes in the province. Similarly, the high rates of kidnapping are indicative of the UCK-run 'informative talks', where Serbs were abducted and either disappeared without a trace or returned days later, often with physical evidence of torture or assault. According to William G. O'Neill, 'every case of killing, disappearance or beating for the Djakovica region in the OSCE report involves UCK, people identifying themselves as UCK, or wearing UCK uniforms'.[48] Abductions of Serbs by men wearing UCK uniforms were reported in Pristina, Gnjilane and Prizren; in many cases the victims never returned. The OSCE noted that Roma were singled out for attacks and evictions, especially in the immediate post-war period.[49] In 1999, NATO discovered evidence of a UCK-run prison where a significant number of Roma and Albanian prisoners were kept and tortured for information about the extent of their collaboration with the Serbs.

Table 5.3 summarizes the crime statistics for 2000, the year in which the shift from intermixed revenge and reprisal attacks to purely reprisal attacks became evident.

The violence during the first wave reflected a variable amount of reprisal violence amidst the revenge attacks that accompanied the return of the thousands of refugees and internally displaced persons (IDPs). Some clear revenge attacks did occur, often between neighbours and former rivals; some Serbs were indiscriminately attacked by returning Albanians who had suffered the loss of loved ones in the war.[50] But there was also significant evidence that UCK units took advantage of the disorder and spasms of violence for highly strategic attacks designed to intimidate and expel Serbs from Albanian-majority regions. In effect, the UCK 'rode the wave' of revenge violence and embedded their campaign of reprisal violence against Serbs amidst the other attacks present in the society.

Second wave (June 2000–December 2001)

By mid-2000, the types of the violence evident in Kosovo shifted towards more strategic violence, due largely to the effective ethnic partition of the province and the increased security presence of KFOR and CIVPOL. At the aggregate level, there was a significant drop-off in violent crime. Between 1999 and 2001, there was a 72.36 per cent drop off in murder, a 26.16 per cent drop off in kidnapping and an 83.43 per cent drop off in arson. The violent crimes which rose between 1999 and 2001 – rape and attempted rape – may not signal an increase in the incidence of that crime but rather in the willingness of the population to report it.[51] The total number of violent crimes against Serbs and Roma decreased, though they

Table 5.3 UNMIK crime data by region, January–December 2000

Crime	Pristina	Gnjilane	Prizren	Pec	Mitrovica	Total
Murder	74	49	30	61	32	246
Attempted murder	81	62	49	49	33	274
Kidnapping	62	58	29	23	19	191
Attempted kidnapping	23	37	22	10	15	107
Aggravated assault	98	95	69	45	49	356
Rape/attempted rape	32	32	21	7	23	115
Arson	160	156	73	72	62	523
Looting	3	0	16	3	0	22
Total	533	489	309	270	233	1,834

Source: CIVPOL data, online, available at: www.civpol.org/unmik/stats/2000/00majoroffreg. htm, adapted by author.

still remained disproportionately high given their numbers and geographic concentration in the population. By 2001, Serbs were the victims of 22 per cent of the murders and 15 per cent of the kidnappings; other minorities experienced 10 per cent of the murders and 22 per cent of the kidnappings.[52]

The violence that did occur was more consistent with reprisal violence than with spasms of revenge attacks. After waves of violence emptied Pec and Prizren of minorities in late 1999 and Mitrovica was partitioned by bloody riots, certain types of violent crime remained disproportionately high in the two Albanian-majority regions, Pristina and Gnjilane. More detailed UNMIK crime statistics suggest that Pristina experienced high numbers of evictions (301) and intimidations (828) in 2000. The high number of arsons (156) and intimidation (407) in Gnilane in 2000 are also consistent with a strategy of forced expulsions of Serbs and other minorities. While these are aggregate crime statistics and do not reveal the exact numbers of revenge or reprisal attacks, the fact that these crime statistics confirm the witness and NGO details of a campaign of abduction, expulsion, intimidation and arson lends additional weight to the argument that an unknown but substantial percentage were reprisal attacks.

In 2000–1, the stylistic details of some attacks – particularly in tactics that betray military training – were particularly important signals of UCK control over violence.[53] Sniper and remote-controlled bombs provided some evidence of UCK involvement in the attacks. On 13 February 2001, the twice-weekly KFOR-escorted convoy of buses carrying Serbs from Strpce to Serbia came under highly accurate sniper fire, resulting in one death and a number of injuries. Only days later, the lead bus of a KFOR-escorted Serb convoy (called the Nis Express) was destroyed by a remote-controlled bomb near Podujevo, resulting in 11 deaths and 40 injuries.[54] Having received advanced warning of the attack, KFOR conducted a search of the route in advance of the convoy and failed to discover the bomb. At the minimum, someone with military training was responsible for this attack, though the timing involved in monitoring KFOR's movements in order to place the bomb after the sweep occurred suggests involvement by a well-trained network or group.[55]

It remains unclear which entities were directing reprisal attacks during this period. The ex-UCK members in the newly formed Democratic Party of Kosovo (*Partia Demokratike e Kosovës*, PDK) disavowed knowledge of the attacks; moreover the lines of control over violence remained blurry. What is clear is that politico-criminal organizations, especially from the remnants of the UCK, continued to operate with impunity during this period and exercised some level of control over the violence.[56] In Albanian-majority regions, the UCK organized parallel structures of governance which operated beneath the surface of the state. These UCK parallel structures operated with a high level of control over violence, as many international officials noticed that UCK appeared to be able to call off demonstrations or violent attacks with ease.[57] The UCK parallel structures – officially forbidden by UNMIK and the provisional government, but widely recognized as the power behind the throne in the province – also appeared to operate its own police structures. The OSCE concluded that 'it would appear that there is an orchestrated campaign, or campaigns organized by, as yet, unidentified elements whose aim was to terrorize minority populations, destabilize the province and prevent democratization and peaceful co-existence'.[58] Other assessments by Human Rights Watch and the International Crisis Group echoed similar conclusions about the extent of the organization of the violence.[59] While tracing the reprisal attacks to Hashim Thaci and the leadership of the PDK is not supportable on the basis of the evidence, both organizations had no doubt that smaller UCK factions continued to engage in attacks against Serbs and other minorities. Their rationale was clear: to expel Serbs and weaken Belgrade's case for continuing control over Kosovo. These reprisal attacks reflected a strategic orientation and indifference to the identity and guilt of the victims which distinguished them from predominantly expressive revenge attacks.

Justifying the violence

Despite the clear strategic orientation of these attacks, the metaphor of revenge was powerful in Kosovo and provided a simplified explanation for what could have been interpreted as reverse ethnic cleansing. Many attacks were described as revenge for wartime suffering, despite the fact that they had a clear strategic purpose, coordination and in some cases employed military tactics and weapons. This assumption about Kosovo – that it was engulfed in uncontrollable spasms of revenge violence – allowed the UCK to embed reprisal attacks within the real expressive violence at low cost and risk. While many on-the-ground observers at the time recognized that there was something more than revenge killings occurring, the prevalence of the metaphor of the revenge affected the international responses to the reprisal violence in four ways.

First, especially in the early days of the mission, there was a false equivalence drawn between the suffering of Kosovo Albanians drawn in the war and the revenge attacks that followed. The deaths of 5,000–10,000 Kosovo Albanians during the war and the expulsion of nearly one million led to calls to 'understand' what was happening in post-war Kosovo.[60] For example, in response to the massacre of 14 Serbs in Gracko, Secretary of State Madeleine Albright remarked that 'We can't forget that there were some pretty disgusting things that took place before, but the system is set up to protect them'.[61] According to former OSCE official William G. O'Neill:

> UNMIK senior leadership, including the SRSG [Special Representative of the Security-General], expressed disgust in private at the ongoing violence documented in the OSCE's report. Public condemnations were also forthcoming, but usually with several qualifiers. UNMIK leadership would not mention the current violations without referring to the past, especially to the recent attempt at ethnic cleansing by the Serbian authorities and 'ten years of apartheid' before that

that. UNMIK press releases and official statements usually included references to Northern Ireland and South Africa and the difficult nature of reconciliation following a conflict. This constant reminder to 'understand the context' and 'to realize what they had been through' was interpreted by Albanian hard-liners as a yellow light to continue their violent campaign.[62]

Drawing a direct connection between wartime and post-war atrocities implied a moral equivalence which subtly justified reprisal killings as a natural response to what had happened during the war. In response to escalating reprisal attacks in the first half of 2000, Albright merely remarked that 'after all that has happened, we do not expect rival communities in Kosovo to immediately join hands and start singing folk songs'.[63] Such a comment was emblematic of the tacit acceptance of revenge violence during this period. That so much of the violence was described as revenge, and linked to the suffering of the Albanians during the war, allowed reprisal attacks to continue to be conducted at lower cost than if it had been clearly seen as an attempt at reverse ethnic cleansing.

Second, this metaphor played directly into the received wisdom – prevalent from authors like Rebecca West and Robert Kaplan – that the Balkans is a region of irreducible hatred and violence.[64] If hatred and revenge is in the blood of the people of the Balkans, it would be hardly surprising that the province should experience serious revenge attacks after the war. This culturalist assumption was reflected when former UNMIK SRSG Bernard Kouchner remarked that 'here I discovered hatred deeper than anywhere in the world, more than in Cambodia or Vietnam or Bosnia'.[65] Many other CIVPOL officials agreed, seeing patterns of tit-for-tat violence as being a natural feature of life in the Balkans.[66] Others ascribed the violence to the Kanun code, which regulated relations between Albanian clans.[67] This tradition of cultural blood feuds would also presumably apply especially for members of the UCK in particular, as they had pledged their allegiance to the 'clan' of the UCK before the war and would be required to avenge their losses on the clan of the enemy (i.e. the Serbs).[68] Aside from the fact that these cultural arguments are of dubious empirical merit, this interpretation implicitly accepts that revenge violence was a natural part of political life in Kosovo, an explanation which does not lead to additional questions about the strategic orientation of reprisal attacks.

Third, the metaphor of revenge left KFOR flat-footed in response to highly strategic forms of violence. In part because KFOR had a fixed set of images about who was the perpetrator and victim in the Kosovo drama, KFOR officers were slow to respond to revenge attacks or to acknowledge that there was a modicum of organization to the violence. Some KFOR officers had been specifically ordered not to respond to the violence and many did not realize that 'their previous mission, to protect Kosovo Albanians from the Serb forces, was now obsolete'.[69] Revenge violence was seen as an unfortunate by-product of the war, rather than a continuation of it. For this reason, KFOR's initial approach was largely reactive. While individual KFOR units sometimes intervened to stop attacks, others did not, which was interpreted as a tacit acceptance of the behaviour. This was particular the case in the event of the looting and seizure of properties, which was interpreted to fall outside of KFOR's initial mandate. NATO commanders were reluctant to admit any kind of organization to the violence, especially as it was important for them to stay on good terms with the UCK leadership. General Wesley Clark remarked that he 'was not going to point fingers at the KLA (Kosovo Liberation Army). The KLA leadership had been very cooperative with us at the top level'.[70] Such tacit support for the UCK – and implicit acknowledgement that a certain degree of rough justice was inevitable – provided a favourable climate for reprisal violence.

Finally, the metaphor of revenge allowed the UCK to disavow responsibility for the reprisal attacks. Throughout the post-war period, UCK leaders Hashim Thaci repeatedly emphasized that the PDK could not be held responsible for individual revenge attacks launched by the returning Albanian population. At the same time, Thaci regularly argued that he was committed to a multiethnic Kosovo, even if it was one in which the UCK was the foundation of the state.[71] But other UCK officials remained silent on the attacks or offered a token condemnation, often with reference to the suffering of the Albanian population during the war. Such weak language was interpreted as a green light by armed groups from within the UCK ranks to continue their reprisal attacks against Serbs. Emphasizing that the violence was 'revenge' for wartime atrocities and permitting or subcontracting unnamed elements from within their ranks to conduct the attacks allowed the UCK leadership to escape moral blame and political responsibility. So long as the metaphor of revenge had plausibility and the lines of control for the violence remained blurry, the UCK could continue to engage in reprisal attacks against Serbs at manageable levels of risk.

Conclusion

The purpose of this chapter was to identify two different types of violence that can emerge in post-conflict states, the expressive, even furious violence that people ordinarily think of as revenge, and its strategic mirror, reprisal violence. As this chapter has demonstrated, these two types of violence are intertwined both conceptually and empirically, yet they serve very different purposes. Revenge attacks are designed to express some form of human emotion, ranging from anger to grief. Reprisal attacks, while they are many descriptive characteristics, are designed to achieve some form of strategic advantage for an armed group. Recognizing these two types, even as heuristics for interpretation rather than as airtight conceptual categories, is essential for unpacking what is commonly called 'revenge' in post-conflict states. Moreover, the violence which occurred in Kosovo from 1999–2001 shows how armed groups can take advantage of spasms of uncontrollable revenge violence to employ reprisal attacks for strategic gain. This case demonstrates how the metaphor of revenge – and fixed notions about who is the victim and perpetrator and about what is natural following wartime atrocities – can inadvertently permit and even encourage reprisal attacks by lowering the risks associated with launching them.

This chapter has policy implications for the protection of vulnerable groups. Far more than in soft post-conflict environments, policy-makers need to consider tougher or more pro-active ways to manage or prevent revenge and reprisal violence. For instance, many international officials later concluded that Kosovo should have been put under martial law in the immediate aftermath of the war, in order to prevent the security vacuum which allowed the UCK to establish control over the province.[72] The UNMIK also started with a severe intelligence gap, with UN officials also in some cases unable to name streets or locate key offices.[73] The delay in arrival of CIVPOL forces, and the ensuring public security gap that these created, did little to put an end to the climate of impunity that existed in Kosovo during this period. To remedy this, the UN will need to consider the preventive deployment of CIVPOL forces and intelligence assets to areas where vulnerable groups are located. Such preventive deployments will act as a deterrent for revenge violence, and send a signal to prospective spoilers that no form of strategic violence, no matter how covert or subtle, will be tolerated.

On a more conceptual level, the interplay of revenge and reprisal violence in Kosovo – which occurred amidst the onset of the most powerful UN peacekeeping mission in the organization's history – also underlines some of the dangers of assuming that the imposition of a democratic government will be sufficient to put an end to the attraction of violence in post-conflict states. The inhabitants of post-conflict states are often haunted by the spectre of the war long after it has ended; for them, the war rarely ends when the peace settlement says it does. Wherever there has been suffering and loss, the instinct to lash out against one's enemies will be compelling. And wherever revenge occurs there will be opportunists who see the blind fury of the mob as an opportunity to achieve their goals. Against this natural tide of violence must be a vigorous law enforcement response. Yet the traditional methods of enforcing the law in well-functioning societies – democratic policing, community engagement, functioning courts and respect for human rights – may be insufficient in a post-conflict environment engulfed in inter-communal violence. Tougher measures – such as martial law, the use of detention and armed force against perpetrators of covert or subversive violence, and a clear effort to hold political leaders accountable for violence emanating from their constituency – may be needed. In post-conflict environments like Kosovo, international officials may find themselves the last line of defence for targeted groups who justly or unjustly are the targets of revenge and reprisal attacks. In these cases, their responsibility is twofold: to dampen the desire for revenge among those who have suffered, but also to send an unambiguous signal that reprisal violence will not be tolerated. Only then can the hard work of reconciliation begin.

Notes

1 An earlier version of this chapter appeared in the *Journal of Conflict, Security and Development*, 10(2) (2010).
2 Tavernese 2006; Karouny 2006.
3 Fearon 2007; Boyle 2009a.
4 Orth 2001.
5 See Paris 2004; Mani 2002; and Minow 1998.
6 See Bowett 1972; on revenge killings, see Balcells 2007.
7 Horowitz 2001: 89–94.
8 This is in part due to extensive under-reporting of the data.
9 The acronym UCK comes from the *Ushtria Clirimtare e Kosoves*, the Albanian name for the Kosovo Liberation Army (KLA).
10 On revenge, see Lowenheim and Heiman 2008; Waldman 2001; Harkavey 2000.
11 Elster 1990: 862.
12 The distinction between expressive and instrumental violence comes from Gurr 1970.
13 Hamlin 1991 and Boehm 1984.
14 Petersen 2002: 62–8.
15 Gould 2000, 1999.
16 Boehm 1984.
17 Waldman 2001.
18 Boehm 1984: 165–73.
19 Kukis 2006.
20 On polyvalent communication (i.e. two distinct groups received different messages from the same violent act) see Tilly 2003: 176.
21 See Scott 1990.
22 Petersen 2002: 40–61.
23 Stedman 1997; Boyle 2009b.
24 *BBC News* 31 March 2004.
25 Rubin 2005.
26 Uniacke 2000.
27 Cottingham 1979; Walker 1999.
28 ICG 1999: 3.
29 Judah 2000: 287.
30 Quoted from Schwander-Sanders 2001: 114.
31 ICG 1999: 3. KFOR reports that the breakdown of murder victims is as follows: 145 ethnic Albanian, 135 Serb and 99 others. Amnesty International reported a KFOR-recorded murder total of 414 by 10 December 1999, with 150 ethnic Albanian victims, 140 Serbs and 124 people of unknown ethnicity. See Amnesty International 2003: 3.
32 ICG 1999: 3. It is unclear how many left under threat of violence and how many left on their initiative.
33 According to the *Kosovo Report*, there were 850,000 returning Albanian refugees, 500,000 Albanian IDPs, 200,000 non-displaced Albanians, 200,000 Serbs and 50,000 other minorities in Kosovo's population.
34 UNMIK CIVPOL (2001–2) 'Offence statistics by motive', unpublished.
35 The data is drawn from OSCE municipal profiles. Online, available at: www. osce.org/kosovo/documents/reports/municipal_profiles/ (accessed 26 May 2003), calculated by author.
36 The statistics were not released to the public and were compiled by the author from a CD-Rom containing the original crime reports for Kosovo during the period 20 June 1999–31 December 1999. Statistics on the other types of crime are not available.

37 Kosovo's crime rate far exceeds that of a comparable conflict-prone European territory of the same approximate population size (1.5–2 million). A tally of six major crime totals in 2001 – murder, attempted murder, aggravated assault, rape/attempted rape, arson and intimidation – reveals that Kosovo's total (2,402) far exceeds that of Northern Ireland (624) (source: UNMIK and unpublished Home Office documents).
38 Human Rights Watch 2002: 9.
39 OSCE 1999d: 7.
40 OSCE 1999d: 7.
41 OSCE 1999c: para. 80.
42 OSCE 1999d: 8.
43 OSCE 1999e: 4.
44 O'Neill 2002: 71.
45 OSCE 1999c: 3.
46 O'Neill 2002: 71.
47 See Human Rights Watch 2002: 8–9.
48 O'Neill 2002: 65.
49 See Amnesty International 2003.
50 Kalyvas 2006.
51 See UNMIK 2003.
52 Unpublished UNMIK crime data.
53 OSCE 1999e: 5.
54 Amnesty International 2003: 12.
55 Amnesty International 2003: 17.
56 ICG 2000.
57 O'Neill 2002: 68.
58 OSCE 1999e: executive summary, p. 1.
59 Human Rights Watch 2001; ICG 1999: 2.
60 American Association for the Advancement of Science 2002.
61 Quoted in O'Neill 2002: 46.
62 O'Neill 2002: 62.
63 Quoted in O'Neill 2002: 53.
64 See Kaplan 1994; West 2006.
65 Quoted in O'Neill 2002: 52.
66 Interview with Andrea Gentile, DPKO, UN Headquarters, New York, 15 April 2003.
67 See Schwander-Sanders 2001: 114–16.
68 Judah 2000: 99.
69 O'Neill 2002: 44.
70 O'Neill 2002: 46.
71 ICG 1999: 6–7.
72 Interview with Christopher Decker, OSCE Headquarters, Pristina, 28 June 2002.
73 Interview with Paul King, UNMIK CIVPOL, Pristina, 20 March 2003.

Bibliography

Albrecht, A.R. (1953) 'War reprisals in the war crimes trials and the Geneva Conventions of 1949', *American Journal of International Law*, 47(4).
American Association for the Advancement of Science (2002) 'Killings and refugee flow in Kosovo, March–June 1999: a report to the International Criminal Tribunal for the Former Yugoslavia', 3 January.
Amnesty International (2003) 'Prisoners in our own homes: Amnesty International's concerns for the human rights of minorities in Kosovo/Kosova'.

Balcells, Laia (2007) 'Rivalry and revenge: killing civilians in the Spanish Civil War', Estudios Working Paper, Juan March Institute, Madrid.

BBC News (2004) 'Liberia hit by "revenge" attacks', 31 March.

Boehm, Christopher (1984) *Blood Revenge: The Enactment and Management of Conflict in Montenegro and Other Tribal Societies*, Philadelphia: University of Pennsylvania Press.

Bowett, Derek (1972) 'Reprisals involving recourse to armed force', *American Journal of International Law*, 66(1).

Boyle, Michael J. (2009a) 'Bargaining, fear and denial: explaining violence against civilians in Iraq, 2004–2007', *Terrorism and Political Violence*, 21: 261–87.

Boyle, Michael J. (2009b) 'Explaining strategic violence after wars', *Studies in Conflict and Terrorism*, 32: 209–36.

Cottingham, John (1979) 'Varieties of retribution', *Philosophical Quarterly*, 29(116): 238–46.

Crawford, Neta C. (2000) 'The passion of world politics: propositions on emotion and emotional relationships', *International Security*, 24(5).

Elster, Jon (1990) 'Norms of revenge', *Ethics*, 100(4): 862–85.

European Commission (1999) Emergency Assessment of Damaged House and Local/Village Infrastructure: Kosovo Damage Assessment.

Fearon, James (2007) 'Iraq's civil war', *Foreign Affairs*, (March/April).

Gould, Roger V. (1999) 'Collective violence and group solidarity: evidence from a feuding society', *American Sociological Review*, 64(3): 356–80.

Gould, Roger V. (2000) 'Revenge as sanction and solidarity display: an analysis of vendettas in nineteenth century Corsica', *American Sociological Review*, 65(5): 682–704.

Gurr, Ted Robert (1970) *Why Men Rebel*, Princeton: Princeton University Press.

Hamlin, Alan P. (1991) 'Rational revenge', *Ethics*, 101: 374–81.

Harkavey, Robert E. (2000) 'Defeat, national humiliation and the revenge motif in international politics', *International Politics*, 37: 345–68.

Hoffman, Bruce and Gordon H. McCormick (2004) 'Terrorism, signaling and suicide attack', *Studies in Conflict and Terrorism*, 27: 243–81.

Horowitz, Donald (2001) *The Deadly Ethnic Riot*, Berkeley, CA: University of California Press.

Human Rights Watch (2001) 'Under orders: war crimes in Kosovo, abuses after June 12, 1999'. Online, available at: www.hrw.org/reports/2001/kosovo/undworld2c.htm.

Independent International Commission on Kosovo (2000) *The Kosovo Report*, Oxford: Oxford University Press.

International Crisis Group (1999) 'Who's killing whom?', Europe Report 79, 2 November.

International Crisis Group (2000) 'What happened to the KLA?', ICG Balkans Report, 88, 3 March.

Judah, Timothy (2000) *Kosovo: War and Revenge*, New Haven, CT: Yale University Press.

Kalyvas, Stathis (2006) *The Logic of Violence in Civil War*, Cambridge: Cambridge University Press.

Kaplan, Robert (1994) *Balkan Ghosts: A Journey Through History*, New York: Vintage.

Karouny, Mariam (2006) 'Sunnis build up their own militia in Iraq', *Reuters*, 6 February.

Kukis, Mark (2006) 'Ethnic cleansing in a Baghdad neighborhood', *Time Magazine*, 25 October.

Lowenheim, Oded and Gadi Heimann (2008) 'Revenge in international politics', *Security Studies*, 17: 685–724.

Mani, Rama (2002) *Beyond Retribution: Seeking Justice in the Shadows of War*, Cambridge: Polity.

Minow, Martha (1998) *Between Vengeance and Forgiveness: Facing History after Genocide and Mass Violence*, Boston: Beacon.

O'Neill, William G. (2002) *Kosovo: An Unfinished Peace*, Boulder, CO: Lynne Reiner.

Oppenheim, L.F.L. (1952) *International Law*, volume II (seventh edition) London: Longman.

Orth, Rick (2001) 'Rwanda's Hutu extremist genocidal insurgency: an eyewitness perspective', *Small Wars and Insurgencies*, 12(1): 76–109.

OSCE (1999a) *As Seen as Told*, volume I – October 1998–June 1999, 5 November.

OSCE (1999b) *As Seen as Told*, volume II – 14 June–31 October 1999, 5 November.

OSCE (1999c) 'Preliminary assessment on the situation of minorities in Kosovo', 10 July.

OSCE (1999d) 'Second assessment on the situation of ethnic minorities in Kosovo', 26 July.

OSCE (1999e) 'Overview of the situation of ethnic minorities in Kosovo', 3 November.

OSCE (2000a) 'Assessment of the situation of ethnic minorities in Kosovo', 15 February.

OSCE (2000b) 'Assessment of the situation of ethnic minorities in Kosovo', 10 October.

OSCE (2001a) 'Assessment of the situation of ethnic minorities in Kosovo', 28 July.

OSCE (2001b) 'Assessment on the situation of ethnic minorities in Kosovo, 1 October.

OSCE/UNHCR (2000) 'Update on the situation of ethnic minorities in Kosovo', 10 June.

Paris, Roland (2004) *At War's End: Building Peace After Civil Conflict*, Cambridge: Cambridge University Press.

Peterson, Roger (2002) *Understanding Ethnic Violence: Fear, Hatred and Resentment in Twentieth Century Eastern Europe*, Cambridge: Cambridge University Press.

Rubin, Alissa J. (2005) 'Revenge killings fuel fear of escalation in Iraq', *Los Angeles Times*, 11 September.

Schwander-Sanders, Stephanie (2001) 'The enactment of "tradition": Albanian constructions of identity, violence and power in times of crisis', in Bettina E. Schmidt and Ingo W. Schroeder (eds), *Anthropology of Violence and Conflict*, London: Routledge.

Scott, James C. (1990) *Domination and the Arts of Resistance*, New Haven, CT: Yale University Press.

Stedman, Stephen John (1997) 'Spoiler problems in peace processes', *International Security*, 22(2): 5–53.

Tavernese, Sabrina (2006) 'As Iraqi Shiites police Sunnis, rough justice feeds bitterness', *New York Times*, 6 February.

Tilly, Charles (2003) *The Politics of Collective Violence*, Cambridge: Cambridge University Press.

Uniacke, Suzanne (2000) 'When is revenge wrong?', *Journal of Value Inquiry*, 34: 61–9.

UNMIK (2003) CIVPOL Annual Report 2000. Online, available at: www.unmikonline.org/civpol/index.html (accessed 23 June 2003).

Von Panhuys, H.F. (1959) *The Role of Nationality in International Law: An Outline*, Leyden: A.W. Sythoff.

Waldmann, Peter (2001) 'Revenge without rules: on the renaissance of an archaic motif of violence', *Studies in Conflict and Terrorism*, 24(6): 435–50.

Walker, Nigel (1999) 'Even more varieties of retribution', *Philosophy*, 74: 595–605.

West, Rebecca (2006) *Black Lamb and Grey Falcon: A Journey Through Yugoslavia*, London: Canongate.

6 Political violence in post-civil war Lebanon[1]

Are Knudsen and Nasser Yassin

Introduction

Lebanon is a multi-religious state that for much of its short history as an independent country has been politically unstable. The devastating civil war (1975–90) left the country in ruins, the economy in a shambles and the populace traumatized.[2] The 15-year-long civil war was very complex, involving many state and non-state actors, who during the course of the war shifted their allegiance many times. The reasons behind the outbreak of the war are contested and have been blamed on multiple economic (Makdisi and Sadaka 2002), political (el Khazen 2000), social (Johnson 2001) and regional factors (O'Ballance 1998).

While the civil war has been thoroughly studied, the post-war violence has not.[3] The civil war ended with a peace deal, the Taif Accords (1989), which instituted Syrian quasi-suzerainty, followed by a General Amnesty Law (1991) granting all leaders and militia members immunity from war crimes. In April 1991, about 25 militias organizing approximately 50,000 fighters disarmed following a general amnesty and an offer of government posts to militia leaders. The 1992 elections provided the most prominent warlords with parliamentary seats and ministerial posts. The war had come to an end, but political violence continued, a trend that persisted throughout the post-war period and peaked after the assassination of former Prime Minister Rafik Hariri in February 2005 (Knudsen 2010). This confirms that post-war states are indeed vulnerable to continued or new violence and makes Lebanon an important case for furthering our understanding of the conflict dynamics in countries emerging from civil war (Silverstein and Makdisi 2006). While third party ('exogenous') involvement in Lebanese conflicts has been very strong, this chapter privileges the country's internal conflict dynamics.

To this end, this chapter provides a narrative account of political violence in post-civil war Lebanon, with an emphasis on assassinations defined as 'a deliberate, extralegal killing of an individual for political purposes' (Havens *et al.* 1970: 4). Political assassinations have been a mainstay in Lebanon since the 1950s attempt on the life of Prime Minister Riad el-Solh followed a year later by his assassination in Amman (Seale 2010). Inspired by Khalaf's (2002) seminal study of 'civil and uncivil' violence in post-independence Lebanon, this chapter traces the origins of political violence from the 1950s, the transformation of violence during the civil war and the return of political violence in post-civil war Lebanon. This diachronic approach enables us to study the patterning of political violence over longer timescales to account for the internal conflict dynamics in post-civil war Lebanon. The data were compiled from secondary sources and interviews with senior politicians, party officials and academics in Lebanon during 2006–8.

Pre-war violence, 1950–74

Lebanon has traditionally been ruled by an urban and rural elite of wealthy and influential patrons known locally as *za'im*, meaning boss or leader (plural *zu'ama*). The term has its roots in the Ottoman Empire, where it was reserved for feudal dignitaries (Attie 2003: 147). The system survived Lebanon's transition to independence and was entrenched both in the countryside (Gilsenan 1996) and in the coastal cities (Johnson 1985). In the latter, clientelistic networks were controlled by an urban-based merchant elite of political leaders or 'city bosses'. The Sunni *zu'ama* of Beirut offered help and services to families or individuals. In return for their help, their clients voted for them at elections. In order to ensure that clients voted for their respective *za'im*, as well as closing ranks behind him, the leaders had at their disposal strong-arm retainers or street leaders whose main job was to recruit and control the *za'im*'s clientele (Johnson 1996). Occasionally, the retainers used violence to coerce them but in general the threat of violence was less than the actual recourse to it.

Nonetheless, violence was an ingrained part of clientelist politics and in a few well-known cases violence was used to root out rivals (Gilsenan 1996: 30). Political rivalry could also end in bloody gunfights such as the 'Mizyara massacre' in 1957, where 20 persons were killed in an intra-Maronite feud (Baroudi 2007: 16). The incident was linked to a deep political crisis that a year later escalated into a short civil war that left 3,000 dead (Kanaan 2005). The large and influential bosses had local power bases where they were in absolute control and often involved in feuds with rival leaders (Johnson 2001). They also founded political parties which provided them with a political platform and a means to recruit clients beyond that secured by traditional legitimacy alone, an example of what has been termed 'political feudalism' (Johnson 2001: 119). Being involved in party politics, however, made them vulnerable to attack and many were targeted in assassination attempts (Knudsen 2010).

Until the 1970s, the rural and urban *zu'ama* had a stranglehold on political power (Ajami 1987; Gilsenan 1996). As the internal conflict escalated, the clientelist system came under pressure from new and larger forms of internal conflict and foreign meddling. Still, the clientelist system worked remarkably well until the eve of the civil war (Johnson 1983), when violence was instituted through the creation of militias, ostensibly as a form of self-preservation as civil unrest spread throughout the country. Many of the *zu'ama* became the political centre for the creation of militias and the rallying point where members of confessional groups sought protection and leadership.

Civil war violence, 1975–88

The Lebanese civil war (1975–90) was one of the bloodiest conflicts in the modern Middle East and atrocities and massacres were committed by all sides (Khalaf 2002). The civil war inflicted physical damage estimated at $25 billion, more than halved the GDP, caused massive human suffering, including an estimated 150,000 deaths (about 5 per cent of the population), displaced some 800,000 people and sped up the already large emigration from the country. The civil war was fought by militias commanded by 'warlords'. Indeed, the Lebanese civil war has been portrayed as the quintessential twentieth-century example of warlords and 'warlordism' in the Middle East (Dib 2004; Randal 1983; but see Giustozzi 2005: 3). The militias were typically associated with a pre-existing political party or religious group. On the eve of the civil war in 1975 the most prominent parties acquired weapons and began military training (el Khazen 2003).[4]

In the first phase of the civil war, the *zu'ama* were able to mediate between factions, but from 1975–6 the traditional clientelist system broke down (Johnson 1983: 190). From that point on, militias commanded by warlords took over control of streets and neighbourhoods, the government collapsed, the army disintegrated along confessional lines and Beirut was cantonized into a Christian East and Muslim West (Picard 2002; Gaub 2007: 6). During the first phase of the war (1975–6), savage murders were committed, often involving the killing of whole families, desecrating the victims or arbitrarily targeting passers-by (Johnson 2001; Makdisi 1999). Most of the killings in this phase of the war were retributive and included vengeance massacres of civilians.[5] As the civil war progressed, the militias carved up Beirut into distinct territories and there were abductions, assassinations and street wars. During the civil war an estimated 3,600 car bombs killed close to 4,500 people (*Time* 1992). In 1981, one of the worst years, more than 550 car bombs exploded with an additional 107 being dismantled (O'Brien 1983: 24).[6] After the signing of the peace accords ('Taif Agreement') in late October 1989, regular battles between former allies continued for another year, illustrating the problem of 'second-order' conflicts following peace accords (Atlas and Licklider 1999).

While some militias included fighters and members from many sects (Rowayheb 2006), the most prominent militias were uni-confessional with members and fighters belonging to a single religious group. The most intense fighting during the civil war was internecine, either between factions of the same militia or between rival militias belonging to the same confession in an attempt to consolidate all the fighters under a unified leadership. Likewise, warlord competition peaked with several assassinations and assassination attempts, but only a few of the most high-profile attacks are properly documented and most remain unrecorded (Knudsen 2010).

During the war, a large, lucrative and complex informal economy developed around the militias (Picard 2000). The larger militias paid regular salaries to their fighters and in their areas of control offered a range of services that in some instances mimicked that of the state (Harik 1993). The militias' finances were a combination of protection rackets, looting and robberies, taxation and trading in drugs and contraband (Picard 1993, 1999). The militias differed in size, personnel and fighters and at the war's end, the approximately 25 militias organized about 50,000 full-time fighters (Makdisi and Sadaka 2002). Despite their wartime exploits, most militias failed to institutionalize their economic and political role and were disbanded after the war. The warlords, however, persisted and the most influential were able to launch illustrious political careers.

From war to peace, 1989–91

By 1989, internal disintegration, internecine wars and high inflation had brought Lebanon to the verge of total collapse. Under internal pressure and with regional brokerage, the Lebanese parliamentarians reached an agreement for a new power-sharing mechanism in late October 1989 (Kerr 2005). The Taif Agreement, or the National Agreement Document, was brokered by Saudi Arabia on Syria's terms and at the expense of Lebanon's sovereignty. The peace deal allowed Syria to continue its tutelage of the country by keeping 14,000 soldiers stationed in Lebanon, to be pulled out within two years, a pledge left unfulfilled. In the years to come, the special relationship between the two 'brotherly nations' was institutionalized in bilateral agreements that cemented Syrian economic and political hegemony. Despite Lebanon's wartime devastation, it did not attract significant foreign aid to help rebuild the country and was forced to fund reconstruction through massive borrowing and costly loans (Zahar 2002).

The transitional period from war to peace (1989–91) was marked by several assassinations, using car bombs to target some of the most senior members of the religious and political elite (Knudsen 2010). There was neither any criminal investigation of these violations nor were any of those responsible brought to trial. Instead, the Lebanese government passed the General Amnesty Law in 1991 (Law 94/91), which granted an amnesty for all crimes committed by militias and armed groups before 28 March 1991.[7] The law effectively stopped legal action against war crimes and war criminals and opened the way for militia leaders to assume ministerial posts and for their militias to be turned into parties. The amnesty law enjoyed widespread political support, but prevented the country from confronting its wartime record, rewarded those who were favoured by Syria and punished those who fell out with the regime.

The General Amnesty Law was part and parcel of the post-war DDR (disarmament, demobilization and reintegration) process and targeted communal and local militias as well as militias linked to political parties but excluded the Palestinian militias, Hizbollah and the Israeli proxy force, the South Lebanese Army (SLA). The extent to which the militias complied with the decree and their willingness to decommission and dispose of their weapons varied, as did their ability to reintegrate ex-combatants (Picard 1999.) When the first (and only) phase of the reintegration process was completed in October 1993, about 6,000 ex-militiamen had been integrated into the army. Many of those not eligible for army service were offered civilian jobs, accorded local integration or left the country. The integration of militiamen into the army was lopsided, with a majority of those integrated being Muslims. Only lower-ranked personnel joined the army. The 'most violent, most experienced and most ideologically convinced fighters' were left out (Gaub 2007: 12). From 1993, mandatory military service was reintroduced, enrolling about 3,000 conscripts a year (Picard 2002: 161). In 2004, the army totalled 60,000 men (Gaub 2007), but did not take full control of Lebanese territory and left the southern part to be controlled by Hizbollah's militia, a non-state actor.

The Lebanese civil war 'came to an end in a state of nearly universal defeat and bitterness' (Picard 2002: 153). Yet 'missing in the transition from war to peace was national reconciliation' (el Khazen 2003: 59). In the absence of both formal and grassroots reconciliation, sectarian tensions remained, but people did not take justice into their own hands and retributive killings were rare. Whether this should be ascribed to 'war weariness' or Syrian suzerainty is a moot point. The Lebanese blamed the war on 'outside forces', often referred to as the *guerres des autres* (Tueini 2002). War, in this perspective, was imposed on Lebanon as an 'externality' rather than an inherent weakness in the country and governance itself. The strong belief in the imposition of the war on the Lebanese meant that there was no need for public scrutiny of the war and its consequences. The war was referred to by the euphemism 'the events' (*al-ahdath*) and considered an aberration, something out of the ordinary and hence unexplained (Makdisi 1999).

Post-war elections, 1992–3

The General Amnesty Law had granted militias and their leaders immunity against war crimes, but they still had to compete for political office. The first post-war parliamentary election in 1992 was an important litmus test of the warlords' transition into politics (el Khazen 1998).[8] The election was controversial and divisive with many undecided about participation and a few, mostly Christian groups opting for a boycott. As is typical for Lebanese elections, there was extensive ballot rigging, engineering of constituencies and late announcement of election lists. The voter turnout for the elections was very low, less than 10 per cent in many places.

The election led to a record number of new deputies, most of them elected unopposed. This was especially the case with leaders of the big militias who, helped by electoral engineering, gained seats in the new parliament. Leaders of minor militias, however, were not able to launch political careers, having lost power and popular appeal. Political office remained the prerogative of the leaders of larger militias. Only one Maronite militia leader, Samir Geagea of the Lebanese Forces (LF), gradually fell out with Syria and boycotted the elections. By 1992, many of the traditional leaders were dead or assassinated, thus the pre-war clientelist system could not be fully reinstated. Yet many of the surviving pre-war Sunni *zu'ama* were re-elected with backing from Syria (Johnson 1996: 338).

The first popularly elected post-war government was headed by Prime Minister Rafik Hariri. Hariri, a self-made businessman and billionaire, was not tainted by a wartime record although he had been accused of funding rival militias (Blanford 2009: 32). Until his death, Hariri was the pre-eminent Sunni *za'im* not only of Beirut but of Lebanon itself. The Taif Agreement increased the prime minister's executive powers, but when Hariri formed his first cabinet he was unable to restrain the former war-lords and militia leaders. Instead, he provided them with cabinet portfo-lios, government posts and privileged access to state funds, which secured them continued voter support and re-election (Picard 1999).[9] No longer needing to fight for political office and clients, warlords-turned-politicians could dispense with violence. This could be one explanation why violence levels during this period were low.[10]

Internal violence and persecution, 1993–9

The 1992 elections marked a return to parliamentary politics, but disen-franchised Maronite groups who, opposed Syria's stewardship, boycotted the elections, as did many of their most prominent leaders. In the first post-war period there was stringent persecution of Maronite Christian activists and hundreds of them were arrested and subjected to physical torture (Zahar 2002). Thus, the early post-war period victimized the Maronites individually by selectively targeting their leaders and collectively by excluding them from political participation; this later led to popular protest against Syria's domination. Hariri's first post-war government not only targeted those opposed to Syria's domination, but also suspended newspapers and closed television and radio stations controlled by political opponents (Perthes 1997). In 1993, the Lebanese army was deployed against civilian demonstrators (Picard 2002: 162) and a year later public demonstrations were banned (Zahar 2002: 581).

From the mid-1990s there was a gradual rise in sectarian attacks on civil-ians, vendettas between rival Islamist groups and bombings of churches, mosques and other places of worship. In 1994, a bomb exploded in a village church near Beirut, killing ten people. The attack was blamed on the LF leader Samir Geagea, who was arrested and tried for his involve-ment in the church bombing. He was found innocent of the bombing charge but sentenced to four death sentences, later commuted to life, on several murder counts (Knudsen 2010). He remains the only warlord to be tried for crimes committed during the war, but his trial and subsequent imprisonment were condemned by Amnesty International (2004).

Hariri's economic policies strengthened the state and the government, yet he was forced to accept Hizbollah's military role in the south as a fait accompli. From 1978, the United Nations Interim Force in Lebanon (UNIFIL) had monitored the southern border with Israel, but was unable to prevent the new wars in 1993 ('Operation Accountability') and 1996

('Operation Grapes of Wrath'), which destroyed thousands of homes, killed hundreds of Lebanese civilians and lead to a mass exodus of 300,000 internally displaced persons (IDPs) from the conflict zone (Hamzeh 2004). The Palestinian militias had retained their light weapons and from the mid-1990s, infighting started among camp-based factions over disagreements concerning the Oslo Accords (Knudsen 2005). Indeed, some of the most intense internecine fighting took place in refugee camps or in their vicinity.

Rafik Hariri prevailed as prime minister in the 1996 parliamentary elections despite very strong Syrian interference (Gambill and Aoun 2000), but towards the middle of his term in office economic growth slowed and the public debt increased (Iskandar 2006: 91). During the summer of 1998, Hariri stepped down and the veteran politician Selim al-Hoss was named his successor. Al-Hoss's slim 15-member cabinet did not include any of the former warlords. The two-year period presided over by al-Hoss (1998–2000) was marked by lower violence and greater flexibility towards Syria. Al-Hoss's cabinet continued Hariri's economic policies but was unable to revive the country's ailing economy, which helped Hariri return as prime minister in the 2000 parliamentary elections.

Syrian crackdown, 2000–3

In 2000 Israel withdrew unilaterally from South Lebanon (Murdon 2000). This was a major military and political victory for Hizbollah, then at the height of its popularity (Murdon 2000). The Israeli withdrawal made the Syrian troop presence all the more glaring: Syria had never made good its pledge to leave the country. Attention now turned to Syria's troop presence and tutelage of the country, and especially to the approximately 17,000 Lebanese who disappeared during the civil war, never to be seen again (Humphrey and Kisirwan 2001). The government exhibited a deep-seated unwillingness to open war-related files and investigate the fate of those missing. Activists were threatened, intimidated and in some cases, jailed. In April 2000, at the twenty-fifth anniversary of the outbreak of the civil war there were large demonstrations demanding information about the fate of missing persons (Johnson 2001: 258).

In 2002, the public reconciliation between the Maronites and the Druze ended the communal conflict and was seen as a significant threat to the Syrian hegemony in Lebanon. Shortly afterwards there was a massive crackdown on the anti-Syrian opposition parties (Gambill 2001). Two years later, two student activists were brutally murdered (Knudsen 2010). Despite the killings, the popular protest against Syria's hegemony grew and student and activist protest marches continued. Mostly, these marches remained non-violent, yet student leaders were arrested and at times kept in police custody for a long time before their release. To prevent further inquiry into the fate of missing persons, the Lebanese army again cracked down on activists. Moreover, abductions and 'disappearances' continued throughout the post-war period, especially targeting Palestinians associated with the main Fatah movement (Sherry 1997).

Targeted assassinations, 2004–5

On 2 September 2004, the UN Security Council passed Resolution 1559. The resolution targeted two of the most critical and sensitive parts of Lebanon's post-war period: the incomplete demobilization of militias, leaving Hizbollah out; and linked to this, the continued Syrian troop presence. Resolution 1559 called for an immediate end to Syrian troop deployment and the disarmament of Hizbollah and Palestinian militias. Additionally, it required the Lebanese army to deploy along the Israeli border, until then controlled by Hizbollah. Each of these demands was a fundamental challenge to the post-war status quo and struck directly at the shaky foundations of Lebanon's post-war consensus, the Taif Accords.

It was widely believed that Hariri had been a key force behind fielding Resolution 1559. This made him a political target. Hariri was summoned to Syria and threatened by Syrian President Bashir al-Assad (Blanford 2009: 100). In 2004, President Emile Lahoud's presidential term was about to expire. Lahoud was favoured by Syria, which sought to have him extended for a new three-year term. This would require an amendment to the Constitution, something Hariri strongly opposed, yet in the end felt compelled to support. Shortly after, one of the MPs who voted against extending Lahoud's term was targeted by a car bomb, which he narrowly survived (Knudsen 2010). Soon after, Hariri stepped down as prime minister but his retreat from politics was considered temporary and it was expected that he would run in the 2005 elections.

In February 2005, while preparations for the parliamentary elections were underway, Rafik Hariri and more than 20 bodyguards in his motorcade were killed in a massive bomb blast in central Beirut. The killing of Hariri led to international condemnation and popular protests, with fingers being pointed at Syria. Considered a 'terrorist attack', investigating the crime was tasked to a United Nations commission.[11] The strong international pressure and huge public demonstrations, known as the 'Cedar Revolution', forced Syria to comply with UN Resolution 1559 and withdrew its troops in late April 2005. Soon, the nation was divided into those opposed to Syrian stewardship and those in favour of it. This internal disagreement spilled over into a dispute on whether to find and prosecute those responsible for Rafik Hariri's assassination, as well as for the many other political assassinations that followed.

The parliamentary elections in May and June 2005 brought an 'anti-Syrian' majority into parliament (known as the '14th March'), but the new unity cabinet for the first time included ministers representing the Shia opposition parties (Amal, Hizbollah). From mid-2005, there was a marked increase in targeted killings of prominent politicians, journalists and intellectuals, as well as in terrorist bombs targeting civilians. None of the murders has been solved and nobody has been arrested and convicted. The assassinations for the most part targeted independent or anti-Syrian politicians and leaders and involved detailed planning, execution and cover-up (Knudsen 2010). Yet in none of the cases mentioned above did victims and their families seek or call for revenge. Instead, they called for unity, dignity and forgiveness. The absence of retributive violence is remarkable given the level of political tension in the country after 2005.

War, communal violence and warlordism, 2006–10

In July 2006, a cross-border raid into Israeli territory by Hizbollah's militia escalated into a major war. When the 33-day 'July War' came to an end a month later, Lebanon had suffered a devastating blow to its infrastructure, lost more than 1,000 civilians and was burdened with many homeless.[12] The biggest fall-out, however, was political and set Lebanon on the slippery slope towards increasing political turmoil. The July War was not only a stark reminder of the devastation of the civil war, but deepened the country's political divisions and ultimately led to a governance crisis. In October 2006, two Shia coalition partners (Hizbollah and Amal) withdrew their cabinet ministers due to disagreements over ratifying the Special Tribunal for Lebanon (STL) to prosecute those responsible for Hariri's murder. As the political crisis escalated, a Maronite minister was assassinated in a drive-by shooting in a Beirut suburb.

In January 2007, the political crisis deepened and violence now took on communal overtones as young men were killed in demonstrations, student clashes, neighbourhood brawls and street fights, fuelling mistrust and sectarian tensions. From this time onwards 'ordinary' parliamentary politics was suspended as street fights and clashes multiplied due to the absence of a national consensus, a precondition for all important political decisions set in the Taif Accords. The UN ratification of the STL to try the suspects in Hariri's murder (Shehadi and Wilmshurst 2007) divided the country and led to new outbreaks of violence.[13] In late May, heavy fighting broke out between the Lebanese army and a new militia group calling itself 'Fatah al-Islam', based in a Palestinian refugee camp near Tripoli. With a death toll of close to 500, this was the biggest violent incident since the civil war ended and added significantly to the country's political turmoil and sectarian tensions. This was followed by the targeted assassinations of two MPs, with a total of eight MPs having been killed since February 2005 (Knudsen 2010).

Confessional concerns now took centre stage and the many assassinations polarized the public and disposed them to take refuge in their own sect. The political deadlock suspended parliamentary politics and made politicians act as confessional leaders. People retreated to their confession, their neighbourhood and their families for reasons of safety, a safety the state could no longer guarantee (Borell 2008). Opinion polls confirmed that members of all confessions perceived their group to be under siege from other groups and would resort to arms if threatened (*iMonthly* 2007). The political tensions induced militias to rearm and for the first time government sources confirmed that groups on both sides of the conflict were undertaking 'armed training'. This was a state of affairs that was in many ways similar to the situation prevailing before the 1975 civil war broke out and continued with a bomb attack killing an army general. The attack, the first on a high-ranking officer, was a significant blow to the army, which had sought to stay outside the political conflict.

In mid-January 2008, amidst soaring internal and regional tensions, new car bombs killed officers involved in investigating the assassination of Rafik Hariri (Knudsen 2010). As the internal political crisis deepened, an attempt to unearth Hizbollah's secret communications network sparked the biggest sectarian clashes in Beirut since the end of the civil war. During the 8–14 May clashes, rival militias took to the streets and the fighting killed 65 people and injured more than 200 (Knio 2008: 449). The political turmoil was resolved by the surprise entente in Doha ('Doha Agreement') that shortly afterwards paved the way for the election of a new president (former General Michel Suleiman) and the formation of a 30-seat 'unity cabinet'. Nonetheless, the political situation remained unstable for the rest of the year. In Tripoli bombs targeted army personnel, killing and injuring soldiers and civilians and in Beirut new car bombs killed MPs and senior Palestinian officials (Knudsen 2010). The closely contested parliamentary elections in May 2009 were a victory for the '14th March' coalition and Prime Minister-Elect Saad Hariri, Rafiq Hariri's son and political heir. However, cabinet formation was held up for five months amidst a growing constitutional crisis. Despite forming a unity cabinet in November and later agreeing to a ministerial statement, the role of Hizbollah's arms remained divisive.

From mid-2010, the conflict levels in Lebanon escalated following claims of a 'politicization' of the STL. In July, the situation took a turn for the worse when the Hizbollah leader Syeed Hassan Nasrallah disclosed that leaked documents showed that the STL would indict 'rogue' Hizbollah members for involvement in Hariri's assassination. This was critical enough to warrant a hurried visit by the heads of state from Saudi Arabia and Syria to defuse tensions. Hizbollah has since upped the ante by terming the STL an 'Israeli project', followed by video footage meant to corroborate Israeli involvement in Hariri's assassination. This has fuelled more political turmoil with the opposition attempting to halt Lebanon's funding of the STL's budget and petitioning the UN to abolish the tribunal and replace it with a joint Arab–Lebanese commission. At the same time, the criminal investigation was stepped up with 3D modelling of the crime scene in Beirut, a full-scale re-enactment of the explosion at a French army base and a request to Hizbollah to hand over all evidence that could link Israel to Hariri's assassination. The conflict levels are expected to rise further when the STL finally issues its indictments.

Conclusion: post-civil war conflict dynamics

This chapter has privileged endogenous variables to explain the conflict dynamics of post-war political violence, but it is important to acknowledge the importance of third party ('exogenous') involvement in 'Lebanese' conflicts of foreign countries, agencies and agents. Despite this caveat, the form, type and magnitude of violence varied over the period under study, as did the internal 'conflict dynamics'. Still, the conflict levels in post-civil war Lebanon were relatively low and collective violence never crossed the threshold of 'civil war' as commonly understood. This notwithstanding, this chapter has demonstrated a remarkable continuity of political violence in Lebanon from the 1950s to the present. Typologically, the continuity is particularly marked with respect to targeted assassinations, which began in the 1950s, despite that fact that there was a transformation in the generation and utilization of violence, both practically and conceptually. As we have shown, Lebanon's clientelist political system was premised on intermittent violence to coerce clients and ward off competitors. The clientelist system was strained during the 1958 'crisis' and collapsed on the eve of the 1975 civil war. The civil war was marked by militia warfare, car bombs and bloody massacres and ended with 'second-order' battles between former allies after the Taif peace accord was signed in October 1989. The transitional period from war to peace (1989–91) saw a series of targeted assassinations that can be considered after-shocks of the war, possibly acting as 'spoilers' seeking to end the fragile peace deal (Zahar 2006).

The early post-war period saw the integration of warlords into the political system under Syrian tutelage, made possible by a General Amnesty Law (1991) that 'closed' the civil war. This was followed by the disarming of militias and reintegration of smaller numbers of militiamen into the expanding army. Former militiamen evidently put killing behind them, although only a few publicly regretted their crimes or sought forgiveness. Likewise, the new class of warlords-turned-politicians did not return to war, but economic and political rivalry continued with Syria as the final arbiter.[14]

The strategy of co-opting warlords and integrating them into the political process by rewarding their wartime exploits reduced violent conflict levels, which fell until the mid-1990s, when violence turned inwards: Maronite Christians and their leaders in particular were targeted due to their opposition to Syrian stewardship. The partial disarmament of militias, leaving out Hizbollah, is one explanation why Lebanon suffered three punitive wars with Israel (in 1993, 1996 and again in 2006). The inter-state wars can be interpreted as a continuation of the civil war and an attempt to reach military, tactical and territorial objectives that the civil war left unfinished. The withdrawal of Israeli forces from the south in 2000 was a victory for Hizbollah, which could boast one of the most disciplined and effective political-military organizations in the Arab Middle East. The Israeli withdrawal, however, increased the opposition to Syrian troops, which, in contravention of the Taif Accords, had remained in Lebanon and instituted Syrian quasi-suzerainty over the country. Popular protests against the Syrian presence grew, despite crackdowns, arrests and the murder of activists and, in particular, Syrian culpability in the fate of those missing since the war.

Syria's tutelage of Lebanon deepened until 2004, when UN Security Resolution 1559 set in motion a new conflict dynamic by demanding an end to Syria's troop presence and the disarming of Hizbollah's militia. The foreign intervention by the UN sharply increased political divisions, drove up conflict levels and began a period of targeted assassinations that was unprecedented in the history of Lebanon (Knudsen 2010). The assassination of Hariri in mid-February 2005 led to massive popular protests that ended the presence of Syrian troops and left a political void. The political stalemate that followed gave rise to bomb attacks against civilians and sectarian clashes, especially in mixed urban neighbourhoods (Yassin 2010). The following re-arming of militias was in many ways similar to the period preceding the 1975 civil war. The return to warlordism reached its apex during the May 2008 Beirut clashes, which brought militias onto the streets and was testimony to the military superiority of Hizbollah's militia and the inability to find a political solution to peaceful disarmament. Only a last-minute political deal in Doha (and a temporary one at that) stopped the country's descent into a new civil war. While a new war was averted, political brinkmanship continued over Hizbollah's arms and the prosecution of those responsible for the murder of the late Rafik Hariri. The conflict over the STL is the most recent and probably the most divisive example of foreign intervention, amidst fears that it could mark a return to violent conflict.

Notes

1 Acknowledgements: The authors would like to thank the editors and anonymous reviewers for detailed comments on previous drafts. The usual disclaimer applies.
2 Lebanon is home to 18 different denominations (as well as about 250,000 Palestinian refugees), which can broadly be fitted into two sectarian blocs: Christians and Muslims.
3 See for example Dib (2004), el Khazen (2000), Fisk (1992), Hanf (1993), Johnson (2001), Khalaf (2002) and Picard (2002).
4 Some groups were already militarized in 1973, if not earlier.
5 Examples include Damour (1976) and Karantina (1976), followed later by the Sabra and Shatila massacres (1982).
6 Several of the car-bomb attacks can be attributed to regional conflicts and foreign intelligence agencies and were not primarily caused by internal conflict dynamics.
7 However, the law (Article 3) does not provide an amnesty for 'crimes of assassination or attempted assassination of religious figures, political leaders, and foreign or Arab diplomats' (Amnesty International 2004).
8 As stipulated in the Taif Agreement (1989), the 124 parliamentary seats are distributed evenly between Muslim and Christian sects. Each sect is accorded a fixed number of seats relative to its numerical strength based on the 1936 census (Jabbra and Jabbra 2001). The country's 250,000 Palestinian refugees lack civil rights and have no political representation.
9 Hariri regretted this, lamenting: 'Some of the people in my cabinet are criminals and should be in jail, but I can't do anything about it' (Norton 2007: 127).
10 However, the negative side of the illegal 'resource extraction' was that corruption boomed (Iskandar 2006).
11 The first UN fact-finding mission into the murder was led by Peter FitzGerald (2005). On the basis of the report, the United Nations International Independent Investigation Commission (UNIIIC) was established shortly afterwards by UN Security Council Resolution 1595 (7 April 2005).
12 The war ended on 14 August following UN Security Council Resolution 1701.
13 The weakness of Lebanon's judiciary, as well as the potential threats to witnesses and defendants, made it mandatory to situate the STL outside the country and place it under the aegis of the UN. The STL is based in The Hague, the Netherlands, STL website, online, available at: www.stl-tsl.org/action/home.

14 Not all warlords benefited from the co-optation process (one was imprisoned and another two assassinated), but the rest of the warlords served as MPs and ministers for the duration of the period under study. Moreover, it is worth noting that Lebanese warlords in most cases had a pre-war political platform and local constituency. This eased their transition to politics after the war, although the recent crises and political stalemates suggest that the transition has been incomplete and could be reversed.

Bibliography

Ajami, F. (1987) *The Vanished Imam: Musá al Sadr and the Shia of Lebanon*, Ithaca, NY: Cornell University Press.

Amnesty International (2004) 'Lebanon – Samir Gea'gea' and Jirjis al-Khouri: torture and unfair trial', *Amnesty International Online Documentation Archive* 23 November 2005. Online, available at: http://www.amnesty.org/en/library/asset/MDE18/003/2004/en/f4dbe07b-d585-11dd-bb24-1fb85fe8fa05/mde1800032004en.pdf.

Atlas, P.M. and Licklider, R. (1999) 'Conflict among former allies after civil war settlement: Sudan, Zimbabwe, Chad, and Lebanon', *Journal of Peace Research*, 36: 35–54.

Attie, C. (2003) *Struggle in the Levant: Lebanon in the 1950s*, London: I.B. Tauris, in association with the Centre for Lebanese Studies.

Baroudi, S.E. (2007) 'Divergent perspectives among Lebanon's Maronites during the 1958 crisis', *Critique: Critical Middle Eastern Studies*, 15: 5–28.

Blanford, N. (2009) *Killing Mr Lebanon: The Assassination of Rafik Hariri and its Impact on the Middle East*, London: I.B. Tauris.

Borell, K. (2008) 'Terrorism and everyday life in Beirut 2005: mental reconstructions, precautions and normalization, *Acta Sociologica*, 51(1): 55–70.

Dib, K. (2004) *Warlords and Merchants: The Lebanese Business and Political Establishment*, Reading: Ithaca Press.

Fisk, R. (1992) *Pity the Nation: Lebanon at War*, Oxford: Oxford University Press.

FitzGerald Report (2005) Report of the Fact-Finding Mission to Lebanon Inquiring into the Causes, Circumstances and Consequences of the Assassination of Former Prime Minister Rafik Hariri, New York: Report submitted by Peter FitzGerald, Head of the United Nations Fact-Finding Mission in Lebanon, New York, 24 March 2005 (S/2005/203).

Gambill, G.C. (2001) 'Lebanon's shadow government takes charge', *Middle East Intelligence Bulletin*, 3.

Gambill, G.C. (2004) 'Dossier: Hassan Nasrallah, Secretary General of Hizbollah', *Middle East Intelligence Bulletin*, 6.

Gambill, G.C. and Aoun, E.A. (2000) 'Special report: how Syria orchestrates Lebanon's elections', *Middle East Intelligence Bulletin*, 2. Online, available at: www.meib.org/articles/0008_l1.htm.

Gaub, F. (2007) 'Multi-ethnic armies in the aftermath of civil war: lessons learned from Lebanon', *Defence Studies*, 7: 5–20.

Gilsenan, M. (1996) *Lords of the Lebanese Marches: Violence and Narrative in an Arab Society*, London: I.B. Tauris.

Giustozzi, A. (2005) *The Debate on Warlordism: The Importance of Military Legitimacy*, London: Crisis State Discussion Papers, no. 13.

Hamzeh, A.N. (2004) *In the Path of Hizbullah*, Syracuse, NY: Syracuse University Press.

Hanf, T. (1993) *Coexistence in Wartime Lebanon: Decline of a State and Rise of a Nation*, London: I.B. Tauris.

Harik, J.P. (1993) 'Change and continuity among the Lebanese Druze community: the civil administration of the mountains, 1983–90', *Middle Eastern Studies*, 29: 377–98.

Harik, J.P. (2004) *Hezbollah: The Changing Face of Terrorism*. London: I.B. Tauris.

Havens, M.C., Leiden, C. and Schmitt, K.M. (1970) *The Politics of Assassination*, Englewood Cliffs, NJ: Prentice-Hall.

Humphrey, M. and Kisirwan, M. (2001) 'Impunity, nationalism and transnationalism: the recovery of the "disappeared" of Lebanon', *Bulletin of the Royal Institute of Inter-Faith Studies*, 3(2): 113–40.

iMonthly (2007) 'Opinion poll: the Lebanese follow their leaders' February-March: 7–11. Online, available at: www.imonthly.com.

Iskandar, M. (2006) *Rafiq Hariri and the Fate of Lebanon*, London: Saqi Books.

Jabbra, J.G. and Jabbra, N.W. (2001) 'Consociational democracy in Lebanon: a flawed system of governance', *Journal of Developing Societies*, 16(2): 71–89.

Johnson, M. (1983) 'Popular movements and primordial loyalties in Beirut', in T. Asad and R. Owen (eds) *Sociology of 'Developing Societies': the Middle East*, London: Macmillan, 178–94.

Johnson, M. (1985) *Class and Client in Beirut: The Sunni Muslim Community and the Lebanese State 1840–1985*, London: Ithaca Press.

Johnson, M. (1996) 'Political bosses and strong-arm retainers in the Sunni Muslim quarters of Beirut, 1943–1992', in J. Gugler (ed.) *Cities in the Developing World: Issues, Theory, and Policy*, Oxford: Oxford University Press, 326–40.

Johnson, M. (2001) *All Honourable Men: The Social Origins of War in Lebanon*. London: I.B. Tauris, in association with the Centre for Lebanese Studies.

Kanaan, C.B. (2005) *Lebanon 1860–1960: A Century of Myth and Politics*, London: Saqi Books.

Kerr, M. (2005) *Imposing Power Sharing: Conflict and Coexistence in Northern Ireland and Lebanon*, Dublin: Irish Academic Press.

Khalaf, S. (2002) *Civil and Uncivil Violence in Lebanon: A History of the Internationalization of Communal Conflict*, New York: Columbia University Press.

Khazen, F. el (1998) *Lebanon's First Postwar Parliamentary Election: An Imposed Choice*, Oxford: Centre for Lebanese Studies Prospects for Lebanon Series, No. 8.

Khazen, F. el (2000) *The Breakdown of the State in Lebanon, 1967–1976*, London: I.B. Tauris Publ., in association with the Centre for Lebanese Studies.

Khazen, F. el (2003) 'Political parties in postwar Lebanon: parties in search of partisans', *Middle East Journal*, 57: 605–24.

Knio, K. (2008) 'Is Political Stability Sustainable in Post-"Cedar Revolution" Lebanon?', *Mediterranean Politics*, 13(3): 445–51.

Knudsen, A. (2005) 'Islamism in the diaspora: Palestinian refugees in Lebanon', *Journal of Refugee Studies*, 18(2): 216–34.

Knudsen, A. (2010) 'Acquiescence to assassinations in post-civil war Lebanon?', *Mediterranean Politics*, 15(1): 1–23.

Makdisi, J.S. (1999) *Beirut Fragments*, New York: Persea Books.

Makdisi, S. and Sadaka, R. (2003) *The Lebanese Civil War, 1975–1990*, Beirut: American University of Beirut (AUB), Lecture and Working Paper Series no. 3.

Murdon, S. (2000) 'Understanding Israel's long conflict in Lebanon: the search for an alternative approach to security during the peace process', *British Journal of Middle Eastern Studies*, 27(1): 25–47.

Norton, A.R. (2007) *Hezbollah: A Short History*, Princeton: Princeton University Press.

O'Ballance, E. (1998) *Civil War in Lebanon, 1975–92*, Basingstoke: Macmillan.

O'Brien, L. (1983) 'Campaign of terror: car bombings in Lebanon', *MERIP Reports*, October, 118: 23–6.

Perthes, V. (1997) 'Myths and money: four years of Hariri and Lebanon's preparation for a new Middle East', *Middle East Report*, Spring: 16–21.

Picard, E. (1993) *The Lebanese Shi'a and Political Violence*, Geneva: UNRISD, DP 42.

Picard, E. (1999) *The Demobilisation of the Lebanese Militias*, Oxford: Centre for Lebanese Studies, Prospects for Lebanon Series, No. 9.

Picard, E. (2000) 'The political economy of civil war in Lebanon', in S. Heydemann (ed.) *War, Institutions, and Social Change in the Middle East*, Berkeley: University of California Press, 292–324.

Picard, E. (2002) *Lebanon – a Shattered Country: Myths and Realities about the Wars in Lebanon*, New York and London: Holmes and Meier.

Randal, J.C. (1983) *Going All the Way: Christian Warlords, Israeli Adventurers, and the War in Lebanon*, New York: Viking Press.

Rowayheb, M.G. (2006) 'Lebanese militias: a new perspective', *Middle Eastern Studies*, 42: 303–18.

Seale, P. (2010) *The Struggle for Arab Independence: Riad al-Solh and the Makers of the Modern Middle East*, Cambridge: Cambridge University Press.

Shehadi, N. and Wilmshurst, E. (2007) 'The Special Tribunal for Lebanon: the UN on trial?', *Chatham House Middle East/International Law Briefing Paper*. Online, available at: www.chathamhouse.org.uk/publications/papers/download/-/id/512/file/10088_bp0707lebanon.pdf.

Sherry, V.N. (1997) 'Disappearances: Syrian impunity in Lebanon', *Middle East Report*, 203: 31–3.

Silverstein, P.A. and Makdisi, U.S. (2006) 'Introduction: memory and violence in the Middle East and North Africa', in P.A. Silverstein and U.S. Makdisi (eds) *Memory and Violence in the Middle East and North Africa*, Bloomington: Indiana University Press, p. VIII.

Tilly, C. (1985) 'War making and state making as organized crime', in P. Evans, D. Rueschemeyer and T. Skocpol (eds) *Bringing the State Back*, Cambridge: Cambridge University Press, 169–91.

Time (1992) 'World Notes Lebanon'. Online, available at: www.time.com/time/magazine/article/0,9171,975156,00.html?promoid=googlep (accessed 26 February 2010).

Tueini, G. (2002) *The Secret of the Trade and Other Secrets* [in Arabic], Beirut: Dar An-Nahar.

Yassin, N. (2010) 'Violent urbanization and homogenization of space and place: reconstructing the story of sectarian violence in Beirut', in J. Beall, B. Guha-Khasnobis and R. Kanbur (eds) *Urbanization and Development: Multidisciplinary Perspectives*, Oxford: Oxford University Press, 205–18.

Zahar, M.-J. (2002) 'Peace by unconventional means: Lebanon's Tai´if Agreement', in S.J. Stedman, D. Rothchild and E.M. Cousens, *Ending Civil Wars: The Implementation of Peace Agreements*, Boulder, CO: Lynne Rienner, 567–98.

Zahar, M.-J. (2006) 'Political violence in peace processes: voice, exit, and loyalty in the post-accord period', in John Darby (ed.) *Violence and Reconstruction*. Notre Dame, IN.: University of Notre Dame Press, 33–52.

7   From regime change to civil war

Violence in post-invasion Iraq

Toby Dodge

Introduction

The evolution of the violence that came to dominate Iraq from the summer of 2003 onwards to some extent marks it out from the other conflicts discussed in this volume. The majority of casualties between 2003 and 2010 occurred after the formal inter-state conflict between the United States and Iraq had finished. In the wake of the invasion and US-led regime change, Iraq experienced a very small but definable post-conflict or post-war period of stability. However, Washington's plans for a post-war settlement were soon challenged by the rise of an insurgency that aimed not only to drive US troops from the country but also to destroy the governing structures and political settlement that America and her Iraqi allies had imposed on Iraq to shape the post-war peace. In 2005 and 2006, the insurgency mutated into a civil war and it is this conflict that has caused the majority of the death and destruction that came to dominate Iraq.

Although the continuing conflict in Iraq started after the invasion and then mutated into a civil war, the common explanatory themes used in the rest of this volume to explain violence after peace settlements can be usefully applied to Iraq to provide powerful insights into the on-going conflict there. It can be convincingly argued that there was nothing inevitable about the scale or form of the violence that erupted after US troops reached Baghdad in April 2003. Once the formal conflict between the United States and the Iraqi state ended the evolution of the insurgency and then the civil war was specifically driven forward by policy decisions taken by the United States and their newly empowered Iraqi allies. Against this background, the Iraqi case study provides a powerful and instructive example of how violent conflict evolves and how it is driven, in part, by the policy decisions of those who thought they had won the initial stage of the war.

On 1 May 2003, President George W. Bush was certain the conflict in Iraq had ended and the United States had won. To mark the cessation of the war he addressed the American people from the flight deck of the USS *Abraham Lincoln*. The hubris surrounding that announcement can in part be explained by an apparently swift victory American troops appeared to have secured. From the start of the invasion on 20 March to that moment, the United States had suffered 139 casualties.[1] In comparison, Iraq Body Count estimates that the invasion had caused the deaths of 7,299 Iraqi civilians, of which 6,882 had been killed by the US military.[2] Casualties amongst the losing side were much harder to assess, though Tommy Franks, the US general in overall charge of the war, estimated that as many as 30,000 Iraqi soldiers had been killed.[3]

George W. Bush's triumphant declaration of the end of hostilities proved to be exceptionally presumptuous. By the summer of 2003 a second phase of the conflict had already started. A resistance movement aimed at driving US forces from the country attacked American soldiers with increasing skill and effect. By April 2004, this insurgency had grown into outright rebellion, with operations launched against the United States by Muqtada al-Sadr's militia across the south of the country and by radical Islamists based in the northwestern city of Falluja. In 2004, the United States suffered 849 military casualties, with its yearly losses peaking at 904 in 2007 (O'Hanlon and Livingston 2010: 3).

The nature of the violence that came to dominate Iraq was transformed for a third time during 2005 and 2006. After two nationwide elections in January and December 2005, what had begun as an insurgency shaped by an assertive Iraqi nationalism mutated into a bloody intra-communal civil war. The death toll caused by this internecine conflict steadily increased, with 16,800 civilians killed in 2004, 20,200 in 2005 and 34,500 in 2006. Violence directed at the civilian population reached its peak in October 2006 when 3,709 were murdered in a single month (O'Hanlon and Livingston 2010: 4, 5, 12).

The damage done by the formal stage of the US invasion of Iraq in March and April 2003 was, in comparison to its bloody aftermath, *relatively* limited. American troops did encounter asymmetrical resistance as they moved north from the Kuwaiti border towards Baghdad but their overbearing technological dominance meant airpower and artillery gave them an unbeatable superiority and victory was relatively swift (Gordon and Trainor 2006). However, although the conventional war was perceived as a success, its aftermath would be far more costly, as the US military's inability to impose order on the country they had conquered became glaringly apparent.

Seeking to understand violence in Iraq

In both British and American government circles there was a marked unwillingness to describe the escalating violence in Iraq as a 'civil war'. This semantic reluctance was primarily shaped by the fear that the public's tolerance of casualties would disappear once the real nature of the Iraq conflict was recognized (Cole 2006). From an analytical as opposed to an instrumental point of view, the definitional issues of when Iraq moved into civil war are focused on the date that indigenous forces on both sides of the conflict, those controlling the state and those seeking to remove them, took responsibility for the majority of violence.

Henderson and Singer (2000: 276) define the indigenous nature of civil war as a 'violent conflict between the military forces of a state and insurgent forces comprised mainly of citizens (or residents) of the state'. Fearon and Laitin (2003: 76) have a comparable definition, though add the caveat that 'involvement by foreign troops does not disqualify a case as a civil war for us, provided the other criteria are satisfied'. Finally, Sambanis (2004: 829) agrees that the government must be the 'principal combatant' but, for the Iraqi case, further complicates matters by adding, 'If there is no functioning government, then the party representing the government internationally and/or claiming the state domestically must be involved as a combatant'.

The US civilian authority in Iraq, the Coalition Provisional Authority (CPA), disbanded the 400,000-strong Iraqi army in May 2003 along with the security services and implemented plans to slowly rebuild them from scratch. As violence across Iraq increased, the United States rapidly rebuilt Iraq's security services. Yet when sovereignty was handed over to an interim Iraqi government in June 2004, the combined numbers of the Iraqi military and police remained less than the number of US troops in the country. It was not until May 2005 that indigenous government forces outnumbered US and allied troops. From then on Iraqi force numbers continued to increase and the weight of responsibility for fighting the insurgency is reflected in the increasing loss of life suffered. In the year and a half from June 2003 to January 2005, 1,300 members of the Iraqi security services were killed with over 2,000 being killed in 2005 and 2006 (O'Hanlon and Livingston 2010: 5, 19, 23).

The more analytically controversial issue is what drove post-regime change Iraq into civil war? Three of the major explanatory themes dominating the literature on the causes of violence: socio-cultural factors, the institutional approach and the nature of the post-conflict political settlement have key roles in the analysis of the rising tide of violence in Iraq.

Socio-cultural factors

When explaining the socio-cultural factors that can lead to post-war violence, Suhrke (2011) focuses on 'a general legitimation of violence stemming from wartime reversal of customary prohibitions on killings'. Just when the 'customary prohibitions on killings' in Iraq were reversed is open to question? The Ba'athist dictatorship that ran the country for 35 years deployed high levels of state-sanctioned violence while seeking to realize its totalitarian aspirations. However, it was the aftermath of the 1990–1 Gulf War that may have had the greatest effect on the customary prohibitions on killing. By the mid-1990s, under the pressure of UN sanctions, the Iraqi state began to lose control over its monopoly on violence. As a result criminality flourished, privatized coercion was put to the service of personal greed as well as state driven repression.[4] It is then that state and societal prohibitions on killing completely lost their purchase. As a result of war and sanctions, by 2003 Iraq was a highly militarized society that had been involved in three inter-state conflicts in 20 years. These conflicts, combined with a large standing army, conscription and the formation by the government of a number of militias, led to a proliferation of small arms across society. All of these factors, societal trauma, violence as a common currency in both politics and crime and a high level of private gun ownership, made the rise of collective violence in Iraq after 2003 comparatively easy to organize (al-Jezairy 2009: 162–3).

However, the socio-cultural factors more commonly deployed to explain Iraq's descent into violence are those that focus on the ethnic and religious divisions within society. Fearon and Laitin (2003: 75–6) in their quantative examination of civil wars are dismissive of ethno-sectarian causalities. However, Sambanis (2004: 856) seeks to add a note of caution to an outright rejection of the ethno-sectarian drivers of civil war. The dominant approach used to explain Iraq's descent into civil war and propositions to end violence discard his caution and impose a reductive primordial template onto the political and societal complexities of the situation.

This argument started with an a priori assertion of a society deeply divided by ethnic and sectarian tensions. The retired US diplomats and policy pundits, Leslie Gelb and Peter Galbraith, were the chief promoters of this approach. For them Iraq had 'three distinct and sectarian communities', Sunni, Shi'a and Kurd (Galbraith 2004; Galbraith 2006).[5] These communities, it was claimed, were largely geographically homogenous, mutually hostile and locked in an artificial, Sunni-dominated state for 85 years. This analysis leads its promoters to view the post-Saddam civil war as an unavoidable tragedy. For this approach, Iraqi politics have always been animated by deeply held communal antipathies; the civil war was simply a by-product of this.

The primordialization of Iraq was also adopted by several political parties who returned to Baghdad from exile after the invasion of 2003 and the two dominant parties in Iraqi Kurdistan, the Kurdistan Democratic Party (KDP) and the Patriotic Union of Kurdistan (PUK). They consistently argued that Iraq was irrevocably divided between sectarian and religious groupings, mobilized by deep communal antipathies. For the KDP and PUK this position was nurtured by their aspirations for greater autonomy, if not outright independence and the horrific repression that the Kurdish communities of northern Iraq suffered at the hands of the Ba'athist government. For the other non-Kurdish party advocating this policy, the Islamic Supreme Council of Iraq (ISCI), the primordial view had the advantage of dividing the Iraqi polity in a way that maximized the returning exiles' influence and their vote in the elections of 2005 (Dodge 2009: 88–99).

From this perspective, there can only be one policy option: the situation would stabilize when the country was divided into three small, ethnically purer and more manageable units. There is a possibility that this could be done through a form of drastic decentralization as proposed in 2006, by Joseph R. Biden and Leslie Gelb. But the primordialization of Iraq led Gelb and others to argue consistently for its complete division into separate states.[6] Biden, as American vice president, has continued to advocate an ethno-sectarian federal, de-centred approach to stabilizing the country as US troops have drawn down and American influence diminished.[7]

From a factual, as well as a policy viewpoint, the primordial approach, although until recently influential, is far from satisfactory. Those studying the social and political evolution of Iraq over the broad sweep of its modern history have long characterized the primordial approach as a static caricature that does great damage to a complex, historically grounded, reality (Dodge 2005: chapter 3).[8] In a series of polls carried out across the whole of Iraq from 2004 to 2009, between 64 and 70 per cent of Iraqis questioned consistently backed 'one unified Iraq with a central government in Baghdad' as their preferred form of government (Dodge 2007b: 23–39). This widespread commitment to a strong centralized state likewise played an important role in the provincial elections of January 2009. ISCI ran a campaign utilizing religious symbolism and a pledge to move towards greater decentralized federalism. This approach badly misjudged the mood of the country. In Baghdad, ISCI took just 5.4 per cent of the vote, compared to 39 per cent in 2005. In the Shia religious heartlands of Najaf and Karbala its share was 14.8 per cent and 6.4 per cent respectively, down from 45 per cent and 35 per cent respectively in 2005.[9]

This is not to deny or indeed minimize the role that sectarian rhetoric and organization played in the Iraqi civil war. However, a more nuanced approach would have to explain why this form of rhetoric became such a key factor after 2003 and not at other times of civil strife such as 1958, 1968 or indeed 1991. This explanation would in part focus on the rapid collapse of state capacity after 2003. Once a state's capacity has collapsed, civil society's ability to positively influence events quickly disappears (Posner 2004: 237, 240). The end of a state's institutional capacity not only means the loss of national authority but also the removal of a central focus for identity formation.

For communalistic identities to triumph as an organizing principle in this fluid and unpredictable situation there needs to be a certain type of sub-national elite. These entrepreneurs have to supply what the wider community desperately needs, a degree of stability and certainty. They can then legitimize their role in terms of communalistic identity and the competition for scarce resources (Rothchild 1981: 29). In these circumstances, people will look to whatever grouping, militia or identity offers them the best chance of survival in times of profound uncertainty (Talentino 2004: 569). This can lead to an unpredictable fracturing of the polity. This unstable and violent process will be shaped by path dependencies built up before the collapse of the state and political entrepreneurs active afterwards. Local, sub-state and ethnic identities will emerge from the wreckage to provide channels for mobilization and the immediate basis for political organization (Laitin 1998: 16).

Once this process has been set in motion, once ethnic entrepreneurs, in the face of state failure, have mobilized a significant section of the population on the basis of communalistic identity, this dynamic can quickly solidify (Wimmer 2003: 120). Previously 'fuzzy' or secondary identity traits can become politicized and 'enumerated' (Kaviraj 1994: 21–32). Survival, or a degree of predictability for yourself and your family, becomes obtainable through the increasingly militant deployment of ethnic or sectarian identity. There is nothing inevitable about the unfolding of this process; the primary cause is the collapse of the state and the subsequent security vacuum, not the communalistic conflict that emerges in its wake. Once the state is reconstituted, as happened in Iraq from 2008 to 2009, this process can be reversed and competing identity traits mobilized for political contestation.

State weakness and the institutional approach

Against this background, an analytical explanation of violence in Iraq after regime change would have to factor in the drastic reduction in state capacity from April 2003 onwards. This would be in line with Fearon and Laitin's argument (2003: 56–8) that 'financially, organizationally, and politically weak central governments render insurgency more feasible and attractive due to weak local policing or inept and corrupt counterinsurgency practices'. In the case of Iraq the rising tide of violence resulted from coalition forces' inability to control the country. Faced with the widespread lawlessness that is common after violent regime change, the United States lacked the troop numbers to control the situation (Chesterman 2004: 100, 112; Dobbins *et al.* 2003: 197).

It was the collapse of the state and resultant security vacuum that played a major role in driving Iraq into civil war after Bush declared the end of major combat operations in May 2003. This sudden security vacuum created, or at least empowered, three distinct groups who deployed violence for their own ends. The first were the 'industrial-strength' criminal gangs that terrorized Iraq's middle class. The high levels of criminal activity reflect opportunism that emerged out of state weakness, not the antipathy of competing groups within Iraqi society. Crime was instrumentally driven, primarily non-communal and a key factor de-legitimizing the occupation and later Iraq's new ruling elite.

The second type of organization comprises the myriad groups making up the Iraqi insurgency. The insurgency was born in a reactive and highly localized fashion, as the US military's inability to control Iraq became apparent (Dodge 2005: 11–19). This saw the creation of a number of small fighting units built around personal ties of trust, cemented by family, locality or friendship. From 2005 onwards, the insurgency consolidated around four or five main groups: the Islamic Army in Iraq, the Partisans of the Sunna Army, the Mujahadeen's Army, Muhammad's Army and Islamic Resistance Movement in Iraq (International Crisis Group 2006: 1–3). As the names suggest, political violence was increasingly justified in religious terms. The main insurgent groups found ideological coherence by fusing a powerful appeal to Iraqi nationalism with an austere and extreme Salafism, which became increasingly sectarian from 2004 onwards (Meijer 2007).

The third group of organizations that deployed violence for political ends were a plethora of independent militias with an estimated 60,000–102,000 fighters in their ranks (Bremer with McConnell 2006: 274; Diamond 2005: 222). Although the US government and sympathetic commentators point to the destruction of the al-Askariyya shrine in February 2006 as causing the rise in militia violence that marked the onset of Iraq's civil war, this is at best a convenient point of reference in a much longer running process (Dodge 2007a: 89; Ricks 2009: 33; O'Hanlon and Livingston 2010: 4). The rate at which civilians were being murdered had been rising rapidly since the start of the year and continued to do so until it reached a peak in October 2006. The militias themselves had been active in Iraq since 2003–4 but 2005–6 saw an increase in their public profile and deployment of violence. The militias overtly organized and legitimized themselves by reference to sectarian ideology but their existence was testament to the inability of the US occupation and later the Iraqi government to guarantee the personal safety of Iraqis on the basis of equal citizenship, not sectarian identity.

The militias can be divided into three broad groups, depending on their organizational coherence and relationship to national politics. The first and most disciplined consists of the Kurdish militias of the KDP and the PUK. The second includes those created in exile and brought back to Iraq in the wake of Saddam's fall. The most powerful of these is the Badr Brigade, the military arm of ISCI, with an estimated 15,000 fighters. The Badr Brigade's colonization of large swathes of the security forces, notably the police and paramilitary units associated with the Ministry of Interior, did much to de-legitimize the already limited power of the state-controlled forces of law and order.

The third group comprises militias created in Iraq since regime change. They vary in size, organization and discipline, from a few thugs with guns controlling a street or a neighbourhood, to militias capable of running whole towns. The largest and most coherent is the 50,000-strong *Jaish al-Mahdi*, set up by Muqtada al-Sadr. The speed with which the militia was built after regime change and two prolonged conflicts with the US military took a toll on its organizational coherence. Mahdi Army commanders became financially independent through hostage-taking, ransom and the smuggling of antiquities and petroleum. In spite of al-Sadr's repeated calls for calm, the Mahdi Army was blamed for the majority of violence in and around Baghdad following the al–Askariyya bombing (Cockburn 2008: 249).

Once a state has institutionally and coercively failed, the population has to quickly seek new, local ways to survive, to gain some degree of day-to-day predictability. This quest haunted the majority of the population in central and southern Iraq from 2003 until at least 2008. During this time, when the state's presence within Iraq society was negligible, the quality of an individual Iraqi's life depended on the discipline, organizational coherence and central control of the militias that dominated their streets, neighbourhoods and towns. The vacuum created by the invasion and the collapse of the Iraqi state in its aftermath is one of the central causal factors that drove Iraq's descent into civil war. Ethno-sectarian politics were certainly deployed to explain and justify the activities of the militias as they fanned out across a society haunted by the lack of law and order. However, the socio-cultural causes of violence from 2003 onwards, are secondary and dependent upon the collapse in the state's coercive and institutional capacity.

The nature of the post-war settlement: elite bargains and the rise of violence in Iraq

Astri Suhrke identifies the nature of peace settlements that follow conflict as a major contributing factor to the possible re-ignition of violence. The shape of the elite bargain placed at the centre of the political settlement in post-2003 Iraq played a central role in accelerating violent conflict after the invasion.

Elite bargains are placed at the centre of successful negotiations to end internal conflicts and any subsequent consolidation of democracy. Whaites (2008: 7) describes such bargains as deep 'often unarticulated, understandings between elites that bring about the conditions to end conflict, but which also in most states prevent violent conflict from occurring'. The elites involved must be the 'principle decision makers', politically, economically and militarily, and have the ability to deliver leadership of the dominant social groups (Burton *et al.* 1992: 8). The bargain between them involves the building of a consensus around 'the basic procedures and norms by which politics will henceforth be played' (Higley and Gunther 1992: xi).

When applying the notion of elite bargains to conflict prone states in Africa, Stefan Lindemann (2008) makes the distinction between elite bargains which are inclusive and hence promote stability and those which are exclusive and are prone to drive countries back into conflict. Inclusive settlements integrate a broad section of the existing national elites into a ruling coalition. The politicians can then use state resources, rents and employment opportunities, as patronage to sustain a strong base of support within society (Lindemann 2008: 2, 10). Exclusive bargains, on the other hand, involve a much narrower set of elites. They thus exclude a number of key politicians and the groups they seek to represent, fostering 'antagonism and violent conflict' (Lindemann 2008: 2, 21).

In Iraq, the political settlement created by the United States after the invasion and defended by Iraq's new ruling elite was clearly a highly exclusive and excluding elite bargain. It was designed to remove key indigenous political elites from any role in government. This, combined with a campaign of violent persecution, drove the excluded elites underground and then into open rebellion against the new political settlement and those it empowered to run the state.

The imposition of a new and excluding elite bargain in Iraq was heralded by the de-Ba'athification edict announced by the US occupation authorities in May 2003. This process was accelerated by the new Iraqi authorities. Running parallel to this political process was a more covert campaign of extrajudicial assassinations, building up to a mass campaign of terror carried out from 2005 to 2007 by militias claiming to represent the Shia population. There is strong evidence that this campaign was supported by key political parties who held ministerial power. The state was dominated by what Lindemann would classify as an exclusive elite bargain. This elite deployed its coercive and institutional capacity to drive Sunni residents from Baghdad.

US policy making on Iraq clearly contributed to the imposition of this destabilizing exclusive elite bargain. Paul Bremer, as head of the CPA from May, 2003 to April, 2004, had paramount authority over the whole of Iraq for his year in Baghdad. The one explicit order Bremer took with him from Washington for implementation in Baghdad was the de-Ba'athification of Iraqi society. The document drafted in the Pentagon, banned the top four levels of the Ba'ath Party's membership from holding government jobs. It also banned *any* former member of the Ba'ath from occupying jobs in the top three management levels of government institutions (Chandrasekaran 2007: 76–7).

The de-Ba'athification of Iraqi society was specifically designed to drive the old ruling elite and those associated with it out of office and place them on the margins of society. In an economy dominated by state employment, excluding large numbers of individuals from working for the government was tantamount to legislating for their forced impoverishment. CPA documents estimated that the order affected only the top 1 per cent of the party's membership, equivalent to 0.01 per cent of the population (Dobbins *et al.* 2009: 115). Bremer cites intelligence estimates that this amounted to 20,000 people (Bremer with McConnell 2006: 140). However, the head of the Central Intelligence Agency (CIA) in Baghdad suggested the order drove 50,000 Ba'athists underground overnight (Woodward 2006: 139). The order forced Tim Carney, then the senior American adviser to the Ministry of Industry, to remove the interim minister and 12 of the top 48 managers of state owned companies. In addition, a third of the Ministry of Health's staff stopped coming to work after the order was issued (Chandrasekaran 2007: 79–80).

In the autumn of 2003, after the initial implementation of de-Ba'athification, Bremer handed this responsibility to the Governing Council, the consultative body of Iraqi politicians set up in July 2003. They in turn created the High National De-Ba'athification Commission, which promptly imposed an even harder line than the one Bremer had pursued (Dobbins *et al.* 2009: 117). The radical nature of the de-Ba'athification imposed by the Governing Council indicates the type of exclusive elite bargain both they and the United States were aiming to impose on post-regime change Iraq.

The formation of the Iraqi Governing Council (IGC) in 2003 was the result of lobbying by Sergio Vieira de Mello, the senior UN representative in Baghdad after the invasion. He persuaded Bremer to form an Iraqi leadership group as a receptacle for Iraq's abrogated sovereignty. However, the IGC became the domain of a small number of formerly exiled political parties who used it as a platform to solidify their grip on the Iraqi state. Members of the IGC were not chosen in an open or indeed consultative process but after a period of extended negotiations between Paul Bremer, de Mello and the six dominant, formerly exiled parties, the KDP and PUK, the Iraqi National Congress (INC), the Iraqi National Alliance (INA), ISCI and the Dawa Party. The CPA claimed the politicians chosen represented the ethnically and religiously divided nature of Iraqi society: 13 Shias, five Sunnis, a Turkoman and a Christian. However, the forced and rather bizarre nature of this arrangement was highlighted by the inclusion of Hamid Majid Mousa, the Iraqi

Communist Party's representative in the 'Shia block' of 13. In reality, the political parties that in exile had done so much to encourage the invasion, quickly and exclusively monopolized the mechanics of Iraqi politics once they had been delivered back to Baghdad by the American military.

The IGC's membership is a good indicator of the post-regime change elite bargain that came to dominate Iraqi politics. First, the six parties that gained prominence in exile by allying themselves with the United States, the INC, INA, KDP, PUK, Dawa and ISCI, dominated the council. Second, 14 of the 24 members were long-term exiles or had lived in the Kurdish regional government enclave beyond Iraqi state control from 1991 onwards. Finally, of the five members of the IGC identified as Arab 'Sunni', only two, Naseer al-Chaderchi and Mohsen Abdel Hamid were members of organized political parties.[10] Al-Chaderchi's party had been set up by his father in the 1950s and 1960s but quickly lapsed into political irrelevance after regime change. Hamid, conversely, was secretary general of the Iraqi Islamic Party. Under the elite bargain, the IIP's role in the Governing Council and every government it has served in since was to deliver the 'Sunni vote', to bring that section of the population from which the former ruling elite originated back into the new post-war political settlement. From 2003 onward, there is a great deal of evidence to suggest that they singularly failed to do this since the IIP were not representative of their social constituency. The IIP's close association with the US occupation and the governing structures it erected meant they were repeatedly out-flanked by more radical political forces in the struggle to mobilize the Sunni section of Iraqi society.

The exclusive elite bargain at the centre of the IGC quickly gained control over the Iraqi state. On 11 November 2003, in the face of increasing violence in Iraq, Paul Bremer was unceremoniously hauled back to Washington where it was decided that sovereignty would be handed back to Iraqis no later than June 2004. What became known as the November 15 Agreement (the date the IGC were told about the plan and gave their assent), would give interim power to a new government ahead of national elections. The premiership was given to Iyad Allawi, a long-term exile and head of the National Accord, and the vice-presidencies to Ibrahim al-Jaafari, the head of the Dawa Party and Rowsch Shaways, a senior member of the KDP. Ministerial posts were liberally divided amongst the other leading parties on the Governing Council. The parties at the centre of the exclusive elite bargain, negotiated in July 2003, had successfully secured their grip on power.

Attempts to gain democratic legitimacy for this exclusive elite bargain were made for the duration of 2005. This involved anointing Iraq's new political elite with two electoral mandates and a Constitution approved by popular referendum. However, the nature of the chosen electoral system, the way the parties decided to fight the elections and the way in which the Constitution was drafted, all combined to exacerbate the exclusive nature of the post-war settlement and alienate a major section of the Iraqi population.

The democratic process was inaugurated by the elections of 30 January 2005, which would select an interim government to rule for a year. The vote itself was held with one nationwide electoral constituency because of security and logistical concerns.[11] This removed local issues and personalities from the campaign; marshalling the politicians and parties that had dominated the IGC into large coalitions, most of which played to the lowest common denominator, deploying ethno-sectarian rhetoric to maximize their vote (Dawisha and Diamond 2006: 93).

This dynamic was exacerbated by the exclusion of the Sunni community. In 2005 they lacked the organizational capacity to effectively mobilize. The Iraqi Islamic Party was heavily tainted by its association with the US occupation. It was challenged by a coalition of mosques, the *Hayat al-Ulama al-Muslimin* (Association of Muslim Scholars, AMS), who emerged to give voice to the alienation of the excluded Sunni section of Iraq's society (Meijer 2007: 7). The AMS channelled the widespread outrage against the US military assault on the town of Falluja in April 2004. The popular anger caused by this operation was such that even the IIP was forced to partially join an election boycott in the wake of the Falluja assault.[12]

Some 8.5 million Iraqis voted in the first set of post-invasion elections, 58 per cent of those were eligible (Marr 2007).[13] However, turnout varied dramatically across the country and amongst Iraq's different ethnic and religious communities. In the northern areas dominated by the Kurdish population, turnout was 82–92 per cent. In the southern districts, where the majority of the population is Shia, 61–71 per cent voted. In Anbar province, an area of northwestern Iraq with a high concentration of Sunnis, only 2 per cent voted, indicating the anger and alienation of that section of society.

The United Iraqi Alliance, the multi-party list designed to maximize the Shia vote, won 48 per cent of the vote and 140 seats in the 275-member assembly. The Kurdish Alliance took 27 per cent and 77 seats. Allawi and his nationalist and secular Iraqi List, damaged by his decision to authorize the attack on Falluja and the military confrontation with Moqtada al-Sadr, only managed to secure 14.5 per cent of the vote and 40 seats.

The divided electoral turnout and the unbalanced government it created was exacerbated by the drafting of Iraq's new Constitution. The main role of the newly elected parliament was to write the Constitution. In the aftermath of the elections a 55-member Constitutional Drafting Committee was formed from the newly elected members of the assembly. However, the assembly and the committee were sidelined by early August. To quote Jonathan Morrow (2005: 15) who was involved in the process on the ground in Baghdad, 'the Iraqi constitutional process was remarkable in the way in which members of the assembly, though legally charged with responsibility for writing the draft, were not involved'. In their place the parties at the centre of the exclusive elite bargain took control. These parties created a 'leadership council' consisting of the new prime minister and head of the Dawa Party, Ibrahim al Jaafari, the leader of the other main Shia party, ISCI, Abdul Aziz al Hakim and the two Kurdish leaders, the president of Iraq, Jalal Talabani and the head of the KDP, Masoud Barzani who wrote the Constitution. Unsurprisingly, the high-handed, non-transparent and undemocratic drafting of the Constitution caused resentment not only in the excluded assembly but across Iraq.

A second nationwide ballot for a full-term government took place on 15 December 2005. Following on from the legacy of the first elections, this poll was again dominated by three broad coalitions, attempting to maximize their electoral power by deploying ethno-sectarian ideologies. This time voter turnout reached 76 per cent. The most important of the coalitions remained the United Iraqi Alliance, with 46.5 per cent of the vote and 128 candidates elected to parliament. ISCI and the Dawa Islamic Party dominated the alliance, but it widened its appeal by joining forces with al-Sadr, whose Mahdi Army had twice led uprisings against the American occupation. The Kurdish Alliance won 19.27 per cent of the vote and took 53 seats.

The increased voter turnout indicated that the Sunni section of the electorate had this time been mobilized in terms of identity politics. The coalition gaining the majority of the Sunni vote was the *Tawafuq*, the Accord Front and was put together by the Iraqi Islamic Party. This coalition took 16 per cent of the vote and 44 seats. A radical grouping, the Iraqi Dialogue Front, took 4 per cent and 11 seats. Once again the main losers were those attempting to rally a secular nationalist vote. This time Allawi built an even wider coalition to form the National Iraqi List, but it only managed to secure 9 per cent of the vote and 25 seats (Diamond: 2006: 12).

From July 2003 onwards, the Iraqi political parties who had obtained prominence during their long exile, successfully leveraged their alliance with the United States to dominate government. This, along with the radical de-Ba'athification pursued by both the United States and the new Iraqi government, created an exclusive elite bargain that consciously excluded and indeed demonized not only the old ruling elite but the whole Sunni section of Iraqi society from the majority of party members had come. This exclusive elite bargain first primordialized Iraqi politics, dividing society into religious and ethnic groups. Political representation was then assigned to the ethnic and religious parties seeking to mobilize voters along primordial lines. The Iraqi Islamic Party was meant, within this rubric, to deliver the Sunni community. However, they faced a series of difficulties in playing this role. First, their close association with the US occupation and the new government severely limited their ability to mobilize the Sunni section of society who were deeply antithetical to the US occupation and the political structures it had created. The IIP, in an attempt to stay within the post-war political settlement, agreed to a series of compromises, personified by their support of the constitutional referendum, which further damaged their ability to represent the community. Finally, within government, the IIP's rewards for collaboration were scant, undermining the party's capacity to deploy the resources needed to tie an already deeply alienated constituency to the state.

The deployment of violence in the struggle to impose or overturn the exclusive elite bargain

Beaton, Richards and Suhrke (in this volume), discuss post-conflict political settlements in terms of a Victor's or Loser's Peace. In deploying these analytical categories they stress the role that violence plays in either solidifying the dominance of the war's winning side or in challenging and attempting to overturn the post-war settlement imposed on the losing side. Richards and then Suhrke describe the conflict arising from the Victor's Peace as being perceived by its protagonist in totality, as an ideological struggle between good and evil with success only achieved by total victory. Once the initial military struggle is over, state power is deployed to 'cleanse' society of the vanquished foe, purging the societal and political organizations associated with the old order (Suhrke 2011). The Loser's Peace, on the other hand, is marked by an upsurge of grass-roots, non-state asymmetrical violence, deployed to overturn the new political settlement. Here local elites, excluded by an exclusive elite bargain, have little choice but to deploy violence in an attempt either to demand a place at the governing table or overthrow the whole settlement. In Iraq after 2003 organized violence was deployed by those who now controlled the state to ensure a Victor's Peace and those excluded from power to overthrow it.

The first political group to exploit the US military's inability to control the country were the insurgents, a disparate movement of independent groups fighting to drive the United States out of Iraq and overthrow the exclusive elite bargain placed at the centre of the new political settlement. US troops were initially their main target, but as they were redeployed to decrease their vulnerability and political visibility, insurgents increasingly focused on Iraqis who served in the police and army. Small bands of highly mobile assailants, making use of their local knowledge, inflicted increasing fatalities on both US and Iraqi troops. By August 2003, car bombs became a weapon of choice, with mass casualty attacks increasingly taking on a sectarian nature, driving Iraq towards civil war. This dynamic was accentuated from 2005 onwards when al Qaeda in Mesopotamia moved to dominate the movement. Using the language of Islamic extremism and deploying mass casualty attacks against Iraq's Shia population, it achieved its aim of driving the country into a sectarian civil war.[14]

On the other side of the equation, the formerly exiled political parties placed at the centre of an exclusive elite bargain by the United States, used their election victories in 2005 to violently impose a Victor's Peace on the whole country. Between 2005 and 2006, the Ministry of Interior became the main vehicle for imposing a Victor's Peace. At this time the Ministry of Defence and the Iraqi army were perceived by Iraqi politicians in government to be under American control. The Ministry of Interior, on the other hand, appeared to be independent of American scrutiny and controlled the Special Police Commandos (later renamed the National Police). This organization was judged to be the most effective fighting force in the country, but since it was had been established by ministerial order was not subject to legal, parliamentary or cabinet oversight (Sherman and Carstens 2008: 2).[15]

After the first elections of 2005, Bayan Jabr, a senior member of ISCI and a former commander in its militia, the Badr Brigade, became Minister of the Interior and inherited complete control of the Special Police Commandos.[16] Through 2005–6, the commandos acted as a sectarian death squad, frequently resorting to extra-judicial execution and torture.[17] Complaints reached their peak in November 2005, when US forces raided a Ministry of Interior detention facility and found 170 detainees (166 of whom were Sunnis) 'who had been held in appalling conditions' (*Amnesty International* 2006: 4).[18] Following this a number of confirmed cases of secret detention facilities and the widespread use of torture came to light.[19] The modus operandi of the National Police in 2006 was summed up by James Danley, who witnessed their actions whilst he was an American troop commander in the Sunni-majority Baghdad suburb of Dora,

> The national police were sectarian murders. They were there to kill people who lived there.... You had what could only be described as liquidation missions in which they would go into a Sunni neighbourhood like ours and this National Police Unit would simply shoot everything they could.[20]

Even after such a public scandal and direct evidence of abuse in the Ministry of Interior, ISCI's power within the government and their support of Jabr was such that he did not leave the ministry until there was a complete change in government and was then promoted to the post of minister of finance.

This struggle between a Victor's and Loser's Peace reached its peak in 2006, when the 50,000-strong militia the *Jaish al-Mahdi* (JAM) Muqtada al-Sadr's military organization, become the main group murdering Sunnis in Baghdad. From mid-2006 onwards, JAM death squads used Sadr city, a slum containing two million people in eastern Baghdad, as a platform from which to drive the Sunni population out of Baghdad. Each night JAM would sweep across the north and west of Baghdad in a pincer movement, which bore all the hallmarks of a well planned operation, to attack the Sunni-dominated areas of western Baghdad. Under the cover of darkness, convoys of armed men would leave Sadr city moving into mixed or predominately Sunni neighbourhoods. As many as 60 men at a time would be seized. Their bodies, bearing the signs of torture, would be dumped the next morning on the peripheries of Sadr city.[21]

The ultimate aim of this campaign was to drastically reduce the numbers of Sunnis resident in Baghdad. Previously affluent suburbs on the western side of the Tigris like Mansour and Yarmouk were targeted for violent population transfer. The militia campaigns of murder and intimidation coincided with the withdrawal of banking services and healthcare provision from the Sunni residential areas on the west bank of the river. There is strong evidence to suggest that government services were withdrawn from targeted areas as part of a coordinated campaign to drive Sunnis from Baghdad (Kilcullen 2009: 126).

Conclusions

The death and destruction wrought on Iraq after George W. Bush declared an end to the invasion in May 2003, clearly qualifies as a civil war. To date that conflict has cost an estimated 107,227 civilian lives.[22] Media punditry and governmental responses to such wholesale carnage have tended to deploy primordial explanations. This stress on the ethnosectarian divisions within Iraqi society shifts the blame from those who invaded the country and failed to plan for the bloody aftermath. Such attempts at absolution also play to dominant Orientalist stereotypes that provide easy, if racist, explanations of complex situations. However, a close examination of how the Iraqi civil war evolved decentres ethno-sectarian divisions, seeing them as at best second order explanations. The main cause of post-war violence was the collapse of state capacity in 2003 and the exclusive elite bargain imposed on the country by the United States and their formerly exiled Iraqi allies.

The looting that dominated Baghdad in the immediate aftermath of the war not only broke the coherence of the Iraqi state but also showed the United State's inability to control the situation. This vacuum in both governance and security was exacerbated by the decision to pursue such a thorough de-Ba'athification process. If the looters in Baghdad took away the fixtures and fittings of the Iraqi state, similarly, US policy destroyed what was left – its institutional memory. The de-Ba'athification pursued by the United States was a conscious and deliberate attempt to drive what was left of the old governing elites and their technocratic allies out of state institutions. The aim was to clear a space for the incoming, formerly exiled politicians, long allied to the United States. Politically an excluding elite bargain was imposed on post-war Iraq as a way of securing US war aims and guaranteeing that the new Iraqi state would align itself with Washington.

However, the US occupation and the nascent new Iraqi state were not strong enough to impose this post-war settlement on the country. The civil war it triggered was a struggle between those seeking to impose a Victor's Peace and those fighting for a Loser's Peace. By 2005, this conflict allowed al Qaeda in Mesopotamia to dominate. Ironically, in 2003 when Iraq was placed on the front line of George W. Bush's global war against terrorism, al Qaeda had no presence within government-controlled Iraq. Al Qaeda in Mesopotamia, still a powerful force in Iraq today, was a creation of US foreign policy mistakes. On the other side of the civil war, those fighting for a Victor's Peace deployed the coercive capacity of the Ministry of Interior and the other government ministries they controlled, to launch a campaign aimed at driving Sunni residents of Baghdad from the city. This was religious cleansing on an industrial scale.

Faced with almost certain defeat and the collapse of Iraq into civil war, the Bush Administration announced a dramatic change in policy on 10 January 2007.[23] The application of counter-insurgency doctrine in Iraq saw an increase in US troop numbers and their aggressive deployment amongst the Iraqi population. According to statistics collated by the Brookings Institution's *Iraq Index*, 3,500 Iraqi civilians were murdered in January 2007, the month before the surge began. This figure dropped to 2,700 in February and continued to steadily decline to monthly figures of below 300 civilians killed from September 2009 until September 2010 (O'Hanlon and Livingston 2010: 4). Statistically, Iraq remains within the midst of a civil war, albeit a much less bloody one than in 2006. The issue is whether the Iraqi government can continue to reduce the levels of violence across the country. Governmentally and coercively the Iraqi state has increased its capacity and driven its institutions into society. The state has again become a presence, albeit a weak one, in the majority of Iraqi's lives. However, the exclusive elite bargain that did so much to drive Iraq into civil war remains in place. The results of the 2010 national elections show that the Sunni population of Iraq were very effectively mobilized by Iyad Allawi's Iraqiyya coalition (International Institute for Strategic Studies 2010). However, this potent vote against the exclusive elite bargain that has dominates Iraqi politics threatens the 'powers that be' that have ruled Iraq since 2003.[24] A complete end to Iraq's civil war can only be guaranteed once the Victor's Peace imposed on the country in the aftermath of invasion is renegotiated to tie the majority of Iraq's population to the state.

Notes

1 See 'The Toll of War' (no date) NPR.org. Online, available at: www.npr.org/news/specials/tollofwar/tollofwarmain.html, accessed 6 October 2010.
2 See Iraq Body Count (2005) *A Dossier of Civilian Casualties, 2003–2005*, 15 July. Online, available at: www.iraqbodycount.org/analysis/reference/pdf/a_dossier_of_civilian_casualties_2003–2005.pdf, accessed 6 October 2010.
3 See the transcript of the secretary of defence's interview with Bob Woodward on 23 October 2003. Online, available at: www.globalsecurity.org/military/library/news/2004/04/mil-040419-dod02.htm, accessed 6 October 2010.
4 See for example, Neil MacFarquar (1996) 'Crime engulfs Iraq', *International Herald Tribune*, 21 October.
5 For a short account of this argument see Leslie H. Gelb (2004) 'Divide Iraq into three states', *International Herald Tribune*, 26 November.
6 See Joseph Biden and Leslie Gelb, 'Unity through autonomy in Iraq' (2006) *New York Times*, 1 May, and Gelb, 'Divide Iraq into three states'.
7 See Reidar Visser (2009) 'Biden, US policy in Iraq and the concept of Muhasasa', 6 July. Online, available at: www.historiae.org, accessed 7 October 2010; and Reidar Visser (2009) 'The second Biden mission to Iraq', 17 September. Online, available at: http://gulfanalysis.wordpress.com/2009/09/17/the-second-biden-mission-to-iraq/, accessed 7 October, 2010.
8 See also Reidar Visser (2006) 'Centralism and unitary state logic in Iraq from Midhat Pasha to Jawad al-Maliki: A continuous trend?', 22 April. Online, available at: http://historiae.org accessed 7 October 2010.
9 For Iraq's provincial elections results see, the Iraqi High Electoral Council (no date). Online, available at: www.ihec.iq/content/file/Election_results/IHEC_Preliminary%20Results_Governorate%20Council%20Elections_2009_EN.pdf, accessed 5 March 2009.
10 See BBC News (2003) 'The Iraqi Governing Council', 14 July. Online, available at: http://news.bbc.co.uk/1/hi/world/middle_east/3062897.stm, accessed 8 October 2010.
11 Mark Turner (2004) 'Poll planning on track but no room for hitches', *Financial Times*, 14 October.
12 Edward Wong (2004) 'Sunni Party leaves Iraqi government over Falluja attack', *New York Times*, 10 November.
13 For electoral data, see also Independent Electoral Commission of Iraq (no date). Online, available at: www.ieciraq.org/English/Frameset_english.htm.

14 See Dexter Filkins (2004) 'Memo urges Qaeda to wage war in Iraq', *International Herald Tribune*, 10 February.
15 See also the interview with Matthew Sherman, deputy senior adviser to Iraq's Ministry of Interior from December 2003 to January 2006, conducted on 4 October 2006,. Online, available at: www.pbs.org/wgbh/pages/frontline/gangsofiraq/interviews/sherman.html, accessed 12 October 2010.
16 See Dexter Filkins (2006) 'Armed groups propel Iraq toward chaos', *New York Times*, 24 May; and Andrew Buncombe and Patrick Cockburn (2006) 'Iraq's death squads', *Independent on Sunday*, 26 February.
17 See for example Hannah Allam (2005) 'Wolf Brigade the most loved and feared of Iraqi security forces', *Knight Ridder Newspapers*, 21 May; and Sabrina Tavernise, Qais Mizher, Omar al-Naemi and Sahar Nageeb (2006) 'Alarmed by raids, neighbors stand guard in Iraq', *New York Times*, 10 May.
18 See also *Associated Press* (2005) 'Iraq inquiry says detainees appear to have been tortured', *New York Times*, 15 November.
19 See interview with Matthew Sherman.
20 James Danley quoted in 'Secret Iraq' (2010) Part 2, BBC 2, 6 October. Online, available at: www.bbc.co.uk/iplayer/episode/b00v8t2t/Secret_Iraq_Awakening/, accessed 12 October 2010.
21 Patrick J. McDonnell (2006) 'Following a death trail to Sadr City: US forces think the kidnap-and-kill forays haunting Iraq originate in the insular Shiite stronghold of Baghdad', *Los Angeles Times*, 24 October.
22 See Iraq Body Count (no date). Online, available at: www.iraqbodycount.org/, accessed on 13 October 2010.
23 See George W. Bush (2007) 'President's address to the nation', 10 January. Online, available at: http://georgewbush-whitehouse.archives.gov/news/releases/2007/01/20070110–7.html.
24 See 'The powers that be', anonymous guest post. Online, available at: http://abuaardvark.typepad.com/abuaardvark/2008/06/guest-post-the.html, accessed 13 October 2010.

Bibliography

Al-Jezairy, Zuhair (2009) *The Devil you Don't Know; Going Back to Iraq*, London: Saqi.
Amnesty International (2006) 'Beyond Abu Ghraib: detention and torture in Iraq', March.
Bremer, L. Paul III with Malcolm McConnell (2006) *My Year in Iraq: The Struggle to Build a Future of Hope*, New York: Simon & Schuster.
Burton, Michael, Richard Gunther and John Higley (1992) 'Introduction', in John Higley and Richard Gunther (eds), *Elites and Democratic Consolidation in Latin America and Southern Europe*, Cambridge: Cambridge University Press.
Chandrasekaran, Rajiv (2007) *Imperial Life in the Emerald City: Inside Baghdad's Green Zone*, London: Bloomsbury.
Chesterman, Simon (2004) *You, the People: The United Nations, Transitional Administration, and State-Building*, Oxford: Oxford University Press.
Cockburn, Patrick (2008) *Muqtada al Sadr and the Fall of Iraq*, London: Faber & Faber.
Cole, Juan (2006) 'Civil war? What civil war? Desperate to convince voters we're winning, Bush is denying that Iraq is having a civil war. But the facts contradict him', *Salon*, 23 March.
Dawisha, Adeed and Larry Diamond (2006) 'Iraq's year of voting dangerously', *Journal of Democracy*, 17(2), April.

Diamond, Larry (2005) *Squandered Victory: The American Occupation and the Bungled Effort to Bring Democracy to Iraq*, New York: Times Books.

Diamond, Larry (2006) 'What civil war looks like: slide rules', *New Republic*, 13 March.

Dobbins, James, Seth G. Jones, Benjamin Runkle, Siddharth Mohandas (2009) *Occupying Iraq: A History of the Coalition Provisional Authority*, Santa Monica: RAND Corporation.

Dobbins, James, John G. McGinn, Keith Crane, Seth G. Jones, Rollie Lal, Andrew Rathmell, Rachel M. Swanger, Anga R. Timilsina (2003) *America's Role in Nation-Building: From Germany to Iraq*, Santa Monica: RAND Corporation.

Dodge, Toby (2005) *Iraq's Future: The Aftermath of Regime Change*, Adelphi Paper 372, London: International Institute for Strategic Studies and Routledge.

Dodge, Toby (2007a) 'The causes of US failure in Iraq', *Survival* 49(1), Spring.

Dodge, Toby (2007b) 'State collapse and the rise of identity politics', in Markus E. Bouillon, David M. Malone and Ben Rowsell (eds), *Preventing Another Generation of Conflict*, Boulder: Lynne Rienner Publishers.

Dodge, Toby (2009) 'Iraq's new ruling elite', *Soundings*, 41, March.

Dodge, Toby (2010) 'The ideological roots of failure; the application of kinetic Neo-Liberalism to Iraq', *International Affairs*, 86: 6.

Fearon, James D. and David D. Laitin (2003) 'Ethnicity, insurgency and civil war', *American Political Science Review*, 97(1), February.

Galbraith, Peter W. (2004) 'How to get out of Iraq', *New York Review of Books*, 13 May.

Galbraith, Peter W. (2006) *The End of Iraq: How American Incompetence Created a War Without End*, New York: Simon & Schuster.

Gordon, Michael and Bernard Trainor (2006) *Cobra II: The Inside Story of the Invasion and Occupation of Iraq*, London: Atlantic Books.

Henderson, Errol A. and J. David Singer (2000) 'Civil war in the post colonial world, 1946–92', *Journal of Peace Research* 37(3), May.

Higley, John and Richard Gunther (1992) 'Preface', in Higley and Gunther (eds), *Elites and Democratic Consolidation in Latin America and Southern Europe*, Cambridge: Cambridge University Press.

International Crisis Group (2006) 'In their own words: reading the Iraqi insurgency', *Middle East Report*, 50, 15 February.

International Institute for Strategic Studies (2010) 'Mistrust prevents formation of Iraqi government', *Strategic Comment*, 32(16), October.

Kaviraj, Sudipta (1994) 'On the construction of colonial power, structure, discourse, hegemony', in Dagmar Engles and Shula Marxs (eds), *Contesting Colonial Hegemony: State and Society in Africa and India*, London: British Academic Press.

Kilcullen, David (2009) *The Accidental Guerrilla: Fighting Small Wars in the Midst of a Big One*, London: Hurst & Co.

Laitin, David (1998) *The Russian-Speaking Populations in the Near Abroad* Ithaca: Cornell University Press.

Lindemann, Stefan (2008) 'Do inclusive elite bargains matter? A research framework for understanding the causes of civil war in Sub-Saharan Africa', Crisis States Discussion Paper 15, Crisis States Research Centre, LSE, February.

Marr, Phebe (2007) 'Iraq's identity crisis', in Markus E. Bouillon, David M. Malone and Ben Rowsell (eds), *Preventing another Generation of Conflict*, Boulder: Lynne Rienner Publishers.

Meijer, Roel (2007) 'The Sunni resistance and the "political process"', in Markus E. Bouillon, David M. Malone and Ben Rowsell (eds), *Preventing another Generation of Conflict*, Boulder: Lynne Rienner Publishers.

Morrow, Jonathan (2005) 'Iraq's constitutional process II. An opportunity lost', United States Institute of Peace, Special Report 155, November.

O'Hanlon, Michael E. and Ian Livingston (2010) *Iraq Index*, 30 September. Online, available at: www.brookings.edu/~/media/Files/Centers/Saban/Iraq%20 Index/index.pdf.

Posner, Daniel N. (2004) 'Civil society and the reconstruction of failed states', in Robert I. Rotberg (ed.), *When States Fail, Causes and Consequences*, Princeton: Princeton University Press.

Ricks, Thomas E. (2009) *The Gamble: General Petraeus and the Untold Story of the American Surge in Iraq, 2006–2008*, London: Penguin.

Rothchild, Joseph (1981) *Ethnopoltics: A Conceptual Framework*, New York: Columbia University Press.

Sambanis, Nicholas (2004) 'What is civil war? Conceptual and empirical complexities of an operational definition', *Journal of Conflict Resolution* 48(6), December.

Sherman, Matt and Roger D. Carstens (2008) *Independent Task Force on Progress and Reform*, Institute for the Theory and Practice of International Relations, College of William and Mary, 14 November.

Suhrke, Astri (2011) 'Introduction', in Mats Berdal and Astri Suhrke (eds), *The Peace In Between: Violence in Post-War States*, Routledge.

Talentino, Andrea Kathryn (2004) 'The two faces of nation-building: Developing function and identity', *Cambridge Review of International Affairs*, 17(3), October.

Whaites, Alan (2008) *States in Development: Understanding State-Building*, DFID Working Paper, Governance and Social Development Group Policy and Research Division. Online, available at: www.dfid.gov.uk/Documents/publications/State-in-Development-Wkg-Paper.pdf.

Wimmer, Andreas (2003) 'Democracy and ethno-religious conflict in Iraq', *Survival*, 45(4), Winter.

Woodward, Bob (2006) *State of Denial*, New York: Simon & Schuster.

Part III

Asia

8   Armed politics in Afghanistan

Antonio Giustozzi

Introduction

The post-conflict transition in Afghanistan is incomplete in more ways than one. Not only has open warfare resurfaced in large parts of the country and is spreading (Giustozzi 2007a) but even where this is not the case the legacy of past wars continues to have a strong impact on several aspects of recovery and reconstruction. The introduction of a political system based on electoral competition is one of the areas where this legacy is felt, due to the continuing presence and influence of non-state armed groups. Such groups intervene in the political process to varying degrees, but their influence is always felt. Inevitably, in the absence of a central monopoly of armed force political competition becomes distorted. Neither the effort to disarm official militias (disarmament, demobilization and reintegration, DDR) nor programmes aimed at disarming unofficial ones (disarmament of illegal armed groups, DIAG) have come even remotely close to resolving the problem (Giustozzi 2006). The introduction of legislation to prevent candidates with links to armed groups from standing for election in 2004–5 only succeeded in forcing about 32 of them to step down, leaving the large majority undeterred (AIHRC–UNAMA 2005b).

This chapter analyses the role of different non-state armed groups in post-2001 Afghan politics and traces their evolution. It starts by developing a concept of 'armed politics' and by identifying 'ideal types' of particular models of armed politics. It then identifies different actors in armed politics, that is, those who, unlike the insurgents, operate within the legal framework of the post-2001 order. After examining the techniques of armed politics used in Afghanistan, the chapter analyses each of these models to establish their use, impact and evolution in the Afghan context. The chapter concludes with a discussion of the prospects of armed politics in Afghanistan.

The non-state armed groups discussed here have their origins in the 1980s jihad against the leftist government and the Soviet army, although some of them fought on the government side as militias. The initial mujahedin were a mixed bag of Islamist, nationalist and Maoist activists, clerics and their supporters, tribal and community leaders with their followers, and outlaws. However, as the war continued the different social origins of the fighters gradually ceased to matter, leading to the emergence of a military class of 'specialists in violence', in Ernst Gellner's words (1995). The process of formation of a military class was not uniform throughout Afghanistan, but after 2001 the remaining non-state armed groups could largely be said to belong to this military class. Political activists were by 2001 a virtually extinct force in terms of their involvement in armed groups, as the original generation of leftists and Islamists alike had been killed during the war. Clerical activism would soon resurface in the shape of the neo-Taliban insurgency, which will not be covered in this chapter. Some communities rearmed after 2001, particularly in areas affected by the insurgency, but their interests were largely local and they did not play a significant role in terms of armed politics as defined here.

Models and actors of armed political competition

Although the term 'armed politics' is used in a variety of ways, including to indicate the intervention of state armies in politics (Keith and Hayes 1976) or political insurgencies tout court (Adejuombi 2004) I use it here to describe the distortion caused by the presence of non-state armed groups on the competitiveness of an otherwise open political system (Neumann 2005) More specifically, I will look at the influence of non-state armed groups over electoral contests and at the competition among those same groups to capture important state offices. The definition of 'armed politics' does not imply that armed force is necessarily physically used to achieve political aims; the simple possession of armed force by private actors and the threat to use it are sufficient to change fundamentally the dynamics of any political system.

Several 'ideal types' of armed politics can be constructed:

- *Self-defensive:* characterized by its reactive character and by the merely local use of violence or threat thereof. In a situation of broken or non-existent state monopoly of violence, or wherever armed state agencies are perceived to be factionally biased and hostile to specific groups, political actors and communities may organize armed militias at least initially for the purpose of defending themselves. This was, for example, the case with several leftist organizations in Europe in the 1920s and 1930s. Often, these armed militias might end up contributing to the general climate of insecurity and threat and push yet other actors to arm.
- *Conservative:* militias are used to establish or consolidate the territorial control and influence of leaders or groups and as a resource to mobilize support by force or prevent other political actors from operating within such an area of influence. It largely occurs at a regional rather than national level. One typical example is that of Latin American 'caudillismo'.
- *Expansionist:* armed politics aimed at expanding the influence of a particular group or individual and/or conveying a particular image. It often means reducing the operating space of competing groups and

its arena tends to be a large region or the whole country. Classical examples include Maoism, which in the early stages of its strategy uses armed force sparingly to achieve psychological gains, and fascism, where the emphasis is on the psychological impact of a display of discipline and strength as a demonstration of the resolution of the group to address core issues of concern among its base of supporters. Expansionism can be driven by personal ambition, ideology or the presence of attractive opportunities. This type of armed activity is different from revolutionary violence in that it does not aim to subvert the state directly, although subversion can remain the ultimate aim of a movement.

These models of armed politics can be matched to a number of different political actors on the Afghan scene. Although initially UN officials were reluctant to discuss the existence of non-state armed groups apart from those engaged in open insurgency, by 2004 both they and the Afghan authorities were openly recognizing this as a major problem. The launch of the DIAG programme was meant to address the problem, but in the end the main contribution of the programme was to map the presence of these groups on the territory and even that not very successfully. At its peak in late 2006, the DIAG database included 5,557 illegal armed groups, including 1,334 already disbanded, and hundreds of thousands of members (Islamic Republic of Afghanistan 2006: 7). Even the most conservative estimate of the number of members of these groups meant in practice the presence of a non-state militiaman for every 140 inhabitants. In addition, there were legal or tolerated irregular formations, such as 63,000 members[1] of the official militias (AMF or Afghan Military Force), gradually disbanded during 2004–5 but possibly in part at least driven underground; 20,000 and rising private security guards, many linked to active politicians; *arbakai* tribal defence groups in the southeast (Giustozzi 2007a, 2007b), a few thousand governor's militiamen and a few thousand members of anti-Taliban militias operating in southern, southeastern and eastern Afghanistan. These irregular formations in turn can be grouped into three 'ideal types':

- *Local communities:* led by elders and other men of influence, they tend to have strictly limited and local aims and interests. Since communities typically include dissident elements and personal rivalries, the elders might want to enforce unanimous compliance, including in political/electoral matters. As noted above, however, in post-2001 Afghanistan local communities played a very small role in armed politics and will therefore not be dealt with here.
- *Strongmen:* autonomous charismatic leaders, initially arising from a local/regional power base, who derive their influence at least partly from some form of legitimization (tribal, kin, provision of patronage and security, mediatory/regulatory role) and from the control of an armed force. In the Afghan context, several strongmen started their careers as religious leaders, but religion played little role in their legit-

imization after the end of the jihad in the early 1990s. In 'ideal' terms, their primary interest as strongmen is to consolidate their influence and prevent challenges. I use the category here to include various types of actor, including 'warlords' (Giustozzi 2009), as for the purposes of this chapter it is not essential to distinguish between them.

* *Parties*: these can be either alliances or hierarchical organizations that are not heavily dependent on a single charismatic leader but have comparatively complex leadership arrangements. In other words, they are at least relatively institutionalized. Their interests are less local than those of strongmen; parties aim to spread their influence as widely as possible or claim a monopoly over a relatively large area.

The relevance of these ideal types for an analysis of post-2001 Afghanistan derives from the fact that not all actors were equally ready to be integrated into the new political system or equally inclined to use armed politics to enhance their position. Another term requiring clarification is 'commanders'. As used here, it denotes members of politico-military organizations with a leadership role. The key difference from the strongmen is that the commanders are not autonomous but belong to a structure with at least an implicit hierarchy.

Techniques of armed politics

The most common form of armed politics in Afghanistan during 2001–7 was latent, i.e. it relied mainly on the power of deterrence and on the universal knowledge that reprisal would follow to any challenge from outsider individuals and groups. Deterrence was usually helped by a good dose of 'soft' intimidation, including through personal visits or anonymous telephone calls, where no violence was used but the possibility of 'incidents' was hinted. Even during the sessions of the Loya Jirgas this type of intimidation was reported.[2] All the protagonists of armed politics in Afghanistan had an established track record of ruthlessness and resilience. This might not contribute towards making them popular but certainly advertised the danger of challenging them in the absence of strong protection from either alternative non-state armed groups or state security agencies. The diffuse presence of factionally aligned armed groups and the unreliability of the police must inevitably have weighed heavily on any political player unable to enlist the support of armed groups (Human Rights Watch 2005). Their interests were taken into account even by the UN body in charge of organizing the elections (JEMB, Joint Electoral Management Board), which often appointed complacent officials to run elections in the more problematic districts. The most blatant example of abuse in this regard concerned the powerful leader of a minor armed faction, Dawat-i Islami (formerly Ittehad-i Islami).[3] Despite the discovery of a massive rigging effort in his home district of Paghman, Abdul Rasul Sayyaf was allowed to enter parliament, although with a much reduced vote.[4]

It should be added that some of these armed groups were officially recognized, which enhanced their influence and status, like the governors' militias, or unofficially tolerated, like the southern anti-Taliban militias. According to Afghan law, governors are allowed to form a personal militia of up to 500 members for protection. In practice, autonomous militias abounded, particularly in southern Afghanistan and when the leaders were personally close to President Karzai and his family. Dismissed officials, like former Uruzgan chief of police Matiullah and former Helmand governor Sher Mohammed, continued to employ militias of several hundred men. These official or tolerated armed groups probably influenced the electoral process more heavily than others, particularly after the first Loya Jirga (2002) when most other armed groups were unable to display their weapons in public. For instance, Sher Mohammad's brother was a candidate in the 2005 parliamentary elections and although he was disqualified at the last minute for having links to armed groups, he did obtain a large number of votes.[5] There is no direct evidence that these militias were engaged in the electoral campaign, but their existence clearly was not conducive to a 'free and fair' environment.

The next most common form of armed politics in Afghanistan is *state infiltration/capture*. This can occur through non-armed means, and also when politicians in mufti use the police or armed forces to strengthen their electoral ambitions. In theory, state capture would mean a reversal of processes of institutionalization and bureaucratization, leading to non-partisan structures of the state becoming factionally aligned. In the Afghan case, the abstraction of the state from factional conflict was never far advanced in the first place. We are therefore talking in practice about groups/factions taking control of chunks of the state with at least the initial consent of the coalition in control of the centre. Such capture is often motivated by the pursuit of personal gain as well as by the promotion of the interests of a specific political group.[6] The infiltration and occupation of the structures of the state by non-state armed groups and political factions affected most institutions of the Afghan state, from the ministerial down to the district level. I will here discuss state capture by armed groups that directly affects electoral politics and the functioning of the political system. The following institutions are relevant for this analysis:

- police;
- National Security Directorate (NSD);
- sub-national administrations, particularly provincial governors.

At the provincial level in late 2001/early 2002, police forces were largely taken over by the dominant faction, group, strongman or coalition thereof and staffed with their followers. The predominance of private interests in the police force was perceived as a problem by at least some sections of the government and the international coalition supporting it (Giustozzi 2011 forthcoming).

Factional control over the NSD was never seriously challenged and by 2005 it remained the stronghold of an Islamist faction, Jamiat-i Islami, both at the centre and in most provinces. The main exception was much of northern Afghanistan, where the NSD was under the control of the primarily Uzbek Junbesh party, led by the powerful strongman General Dostum, although by 2004 there were signs that Junbesh's control over provincial NSD units was eroding, with some officials refusing to follow the directives of Junbesh leaders.[7] At least one case of NSD involvement in the electoral process occurred during the 2003–4 Constitutional Loya Jirga elections, when the police and NSD tolerated a plot orchestrated by some jihadi groups to oust Baghlan candidate Sayyid Mansur Naderi. Unauthorized individuals were allowed into the election site and reportedly put pressure on the grand electors[8] to support specific candidates; NSD agents were also present inside the site, contravening the regulations, and did not intervene. In addition, harassment of political opponents was reportedly carried out by NSD on behalf of powerful political groups, including Shura-i Nezar,[9] Junbesh and Dawat-i Islami. As long as Shura-i Nezar and Karzai were allied, the NSD served the purposes of the president too, for example by putting pressure on delegates to the Constitutional Loya Jirga to agree on Karzai's draft (Human Rights Watch 2002).

Often, the police and NSD were guilty of failing to protect potential victims against threats rather than of active harassment or repression on behalf of their local patrons. The knowledge that the security agencies were aligned with certain political players is likely to have contributed to discouraging electoral competition, particularly in its most aggressive forms. Several governors were also reported to be involved in intimidation and threats through their militias, including Sher Alam and Asadullah Khalid of Ghazni province (Human Rights Watch 2005).

Armed politics 'in being' of course tends to offer diminishing returns over time unless it is actually used, at least occasionally. Potential challengers need to be periodically reminded that the threat still stands. In Afghanistan, apart from conflicts among armed strongmen and factions, which steadily declined after 2003, direct challenges to local/regional monopolies over political activity emerged periodically and were mostly met by '*controlled violence*'. This typically consisted of instances of beatings and harassment, which were reported during the presidential and parliamentary elections particularly but not only in northern Afghanistan. The main targets were reluctant notables and party activists trying to establish a foothold in the fiefdom of some militia (Human Rights Watch 2005; AIHRC–UNAMA 2005a, 2005b). More extreme forms of violence such as the *assassination* of candidates, delegates and MPs took place in a number of cases in Badakhshan, Ghor, Laghman and Balkh. Usually, local strongmen and militias were accused of their deaths.[10]

Violence on a larger scale and prevarication also occurred, although it was not the norm. During the initial years of the post-Taliban transition the hold of non-state armed actors was still precarious, mainly due to the need to assess the intentions of international players, now present on the Afghan scene with relatively large military contingents and the much feared US Air Force.[11] During 2002–3 non-state armed actors needed to show to an uncertain public that they meant business and that international intervention was neither diminishing their resolve nor should it be taken as implying open political competition everywhere. By the end of 2003 and even more so by the end of the summer 2004, their bluff had been called, following a series of incidents in which they opted to back down from confrontation with Kabul and its international patrons. From 2004 onwards, the large-scale display of armed force and violence was mainly the preserve of actors who were being marginalized from state power and patronage. They needed to show that they still had the potential to destabilize large regions of the country and had to be incorporated into the ruling alliance. On the whole, the most blatant forms of armed politics in action used after 2001 can be summed up within three categories:

- armed rioting;
- blockading;
- direct seizure of the electoral process in specific localities/regions.

During 2002–3 armed politics was practised quite aggressively and assertively in trying to establish a monopoly of political representation over specific areas. During the first phase of the Emergency Loya Jirga elections of 2002, for example, northern Afghanistan witnessed the *blockading* of specific areas with the aim of keeping 'hostile' candidates out of the competition or of preventing voting in some communities known to be hostile (Noelle-Karimi 2002).

Seizures of the electoral process mostly occurred during the first Loya Jirga (2002) and took different forms. Sometimes the tactics used would consist in seizing control of the whole selection process and pre-selecting the candidates. At other times militiamen would be present in the polling station to intimidate the electors (Noelle-Karimi 2002). After 2002 such tactics became difficult to implement on a large scale, due to increased international scrutiny. During the elections to the Constitutional Loya Jirga of 2003–4, no seizure of the first phase of the process (local selections) was reported. During the second phase at least one incident occurred. Up to 200 individuals external to the selection process managed to storm the polling station in Kunduz to protest against the candidacy of Sayyid Mansur Naderi, who had been pre-selected, eventually forcing him to withdraw.[12]

As outright military confrontation came to be seen as an unacceptable challenge to the occupation and peacekeeping foreign forces deployed in Afghanistan, non-state armed actors used their supporters to create 'popular revolts', which were aimed at legitimizing their demands and embarrassing the government and its foreign sponsors. In 2004, large *riots* organized by the militias occurred in Maimana and Sar-i Pul, in both cases succeeding in dislodging administrators appointed by Kabul. In Herat (also 2004), the aim was to prevent the removal of Ismail Khan from the position of governor. The riots did not succeed, although Ismail Khan was later appointed minister to compensate for the loss of the governorship. In 2005, demonstrations against the provincial governor at least in part organized by non-state armed actors took place in Baghlan, again with success.[13] There seems to be sufficient evidence that actors of the same kind were involved in the Kabul riots of June 2006.[14] Their involvement may also have occurred in a number of riots in eastern and southeastern Afghanistan in 2005 and 2006, of which the Jalalabad riots of May 2005 were the largest, but this is not proven.

The last form of armed politics to be reviewed is *armed propaganda*. In post-2001 Afghanistan, the only significant manifestation of this has been the effort of Hizb-i Islami to mount a symbolic insurgency, mainly in eastern Afghanistan. As of early 2007, tens of small armed groups, mostly number-ing 3–15 men, were involved in small-scale military activity. On the basis of the analysis of their military operations and of the fact that the party cer-tainly did not lack experience on how to mount an effective insurgency, I argue that the leadership of the party deliberately kept insurgent activities 'soft'. In the light of later developments, which saw Hizb-i Islami escalate its activities, this might have been a typical expansionist tactic, as discussed above. Armed activity and violence were meant to convey an image of strong opposition to the presence of foreign troops, against whom most attacks were targeted. The Afghan police and army were mostly spared or at least not actively targeted.[15] These military activities seem to have been meant to work in tandem with a 'political front' and attract the support of (expand-ing) sections of the population who resented the foreign presence in the country. The task of the political front was to capitalize on the image of opposition to the foreign presence in the country, which armed resistance created or reinforced, and turn that positive image into political gains (see *Ideologies, parties and expansionist armed politics* above). The creation of polit-ical fronts is far from unusual among insurgent groups, but what qualifies Hizb-i Islami's insurgency as 'armed propaganda' is the fact that its purpose at the stage described here was not to conquer control of the state directly, but to create an image of strength and resolution.

In terms of the ideal types proposed at the beginning of the chapter, it might be worth comparing this to the violent tactics used by fascist move-ments in 1920s–30s Europe: violence was used on a limited scale to weaken opponents seriously; its real purpose was to mobilize specific sections of the population around a leadership and conquer power through 'legal' means. The difference is that fascist movements mainly relied on a display of military discipline to achieve their aim, an aspect absent in Hizb-i Islami. A strictly 'fascist' style of armed propaganda never had much cur-rency in Afghanistan, despite long years of war and the rising issue of eth-nicity and ethno-nationalism. The weakness of the state and of its ability to indoctrinate and train, as well as the fact that the Afghan jihad was never about large battles, and therefore did not require much discipline, are probably the key factors in explaining why the specific fascist model of armed propaganda, with its stress on discipline and *esprit de corps*, never made it very far. Despite some influence from Turkish far-right groups among Uzbeks after 2001, not even the most radical wing of Junbesh – its youth movement – flirted with demonstration styles and tactics which remotely resembled the fascist model. Even the most successful of Junbesh's street demonstrations, when in Maimana (2004) they succeeded in dislodging an unwanted governor and the commander of the local 200th Division of the Ministry of Defence, bore a stronger resemblance to riots than displays of discipline and efficiency.[16]

Conservative armed politics or 'caudillism' in Afghanistan

Armed politics in post-2001 Afghanistan has had a predominantly conservative character. Until 2001, Afghanistan's 'caudillos', the strongmen, had mostly been playing feudal politics (i.e. using their regional influence to bargain with factional leaders and form alliances on as favourable terms as possible). The strongmen should not simply be confused with the so-called 'commanders' (*kumandanan*), as the strongmen have an autonomous power base and are virtually independent, even when they maintain some formal affiliation with a faction. In a sense they could be described as the top tier of the 'commanders'. The power of the strongmen had been rising throughout the 1980s and 1990s as the Afghan state grew weaker and became unable to exercise direct control over the countryside. At the same time, opposition political organizations based abroad were in most cases too weak and too keen to expand their influence in the easiest and fastest possible way even to try to exercise effective control over their affiliates inside Afghanistan. The only interruption to the power of the strongmen was the emergence and consolidation of the Taliban movement in 1994–2001, which almost eliminated the strongmen from the scene. By the end of 2001, however, the strongmen were re-emerging fast, filling the vacuum left in much of the countryside by the collapse of the Taliban regime (Giustozzi 2003). I will here distinguish between *independent strongmen*, who rely on a personal following without significant organized support, and *factional strongmen*, who were part of, or leaders of, organizations and could rely on their support in exchange for protecting organizational interests.

After 2001, the independent strongmen increasingly adopted four survival strategies in order to adapt to the post-conflict environment. The first was a modified version of the old 'feudal politics' of the 1980s and 1990s, whereby the strongmen tried to strike alliances with individuals and factions in power in Kabul in order to secure their regional influence and possibly gain a foothold in the capital as well (Giustozzi 2004). The alternative strategy was to enter electoral politics, either directly or indirectly supporting allies and relatives. The two strategies were not mutually exclusive, although inevitably the weaker the link with Kabul, the stronger the temptation to seek alternative sources of legitimation and influence through elections (Giustozzi 2008). The third option was to seek employment by the state in high status positions, and the fourth to enter money-making activities such as business and crime (Giustozzi 2007c). The slim chances of making it into parliament were a factor in the decision of many to stay away from politics. The 'withdrawal from politics' option was mainly the choice of the smaller strongmen, who usually controlled not much more (and often significantly less) than a single district. Lack of resources might have been another factor for the poorer strongmen, as the electoral campaign was widely expected to be expensive. Finally, a few strongmen were banned from competing in electoral politics because of allegations of maintaining armed militias, or opted to stay out fearing that they would otherwise attract unwarranted attention to their 'underground' activities. Badly connected strongmen were particularly ill positioned for an entry into electoral politics: since all strongmen maintained underground militias, being singled out for exclusion was likely to be a political choice made in Kabul. In what follows, I shall deal exclusively with the electoral strategy.

The first manifestation of the strongmen's involvement in competitive politics was during the 2002 Emergency Loya Jirga elections. These were indirect elections, in which 30,000 grand electors were to be selected by the different districts and in turn would elect 500 delegates to the Loya Jirga. Several independent strongmen were prepared to run, but were initially prevented from doing so by UN-sponsored regulations that banned leaders of armed groups from the contest. As the selection process proceeded, however, this principled stand was abandoned and the strongmen were allowed to compete.[17] In the following Constitutional Loya Jirga elections of 2003, which used a similar selection system, the strongmen were allowed to participate from the beginning. Finally, in the parliamentary elections of 2005 the independent strongmen also did well and several of them were elected as MPs, although a few were prevented from running because of links to armed groups. In many cases, they ranked at the top in terms of votes at the provincial level (see Table 8.1). The strongmen's involvement in politics did not end with their national electoral campaigns, as others ran for election in the provincial councils.

All these strongmen were staking a claim to local/provincial leadership and to represent local, tribal, ethnic or regional interests. Apart from benefiting from the support of armed militias, they also invested sizeable resources in running a strong campaign, legitimizing their claims and consolidating their status as strongmen.[18] Winning was in a sense a requirement for justifying their claim to provincial leadership. To what extent did they rely on armed politics to secure election to representative bodies? Particularly after the two Loya Jirga elections, i.e. after 2003, there is only limited evidence that most of them used armed followers to intimidate voters and threaten alternative candidates (AIHRC–UNAMA 2005a and 2005b). The parliamentary electoral system, based on provincial constituencies, and an election system (single non-transferable vote) that encouraged extreme electoral fragmentation contributed to making threats to other candidates redundant: in some cases it was possible to become the best supported candidate at the provincial level with only just over 3 per cent of the votes. Most of the strongmen also had access to substantial financial resources, thereby enjoying a key advantage over most other candidates. The sources of financial strength varied – ability to tax sections of population, involvement in smuggling and trafficking of various sorts, proximity to foreign powers, support from sections of the trading class, land and property grabbing and exploitation of state resources through alliances with local authorities (Giustozzi 2007c). As a result, violent incidents and abuses occurred only on a small scale and armed force was rarely displayed, contrary to what had happened

Table 8.1 How well the independent strongmen did in the elections

	Province	Percentage obtained	Provincial ranking
Ahmad Khan	Samangan	23.9	1
Piram Qul	Takhar	6.2	1
Hazrat Ali	Nangarhar	3.4	1
Padsha Khan	Paktya	4.7	3
Alam Khan Azadi	Balkh	5.4	2
Fataullah	Faryab	5.3	2
Dr Ibrahim	Ghor	11.2	1
Amir Lalai	Kandahar	5.0	5
Haji Abdur Raouf	Kunduz	3.8	2
Ismatullah Mohabat	Laghman	7.3	3
Payenda Mohammad Khan	Sar-i Pul	8.8	2

Source: JEMB electoral results.

during the 2002 and 2003 Loya Jirga selection processes. Some presence of militiamen was reported in parts of Parwan province, Ghor and Kunar, while threats and physical attacks occurred at least in Dai Kundi, Herat, Ghor and parts of Nangarhar.[19] As mentioned in *Techniques of armed politics* above, the main contribution of armed politics in securing elected positions for the strongmen came from the climate of fear which they had successfully established in their respective areas between 2001 and 2005. This combined with other factors, such as patronage and protection against local rivals, to deliver electoral success. Some of the strongmen might have benefited from a falsification of the electoral process. This was alleged, for example, in the case of Piram Qul in Takhar province, although it was never proven.[20]

Fraud cases apart, the votes received by the strongmen seem mostly to have been real enough. As well as the implicit threat of violence and financial strength, their electoral success was probably the result of their ability to provide a modicum of security in the absence of strong state institutions, similarly to what had been the case with the Latin American caudillos. The provision of security to specific sections of the population was more pronounced in some cases, such as those of Ahmad Khan and Hazrat Ali (see Table 8.1), who during the 1990s had built strong constituencies among respectively the Uzbeks of Samangan and the Pashais of Dara-I Noor. Moreover, several strongmen tried to improve their political standing and legitimize themselves by sponsoring popular causes. Ethnic and tribal causes were the most common choices. Ahmad Khan, for example, openly sympathized with the cause of Uzbek ethnic rights and was linked to General Dostum's Junbesh-i Milli Islami from its early days until 2006. To a lesser extent, Payenda Mohammad Khan (an Arab from Sar-i Pul) and Haji Abdur Raouf (an Uzbek from Imam Sahib) did the same and were also involved with Junbesh, although the latter only superficially. Both maintained a high degree of autonomy in their relationship with Junbesh, which is why I regard them as 'strongmen'. Hazrat Ali did not so obviously stress his Pashai ethnicity as a legitimation tool, probably because he hoped to gain supporters beyond his small ethnic minority. Yet in the end his distribution of patronage among Pashais was the key factor that got him elected to parliament. He appears to have received very little support from non-Pashai voters. Others, such as Alam Khan Azadi, played both the ethnic (in his case Arab) and the religious/ideological cards (in his case Islamist links). Some, like Piram Qul in Rustaq, stressed their role in the jihad and their anti-communist profile, while Padsha Khan in Paktia campaigned on a platform 'more royalist than the king's'. In Kandahar, Amir Lalai tried to cast himself as a jihadi figure and at the same time appealed to tribal voters.[21]

The relative 'ideologization' of the strongmen blurred the boundaries between independent strongmen and factional strongmen or parties as defined here. Apart from tactical considerations, the development of a political or ideological platform can be taken as a sign of the ongoing evolution of the Afghan political scene, but major differences remained. In particular, the extremely patrimonial character of their modus operandi set them apart from their more sophisticated colleagues, who invested in the development of organizations, allowing a degree of institutionalization.

Between conservatism and expansionism: the factional strongmen

The importance of organizational capacity and institutionalization is well illustrated by the case of Hazara factional strongman Mohammed Mohaqqeq, whose fast (and short-lived) conversion into charismatic political leader was in a league of its own. Contrary to Junbesh or Jamiat, the Hazara-dominated party Hizb-i Wahdat did not include many strongmen in its ranks and most factional commanders were small and politically weak. The only significant exception was Haji Mohammad Mohaqqeq, who had risen to prominence during the resistance against the Taliban, when he had led Hazara resistance in northern Afghanistan. Tension between political leaders of Wahdat and Mohaqqeq surfaced in 2003, when he was expelled from the government following a controversy with Finance Minister Ashraf Ghani (Tarzi 2004). His expulsion opened a gap between the political leadership, embodied by Deputy President Karim Khalili, who remained associated with Karzai, and Mohaqqeq, who proceeded to mobilize the small field commanders of Wahdat, who mostly lacked both occupation and status. Mohaqqeq also attracted Hazara youth, the intelligentsia and the junior clergy around a platform of resentment and ethno-nationalist claims. He launched his own party, Hizb-i Wahdat-e Mardom-e Islami (Unity Islamic Popular Party) and became a serious rival for Khalili's claim to leadership. Although Khalili ran on Karzai's ticket during the presidential elections of 2004, Mohaqqeq ran as an alternative candidate and received a large majority of the Hazara vote. During the parliamentary elections the following year, Mohaqqeq not only entered parliament with the highest number of votes in the country, but out of the

38 Hazaras in the Wolesi Jirga, 13 more were loosely affiliated with his party.

Although there were allegations that Mohaqqeq utilized his armed force in northern Afghanistan in order to limit access to alternative Hazara candidates (Human Rights Watch 2005), it is clear that he succeeded at least temporarily in mobilizing political support in Kabul, Bamian and other Hazara-populated areas outside his northern fiefdom. Mohaqqeq's decisive exploitation of ethnic feelings was a key to his success, partly because ethnic consciousness appears stronger among the Hazaras than other Afghan ethnic groups. Mohaqqeq's example illustrates how the transition from strongman to politician could happen quite quickly even without reliance on armed politics. It also shows, however, that the qualities and skills required as a politician differ markedly from those of a strongman or military commander. Mohaqqeq rapidly lost the support that he had gathered once he involved himself in political machinations in Kabul. In particular, his supporters did not forgive his alliance with the political leader most hated by the Hazaras, Abdul Rasul Sayyaf, whose bid for the position of speaker of the lower house of parliament Mohaqqeq supported. His popularity was reportedly in rapid decline during 2006. Despite having launched a party, Mohaqqeq was never able to give it any effective organization. Once his charismatic leadership started to evaporate, nothing was left to retain the support previously earned.[22]

In terms of the ideal types outlined earlier in this chapter, after leaving Wahdat to form his own faction Mohaqqeq resembled more of an individual strongman than a factional one. In the new post-conflict context, a strong rationale for maintaining organizational structures continued to exist in the eyes of most of their members. It is clear that the influence of the independent strongmen was significant at the periphery but less so at the national level. Their numbers in parliament were small and their ability to influence legislation or even the main political trends was at best modest, particularly since they had difficulties in organizing collective action among themselves. Other 'caudillos' who tried to send their men to parliament without the support of a strong organization usually performed poorly. This is, for example, the case of Gul Agha Shirzai,[23] who could only get one of his men elected in Kandahar province (Khalid Pashtun). By contrast, the real factional strongmen proved able to cast their influence and domination much wider than independent strongmen. They also proved to be much more resilient. Their power was based on two developments.[24] One was the establishment of alliances of strongmen, often formed under external pressure, where one was recognized as leader. The other was the establishment of formalized and occasionally institutionalized hierarchical structures that resembled a political party. Using both strategies, factional strongmen such as Ismail Khan and General Dostum were able to cast their influence over large regions, get several of their supporters elected to parliament (respectively 8 and 22)[25] and, most importantly, maintain their influence despite the ups and downs of Afghan politics.

In Herat, Ismail Khan considered himself above membership of parliament, but placed his resources at the disposal of allies and followers who were competing for seats in parliament and in the provincial council. Combined with his appeal to conservative Islamic networks, this enabled supporters and allies to win half of Herat's parliamentary seats in 2005. The winners were mostly ideological mujahedin rather than strongmen or commanders themselves (Giustozzi 2009).

In northern Afghanistan the power structure developed by General Dostum differed substantially from Ismail Khan's. In some respects his party, Junbesh-i Milli was more complex and sophisticated, mainly thanks to the contribution of remnants of the left-wing party which had been in power in Kabul during 1978–92 (HDK, *Hizb-i Demokratik-i Khalq*). After 2001 Dostum turned it into a political party with a programme and a developed civilian structure, but also maintained the affiliation of many militia commanders. In addition to the effect of intimidation deriving from the existence of non-state militias, Dostum relied on KGB-like structures, sometimes hijacked from the official NSD and sometimes existing separately. These structures were responsible for most of the intimidation and harassment of potential political rivals. On the other hand, Dostum was not able to enforce the same degree of discipline on his militias as Ismail Khan did. In fact several of Dostum's supporters were almost autonomous strongmen, such as Ahmad Khan and Payenda Khan, or lesser figures (see Giustozzi, 2009, on Junbesh and the 2005 elections).[26]

Ideologies, parties and expansionist armed politics

Because the militias of Jamiat-i Islami had occupied Kabul at the end of 2001, they had a golden opportunity to use state infiltration as a route to hijacking the political process. A composite group which expanded greatly during the 1980s jihad and the 1990s civil wars, Jamiat included plenty of loosely affiliated strongmen, ranging from small ones to others like Ismail Khan, who claimed control over several provinces, as well a more tightly knit party militia (Shura-i Nezar, see above), which had been developed by late commander Ahmad Shah Massud. Despite their increasing internal fragmentation, the Jamiatis were united in pursuing the capture of state institutions, particularly at the centre, where it monopolized the Ministries of Defence and the Interior. Under Massud's skilled leadership, these militias had developed a strong *esprit de corps*, which distinguished them from the independent strongmen discussed above. At the provincial level, they monopolized positions in the regions under their control (northeast, west, Kabul region), while having to concede positions to the other factions which controlled territory in the rest of Afghanistan. Where a vacuum existed, as in Logar, Wardak and Paktya provinces, they put their men in place, but were rarely able to consolidate their positions. Indeed, neither in Wardak nor in Paktya were Jamiat's factions able to elect anyone to parliament in 2005: two Jamiat MPs were elected from Logar, but as Jamiat had had a significant presence in Logar since the 1980s it cannot be considered an area of new expansion.

As in Junbesh's case, reconciling the two elements of 'armed politics' was problematic. Minister of Defence Fahim was caught between participation in the political process and unwillingness to break completely with the militia commanders; eventually he lost on both counts. He was dropped from Karzai's presidential ticket, where he was supposed to occupy one of the two vice-presidential posts, and sacked from his position as Minister of Defence. He also lost much of his support base among the mid-ranking commanders because of his concessions to foreign pressure for disarmament (Giustozzi 2009).[27]

Jamiat's armed politics did not manifest exclusively in terms of state seizure. Even after the end of the official DDR in 2005, small armed groups continued to patrol many parts of Parwan, Kabul and Kapisa provinces. The purpose seemed to be to maintain territorial control and reassure/convince local communities that the militias of Jamiat-i Islami and related groups were there to stay. In much of Parwan and Panjshir this had a clear impact on the electoral campaigns of 2004 (presidential) and 2005 (parliamentary). Candidates not aligned with Jamiat reported feeling intimidated by the presence of armed men even when they had good personal relations with Jamiati leaders. Those who could afford it hired armed escorts in order to be able to campaign.[28]

The Jamiatis were not alone in pursuing 'expansionist' armed politics. Apart from the smaller groups, which I shall not mention here, the other main branch of Afghanistan's Islamist movement, Hizb-i Islami, used armed propaganda after 2001, mainly in eastern Afghanistan, as discussed above. An essential component of Hizb's armed propaganda was the formation of a political front able to capitalize on the image of resilience and opposition to foreign presence. The political front had a difficult start during 2002, when attempts to bring together militarily inactive members of the party met with severe repression in Kabul from the Jamiat-dominated NSD and police. Hundreds were arrested, although most of them were not detained for long following the intervention of foreign diplomats. Subsequent attempts to organize a 'political' Hizb-i Islami simmered for a while, until in 2004 the decision was made to launch a party of the same name under the leadership of Arghandiwal and Farouqi, two long-standing functionaries in the organization led by its founder, Gulbuddin Hekmatyar. Again the attempt met resistance in Kabul in the form of the rather spurious claim that a party of that name already existed. Finally, registration succeeded in 2005.

The election law did not permit individual candidates for parliament to run on a party ticket. Hence, like all the political parties at the time the legal Hizb-i Islami did not play much of a role during the elections. Nevertheless, a substantial number of members and sympathisers won parliamentary seats. According to one count, as many as 42 former members of Hizb-i Islami made it into the Lower House, although quite a few had cut their relations with the party long before. The actual number of MPs with some ongoing connection with Hizb-i Islami was probably no more than 30, still enough to represent one of the largest blocs in parliament if they were formally united under a single banner. After the elections, Farouqi's Hizb-i Islami engaged in a campaign to bring together the many MPs linked to Hizb-i Islami under his banner, with some success. Although formally Farouqi's Hizb-i Islami claimed to have broken with Hekmatyar, when challenged on this issue all the members refused to condemn Hekmatyar. Quite the contrary, they maintained that he had been 'a great leader' and that he had 'done a lot for Afghanistan'.[29] This, together with the then half-hearted insurgency of Hekmatyar and a few commanders of the party, confirms that the political front and the armed insurgency are two components of a single strategy of armed propaganda. While it is very difficult to judge the extent to which armed propaganda contributed to the electoral successes of Hizb-i Islami, the geographical distribution of the successful candidates shows a concentration in areas where Hizb-i Islami was most active militarily, that is eastern Afghanistan.

Conclusion: the uncertain transition of armed politics

Several factors explain the continuing importance of armed politics in Afghanistan. Quite central, of course, is the inability of the post-2001 government to establish an effective monopoly of armed force, that is, to disarm the factions and the strongmen. There are other reasons too. The most important is the inability of the renascent Afghan state to act as an effective regulatory force and a broker among the armed groups, which in turn made disarmament more difficult. It is debatable whether the government in Kabul should have been more inclusive or not, but the slow progress in depatrimonializing the security agencies prevented the state from being able to appear as impartial to many major players. The internationally-imposed adoption of meritocratic criteria at the Ministry of Interior, for example, collided with ingrained practices of patronage and factionalism in the appointment of key personnel. After many years of civil war, different organizations and individuals had little trust in each other. Initially, the UN in part replaced the government as a regulatory body and broker and successfully started processes of reconciliation, particularly in parts of the north and northeast, but also in the south and southeast. This led to a very partial process of disarmament and to a decline in factional fighting after 2003. However, the UN's efforts to defactionalize the state were repeatedly frustrated, which prevented the process of reconciliation from going very far. Under these conditions, an effective disarmament was probably never a real possibility in post-2001 Afghanistan. Even if a fully inclusive government had been formed after 2001, it would probably have taken several years for some degree of mutual trust to develop among formerly rival groups. By 2005–6, the expanding insurgency was further removing any incentive for the armed groups to disarm. Indeed, there were signs of rearmament in the north and northeast. Three years later, the United States supported the formation of village self-defence units in contested areas to fight the Taliban insurgents.

The logical conclusion is that a more realistic approach towards the realities of armed politics in Afghanistan would have been required to achieve greater success in gradually removing arms from the political arena. After 2001, virtually all the most powerful armed actors present on the Afghan scene tried to convert themselves into political parties and to establish a foothold in the new parliament (although many independent strongmen opted to retire from public life). Their main concern seems to have been to legitimize their political role in the new post-conflict environment. Voter support, whether genuine or not, came to be seen as the best way to prevent marginalization at the national level and secure entrenchment as local leaders. As discussed above, the process was necessarily controversial: in order to maximize their chances of success, strongmen of various kinds had to use their original source of influence, that is armed force, while at the same time distancing themselves from it. This is indeed the nature of armed politics. For the more sophisticated factional strongmen and the ideological groups, the transition to political legitimacy meant not only the need to overhaul their image, a problem which they shared with the independent strongmen, but also a conflict of interest between the actual commanders of militia groups and their more political leaderships. This was most evident in the cases of Jamiat and Junbesh. The fact that Kabul opted to exploit the divide between commanders or strongmen and the organizations to which they were affiliated, in the hope of crucially weakening them, might have slowed the transition away from arms, but this conflict of interest opened a window of opportunity in which the process of transition away from armed politics might have been strengthened and accelerated had these organizations been given the right incentives.

Nevertheless, Kabul's courting of (or forcing) small and large strongmen and commanders to lure them away from the large non-state organizations, combined with the varying degrees of success of some of their members in achieving status and power within the post-conflict environment, meant that the organized armed factions gradually lost cohesion. The decreasing pressure from a threat such as the expanding pre-2001 Taliban also contributed to make factional alignments less important. From 2002 it was instead the rise of narco-mafias throughout the country that increasingly dominated the political landscape, leading to new cross-ethnic, cross-regional and cross-ideological alliances. Time will tell whether this development has the potential to bring about the appearance of a new type of armed politics, based on the desire of narcotics producers to have at their disposal tools to pressure local and national authorities and to ensure that elected representatives respect their wishes.

Notes

1 This is the official figure of those DDRed according to the Afghanistan New Beginnings Program (ANBP) run by the United Nations Development Programme (UNDP).
2 The two Loya Jirgas of 2002 and 2003 were meant to legitimize the transitional government (2002) and ratify the new Constitution (2003). The Loya Jirga is a nationwide tribal assembly convened by the rulers of Afghanistan to obtain legitimization for their actions (Human Rights Watch 2005, 9–11 and 2003, chapter IV; 'Christian Parenti in Afghanistan: Saturday's elections were a farce' (2004) *Democracy Now*, 12 October. Online, available at: www.democracynow. org/article.pl?sid=04/10/12/1347201; AIHRC–UNAMA (2005b).

3 Although Ittehad was never a major military force, Sayyaf has always been well funded from Arab sources and able to exercise influence over other groups and individuals, including President Karzai. He also exercises significant influence over Afghanistan's judiciary.

4 Personal communication with UN official, Kabul, October 2005; Mudassir Ali Shah (2005).

5 Personal communication with UN officials, Kabul, February and March 2007; personal communication with Afghan journalist, Kabul, October 2006; Coghlan (2007).

6 The concept of state capture is mostly used in the context of the area of the former Soviet Union. For its application to Afghanistan, see O'Donnell (2008).

7 Personal communications with UN officials, Mazar-i Sharif, June–September 2004; personal observation, Kunduz, November 2003; Human Rights Watch (2003), chapter IV. Naderi would later stand as a candidate in the parliamentary elections, winning the largest number of votes in Baghlan.

8 The Loya Jirgas were elected by grand electors, who were in turn elected by gatherings of elders and men of influence in the provinces.

9 The 'Coordination Council', originally led by Ahmad Shah Massud, emerged as the leading faction inside Professor Rabbani's Jamiat-i Islami in the late 1980s and maintained a separate identity even after its formal disbandment in 1992.

10 This list of provinces is limited to cases in which the involvement of non-state armed groups (excluding the insurgents) was reported. Personal communication with Loya Jirga delegates from Badakhshan, October 2003; United Nations (2002) *Daily Highlights*, 21 May; *Pajhwok News Agency* (2005) 15 March; Radio Liberty (2006) 15 December, online, available at: www.rferl.org/featuresarticle/2005/12/216ef1be-d4dd-4d09-b17b-a461db18f501.html; UNHCR (2002); 'Candidate killed in Afghanistan' (2005) *BBC News*, 27 September.

11 Interview with former Loya Jirga commissioner, Kabul, May 2003.

12 See note 7 above.

13 Personal communications with UN officials, Mazar-i Sharif, June-July 2004, and in Kabul, September 2004; 'Afghans stop governor from assuming office' (2004) *Arab News*, 13 June. Online, available at: www.arabnews.com/?page=4&section=0&article=46704&d=13&m=6&y=2004&pix=world.jpg&category=World; Gall (2004); Constable (2004); *Arman-e-Milli*, (2005) 6 September; Rahmani (2005).

14 Personal communication with ISAF officer and journalist Carlotta Gall, Kabul, June 2006.

15 For more details about the military activities of Hizb-i Islami, see Giustozzi (2007a).

16 Personal communication with UN officials, Kabul and Mazar-i Sharif, June-July 2004.

17 Personal communications with former Loya Jirga commissioners and UN officials.

18 Personal communications with candidates and UN officials, Kabul and provinces, August–September 2004 and October 2005; Wilder (2005) pp. 27–8.

19 'Afghanistan: where the rule by the gun continues' (2007) *IRIN*, 7 April; AIHRC–UNAMA (2005a and 2005b); personal communication with party activist returning from Kunar, Jalalabad, February 2006. This list of course excludes the insurgency-affected provinces of the south, southeast and east.

20 Telephone communication with UN official, Kunduz, October 2005.

21 Personal communications with UN officials, Kunduz, Mazar-i Sharif, Kabul, Jalalabad and Kandahar, January 2004-February 2007.

22 Personal communication with Niamatullah Ibrahimi, Crisis States Research Centre, Kabul, March 2007.
23 Gul Agha emerged as one of the key recipients of US support in late 2001, in the context of Operation Enduring Freedom, to mobilize support and start fighting the Taliban in Kandahar.
24 On Herat see Giustozzi (2006).
25 This number includes some of the strongmen mentioned in the previous paragraph: Ahmad Khan, Payenda Khan, Fataullah.
26 Giustozzi (2005); personal communications with UN officials, Mazar and Kabul, June 2004–September 2004.
27 Personal communication with UN official, Kabul, May 2005; personal observation, Shamali plains, February 2005; interview with former official of the Minister of Interior, Kabul, January 2006.
28 Interview with candidates from Parwan, Kabul, October 2005 and October 2006.
29 Interviews with former and current members of Hizb-i Islami, Kabul, London, Jalalabad 2006–7.

Bibliography

Adejumobi, Said (2004) 'Conflict and peace building in West Africa: the role of civil society and the African Union', *Conflict, Security and Development*, 4(1): 59–77.

AIHRC–UNAMA (2005a) *Joint Verification of Political Rights, Wolesi Jirga and Provincial Council Elections*, First Report (19 April–3 June 2005), Kabul.

AIHRC–UNAMA (2005b) *Joint Verification of Political Rights, Wolesi Jirga and Provincial Council Elections*, Second Report (4 June–16 August 2005), Kabul.

Coghlan, T. (2007) 'Taliban flee Afghan-led NATO offensive', *Daily Telegraph*, 30 March.

Constable, P. (2004) 'Afghans riot over dismissal of governor in Herat', *Washington Post*, 13 September.

Gall, C. (2002) 'Ex-president says he'll back Afghan leader', *New York Times*, 4 October.

Gall, C. (2004) 'Afghan crowds loot and burn over governor's dismissal', *New York Times*, 13 September.

Gellner, E. (1995) *Anthropology and Politics*, Hoboken: Wiley-Blackwell.

Giustozzi, A. (2003) *Respectable Warlords? The Politics of State-Building in Post-Taleban Afghanistan*, Working Paper 33 of the Crisis States Programme, London: London School of Economics and Political Science.

Giustozzi, A. (2004) *Bad State vs. Good Warlords? A Critique of State-Building Strategies in Afghanistan*, Working Paper 51 of the Crisis States Programme, London: London School of Economics and Political Science.

Giustozzi, A. (2005) *The Ethnicisation of an Afghan Faction: Junbesh-i Milli from the Origins to the Presidential Elections (2004)*, Working Paper 67, London: Crisis States Research Centre.

Giustozzi, A. (2006) *Genesis of a Prince: The Rise of Ismail Khan in Western Afghanistan, 1979–1992*, Working Paper 4 Series 2, London: Crisis States Research Centre.

Giustozzi, A. (2007a) *Kuran, Kalashnikov and Laptop: The Neo-Taliban Insurgency in Afghanistan, 2002–2007*, Columbia University Press.

Giustozzi, A. (2007b) 'The privatizing of war and security in Afghanistan: future or dead end?', *The Economics of Peace and Security Journal*, 2(1): 19–23.

Giustozzi, A. (2007c) 'War and peace economies of Afghanistan's strongmen', *International Peacekeeping*, 14(1), January: 75–89.

Giustozzi, A. (2008) 'Afghanistan: political parties or militia fronts?', in J. de Zeeuw (ed.) *Transforming Rebel Movements after Civil Wars*, Boulder: Lynne Rienner, Chapter 8.

Giustozzi, A. (2009) *Empires of Mud*, London: Hurst.

Giustozzi, A. (2011, forthcoming) *The Politics on Policing in Afghanistan*, Kabul; Afghan Analyst Network.

Human Rights Watch (2002) 'Loya Jirga off to a shaky start', press release, 13 June.

Human Rights Watch (2003) *'Killing You is a Very Easy Thing for Us'*: *Human Rights Abuses in Southeast Afghanistan*, New York, July.

Human Rights Watch (2005) *Afghanistan on the Eve of Parliamentary and Provincial Elections*, New York.

Islamic Republic of Afghanistan (2006) 'Afghanistan National Development Strategy (ANDS), implementation of the Afghanistan compact benchmarks March–August 2006', Prepared by Working Groups (WGs) and Consultative Groups (CGs) supported by ANDS Office, Kabul, Afghanistan. Online, available at: www.undpanbp.org/diag-fast-fact/.

Keith, Henry H. and Hayes, Robert A. (eds.) (1976) *Perspectives on Armed Politics in Brazil*, Tempe: Arizona State University.

Mudassir Ali Shah, S. (2005) 'A fractured parliament', *Nation*, 14 October.

Neumann, Peter R. (2005) 'From revolution to devolution: is the IRA still a threat to peace in Northern Ireland?', *Journal of Contemporary European Studies*, 13(1): 79–92, April.

Noelle-Karimi, C. (2002) 'Report on Loya Jirga elections phases I and II, Provinces of Balkh and Samangan May 1–28, 2002, Loya Jirga elections phases I and II, Kabul, May 29–June 7, 2002', unpublished report, courtesy of the author.

O'Donnell, M. (2008) 'Post-conflict corruption: a rule of law agenda?', Agnès Hurwitz with Reyko Huang (eds.), *Civil War and Rule of Law*, International Peace Academy.

Rahmani, W. (2005) 'Two northern Afghan governors replaced', *Pajhwok Afghan News*, 4 September.

Rossi, S. and Giustozzi, A. (2006) *Disarmament Demobilisation and Reintegration of Ex-combatants (DDR) in Afghanistan: Constraints and Limited Capabilities*, Working Paper 2 Series 2, London: Crisis States Research Centre (LSE).

Tarzi, A. (2004) 'Dispute erupts over Afghan minister's purported resignation', *RFE/RL Report*, 3(10), 11 March.

UNHCR (2002) *Chronology of Events in Afghanistan*, May. Online, available at: www.unhcr.org/home/RSDCOI/415c614b4.pdf.

United Nations (2002) *Daily Highlights*, 21 May.

Wilder, A. (2007) *A House Divided? Analysing the 2005 Afghan Elections*, Kabul: AREU: 27–8.

9 Warlordism

Three biographies from southeastern Afghanistan[1]

Kristian Berg Harpviken

How do 'warlords' – defined in the Afghan context both by their military skills and capacity to strike a balance between local and external sources of support – respond when the war they are fighting ends? Why do some choose compliance with the new political order while others remain engaged in various forms of opposition? The political biographies of three longstanding warlords of the largely Pashtun southeast of Afghanistan – Mullah Rocketi, Qari Baba and Jalaluddin Haqqani – enable us to explore the dynamics of quite different responses. The 2001 US-led intervention and the transitional challenges that followed led the three men in different directions. Why was this so? Why did one man lay down his arms to become a politician, another place his capacity for commanding violence at the service of the new Karzai government, while the third continued to challenge the new rulers with armed force? The analysis of these different trajectories provides an insight into the nature of violent warlordism during the formal transition from war to peace and into the post-conflict period.

The historical context for the emergence of Afghan warlords

The 1978 coup by the People's Democratic Party of Afghanistan (PDPA), followed by the late 1979 Soviet intervention, led to the emergence of a large set of resistance commanders in Afghanistan. Initially, the resistance was largely in the form of local defence against the coercive reforms of the PDPA, sometimes led by traditional notables, including Islamic scholars. By the beginning of the 1980s, political parties based in Pakistan and Iran formed to lead the resistance.

Most of them were loosely organized and had limited control over their field commanders. I will here refer to such local and regional leaders as warlords, without giving the term a derogatory meaning, but simply to designate individuals who built personal power in the context of war, deriving their main legitimacy from their capacity for organized violence (Giustozzi 2003). These warlords – then commonly referred to as commanders – remained the central actors in the armed resistance of the jihad and held key positions in the governments that followed the fall of the PDPA in

1992. When the Taliban took Kabul in 1996, some former commanders were incorporated in the new regime, while others went into exile or the mujahedin-controlled areas in Afghanistan's northeast.

The US-led intervention in 2001 enlisted the anti-Taliban warlords – now loosely joined in the Northern Alliance – in fighting the Islamist regime. Those who took part were generously rewarded for their services by President Karzai, who, encouraged by his US allies, based his rule in part on accommodating former warlords and rewarded many with government positions.

Understanding warlords

The literature suggests three dominant explanations for the emergence of warlords: political economy; ideological; and relational. These are not mutually exclusive. In the political economy approach of Mancur Olson (1993) the warlord is a rational actor. Once he gains control over a certain area, it is in his interest to provide minimal security to the subjects within so as to facilitate further economic accumulation. When warlordism develops into a relatively stable system of governance that provide public goods, 'roving bandits' turn into 'stationary bandits'. A variation on this theme is found in William Reno's work on Africa (1998; 2002). Warlordism emerges here in response to the fragmentation of state authority. Like Olson, Reno's warlords are self-interested actors aiming to strengthen their own economic and political position, but are less interested in providing goods than those in Olson's model. Other analysts have developed the economic self-interest theme further (Keen 1998; Collier and Hoeffler 2002).

In a political economy perspective, warlords are pragmatic actors with little interest in ideology or reforms of the state. As we shall see below, however, this does not quite fit the Afghan scene. For a start, many warlords, held religious positions and legitimized their role in Islamic terms (Giustozzi 2007). Some were constrained by everyday ideologies inherent in shared norms, (Bhatia and Sedra 2008: chapter 3), and all were exposed to ideology through their relationships with external backers.

The third approach to understanding warlords is relational (Tilly 2003; Wood 2008). Most analysts agree that warlords rely on pre-existing social bonds. Ties via family, tribe, ethnicity, religion or shared locality are important both for recruitment and support (Harpviken 2009). As a result, warlords are also accountable to their local constituents (Marten 2007). In this understanding, warlordism can be a fairly stable political system, and it can be partially responsive to the local population's need for security and welfare.

With these three explanatory dynamics in mind, let us explore the trajectories of our three Afghan warlords.

Three Afghans

The three Afghans – Mullah Rocketi, Qari Baba and Jalaluddin Haqqani – are chosen here for several reasons. First, all emerged as military commanders in the resistance against the PDPA and the Soviets in the 1980s. They are all from the Pashtun heartlands in the southern and southeastern part of the country, an area where tribal solidarity has proven remarkably resilient in the encounter with war. While this was the home area for many members of the PDPA, it was also the core area for the resistance parties, particularly those of a traditionalist Islamic orientation. In 1994, the Taliban emerged, first further south, around Uruzgan and Kandahar, then quickly spreading eastwards throughout the Pashtun belt. They met minimal armed resistance. Local commanders were faced with a choice between resisting, going underground, fleeing, or subordinating themselves to the Taliban. Joining meant at worst that the Taliban would deprive them of their armed forces, and at best appoint them to official posts.

Second, the three followed different strategies for adapting to the post-Taliban situation. Third, the background of all three is sufficiently well known that the present analysis does not violate privacy concerns. The chapter is primarily based on interviews with key informants who have first-hand knowledge of the three men.[2] The interviews have been supplemented by written sources in the form of both academic analysis and journalistic accounts. Finally, I have followed the political landscapes in which these individuals have operated through almost two decades, and I have personally met several times with Jalaluddin Haqqani and Qari Baba.

Mullah Rocketi: tribal-traditional warlord

Mullah Rocketi was elected to parliament in 2005, representing Zabul province, where he had been the major commander for most of two decades. The nickname 'Rocketi' signifies his reputation as a marksman with the rocket propelled grenade (RPG) launcher. His real name is Mullah Abdul Salam. Rocketi was a commander of Sayyaf's Ittehad-e Islami, an Islamist group with a Wahabi orientation – a rigorous school of thought originating in what is today Saudi Arabia – despite feeling more at home with traditionalist Afghan groups. Never an active builder of local welfare, Rocketi emphasized local security and always displayed a strong interest in pragmatic deals. Representing classic Pashtun values, Rocketi was never attracted by new types of religio-political ideology. He represents the type of commander that is rooted in local networks and values, acting as a middleman in relation to strong political currents that originate externally. As such, Rocketi may be the one, amongst the three discussed here, that comes the closest to an ideal-type warlord as conceptualized in this chapter. Ironically, he is also the one who – although not without pains of transition – has become an integral part of the post-2001 power structure.

Mullah Abdul Salam was born in Sinak village, close to Qalat, the provincial capital of Zabul, around 1957. He is married and has eight children (five sons and three daughters); the eldest son is now (2009) 19 years old. Mullah Rocketi has basic madrasa training, but is not fully literate. He led a local madrasa in Zabul prior to the war, but was still in his early twenties at the time of the Soviet intervention in late 1979, after which he joined the resistance. In the words of one informant, 'he has a divine gift for military strategy'. Quickly gaining a reputation as an effective military commander, Mullah Rocketi also played on his background within the Suleiman Khel lineage of Pashtuns, and tribal solidarity was probably more important than religious legitimization for his support.

Mullah Rocketi soon emerged as a major commander of Ittehad-e Islami. His relationship with the party leader, Abdul Rasool Sayyaf, became increasingly antagonistic, both as a result of ideological differences and because Rocketi was sceptical about the strong Pakistani influence in Sayyaf's movement. His political orientation brought him closer to Maulawi Nabi's Harakat-e Islami, with its traditionalist religious leaning, and in the late 1980s he shifted his party affiliation, much to Sayyaf's chagrin. Throughout the late 1980s and early 1990s, Rocketi's position as Zabul's main commander was never seriously contested. Commanders affiliated with other parties made sure to coordinate and keep in line with Rocketi. In the latter half of the 1980s, the Mullah was, in most people's eyes, functioning as the resistance governor in a province where the PDPA government – apart from the provincial capital Qalat and along the Kabul–Kandahar highway – had minimal say.

Rocketi's pattern of mobilization was of the traditional sort; his main support was through the tribal networks, and it was also here that he recruited his combat personnel. The Suleiman Khel tribe does not dominate the tribal landscape in Zabul, and based on his military proficiency, Rocketi gained support also from other tribes, including the Kharoti, Taraki and Tokhi. Through the Suleiman Khel network, he gained influence also outside Zabul, in Ghazni, Helmand, Kandahar, Logar and in Paktika. While a famously effective fighter, Rocketi never had a sizeable professional salaried army, or – as many other warlords – even a semi-professional one rewarded by booty. As the main commander in the province, he certainly had access to generous external resources. This enabled him to reward loyal supporters and convince others to join in. He never attempted, however, to build an economic base of his own. Neither did he have multiple sources of external support. For this reason, he was vulnerable to shifts in the larger political landscape.

Despite his harsh criticism of the Pakistani influence on Afghan politics in general and on the 1980s resistance parties in particular, Rocketi also relied on Pakistan for money and arms. Like Qari Baba, he never established himself in Pakistani exile but maintained a liaison function and visited regularly. His capacity to fight was dependent on Pakistani sanctuary, as were most of the other groups in the south and east. Yet his contact with the Pakistanis made him more hostile to their interference. The killing of his brother in the early 1980s, allegedly by Pakistani intelligence services, stayed with him. In mid-1994, one of his bases was allegedly searched by Pakistani forces looking for valuable heat-seeking Stinger missiles. Rocketi hit back by taking two Pakistanis and seven Chinese hostage, demanding payment for his Stingers and the release of his brother from a Pakistani jail. After several months, the hostages were released, reportedly having been maltreated and tortured while in custody (US Department of State 1995).

At the very end of 1994, the Taliban movement closed in on Zabul. The takeover was virtually bloodless and not a single shot was fired (Rashid 2000: 33). Mullah Omar, the head of the Taliban, knew Rocketi. He was impressed by Rocketi's reputation and positively inclined as a result of their joint background in Harakat-e Enqelab, a traditionalist party rooted in clerical networks set up in the early days of the jihad. Mullah Rocketi saw that Taliban rule was coming and weighed up his position: should he resort to passivity or should he offer his services to the new regime? He decided on the latter and established contact with the Taliban leader prior to the takeover of Zabul. He served as a go-between with Ahmad Shah Massoud, the main commander of the Northern Alliance. Omar had hoped to get Massoud on board with the Taliban, but failed. In a 2006 interview, Rocketi said: 'When the Taliban came along, I gave everything to them because I wanted the country to improve and the people to be safe' (Sands 2006).

After a few months, the Taliban offered Rocketi the job of commander of the 1st Army Corps in Jalalabad, a post he retained until the fall of the Taliban regime in late 2001. In this capacity, he led operations in the north, which had an enduring negative impact on his relationship with Northern Alliance leaders who came to power after 2001. Abdul Salam's attachment to the Taliban is unsurprising; most Pashtun commanders with a similar religious background and political orientation did the same. Nonetheless, the level of trust that the Taliban gave Rocketi is special, first as an envoy to Massoud in 1994–5 and later as a key corps commander until their 2001 fall from power. Few warlords with his previous stature gained such confidence from the new rulers.

When the United States invaded in 2001, Rocketi left his commander post and sought sanctuary at the shrine of the Gilani family in Jalalabad, a confirmation of his long-term links with this influential Sufi family network. After a while, he went to Zabul. In late December, he received Ismael Gilani, who now had a mandate from President Karzai, and the two agreed that Rocketi would hand in his weapons, including a handful of Stinger missiles (Kibel 2001). Rocketi then went to Kandahar where he got protection from Gul Agha Shirzai, the first post-Taliban governor. Like some other commanders, he was also granted what was understood to be an amnesty from Karzai (Yusufzai 2002). In May 2002, however, US forces arrested him, took him to Bagram air base north of Kabul and held him for interrogation for eight months. He was released at the initiative of Karzai, but the main interlocutors were again from the circle around Pir Ahmad Gilani, a political and spiritual leader who was close to Karzai. Upon Rocketi's release, Gilani's men suggested an appointment as governor of Zabul, but the president declined, probably reflecting US pressure.

Rocketi proved very loyal to the new regime. He took a particularly active stand in the DDR (disarmament, demobilization and reintegration) process, first handing in his own weapons and then working with the government to convince other Zabul commanders to do the same. In the run-up to the 2004 presidential elections, Rocketi campaigned for Karzai in Zabul and in the 2005 parliamentary elections he was himself a candidate. He campaigned extensively in the province, apparently with generous access to money that could buy support. He won a seat in parliament and settled in Kabul with his wife and children. At the same time, the Taliban was gaining strength in Zabul, controlling some 80 per cent of the province already by late 2003, (Rashid 2008: 247). Defectors were targeted by the Taliban, and personal security was becoming a serious concern for people like Rocketi. Nonetheless, Rocketi continued to respond to calls for intervention in local conflicts and occasionally travelled to his home province for this purpose. In this, he collaborated closely with the US forces operating in the province. When 21 South Koreans were held hostage in Ghazni in 2007, Rocketi was part of a delegation sent to negotiate with the Taliban captors. In June 2008, when endorsing the principle of reconciliation with Taliban, British Foreign Minister David Miliband held up Rocketi as a prime example of success (Miliband 2008).

In parliament, Rocketi surprised many by distancing himself from his Taliban past and by speaking up against warlords, even to the extent of expressing support for Malalai Joya, parliament's most vocal warlord critic. Like many others, however, he grew more and more frustrated by the limited influence of parliament and become increasingly critical of the government, as in this interview:

> When the current government came along, I gave everything to them because I thought they would make the county better. But I regret that. Everything is gone now, we have nothing. I regret it not because I am no longer with the Taliban, but because our government does not have the power to improve our country.
>
> (Sands 2006)

Rocketi has continued to distance himself from the Taliban, but distinguishes between their original aims (security, Islamic state) – for which he expresses qualified sympathy – and their means (repression, violence, terrorism) (Sennott 2007: 9). There is little sign that his gifts in the military domain are paralleled in the political sphere and his influence in parliament is limited. At best, he serves a symbolic purpose as a 'reconciled' warlord.

Immediately after the 2001 intervention, Rocketi laid down arms. This did not prevent the US forces from jailing him for eight months, but in the longer run Rocketi's strategy worked. Few Taliban commanders of his stature were similarly brought into the political arena. Admittedly, he had limited choice. Despite considerable tribal and local support, he lacked steady sources of finance. He was already uncomfortable with the increasing political radicalization of the Taliban. Some of his long-term protectors strongly pressured him to side with the Karzai government. His reconciliation seems genuine. Unlike other parliamentarians, he has not associated himself with any standing armed force. Despite the obvious threats to his life, he does not even entertain bodyguards. He does his best to counter his reputation for brutality. At the same time, informants who know Zabul well do not doubt that he could easily remobilize support if the situation changes.

Qari Baba: tribal compromise, builder of proto-state

Qari Taj Mohammad, more commonly known as Qari Baba, was killed in 2006, allegedly by local Taliban sympathizers. He emerged in the early 1980s as the most prominent commander in the area surrounding Ghazni city, located on a strategic stretch of the Kabul–Kandahar road. His main support base was in Andar district outside Ghazni. A local Islamic scholar in charge of his own madrasa before the war, Qari Baba was an archetypical commander of Harakat-e Enqilab, an Islamic traditionalist party with broad support among the clergy. He was reputed to be firm on his enemies – the 'dictator' being one of his many nicknames – and he played on this violent reputation to instil fear and respect. At the same time, he built a proto-state, encouraging local business, promoting health and education services and collecting local taxes.

Qari Baba was born in Attal village of Andar district in Ghazni. At the time of his death, he was somewhere in his mid-seventies. He was from a religious family, his father Mawlawi Abdul Wakil being an *alim*, a trained Islamic scholar. Qari Baba himself pursued Islamic education at the well-known Noorul madrasa in Ghazni, but did not make it to an advanced level and never called himself an *alim*. He gained a reputation for both his handwriting and his prose. For a while he worked as a scribe, stationed in front of the Ghazni governor's office, where he wrote petitions and letters to the governor. Around 1973, he set up a small madrasa in Andar district. Qari Baba fathered one son and four daughters, one of whom married one of his main commanders, Khail Mohammad Hussein (a member of the 2005 parliament).

Qari Baba was of Tajik ethnic origin, which is fairly common in Ghazni city and the surrounding areas. A fluent Pashtu-speaker, he was generally seen as a commander of Pashtuns. Tribal structures persist in Andar, where he had his main power base, and Qari Baba was a compromise candidate between four local Pashtun tribes that were unable in the early 1980s to agree upon a candidate from their own ranks. Qari Baba's political talents as well as his religious background undoubtedly served him well. As a compromise candidate not belonging to any of the main local tribes, he was shielded from accusations of only looking after his own interests. A system of tribal sub-commanders serving under him also helped to ensure accountability to his local support base. Yet as a compromise candidate with no primary constituency of his own, Baba was vulnerable. In the Ghazni area, it was common for resistance leaders to have a religious background, almost entirely replacing the traditional notables who had constituted the main elite prior to the war (Roy 1986: 114). Baba is himself reputed to have purged more than one *khan* from Andar in the early days of the war. In the words of one informant, 'he had more enemies than I can possibly list'.

Ghazni was one of the few places where, large-scale revolts were organized against the PDPA government before the Soviet intervention. The networks of religious leaders constituted the core of the revolts, the first of which was reported in September 1979. Mohammad Nabi, who became the leader of one of the main Sunni parties, Harakat-e Enqilab, had taught at the Ghazni madrasa and was widely respected among the local *ulama*. As Olivier Roy points out, 'the *ulama* saw the Harakat as an apolitical party, a sort of clerical association. Decentralized ... without political militants and without ideology' (Roy 1986: 114). Within this network, Qari Baba was a pioneer in opposing the communists with armed force. There are no signs, however, that he was engaged in any political activity prior to the 1978 communist coup. Once engaged in resistance, he quickly gained a reputation for cruelty and mercilessness, which was an essential part of his political capital. Anybody suspected of being 'a communist' – reportedly it would suffice to be a teacher, wear jeans, or have a moustache but no beard – would be killed, often in brutal ways.

Qari Baba also had a long-term, 'state-building' perspective. He held back on offensive military action. He instituted regular tax collection (*usher* and *zakat*), used in part to support his fighters and in part to offer both medical services and education to the population in areas under his command, even at an early stage in the war.[3] The development of a local proto-state, where the leader claimed both tax and military services from the population but also provided welfare services in return, was atypical among warlord commanders in the Pashtun south and southeast. In line with this approach, Baba acted responsibly when, already in 1988, he gained control over two major Soviet-built projects, Chardewal, an uncompleted collective farm, and Band-e-Sardeh, a large dam built for irrigation purposes. In contrast to the general pattern throughout much of the Pashtun south (Rubin 2002), Qari Baba protected the infrastructure and the equipment carefully and handed it over to the mujahedin government when it took power in 1992. He was immediately appointed provincial governor and had relative success in accommodating the interests of different and mostly ethnically-based political groups. Increasingly, he came to be seen as a trusted ally by leaders in the mujahedin government; he would later spearhead the resistance to the Taliban. In his province, he acted as a sovereign ruler, but his ability to maintain relative calm instilled respect amongst many and Ghazni quickly became a vibrant business hub.

Qari Baba portrayed himself as an Afghan nationalist and he was extraordinarily vocal about the detrimental role played by foreign countries, particularly Pakistan. At the same time, he cultivated relations with all sides. He worked with Pakistan, both through Harakat and directly with Inter-Services Intelligence (ISI). He also cultivated relations with agents of the PDPA government, who were working to pacify the resistance. In 1989, when the Soviets pulled out, Baba entered into what was effectively a ceasefire agreement with the Najibullah government, which paid him handsomely to limit his military activities. Qari Baba was critical of the radical Islamists, particularly Gulbuddin Hekmatyar's Hezb-e Islami, which not only challenged the traditional Sunni Islamic clergy but also had close relations with Pakistan and transnational political networks. In Andar, the local chapter of Hezb-e Islami was a constant challenge to his authority throughout the 1980s and first half of the 1990s. In one version of the events that eventually led to the Taliban takeover in late January 1995, Hezb-e Islami had launched a counterattack on the Taliban in Ghazni, but Qari Baba struck a deal with the Taliban (Dorronsoro 2005: 250). The story about the Taliban deal remains unclear, but there is no doubt that one of Qari Baba's seconds-in-command (and a tribal appointee) was the main facilitator of the Taliban's entry to Ghazni. His second-in-command had been negotiating with them for quite a while without Qari Babar's knowledge, which also led to a breakdown in the long-standing relationship between the two men.

In the early months after the Taliban takeover, Qari Baba continued to serve as the governor. This is not surprising; the Taliban objectives harmonized with the traditional Islamic order maintained by Qari Baba in Ghazni, and Harakat supporters in general seemed to integrate easily into the new regime (Dorronsoro 2006 [1994]). Qari Baba's relationship with the Taliban deteriorated, however, and not long afterwards he left his governor post and sought protection with the enemy, that is, with Massoud, first in Taloqan and later in the Panshjir valley. Eventually he left for Iran, where he spent almost four years before returning to Panshjir in 2001.

After 9/11, Qari Baba's competence was again in demand. Realizing his record of being brutal but effective, Karzai reappointed Baba as provincial governor. From the beginning, Baba was critical of the presence of international forces and this evolved into a major disagreement with Karzai. He served as governor only until late 2002, when Karzai removed him. Baba remained in Ghazni and is widely credited with having played an active role in encouraging local warlords to cooperate in the DDR process. It therefore came as quite a surprise when, in August 2005, Qari Baba was arrested by US troops on charges of hiding arms in his home (Tarzi 2005). It was even implied that Baba had participated in the insurgency against Afghan and US forces. This seems unlikely and has not been confirmed by any local sources. Even after this, however, Qari Baba was called upon by the government. In 2006 he served as an advisor (sometimes described as the de facto police chief) to the new governor, Sher Alam. Although his armed forces had long since been dismantled, his military competence as well as his skills as a mediator continued to be in demand in a province which was becoming increasingly conflict-ridden.

Qari Baba was killed on 17 March 2006, along with his son-in-law and four other men. He was returning from a visit to Ghazni city when the car was attacked by gunmen close to his house. Later on the same day, there was a failed attempt on the life of the governor as well. Taliban spokesmen claimed responsibility for both attacks. While few observers dispute the involvement of the Taliban, there are several versions of the story. Possibly it was a central Taliban decision, part of a larger campaign to eliminate religious leaders and others with local legitimacy and an agenda reminiscent of their own (Sinno 2008: 241). Others think Qari Baba's former enemies, now part of the Taliban, had taken the initiative. These sources mention both opponents from his own mujahedin and contending groups in the same area, as well as the descendants of the 'communists' whom he so mercilessly took on in earlier days.

Jalaluddin Haqqani: tribal-ideological warlord

One of Afghanistan's most effective resistance commanders throughout the 1980s, Jalaluddin Haqqani held posts in the mujahedin government before he joined the Taliban in 1995. His primary base is within the Zadran tribe. Haqqani was a graduate of the Darul-Uloom Haqqania madrasa in Pakistan and a trained Islamic scholar. Despite attempts to bring him over to the government's side in 2001, he has remained with the Taliban, but with a considerable degree of independence. A favourite of the United States in the 1980s, Haqqani was always closely connected to radical Islamist forces both in Pakistan and in the Gulf, and also had longstanding relationships with Al Qaeda leaders, whom he helped to set up training camps in Afghanistan. Haqqani, and increasingly his son, Sirajuddin, have played an active role in the Taliban insurgency in Pakistan's Waziristan districts as well and may be described as a transnational warlord. Haqqani has never focused on civilian affairs, but rather on military action. In recent years, he has also been identified as a core promoter of terrorist tactics, particularly suicide bombers (Ruttig 2009).

Born in Saraneh village in Paktia in 1930, Jalaluddin Haqqani pursued religious studies, first locally and later at the famous Darul-Uloom Haqqania madrasa at Akhora Khattak in Pakistan, from where he also took his name. The Haqqania madrasa has long been the main Deobandi teaching centre in Pakistan. Several central Taliban leaders have had their training there, as well as some of the key mujahedin figures of the 1980s. After completing his studies Jalaluddin took up teaching at the madrasa and developed close relations with both Mawlawi Fazlur Rehman and Qazi Hussain Ahmad, who went on to lead Pakistan's two most important Islamist parties, the Jamiat Ulema-e Islam and the Jamiat Islami respectively. Mawlawi Haqqani has two wives, at least one of whom is of Arab origin and possibly from bin Laden's family. While the family background of the second wife is unclear, it seems likely that his second marriage was used to cement political relationships with some of his radical contacts in the Gulf. Haqqani is reported to have 11 sons, of whom Sirajuddin and Khalil have followed in their father's footsteps. By 2007, Sirajuddin was increasingly the one in charge of day-to-day affairs on both sides of the border.

In general, politics in the part of Afghanistan where Haqqani hails from, the provinces of Paktia, Paktika and Khost in particular, are closely linked to tribal structures and tribal values (Glatzer 2002). The traditional consensus-oriented *jirga* is commonly used to resolve conflict both within and among various tribes. The *arbaki*, a tribal force set up to maintain security in the event that *jirga* deliberations are unsuccessful, is widespread. In this environment, Jalaluddin Haqqani stands out from the crowd of warlords, deriving legitimacy more from his religious status than from his tribal background (Dorronsoro 2005: 114). Yet as Olivier Roy pointed out in the mid-1980s, Haqqani's front was 'very tribal in character' (Roy 1986: 128). His immediate support base was within the large Zadran tribe, but not at any stage was he close to being its undisputed leader. Haqqani had considerable success in building support within several of the neighbouring tribes as well – Mangal, Tani and Waziri – whose territory spans the Pakistani–Afghan border. As an Islamist, Haqqani represented a new breed of leaders in the Pashtun tribal heartlands, yet, unlike many of the other Islamist commanders, he has always had a good sense of tribal politics.

While Jalaluddin Haqqani was in close contact with several leading Islamists, certainly on the Pakistani side, it does not seem that he was politically active prior to the 1978 communist coup. By 1979, however, Haqqani was firmly with Younos Khales, who had just broken out of Hekmatyar's Hezb-e Islami and established his own party under the same name. Khales, like Haqqani, was a blend of Islamist and traditionalist-tribal outlooks and recruited through both types of network. Haqqani remained a member of the Hezb (Khales) until joining the Taliban in 1995, but operated virtually as an independent commander. A fluent Arabic speaker with good contacts in the Gulf, Haqqani got money from a number of wealthy supporters and hosted many international Islamic warriors in his bases on both sides of the border. Already by the mid-1980s, he was reputed to have very good contacts with the ISI and the Central Intelligence Agency (CIA), and was a favoured recipient of international military aid throughout the anti-Soviet war (Jalaluddin Haqqani 2006). He was one out of ten commanders who received direct support from the CIA (Rubin 2008). All in all, Haqqani's variety of contacts, both in Pakistan and internationally, by far outweighed that of his party leader, Khales. More importantly, not being dependent on any single actor gave Haqqani considerable room for manoeuvre. The case of Haqqani contradicts Sinno's claim (2008: 14) that foreign sponsors tend to demand exclusivity, leaving warlord clients highly vulnerable to political shifts. With a strong reputation as an effective fighter, sponsors wanted Haqqani as a recipient and, through combining income from multiple sources, Haqqani protected himself against fickle patrons.

Unlike Qari Baba, Haqqani was never a provider of quasi-state services for the local population. His focus was always on armed struggle and on mobilizing the resources required to maintain the resistance. Most of his resources came from external sources, both in Pakistan and internationally. Both he and his sons made fund-raising trips to Saudi Arabia and the Gulf countries. He also profited from various businesses, including drug smuggling, arms trading and timber exports. Hence, Haqqani never needed to be accountable to the population within his territory.

In March 1991, the city of Khost fell to an alliance of mujahedin, the first provincial capital to be lost by the communists. The alliance, which was led by Haqqani, quickly disintegrated, in part because Hekmatyar's group, which had played a minor role in the battle, tried to take a disproportionate part of both the credit and the control (Rubin 2002: 255). In any case, the end result was that Khost city was systematically looted by the various mujahedin groups, with a heavy impact on the civilian population. Being the first city to be captured by the mujahedin, the looting of Khost sent a loud signal about the mujahedin's disregard for civilian lives and infrastructure.

Haqqani's relationships with key personalities in Al Qaeda, including Osama bin Laden, goes back to the first half of the 1980s, when he was hosting groups of international Islamist warriors based in Pakistan's Miram Shah and the Khost region of Afghanistan. By the mid-1980s, Haqqani was already a close associate of bin Laden and his then-mentor, the late Abdullah Azzam. At the time Haqqani had his own advance base with underground facilities at Zhawar, just across the border from Pakistan. The Zhawar base was a key logistical stronghold for the mujahedin in the 1980s. Bases in Zhawar were also used by the international Islamists who in 1988 took the name Al Qaeda. The Zhawar base was the target of numerous attacks by PDPA and Soviet forces (Grau and Jalali 2001) and, a decade later, for the Clinton Administration's missile attacks after the bombings of the US embassies in Dar-es-Salaam and Nairobi, when it served as a main base for Al Qaeda.

Khost and the surrounding Paktika province fell to the Taliban in early 1995. For the Taliban, dominated by Kandahari clerics, the early inclusion of Haqqani was important for building credibility in the eastern areas (Sinno 2008). Haqqani made a deal with the Taliban, contributing a sizeable force to its campaign, which continued eastwards and ended with the takeover of Kabul in September 1996 (Rasanayagam 2003: 149). Haqqani was ideal for Taliban co-optation:

> The Taliban also astutely used their knowledge of the Pashtun landscape to decide whether to co-opt, discard, or assassinate different commanders. The Taliban co-opted leaders who wouldn't tarnish their finely calibrated image as heralds of a better order and who could enhance their military potential. Jalaluddin Haqqani, the master guerrilla leader and uncompromising learned scholar without independent ambitions, was the epitome of the co-optable commander.
>
> (Bhatia and Sedra 2008: 241)

Just as in the early days of the mujahedin government some three and a half years earlier, Haqqani was appointed a minister, this time for Borders and Tribal Affairs. Haqqani was only moderately engaged in his ministerial duties, which he left largely to his brother Khalil. Jalaluddin himself was now heavily engaged in the war against the Northern Alliance. He played a central role in the brutal trench warfare on the Shamali plains to the north of Kabul, demolishing virtually all infrastructure and driving out most of the local population. The Shamali campaign, at its most intense in 1996–7, has often been referred to as 'ethnic cleansing' of the majority Tajik population (Human Rights Watch 2007). Again, Haqqani's talents for warfare were put to use. As at earlier crossroads, Haqqani shied away from political and administrative duties, privileging armed action.

In the run-up to the intervention in 2001, US and Pakistani intelligence jointly decided to try to convince Haqqani to support the new order. Several meetings took place in Islamabad and Rawalpindi, with little result. It has been speculated that some of Haqqani's longstanding ISI contacts encouraged him to keep up the fight, given their mixed sympathy with the US-led intervention (Gannon 2005: 269; Rashid 2008). The negotiations took place while Haqqani was hosting a number of Al Qaeda leaders. One of Haqqani's guests, according to Ahmed Rashid, was Osama bin Laden himself, in one of his safe houses in Pakistan's North Waziristan, close to the Afghan border (Rashid 2008: 99). Journalist Kathy Gannon believes Haqqani could have handed over the whole network, had he wanted to. In December 2001, at the time of Karzai's inauguration, Haqqani declared that the time to fight was over and sent a delegation of Zadrani tribesmen to Kabul to attend. The convoy was bombed by the United States, probably misinformed by one of his rivals, and some 60 people were reportedly killed (Rubin 2008). While it is hard to say how sincere Haqqani was in reconciling at this point, there is little doubt that the US bombing effectively blocked it.

Over the next couple of years, Haqqani kept a low profile, knowing that he was a prime target. Yet, he and his sons were deeply involved in much of the unrest that took place on both sides of the border. He appears to have been able to rebuild his armed capacity as well as his sources of finance, although a significant part of his former infrastructure had either been bombed or closed down. Haqqani increasingly recruited among the Pashtuns on the Pakistani side of the border, who were handsomely paid to protect the foreign guests, over time forming the backbone of the so-called 'Pakistani Taliban'. With his ability to lead, or at least inspire, violence on both sides of the border, Haqqani had become a genuine transnational warlord.

The adoption of terrorist tactics in Afghanistan – the use of suicide bombers, hostage-taking and beheadings – is often said to be Haqqani's work (Giustozzi 2007: 91–2). Sirajuddin Haqqani, his son, is talked about as a representative of a new generation of Taliban, far more militant than Jalaluddin's generation (Burke 2007). Haqqani is a member of the inner leadership council of the Taliban. Until 2006, it seems unlikely that

Haqqani played a key role in the military strategizing of the Taliban. The so-called Haqqani front was often perceived as an entity of its own, only loosely connected to the Taliban (Cordesman 2006). After the death of Mullah Dadullah in 2006, however, there were a number of reports, probably planted to enhance his standing, that Haqqani had been appointed the general commander of the Taliban (Ruttig 2009: 61). The Afghan government, backed by US sources, has accused Haqqani of the attacks on Kabul's Hotel Serena in January and on the Indian embassy in July 2008 (Mazzetti and Schmitt 2008).

In sum, since the end of the 1970s Haqqani has been known as an effective and merciless warrior. When fighting the PDPA and its Soviet supporters, his long-term perspective and use of advanced technology made him considerably more sophisticated than many contemporary warlords. The combination of a will to exert massive violence and his strategic and tactical skills made him quite an asset for the Taliban regime, particularly in its battles with the Northern Alliance from 1996 onwards.

As a warlord type, Haqqani was initially reliant on local support, but expanded beyond the limitations set by local checks and balances. His interest in local welfare has been negligible. While expressing some interest, he ended up rejecting invitations to become part of the post-2001 regime, remaining loyal to his long-term associates within Al Qaeda and in Pakistan. Since then, he has been a key actor in Taliban's expanding repertoire of violence. He and his sons have been instrumental in transnationalizing the Taliban, transforming the movement into a network that fights the governments of both Afghanistan and Pakistan. In this sense, Haqqani is the archetypical transnational warlord. Remaining close to his one-time teachers and colleagues at the Akhora Khattak madrasa, he has himself been a key agent in the radicalization of traditional religious networks on both sides of the border.

Comparing the trajectories of Afghan warlords

The political biographies examined above suggest that military capability and reputation remain the core of a warlord's status when the war ends. All three men – Rocketi, Baba, Haqqani – were known as effective military commanders. They were able to economize on resources and not engage in fighting when no gains were to be made; they were also capable of using extensive violence against anybody seen to threaten their rule. It is commonly assumed that the status of warlords, in order to be upheld, hinges on regular involvement in military action. However, both Baba (after deserting the Taliban in the 1990s) and Rocketi (after joining the post-2001 government) continued to be respected – even feared – years after they had disengaged from military action and even long after their military infrastructure had been dismantled. A violent reputation can be an effective means of gaining respect and obedience in wartime; in politics, however, it may prove counterproductive. Indeed, Rocketi, the only one who pursued a political career, has gone to considerable lengths to distance himself from his violent past. He has had only limited success, in part because his political talent does not match his military skill. Baba, balancing his military reputation with an interest in local welfare, might have been more successful had he been given the opportunity. Haqqani, with a reputation for being both merciless to his opponents and already in the 1980s strongly against non-Pashtuns, decided not to give politics a chance, perhaps realizing the insurmountable legitimacy problems he would face.

In terms of a relational approach to explaining warlordism, we see that all three men initially relied on local support and would never have made their mark as warlords had they not been able to continue to muster the support of local tribal networks. All three had some sort of religious stature, as was common throughout the Pashtun southeast, although less so in the cases of Rocketi and Baba. While religious position carries an element of legitimacy, the key was tribal support. At this point, the patterns differ widely. Rocketi had support from one of the less significant tribes in the area (albeit significant across the larger south and southeast), but gained wider local support because of his military skills. Baba was elected as a compromise candidate from the four major local entities, himself being an outsider, but he was encumbered by a system of sub-commanders from the respective tribes who held him accountable. Hence, Baba's experience contradicts the notion, formulated at the outset, that warlords over time become increasingly sovereign by freeing themselves from local checks and balances. Haqqani conforms to the notion, however: his initial basis of power was within a dominant local tribe, but accountability to local constituencies declined as his external financing increased. He also increasingly recruited beyond the Zadran tribe on both sides of the Pakistani–Afghan border. It is possible that in adapting to post-conflict politics, warlords such as Rocketi and Haqqani faced much larger problems in that they had moved beyond the ties with their original constituency, whereas the one who was kept partially accountable – Qari Baba – was better placed to play a genuine political role. The problem in Qari Baba's case is that the very reason he was held accountable was that he did not himself emerge from any of the tribal entities that backed him during the war, which in turn made him vulnerable.

In a political economy perspective, the first point to note is that none of the three warlords was driven by economic concerns. Rather, economic resources were only a means to an end. Apart from that, there are interesting differences. The politically most vulnerable candidate, Baba, invested most heavily in local welfare. He actively sought to develop local health and education systems in areas under his control and used this to justify both taxation and conscription amongst his subjects. Neither Rocketi nor Haqqani attempted to expand popular support through a social contract of welfare provision. Haqqani conformed more to the standard image, relying in part on income from a grey economy, but overwhelmingly on external support. In Haqqani's case, however, this does not seem to have instilled the vulnerability to external controls suggested by many analysts. Rather, being in demand for his skills at waging war, he was able to maintain support from different sources. Haqqani's relative success in this regard, however, relied on his ability to operate with considerable freedom on both sides of the Pakistani–Afghan border. More importantly, a comparison of the three men indicates that warlords who rely on local support for financing are less likely to engage in oppositional violence when the war ends. Yet, as with Rocketi, such warlords may find it difficult to maintain political influence, which also takes political skill that many warlords lack. In the absence of external support, warlords have to be responsive to the financial promises of a new government, as was the case with both Baba and Rocketi when the mujahedin took power in 1992.

Ideologically, the differences among the three are marked. Haqqani is so ideologically committed that he challenges the conventional concept of the warlord as a non-ideological leader, yet he appears not to have taken a lead in formulating general political strategies or objectives. His strength lies in providing and developing the means needed to reach radical ends. Baba, while not articulating a vision of the state and the polity, was committed to local security and welfare, possibly for reasons beyond narrow self-interest. In terms of the model of the non-ideological warlord, Rocketi is the ideal type, not committed to a radical cause but preoccupied with local security, and, of course, his own power. Historically, all three men owed their emergence as warlords to a degree of religious legitimacy. While their religious leadership roles as such had little impact on their conduct as warlords, they carried networks and influences that were decisive for later choices. Thus, Haqqani stayed committed to contacts from his madrasa days in Pakistan, whereas Rocketi was persuaded by a member of one of Afghanistan's most influential Sufi families to join the Karzai government. Hence, while warlords may not be the chief ideologues, ideology – at least in its religious form – matters. It defines the lines of commonality and difference on which solidarity and work relationships are based. Such relationships interact with economic and ideological factors to define the military capacity of any warlord. Ultimately, military capacity itself is an uncertain foundation for power; it is at the interface between the three other types of factors that we can understand its robustness.

Where does this leave us when it comes to accommodating warlords within a new political order? In his influential work, Stedman (1997) suggests three principal ways of accommodating potential 'spoilers': through coercion (the use of armed force, or the threat of using it); inducement (offering political positions or other alternatives); and socialization (the process of building a common normative foundation). A fourth way, as the above analysis shows, would be to attack the relational base of a warlord by rebuilding structures of accountability and possibly by supporting aggrieved groups that may overturn warlords who have lost touch with their erstwhile supporters. These four strategies for dealing with warlords correspond with the broad framework informing this chapter: military skill (i.e. coercion), political economy (i.e. inducement), ideology (i.e. socialization) and relationships (i.e. accountability). The four are not necessarily mutually exclusive. In the case of Rocketi, for example, all seem to have been at work: the threat of coercion was instrumental in convincing him to lay down arms, the promise of a political future solidified the decision, and his responsiveness to local supporters (and political mentors) did likewise insofar as his participation in the political process was meant to convince them he would not to revert to violent means. With Haqqani on the other hand, this combined strategy did not work. He was largely unresponsive to a local constituency, he had access to generous external support that made an alternative course of action possible, he was deeply embedded with individuals and organizations committed to the insurgency, and, when he explored accommodation by sending a delegation to Kabul to attend Karzai's inauguration, the international coercive apparatus (probably intentionally misled) responded by killing 60 of his men and thus effectively sealed off the path of co-option.

Notes

1 In researching this chapter I owe a great debt to two Afghan research assistants, who must remain anonymous. I am also grateful for comments on earlier versions from Arne Strand and Astri Suhrke, and deeply grateful to all those Afghans who volunteered their time to be interviewed for this study but whose identities I promised not to reveal.
2 A total of 30 interviews have been conducted specifically for this project (11 focusing on Rocketi, ten on Baba, six on Haqqani and three interviews dealing with all of them).
3 The Norwegian Afghanistan Committee (NAC), a small NGO set up in solidarity with the Afghan resistance in 1980, worked closely with Qari Baba in the period 1986–91 (Skaufjord 2006). The author worked for NAC from 1990 to 1992.

Bibliography

Bhatia, Michael and Sedra, Mark (2008) *Afghanistan, Arms and Conflict: Armed Groups, Disarmament and Security in a Post-War Society*, London: Routledge.

Burke, Jason (2007) 'The New Taliban', *Observer*, 14 October.

Collier, Paul and Hoeffler, Anke (2002) *Greed and Grievance in Civil War*, Oxford: Centre for the Study of African Economies.

Cordesman, Anthony H. (2006) 'One war we can still win', *New York Times*, 13 December.

Dorronsoro, Gilles (2005) *Revolution Unending: Afghanistan, 1979 to the Present*, New York: Columbia University Press.

Dorronsoro, Gilles (2006 [1994]) 'Le mouvement des Taleban en Afghanistan', *Cemoti*, 19.

Gannon, Kathy (2005) *I is for Infidel: From Holy War to Holy Terror*, New York: Public Affairs.

Giustozzi, Antonio (2003) *Respectable Warlords? The Politics of State-Building in Post-Taleban Afghanistan*, Crisis States Programme Working Papers series 1, 33, London: Crisis States Research Centre, London School of Economics and Political Science.

Giustozzi, Antonio (2007) *Armed Politics and Political Competition in Afghanistan*, CMI Working Paper, Bergen: Chr. Michelsen Institute.

Glatzer, Bernt (2002) 'The Pashtun tribal system', in Georg Pfeffer and Deepak Kumar Behera (eds) *Concept of Tribal Society*, New Delhi: Concept Publishers, pp. 265–82.

Grau, Lester W. and Jalali, Ali Ahmad (2001) 'The campaign for the caves: the battles for Zhawar in the Soviet-Afghan War', *Journal of Slavic Military Studies*, 14(3): 69–92.

Harpviken, Kristian Berg (2009) *Social Networks and Migration in Wartime Afghanistan*, Basingstoke: Palgrave Macmillan.

Human Rights Watch (2007) *The Human Cost: The Consequences of Insurgent Attacks in Afghanistan*, New York: Human Rights Watch.

'Jalaluddin Haqqani' (2006) *Frontline*.

Keen, David (1998) *The Economic Functions of Violence in Civil Wars*, Adelphi Paper 320, London: International Institute of Strategic Studies.

Kibel, Amanda (2001) 'Live from Afghanistan', *CNN*, 18 December.

Marten, Kimberly (2007) 'Warlordism in comparative perspective', *International Security*, 31: 41–73.

Mazzetti, Mark and Schmitt, Eric (2008) 'Pakistanis aided attack in Kabul, US officials say', *New York Times*, 1 August.

Miliband, David (2008) 'British troops have a clear mission in Afghanistan', *Telegraph*, 21 June.

Olson, Mancur (1993) 'Dictatorship, democracy and development', *American Political Science Review*, 87(3): 567–76.

Rasanayagam, Angelo (2003) *Afghanistan: A Modern History*, London: I B Tauris

Rashid, Ahmed (2000) *Taliban: Islam, Oil and the New Great Game in Central Asia*, London: I B Tauris.

Rashid, Ahmed (2008) *Descent into Chaos: How the War against Islamic Extremism is being lost in Pakistan, Afghanistan and Central Asia*, London: Allen Lane.

Reno, William (1998) *Warlord Politics and African States*, Boulder, CO: Lynne Rienner.

Reno, William (2002) 'Mafiya troubles, warlord crisis', in Mark R. Beissinger and Crawford Young (eds) *Beyond State Crisis? Postcolonial Africa and post-Soviet Eurasia in Comparative Perspective*, Baltimore, MD: Johns Hopkins University Press, pp. 105–27.

Roy, Olivier (1986) *Islam and Resistance in Afghanistan*, Cambridge: Cambridge University Press.

Rubin, Barnett R. (2002) *The Fragmentation of Afghanistan: State Formation and Collapse in the International System*, second edition, New Haven: Yale University Press.

Rubin, Barnett R. (2008) 'New York Times on ISI: Serena Hotel attack (plus update connecting the two and historical background)'. Blog post, online, available at: http://icga.blogspot.com/2008/01/new-york-times-on-isi-serena-hotel.html.

Ruttig, Thomas (2009) 'Loya Paktia's insurgency: the Haqqani network as an autonomous entity', in Antonio Giustozzi (ed.) *Decoding the New Taliban: Insights from the Afghan Field*, New York: Columbia University Press, pp. 57–88.

Sands, Chris (2006) 'Afghan MPs predict "very big war"', *Dominion*, 19 December. Online, available at: www.dominionpaper.ca/accounts/2006/12/19/afghan_mps.html.

Sennott, Charles (2007) 'Afghanistan at the tipping point', *Carnegie Reporter*, 4(3): 2–11.

Sinno, Abdulkader H (2008) *Organizations at War in Afghanistan and Beyond*, Ithaca, NY: Cornell University Press.

Skaufjord, Terje (2006) 'Qari Baba drept av Taliban', *AfghanistanNytt*, 1–2006.

Stedman, Stephen John (1997) 'Spoiler problems in peace processes', *International Security*, 22: 5–53.

Tarzi, Amin (2005) 'Afghanistan report', *Radio Free Europe/Radio Liberty*, 18 August.

Tilly, Charles (2003) 'Armed force, regimes and contention in Europe since 1650', in Diane E. Davis and Anthony W. Pereira (eds) *Irregular Armed Forces and their Role in Politics and State Formation*, Cambridge: University of Cambridge Press, pp. 37–81.

US Department of State (1995) 'Afghanistan human rights practices: 1994'. Online, available at: http://dosfan.lib.uic.edu/ERC/democracy/1994_hrp_report/94hrp_report_sasia/Afghanistan.html.

Wood, Elisabeth Jean (2008) 'The social processes of civil war: the wartime transformation of social networks', *Annual Review of Political Science*, 11: 539–61.

Yusufzai, Rahimullah (2002) 'Still on the run: the hunt for top Al-Qaeda and Taliban leaders continues…', *Newsline*.

10 Violence in post-war Cambodia

Sorpong Peou

A significant number of violent conflicts end in peace agreements that commit the warring factions to democratization – thus allowing competition for power through elections rather than combat – and marketization. Accordingly, this chapter seeks to answer the following questions: Does violence end the moment that warring factions sign their peace agreements? And if it does not, why does post-agreement violence continue?

Scholars have acknowledged that violence often continues after peace agreements are signed, but disagree on the factors that perpetuate violence. Two general approaches emphasize the 'legacies of war' and the 'nature of the peace'. Legacies-of-war perspectives emphasize the structural legacies of socio-cultural, historical, economic and institutional factors. Nature-of-the-peace perspectives are critical of neoliberalism: some proponents argue that a general framework for peace based on neoliberalization creates new sources of violence, while others regard violence as being rooted in growing socio-economic inequalities associated with economic liberalization.

These two broad approaches are not mutually incompatible, however. Legacies matter, especially in institutional terms. The culture, ideology and history of violence may linger after a peace agreement is signed, but above all else the fact of an extremely weak system of government, without effective institutional checks and balances at the state level, is the main permissive cause. Hegemonic-party politics continues, perpetuating mutual animosities among former adversaries, their mutual distrust and hence their tendency to resort to violence. Violence in post-war states is less correlated with the introduction of democratization and marketization than with the ongoing fragility of democratic institutions that are incapable of guaranteeing mutual trust based on security among former foes, of checking any hegemonic ambitions that might perpetuate the legacies of violence and of responding to unscrupulous market forces. For their part, external actors have difficulty building institutions because of their self-interest and their unwillingness or/and inability to engage in long-term projects.

To shed empirical light on these arguments, this chapter relies on the Cambodian experience and is divided into three parts. The first part describes change and continuity in the various forms of violence prior to and following Cambodia's 1991 peace deal. The second part evaluates the causes of violence by closely examining cultural, historical and institutional legacies and concludes that the lack of an effective system of institutional checks and balances remains a permissive cause of violence. The third part shows that the neoliberal peacebuilding agenda based on democratization and marketization has also contributed to political and economic violence, but that the more serious challenge lies in the limitations on institution building. Members of the international community appear to have been unable to help build effective state institutions capable of holding powerful members of the political, military, security and economic elites to account for their violent actions. They not only preferred political stability, thus allowing the Cambodian People's Party (CPP) to consolidate power (a case of victor's peace and violence), but also pursued their interests and were thus inclined to support the authoritarian behaviour of Prime Minister Hun Sen. The main contention of this chapter is that various forms of violence in post-war Cambodia can be traced to their cultural, ideological, historical, socio-economic and institutional roots and that the neoliberal peacebuilding agenda has had very limited success in ensuring better socio-economic equity and democratic institutionalization (simply defined as the process of democratic institution building and strengthening), which has largely been trumped by security politics.

Violence in post-war Cambodia

Throughout the 1980s, the warring factions included the People's Republic of Kampuchea (PRK, later renamed State of Cambodia or SOC, which formed the CPP in the early 1990s); the Khmer Rouge (officially known as Democratic Kampuchea); and two other major armed resistance forces (the National United Front for an Independent, Neutral, Peaceful and Cooperative Cambodia (FUNCINPEC) and the Khmer People's National Liberation Front (KPNLF)). The PRK/SOC was thus fighting against three armed enemies, the Khmer Rouge, FUNCINPEC and KPNLF, which formed the Coalition Government of Democratic Kampuchea (CGDK, a government-in-exile representing Cambodia at the UN). The CGDK received support from Western powers such as the United States, as well as from China and the Association of Southeast Asian Nations (ASEAN), whereas the PRK/SOC was deprived of a seat at the UN but received active support from members of the Soviet bloc. The early 1990s saw a triple transition in Cambodia: from war to peace, from political authoritarianism to liberal democracy and from socialism to capitalism.

Peace agreements

Four Cambodian factions signed the Agreements on a Comprehensive Political Settlement of the Cambodia Conflict on 23 October 1991. According to the agreements, the four Cambodian signatories were to end their armed conflict by, among other things, respecting a ceasefire, ceasing outside military assistance, swapping the battlefield for the ballot box, complying with international instruments covering human rights and moving toward capitalism. A transition from war to peace meant that the Cambodian signatories agreed to observe a comprehensive ceasefire, to 'order their armed forces immediately to disengage and refrain from all hostilities and any deployment, movement or action that would extend the territory they control or that might lead to a resumption of fighting', and to plan for the regrouping, cantonment and disarmament of their forces (annex 2, Article 1). A transition from authoritarianism to democracy meant that the signatories agreed to compete for power in the electoral process. They would allow the Cambodian people to have the right to determine their own future through free and fair elections and had to 'commit themselves to respect the results of these elections once certified as free and fair by the United Nations' (part II, Articles 12, 13; see also annex 3). The peace agreements also stated that the process of reconstruction 'should promote Cambodian entrepreneurship and make use of the private sector, among other sectors, to help advance self-sustaining economic growth' (United Nations 1991: 49).

It should be noted, however, that the warring factions did not end the war right after they had put their signatures on the peace agreements. The CPP armed forces and those belonging to FUNCINPEC and the Khmer Rouge still engaged in armed clashes. The Khmer Rouge army was responsible for most of the violations of the ceasefire and effectively resisted disarmament efforts, but it was not the only signatory to do so: the CPP leadership was never keen to see its armed forces disarmed, either.

As the result of their refusal to play the game by its rules, the military aspect of the peace agreements failed: the factional forces were unwilling to comply properly with their initial formal agreement to report to regrouping areas and to surrender their arms, ammunition and military equipment to the designated cantonment areas. The election took place in May 1993, but the Khmer Rouge army continued its armed rebellion. This time, however, the rebels were on their own and discredited, battling both their former CGDK allies and their old enemy, who shared power in the newly elected coalition government (led by First Prime Minister Norodom Ranariddh of FUNCINPEC and Second Prime Minister Hun Sen of the CPP). The war ended early in 1999, but only after the Khmer Rouge leadership had disintegrated. Intra-factional friction led to a series of events that spelled the end of this armed rebellion. It thus took Cambodia another eight years after the signing of the Peace Agreements before the armed conflict came to a complete end; however, other forms of violence have continued.

Post-war political violence

Political violence had intensified in the years leading up to 1998, as the CPP relied on violent tactics to repress other members of the coalition government. The violent incidents included the 1997 grenade attacks on the ex-KPNLF Buddhist Liberal Democratic Party (BLDP), which left at least 17 people dead, and the growing tension between the two prime ministers, which led to a violent putsch against Prince Ranariddh in July 1997, resulting in more than 100 political killings.

After removing his co-prime minister from power, Second Prime Minister Hun Sen proved successful in consolidating his political and military power; however, violent opposition to his rule did not end quickly. Coup attempts and rumours about possible coups against Hun Sen continued after the CPP won the 1998 election. The resistance movement Cambodian Freedom Fighters (CFF), led by its president Yasith Chhun, a California-based Cambodian-American, challenged the Hun Sen regime. The CFF orchestrated a coup attempt known as 'Operation Volcano' in November 2000 aiming to overthrow Hun Sen, which led to an armed clash in Phnom Penh with government forces. The coup resulted in three deaths and an unknown number of injuries, but failed. The CFF has since disintegrated, after its leader was jailed by the United States.

When assessed in terms of the number of assassinations, grenade attacks and coups, the overall trend shows that the level of political violence in the 2000s declined noticeably. Hun Sen has since consolidated his authoritarian power base, using political tactics to weaken the opposition. The 2003 and 2008 national elections saw the political trend moving in favour of the prime minister. The main opposition parties, particularly the BLDP and FUNCINPEC, disintegrated. The BLDP did not even complete in 2003 and the royalist party fell apart when it ousted its president, Prince Ranariddh. Although the 2008 election went far more smoothly and peacefully than the previously ones, the results remained controversial. Political violence, though growing less intense over recent years owing to Hun Sen's consolidated power, has not disappeared.

Political rights and civil liberties (especially freedoms of expression, strike and demonstration) have been increasingly suppressed in recent years. Violence against civil liberties has not been limited to party members, with violence often directed at religious elements, including Buddhist monks, involved in peaceful demonstrations.

Post-war social violence

Although not widespread and regular or frequent, violence by members of the military and security apparatus has persisted. Individual military and police officers continue to stand above the law. Various NGOs have reported incidents of violence in which military and police officers were involved in a spate of shootings (LICADHO 2008b).

Moreover, Cambodia has often witnessed high homicide rates, as well as 'mob violence' or 'street justice'. Homicide includes armed robbery, and street justice was often carried out when local crowds took matters into their own hands, confronting criminals such as thieves and often lynching them. This type of violence is known as 'people's courts', with police officers turning a blind eye or on many occasions being complicit. At least 65 such incidents had occurred by June 2002 (United Nations 2002).

A positive trend in ethnic violence can be observed, however. In the early 1990s, this form of violence frequently occurred when ethnic

Vietnamese were subject to armed attack, especially by the Khmer Rouge army. Other opposition parties also adopted a nationalist stance in an attempt to discredit the pro-Vietnam SOC-turned-CPP. After the Khmer Rouge rebellion ended in the late 1990s, ethnic violence against Vietnamese declined. Early in 2001, the UN Special Representative reported on the difficult situation of ethnic Vietnamese. The report adds that 'ethnic minority groups have been victims of discrimination and inadequate consideration of their cultural and traditional beliefs' (United Nations 2001: 22). In 2003, ethnic violence began to disappear from the electoral scene across the country, although xenophobic politics still continued at the attitudinal level. The last act of ethnic violence occurred in January 2003, when anti-Thai riots broke out. Overall, serious physical violence against ethnic minorities has since disappeared. This does not mean that ethnic minorities now enjoy full personal security. Subsequent reports by the UN representative have not focused their attention on this issue, however. They have expressed concerns about indigenous minority groups, which are said to be losing traditional lands as a source of their livelihood and identity, but as will be discussed later, other Cambodians have also faced the same problem.

The Cambodian authorities also mistreated the ethnic minority groups which fled to Cambodia from Vietnam in early 2001 (who became known as the Montagnard asylum seekers), but this issue has now been muted. Initially, Cambodia decided to close down the refugee camps, said that newcomers would no longer be accepted and denied the UN High Commissioner for Refugees (UNHCR) access to border areas where asylum seekers were making claims about their refugee status. Some of the asylum seekers were subjected to harassment and forced deportation. Since the governments of Cambodia and Vietnam and the UNHCR signed a Memorandum of Understanding in January 2005, this ethnic problem has no longer captured the attention of human rights organizations.

Economic violence

What have become more widespread in recent years are new forms of economic violence directed at the poor and powerless individuals within society. Poverty remains widespread. Land-grabbing is one form that has now drawn the attention of local and international organizations alike. This form of economic violence has been committed mainly by members of the politically and economically powerful elites who 'secured ownership of lands already rightfully owned or occupied by powerless and poor people'. Through the use of illicit and arbitrary means, these powerful elements 'also secured cooperation from law enforcement agencies and courts of law to enforce their ownership and to evict the owners or residents' and 'offer to pay compensation that is not commensurate with the market prices of the affected lands and the hardship of relocation' (Hay 2008: 1). Unlawful land-grabbing by members of the elites appears to have gone on unresolved (Asian Legal Resource Centre 2007: 2; United Nations 2009: 13; Amnesty International 2008). As of 2009, land-grabbing had not ended, although the number of complaints of such violence had dropped in 2007, as noted earlier. The drop may have resulted in part from repression. Powerful individuals also grabbed forestry land, including national parks, cleared forests for personal purposes and even threatened park rangers (Hay 2008). The overall situation worsened to the point that it grabbed the attention of Hun Sen, who declared on 3 March 2007 that his government would set out to wage 'a war against land-grabbers', but the war is considered to have been ineffective.

Based on the above observations, we can generally conclude that eight years after the signing of the peace agreements Cambodia has witnessed the end of military violence but not of other forms of violence. Violence against ethnic groups diminished, although discrimination against them still existed. The level of political violence decreased, as shown by the decline in the overall number of people killed and injured, but still persisted. Homicide and mob violence remained common and economic violence grew worse in more recent years.

The legacies of war and violence

What explains the continuation of the war until it ended in 1999 and the different forms of violence in Cambodia after the peace agreements were signed? Historical, cultural, ideological and institutional legacies have some explanatory power.

Historical and cultural legacies

Cambodian history is replete with struggles for power, war and violence. Military violence between Cambodia and its neighbours, for instance, resulted from the ambitions of Siam (now Thailand) and Vietnam to establish their suzerainty over Cambodia. Armed violence between these countries, however, often had its roots in Cambodia's domestic politics, in particular struggles for political supremacy. For instance, King Ang Chan II (1791–835) had a brother who sought to overthrow him in 1811 by soliciting Siamese support. The Siamese king, Rama II (1768–824), responded by sending in an army to oust Ang Chan, who then fled to Vietnam in search of aid to regain his throne. The Vietnamese emperor Gia Long (1762–820) responded by dispatching to Cambodia a large army, which forced the Siamese troops to withdraw from Cambodia without war and helped restore Chan's throne in 1812 (Chandler 1993: 118–19). This story of power struggles reveals both the old problem of royal sibling rivalry (a kind of rivalry that often led to military violence) and the persistent nature of violence that was deeply rooted in personal power politics. Socio-culturalists also tend to refer to Cambodia's cultural tradition of absolute power, its anti-democratic or illiberal political culture, or its 'culture of disproportionate revenge' based on the notion of 'a head for an eye' (Hinton 2002).

Contemporary history still showed the persistence of such violent practices. When still in power as head of state, for instance, Prince Norodom

Sihanouk mounted verbal and physical attacks on his opponents and was complicit in his security agents' use of terror as a weapon against them. Rebels such as those involved in the Samlaut peasant revolt in the late 1960s were harshly dealt with. The heads of some villagers accused of participating in the revolt were severed and these 'grisly trophies' were brought to Phnom Penh 'as evidence of the army's success' (Osborne 1994: 192). Of all the regimes in living memory, the one presided over by the Khmer Rouge revolutionaries was by far the most ruthless. Accused enemies of the state were arrested without warrant and were never put on trial. They lived in festering hells of lost hope and in inhumane squalor. They were extra-judicially executed and tortured in various cruel forms, such as the use of steel clubs, cart axles and water pipes to hit the base of the neck. Khmer Rouge leaders have now been charged with genocide, war crimes and crimes against humanity. War and repressive violence were less intense throughout the 1980s but still persisted.

Ideological and socio-economic legacies

Ideological legacies rooted in socialism further help explain violence. As noted, the SOC/CPP leadership is made up of some Khmer Rouge remnants who survived the purges by the Pol Pot group. This group is said to have adopted a type of ideology inspired by Maoism and radical egalitarianism under the dictatorship of the Communist Party of Kampuchea (PKK), which justified its use of violence as a necessary political instrument to build and maintain an egalitarian society (Jackson 1989). Although it has officially embraced liberal democracy and capitalism, the CPP was the offspring of the People's Revolutionary Party of Kampuchea (PRPK), whose objective was to build socialism. The legacy of this ideology is that the CPP has a history of enjoying a monopoly of political power and has thus found it difficult sharing power with opposition parties, such as the royalists and democrats. Because of its ideological background, the CPP leadership could not afford to trust its political opponents either, especially those who were pro-Western and supportive of international criminal justice.

Because of the wars and the Khmer Rouge reign of terror, much of the Cambodian economy was destroyed. In its aftermath the socio-economic conditions were appalling. Cambodia remains one of the poorest countries in the world. The percentage of people living below the poverty line has declined only slowly, from 40–50 per cent in 1994 to 36.1 per cent in 1997 and to 35 per cent in 2004. Overall, per capita gross national income (GNI) appears to have risen gradually from $247 in 1998 to $320 in 2005, and may have reached $340 in 2008. In 2005, the monthly income of a soldier was about $15, of a public school teacher no more than $30 per month and of a factory worker about $45 per month. Socio-economic inequalities persist and continue to widen. When measured in terms of the UN Development Programme's Human Development Index (HDI), social exclusion on the basis of poverty, education or gender discrimination remains both quantitatively and qualitatively extensive and structurally ingrained. The HDI score stood at 0.541 in 2001, ranking Cambodia 121st among 174 countries. In 2002, it ranked 131st out of 175 nations. When measured against the increase in socio-economic inequality, which rose from a Gini coefficient of 0.35 in 1994 to 0.40 in 2004 (a Gini score of 1 represents perfect inequality, whereas a Gini of 0 represents perfect equality), per capita GNI reveals that the poor have made no significant improvement. Cambodia still faces a growing unemployment problem, as the labour_force continues to expand because of rapid demographic growth. The economy remains uncompetitive and based on a few sectors (tourism, textiles and construction), which have not generated enough jobs for the unemployed. The discovery of major offshore oil and gas fields has improved Cambodia's economic prospects, provided that the revenues from such resources are not squandered through corruption. The exploitation of timber resources is an environmental challenge facing the country. This socio-economic legacy has encouraged the Cambodian regime to regard the need for economic development as more urgent than the demand for democracy. The legacy has thus limited the progress of democratic institutionalization, and is used to justify the need for restoring and maintaining political stability and for tolerating the use of repressive violence.

Cultural, historical, ideological and socio-economic perspectives on violence have insufficient explanatory power, however. Can Cambodian culture always be characterized as one based on 'a head for an eye'? Do most Cambodians always seek revenge in this form? The signing of the Paris Peace Agreements in 1991 and the end of the Khmer Rouge rebellion in 1999, for instance, did not, as noted, result from vengeance and violence or war but from a form of political compromise that allowed all former enemies to take part in the negotiation and political processes. The Khmer Rouge movement became de-legitimated after it pulled out of the electoral process in 1993 and disintegrated in 1998, following a series of formal and informal amnesties given to its top leaders and the subsequent reintegration of its army into the national armed forces. Government leaders have resisted efforts at putting Khmer Rouge leaders on trial.

Historical legacies help to shed additional light on the more recent animosities driven by mutual mistrust among the factional power contenders, but they do not tell us how Hun Sen succeeded in consolidating political power – a case of victor's peace. History does not forever determine political events or perpetuate violence. Recent growth in peace and political stability has had more to do with Hun Sen's growing sense of self-confidence and security – a condition for making his political regime less prone to violence. The successful consolidation of his political power has also made it possible for the regime to weaken ethnic politics in the country, especially violence against ethnic Vietnamese. As noted, the SOC/CPP enjoyed the support of Vietnam throughout the 1980s and has still maintained close relations with the latter.

Ideological and socio-economic legacies also matter but still have limited explanatory power. Members of the CPP elite today do not seem to have a coherent ideology and have instead pursued an unscrupulous form of capitalism, as noted elsewhere in this chapter. Poor socio-economic conditions help explain economic violence, such as illegal land grabbing and land disputes, but this form of economic violence also appears to have resulted from Cambodia's weak institutions.

The persistence of institutional weaknesses

The Cambodian political elites have shown little interest in building state institutions. There seems to be 'little difference between the way Cambodia was governed when the French turned the country into its colony in the 1860s and the way Angkor had been governed almost a thousand years before' (Chandler 1993: 142). If the elites resisted institution-building efforts, it was because they regarded them as jeopardizing their security interests. The French colonialists, for instance, learned that King Norodom behaved in 'an arbitrary, authoritarian way' and 'was drawn less by the idea of a sound administration than by the imperatives of personal survival' (Chandler 1993: 142). Post-independence history also saw little institutionalization of politics, and the Khmer Rouge regime was most responsible for the destruction of all existing institutions.

It thus should come as no surprise that the political elites have since the early 1990s shown little interest in building effective institutions. Instead of strengthening democratic institutions, Hun Sen has succeeded in monopolizing power at the expense of the opposition. There still exists no effective system of institutional checks and balances among the three branches of government: executive, legislative and judicial. Institutional weaknesses have allowed the CPP elite to use violence against its political opponents with impunity. It may be worth stressing that Hun Sen has effectively been in power since the mid-1980s. Although he was second to Ranariddh from 1993 to mid-1997 (within the coalition government), he wielded most of the political power.

State institutions have not become stronger over time, however. Instead of functioning solely as the institutionalized force protecting national security and domestic stability based on the rule of law, the armed forces remain factionalized and still function as coercive political instruments of the CPP. Policing institutions also remain institutionally ineffective. Their employees remain underpaid and still succumb to bribery and other forms of corruption. As one scholar puts it, 'the current situation ... is not simply a product of lawless behavior but the absence of a law reflective of indigenous and legitimate institutions to enforce them' (Broadhurst 2006: 373).

Members of the political and military elites have often pursued their interests by relying on illegal, secretive or even coercive means. Some have committed acts of economic violence. For instance, government ministries were allegedly responsible for granting private companies (both local and foreign) economic land concessions (over 943,069 hectares of land as of 2006) which had a negative impact on the human rights and livelihoods of people in rural communities, who depended on land and forest resources for survival. The Land Law adopted in 2001 has lacked effective implementation. Global Witness, based in London, has exposed the fact that members of the armed forces were involved in illegal logging. The Brigade 70 Unit in particular ran a nationwide timber trafficking and smuggling service that catered to prominent business tycoons, generating between $2 million and $2.75 million in profits (Global Witness 2007). According to the UN Representative for Human Rights in Cambodia, 'if the Land Law was effectively implemented, many land conflicts would not arise, those arising would find fair solutions' (United Nations 2009: 13). This is a valid point, but it also tends to assume that the highest authorities were able to implement laws effectively. Other rich and powerful elements of the ruling elite have also pursued other personal interests, such as illegal logging. At a conference on military reform in January 2010, for instance, Hun Sen has threatened to dismiss some high-ranking military officers (Rith and Sokheng 2010), but he has been ineffective in his war against land-grabbing and has proved unable to prevent local authorities from abusing their power.

The bicameral legislative branch too remains insufficiently institutionalized and unable to hold government leaders to account for their actions. A number of members of the Senate have been business tycoons, who can still pursue their personal interests. According to a UN report in 2007, for instance, 'prominent Cambodian political and business figures, including senators ... own shares in at least 11 economic land concessions' (United Nations 2007b: 20). Now that the CPP has 90 out of 123 seats in the National Assembly, more than the simple majority required to form a new government, it has been able to exercise power in a more or less authoritarian manner. Coercive power has been highly concentrated in the hands of top CPP leaders, especially the prime minister, who has turned the legislature into a rubber stamp institution that continues to act in support of his political game. The prime minister, for instance, has almost always successfully persuaded the National Assembly to lift the parliamentary immunity of opposition lawmakers. On 23 June 2009, it voted to lift the parliamentary immunity of SRP lawmaker Mu Sochua. The parliamentary immunity of another SRP lawmaker, Ho Vann, was also lifted: he was simply alleged to have made the false claim in April 2009 that 22 senior military officers had obtained meaningless awards from Vietnam.

The judicial system was destroyed by the Khmer Rouge, but the PRK/ SOC made no serious effort to build a judicial system that was politically independent of the executive branch. Political organizations (such as the People's Revolutionary Party of Kampuchea and the United Front for the Construction and Defense of the Kampuchean Motherland) were in a position to exercise a large degree of influence and control over the judiciary. Most of the current judges are political appointees from and since the SOC period, and most of them thus remain loyal to the CPP and toe the party line. The court system remains institutionally weak, corrupted by money and partisan politics and ineffective by virtue of technical incompetence (Ford and Seng 2008).

The courts remain resource-poor and subject to the influence of powerful elites – political, military and economic. This institutional legacy helps to explain why there has been little accountability within the judiciary and why political criminals, such as those in the security forces who committed violence against opposition elements in 1997, have never been brought to justice. The CPP successfully tightened its control over the judicial system. The courts remain deeply politicized and have proved useful to the ruling party's pursuit of hegemonic power. In 2005, for instance, Sam Rainsy and another SRP member fled the country. The SRP leader was sentenced in absentia. CPP leaders have usually won their lawsuits, while anti-government lawsuits have almost always failed.

The executive branch has kept or prevented the judiciary and the legal system from becoming more politically independent and capable of administering justice. The annual budgetary allocation to the judiciary remains far from sufficient (less than 1 per cent of the national budget), and is much less than that for the armed forces. It comes as no surprise that the prison system remains under-institutionalized. Surya Subedi, the UN Special Rapporteur for Human Rights in Cambodia, observed that 'more and more citizens had been jailed because of flaws in the court system' (*Mirror* 2010).

Due to political interference, abuse of power, the lack of resources and other institutional problems, citizens still do not trust the judicial system and take matters into their hands. In June 2010, Surya Subedi expressed his concerns about the lack of judicial independence and the fact that the public had no confidence in the judicial system. In his words, 'if you are poor, weak and dispossessed of your land, you seem to have limited chance to obtain redress either through existing administrative land management, or through courts' (*Agence France-Presse* 2010). Cambodians have, especially, learned that judges cannot provide them with justice when dealing with members of the armed forces and that only the prime minister can do something for them. For instance, a group of 50 veterans, representing 338 families living in Malai district in Banteay Meanchey province who were involved in a land dispute with a high-ranking member of the military in late 2009, apparently did not take their case to court, but instead filed a complaint with Prime Minister Hun Sen's cabinet. In June 2010, they camped out for days in Phnom Penh awaiting its response. As noted earlier, Hun Sen had threatened to fire military commanders allegedly involved in illegal activities. Mob violence associated with street justice, as noted, was also symptomatic of this institutional malaise.

In short, the persistence of institutional weaknesses helps explain the practice of violence and the culture of impunity. The system of institutional checks and balances still remains rudimentary. Powerful members of the political, military, security and economic elites can still commit acts of violence against their opponents and citizens in pursuit of their own interests and get away with it. Critics of the government and ordinary citizens can do little to protect themselves from being victimized. However, these institutional weaknesses need to be explained. External factors help shed further light on this.

Nature-of-the-peace perspectives and the challenge for institution-building in Cambodia

The cultural, ideological, historical and institutional legacies of violence help to explain the trend toward a victor's peace and violence in Cambodia, but a question remains: did the ongoing violence also result from the process of neoliberalization, as some scholars suggest? As will be shown, neoliberalism has its flaws, but is not the main culprit.

Nature-of-the-peace perspectives

Roland Paris and others make an important contribution to the debate on liberal peacebuilding with the thesis that democratization and marketization before institutionalization poses a real challenge to peacebuilding, since it destabilizes post-conflict countries. Electoral and economic competition is not the best recipe for peace and stability in post-war societies (Paris 2004: 79–96). From this perspective, to avoid violence in general and political and economic instability or violence in particular, the rule of law must be built first. Other critics of Neoliberalism also blame marketization for its tendency toward economic violence, which in this case is associated with the transition to a free-market economy and the mass privatization and rampant exploitation of natural resources carried out by members of the CPP elite.

These perspectives help to throw some light on this type of violence, because they pay attention to the process of neoliberalization, most notably marketization, which is regarded as a force that widens socio-economic inequality. Individual members of the ruling elite have committed this form of violence, such as the forceful evictions and land-grabbing which have been more evident since the early 2000s. Global Witness also accused members of the political elite of both filling their pockets with money earned from illegal logging and using some of the money to fund the activities of a 6,000-strong private army controlled by Hun Sen, with some of the profits also went to his Bodyguard Unit led by Lieutenant-General Hing Bun Heang (Global Witness 2007).

Donors also tend to see political stability as necessary for neoliberal economic development. Although they have often expressed their dissatisfaction with the CPP-dominated governments, donors continue to lend the Hun Sen regime active support. Some donors suspended their aid after the violent 1997 coup, but then resumed their pledging. Between 1998 and 2008, the total amount of aid amounted to $5.5 billion. In 2007, Global Witness accused donors of policy inaction while members of the ruling elite surrounding Prime Minister Hun Sen looted the forests (Global Witness 2007). The donor community nevertheless continued to pledge more aid to help sustain economic growth, despite all the challenges described earlier. In 2009, donors pledged to give Cambodia $950 million, despite the government's failure to implement various reforms. In June 2010, they pledged another $1.1 billion – the largest aid package in Cambodian history. While this international assistance has done much to help ensure political stability, it has also enabled the Hun Sen regime to consolidate power through violent repression.

Critics of neoliberalism tend to generalize claims that neoliberalization is responsible for all sorts of violence in Cambodia, but still have difficulty explaining the causal relationship between the two variables. They tend to put exclusive blame on neoliberalism, as if this ideology bears full responsibility for all forms of violence in Cambodia. In fact, the most violent period in Cambodian history took place under the revolutionary Khmer Rouge regime, which violently abolished capitalism and destroyed any ideological traces of liberalism. This theoretical approach also does not give liberalism much credit for the recent decline of violence in other forms.

Moreover, it is far from clear that neoliberalism per se is primarily responsible for political and economic violence in Cambodia. Evidence suggests that economic violence has resulted more from the Cambodian elites' authoritarian behaviour. They have exploited the new market environment to their own advantage and this seems to have prevented the new free market economy from becoming institutionalized. The problem with socio-economic inequality associated with marketization lies with the inability of donors to build effective institutions to keep members of the elites in check. This does not mean that they have never been critical of the Hun Sen government but that their criticisms have not been strong or effective enough. In fact, there is a tendency among donors to paint a positive picture of the progress the government has made so far.

The limits of intervention

The limited attention paid by donors to institution-building, especially in the area of building political parties (Peou 2007), further means that the task of establishing a system of checks and balances is difficult. Cambodia has a long history of efforts by ruling elites to consolidate power, to pursue hegemonic status when and where possible and to deinstitutionalize politics. If various forms of violence still persist in Cambodia, it is not simply because democratization and marketization took place before institutionalization but also because they were not accompanied by the building of effective democratic state institutions. There are several reasons for this failure. The CPP has been able to prevent democratic institutionalization by personalizing power, as demonstrated above. Members of the international community, as will be further explained, have also proved unable to build democratic institutions that could prevent violence-prone elite behaviour.

Members of the international community, especially states and multilateral institutions, have been either unwilling or simply unable to stop or prevent the Cambodian parties from using violence to get their way. From early on, UNTAC was certainly unable to create a political environment that ensured full security for the former resistance forces. Perhaps most threatening to the Khmer Rouge faction was the fact that the disarmament plans to be implemented by UNTAC would eventually render them defenceless and subject to future prosecution. Their fears were justifiable at the time because of an international commitment to making sure that they would not return to power and would eventually be punished (Marks 2001: 245–7). The ongoing trials of Khmer Rouge leaders have proved them right. The disintegration of the Khmer Rouge movement was a most welcome development in that it brought about peace and greater stability, but it also contributed to the CPP's successful consolidation of power. With the royalist and Khmer Rouge forces destroyed and reintegrated into the armed forces under CPP control, the Hun Sen regime has been able to run the country unchecked.

Some international actors appear since to have adopted a more realistic approach to peacebuilding. They have been either unwilling or unable to put collective pressure on the Cambodian government because of their preference for political stability. As noted earlier, they have continued to reward Hun Sen's authoritarian behaviour by pledging more assistance. Moreover, they have been unwilling or unable to coordinate their aid activities effectively because they have often operated at cross-purposes. The question of aid effectiveness has been raised again and again. According to critics, official development assistance has been mostly supply-driven and poorly coordinated.

Geo-strategic interests

State donors, including democratic ones, have pursued their national interests more consistently than the policy of promoting democracy they publicly claim to pursue. Japan and the United States, for instance, have adopted a more or less 'realist' approach because of the war on terrorism after the attacks on US territory in 2001 and because of their shared concern about the 'China threat'. These democracies have allowed the CPP to consolidate power at the expense of the opposition and have shown no real political will to do what was necessary to reverse the CPP's consolidation of political power, largely because they saw no reason to push Cambodia deeper into the China camp.

The geo-strategic thinking of Japan and the United States appears to be more in line with realism than with liberalism. Rivalry between China and the US/Japan security alliance seems to correlate with the steady rise of Chinese power and the growth of Chinese influence over Southeast Asia. In 1994, for instance, Tokyo issued a new national defence programme outline, which touched on nuclear arsenals in neighbouring states and justified the need to enhance military forces in the south (close to China and North Korea). The document did not then mention China as a threat; ten years later, however, the 2004 National Program Defense Guidelines 'was the first national security document to openly identify a potential threat from the People's Republic of China, noting that the PRC was modernizing its forces and expanding its range at sea' (Samuels 2007: 69). The Bush Administration then signed a congressional appropriations resolution for the 2007 fiscal year, which 'contains no restrictions on direct US government funding of the Cambodian government activities'. According to US Ambassador Joseph Mussomeli, the US move was also 'yet another sign of the deepening and strengthening of the promising relationship between our two countries' (*Associated Press* 2007a). Diplomatic sources unofficially revealed that Washington entertained the idea of establishing a military base in Cambodia. In February 2007, a US warship paid a visit to Cambodia's seaport for first time in 30 years.

Washington's fears of Islamist militancy have further tempered its criticism of the Cambodian government and it recently considered Cambodia (relative to the other ASEAN states) 'most willing' to cooperate with its efforts to combat global terrorism. As Hun Sen succeeded in consolidating his power, he presented himself as a leader committed to combating terrorism in the region. The dubious arrests of foreign Muslim men in Cambodia, who were later charged with terrorist offences, and Cambodia's plan to expel Islamic foreigners prior to the holding of the 2003 ASEAN Regional Forum conference, must have pleased the US government. In April 2007, General Hok Lundy, Cambodia's notorious National Police Chief, was even allowed to hold bilateral talks on counter-terrorism with the FBI in Washington. Senior US officials also met with the general at the State Department. All this took place amid criticism from human rights activists and others that Washington had changed its policy by granting the general a visa to enter the United States after it had refused to do so in 2005 because of his alleged complicity in human trafficking and involvement in unresolved political killings, especially those committed in March 1997 and during the coup in July 1997. Cambodia must have also pleased Washington when the Hun Sen government signed an 'Article 19' agreement with the United States that contained a Cambodian commitment not to send any US citizens to the International Criminal Court (ICC).

Even if Western donors had been willing to give priority to democratic institution-building, it is far from clear that they could have done so. As mentioned earlier, the Cambodian elites have a history of resisting institution-building efforts, regarding them as jeopardizing their personal interests. They were driven by the imperatives of personal and regime survival and could often find a way to thwart institution-building efforts. The CPP government has maintained close relations with other authoritarian regimes in the East Asian region, such as Vietnam, Myanmar and China. Close ties with Vietnam have resulted in one positive development: the disappearance of anti-Vietnam ethnic violence; however, they have also enhanced Hun Sen's grip on power.

The overall impact of Chinese influence on Cambodia has been more negative than positive when assessed in institutional terms. Over the past several years, the Hun Sen government has approved approximately $6 billion worth of Chinese investment and received at least $2 billion more in Chinese grant aid and loans. Critics have, however, expressed concerns about the growing influence of China, which has had little to do with democratic institution-building. They regard the Chinese generosity as fulfilling part of Beijing's broader strategic interests in the region. China has provided Cambodia with military assistance and seems ready to step in when Western donors suspend their military aid to the country. For instance, China announced that it would donate more than 250 trucks and 50,000 uniforms to the Cambodian military after Washington announced its decision on 1 April 2010 to suspend the supply of about 200 military trucks and trailers to Cambodia. Chinese investment in Cambodia's infrastructure also ends up benefiting state-owned Chinese companies involved in the building of roads and hydropower dams. Moreover, Chinese grants and loans have been provided to maintain or strengthen authoritarianism in both countries. In December 2009, for instance, just two days after Cambodia had deported 20 ethnic Uighur asylum seekers to China, where they could face persecution, Beijing signed a $1.2 billion deal with Phnom Penh.

China has also funded Cambodian government building projects, such as the gigantic headquarters for the Council of Ministers, but such efforts have contributed little to the process of promoting democratic governance. Unlike Western democratic donors, which usually demand that Cambodia comply with standards of good governance and environmental safety, China has imposed no such conditions: it usually provides aid with 'no strings attached'. At a ground-breaking ceremony for two Chinese-financed bridges in 2006, for instance, Hun Sen made the following remarks: 'China talks less but does a lot. There are no conditions. We talk back and forth directly'. China 'didn't need to announce "If you amend this or do this, I will give you the money". China doesn't do that' (*International Herald Tribune* 2009).

What all this means is that the neoliberal agenda for peacebuilding that encourages democratization, marketization and justice institutionalization is a potential source of competition and conflict, but there is another important culprit. Members of the international community have either allowed the CPP under the leadership of Hun Sen to consolidate power or proved unable to stop him doing so. Donors have also been either unwilling or unable to coordinate their aid activities effectively and to take collective action to help Cambodia build an effective system of institutional checks and balances, because they have often pursued their own national interests and priorities.

Conclusion

Developments in post-war Cambodian politics have been far more positive than negative. The country has been at peace since the Khmer Rouge's armed rebellion ended and has enjoyed political stability as well as noticeable economic growth. Serious ethnic violence has disappeared. Political violence has declined. Unfortunately, other forms of violence continue. This chapter has shown that 'legacy-of-war' and 'nature-of-the-peace' perspectives contribute to our understanding of post-war violence, but that neither one should be given too much credit for its exclusive explanatory power. Cultural, ideological, historical and socio-economic legacies matter, but weak institutional structures matter more. In institutionally weak states, former foes often find it difficult to overcome their mutual distrust and are subject to the temptation of monopolizing power. Institutional weaknesses have also permitted powerful members of the ruling elites to pursue their interests at the expense of others and often to commit acts of violence with impunity.

The Cambodian case further confirms that the triple neoliberal process of democratization, marketization and justice institutionalization may have encouraged violence and authoritarianism as former foes competed for power at the ballot-box, as powerful elements took advantage of marketization at the expense of society, and as some political elements (most notably the Khmer Rouge) feared legal punishment for their crimes. However, these post-war tendencies should not be interpreted to mean that neoliberalism per se is the sole culprit for all that has gone wrong. The main factors perpetuating violence can be found in the persisting lack of effective democratic institutions capable of checking the political, military, security and economic elites' pursuit of self-interest and in the limited role of the international community in the process of peacebuilding. External actors have proved either unwilling or unable to shape Cambodia's domestic power relations in ways conducive to the establishment of an effective political system. State donors have often pursued their interests, as is evident in the support they have given to the increasingly authoritarian regime of Hun Sen. More often than not, the neoliberal vision for peace has been blurred by political realities.

Bibliography

Agence France-Presse (2008) 7 January 2008.

Agence France-Presse (2010) 'UN says poor lose out in Cambodian courts', 17 June.

Amnesty International (2008) 'Forced evictions in Cambodia: homes razed, lives in ruins', 11 February.

Asian Legal Resource Centre (2007) 'Cambodia: the absence of the rule of law aggravating the human rights situation in the country', 31 May. Online, available at: www.alrc.net/doc/mainfile.php/alrc_statements/419 (accessed 5 November 2008).

Associated Press (2007a) 27 February 2007.

Associated Press (2007b) 'Buddhist monks clash with police during protest in Cambodia', 17 December.

Associated Press (2008) 1 June.

Broadhurst, R. (2006) 'Lethal violence, crime and political change in Cambodia', in A. Croissant, B. Martin and S. Kneip (eds) *The Politics of Death: Political Violence in Southeast Asia*, Berlin: Lit Verlag.

Cambodia Daily (2001) 15–16 September.

Chanboreth, E. and Hach, S. (2008) *Aid Effectiveness in Cambodia* Washington, DC: Wolfensohn Center for Development, Working Paper 7, December.

Chandler, D.P. (1993) *A History of Cambodia*, Chiang Mai, Thailand: Silkworm Books.

Daguan, Z. (2007) *A Record of Cambodia: The Land and its People*, trans. P. Harris, Chiang Mai, Thailand: Silkworm Books.

Dosch, J. (2007) *The Changing Dynamics of Southeast Asian Politics*, Boulder and London: Lynne Rienner.

Ford, S. and Seng, T. (2008) 'Corruption in the judiciary of Cambodia', in I. Denker and M. Sidwell (eds) *Annual Report 2007*, Transparency International.

Global Witness (2007) 'Cambodia's family trees', unpublished, London, UK.

Hay, L.M. (2008) 'Hun Sen's ineffective war on land-grabbing', UPI Asia Online, 5 March.

Hinton, A.L. (2002) 'A head for an eye: revenge in the Cambodian genocide', in C. Besteman (ed.) *Violence: A Reader,* New York: New York University Press.

Human Rights Watch (2007) 'Cambodia: ensure safety of Buddhist monks; prosecute police involved in "Burma-style" crackdown', Press Release, 24 December.

Hughes, C. (2006) 'Violence and voting in post-2003 Cambodia', in A. Croissant, B. Martin and S. Kneip (eds) *The Politics of Death: Political Violence in Southeast Asia,* Berlin: Lit Verlag.

International Herald Tribune (2006) 2 November.

International Herald Tribune (2008) 'Longtime Cambodian leader looks set to win another term', 28 July.

International Herald Tribune (2009) 23 December.

Jackson, K.D. (1989) 'Introduction: the Khmer Rouge in context', in K.D. Jackson (ed.) *Cambodia, 1975–1978: Rendezvous with Death,* Princeton, NJ: Princeton University Press.

Khmer Intelligence (2002).

LICADHO (2006) 'Land grabbing in Cambodia leaves communities campaigning out on the government's footsteps waiting for justice', Phnom Penh: LICADHO, 4 October.

LICADHO (2007) 'Prison conditions in Cambodia 2005 and 2006', Phnom Penh: LICADHO, January.

LICADHO (2008a) 'Prison conditions in Cambodia 2007: the story of a mother and child', Phnom Penh: LICADHO, March.

LICADHO (2008b) 'Impunity at work in Cambodia: soldiers and police escape prosecution', Phnom Penh, Cambodia: LICADHO, 15 October.

Marks, S.P. (2001) 'Forgetting "the policies and practices of the past": impunity in Cambodia', in S. Peou (ed.) *Cambodia: Change and Continuity in Contemporary Politics,* Aldershot: Ashgate.

Mirror (2008) 'The condition of prisons in Cambodia remains difficult', 12(562), 31 May.

Mirror (2010) 'Subedi: The court system in Cambodia still has difficulties in providing justice for Cambodian citizens', 14(669), 21 June.

Osborne, M.E. (1994), *Sihanouk: Prince of Light, Prince of Darkness,* St. Leonards, NSW: Allen & Unwin.

Paris, Roland (2004) *At War's End: Building Peace after Civil Conflict,* Cambridge: Cambridge University Press.

Peou, S. (1997) *Conflict Neutralization in the Cambodia War: From Battlefield to Ballot-Box,* Kuala Lumpur, New York and Singapore: Oxford University Press.

Peou, S. (2007) *International Democracy Assistance for Peacebuilding: Cambodia and Beyond,* Hampshire and New York: Palgrave Macmillan.

Peou, S. (2010) *Peace and Security in the Asia-Pacific: Theory and Practice,* Praeger.

Rith, S. and Sokheng, V. (2010) 'Cambodian prime minister points finger at corrupt army chiefs', *Cambodia Tonight,* 29 January. Online, available at: http://cambodiatonight.blogspot.com/2010/01/cambodian-prime-minister-hun-sen-points.html (accessed 23 June 2010).

Samuels, R.J. (2007) *Securing Japan: Tokyo's Grand Strategy and the Future of East Asia,* Ithaca and London: Cornell University Press.

United Nations (1990) *Report of the United Nations Fact-Finding Mission on Present Structures and Practices of Administration in Cambodia,* New York: United Nations, 24 April–9 May.

United Nations (1991) *Agreements on a Comprehensive Political Settlement of the Cambodia Conflict*, Paris, 23 October.

United Nations (1999) *Report of the Group of Experts for Cambodia Pursuant to General Assembly Resolution 52/135*, New York: United Nations.

United Nations (2001) Document E/CN.4/2001/103, United Nations, 24 January.

United Nations (2002), 6 June.

United Nations (2007a) Document A/HRC/4/36, United Nations, 30 January.

United Nations (2007b) June.

United Nations (2007c) Cambodia Office of the High Commissioner for Human Rights 'Economic land concessions in Cambodia: a human rights perspective', Phnom Penh, June.

United Nations (2009) Document A/HRC/12/41, United Nations, 5 August.

United Nations (2002) Special Representative of the Secretary General for Human Rights in Cambodia 'Street retribution in Cambodia', 6 June 2002.

11 Conflict and violence in post-independence East Timor

Dionísio Babo-Soares

Introduction

On 30 August 1999, after 24 years of Indonesian occupation and local resistance, the population of the eastern half of the tiny island of Timor voted overwhelmingly in a United Nations-sponsored referendum to separate from Indonesia (Security Council Resolution 1272/1999). For over two years after the referendum, East Timor was administered by the United Nations and gained full independence on 20 May 2002. In the following eight years – often called the peacebuilding period – the institutions and infrastructure of the state were established, including a Constitution, a Parliament, a government, courts, administrative regions, a public service and laws.

East Timor started this post-independence journey by struggling to deal with the wounds created by its long history of conflict, both with Indonesia and amongst the Timorese themselves. As has been well documented elsewhere (Gusmão 1998: 23–37), the struggle for independence had been marked by friction, division and violence among the nationalist forces. Feeding on these divisions, the complex post-independence hostilities and grievances coalesced around numerous divisions – sacrifices made during the war, geographical distinctions, generational divisions and divisions between those who had fought in the jungle and those who had not. Past power struggle among the nationalists also lingered. Failure to resolve such conflicts inhibited post-independence efforts to introduce democracy and promote reconciliation.

This chapter begins by describing the context of post-independence conflict in East Timor. It maps the legacy of past conflict and discusses its impact on post-independence violence. It then looks at actions taken by the state to address the problems and, in conclusion, reflects on the forces of continuity in the violence that has occurred in East Timor.

Political divisions

Most East Timorese participated in some way in the long resistance against Indonesian occupation. Some took part in the war directly, e.g. by joining the armed wing of the resistance, *Forças Armadas da Libertação Nacional de*

Timor-Leste (FALINTIL). Others contributed indirectly and some participated passively, while others again resisted silently behind the walls of prison. After victory, all demanded to be respected, praised and rewarded for the contributions made during the struggle. Their demands were a basic fact of the post-independence political context.

Most of the political groups that emerged in post-independence East Timor identified themselves with the past resistance against Indonesia. Each group attempted to gain political leverage on the basis of their contribution to the struggle. Various political groups which claimed to have participated directly in the struggle for independence and identified themselves with the nationalist front prior to 1999 reappeared and joined the political context in post-independence democratic elections, now as different factions with different political perspectives. One example is the upsurge of the group *Sagrada Familia* (the Holy Family) in 2005, led by a former resistance commander who traced the group's foundation to the long period of struggle and its members' particular beliefs (Babo-Soares 2003: 264–97). The group was formed during the resistance years with a strong adherence to the 'Holy Family' as their protector. Colimau 2000, another organization that had helped organize mass protests during the Indonesian occupation and the referendum, also came to the fore. Both these groups attempted to claim political status and recognition on the basis of their participation in the resistance.

As part of the same logic, many ex-combatants argued that their group had fought more in the resistance than other groups and should therefore be given privileges in the post-independence political hierarchy. As a result, various groups similarly sought to highlight the significance of their often unreported role in the war against Indonesia.

Other issues surfaced concerning people's roles during the war, especially the question of whether people had been nationalists (fighting against Indonesia) or integrationists (accepting Indonesian rule) during the occupation. Geographical location was important. Home-stayers (people living in East Timor) were regarded as having fought in a physical sense in the war against Indonesia, whereas the diaspora living abroad were accused of having led a good life and suffered less than their compatriots at home. The division was accentuated as former diaspora Timorese began entering politics and competing with home-stayers in the elections. Rivalry also arose from the different language proficiencies of diaspora Timorese and home-stayers; the diaspora had the advantage of having acquired additional language skills such as English and Portuguese while abroad. Among the home-stayers, geographical divisions were important. Those living in the eastern part of the country were regarded as having resisted Indonesia's military regime in a true sense, while those in the western part were accused of having participated less in the struggle.

Hence, while the involvement of former political activists and guerrillas in politics was welcomed, their means of establishing political parties and claiming political advantage were not necessarily democratic. Their claim to participation rested on the question of who had fought most during the struggle. It was essentially a demand that only true advocates of independence be given space in the bid for power in independent East Timor.[1] A similar power struggle also developed among factional leaders within the resistance. Accusations of misdeeds and wrongdoings during the struggle among former members of the resistance were used in the struggle for power and control of the new state and its institutions (see for example *Suara Timor Lorosae* and *Diário*, 16–20 February 2009; also Silva 2009b). Individual claims about 'who did what' came to dominate the political debate.

The classification of war veterans must be understood in this context. A three-level system was constructed: armed combatants; former clandestine members; and members of the diplomatic front. Members of the diplomatic front (diaspora East Timorese) typically enjoyed less respect, since they were seen as having made a less direct contribution during the war than their fellow home-stayers. Although the parameters for being classified as a 'veteran' were unclear, some student groups that had organized protests in cities throughout Indonesia, and individuals who claimed to be sympathizers of the struggle, were excluded from the three levels and complained that they had been given insufficient recognition in post-independence politics (e.g. student resistance organizations such as *Resistencia Nacional dos Estudantes Timor-Leste* (RENETIL); Frente *Clandestina Estudantil de Timor-Leste* (FECLETI); and *Liga dos Estudantes Patriotas* (LEP)).

Controversy over institutions

The fight for political leverage and control of the resistance's memorabilia was an enduring phenomenon. The competing claims over institutions that belonged to the resistance began with the controversy over the umbrella organization of the resistance, the *Conselho Nacional da Resistência Timorense* (CNRT). This organization was established in April 1998 in Peniche, Portugal as a metamorphosis of the previously disputed *Conselho Nacional da Resistência Maubere* (CNRM). CNRT was hailed as the forum that represented the various political interests of the East Timorese people. Its aim was to unite all factions within the resistance and to lead East Timor towards independence. It was the CNRT that represented East Timor during the UN-administered referendum in 1999. After September 1999, the various political parties that constituted this umbrella organization, particularly the smaller political parties – *Associacão Popular Democratica Timorense* (Timorese Popular Democratic Association, East Timor, APODETI); Trabalhista; *Partido Socialista Timor* (PST); and KOTA (a local feudally-oriented political party) wanted to maintain the CNRT and its leadership and retained this former national independence front as the first government of Timor Leste in a national unity style of government. However, traditional political parties such as *Frente Revolucionária de Timor-Leste Independente* (FRETILIN) and *União Democrática Timorense* (UDT) began restructuring and positioning themselves for the general election, thus distancing themselves from CNRT. They demanded that CNRT be dissolved (Babo-Soares 2003: 222–56).

FRETILIN was led by two resistance veterans, Lu-Olo (president) and Mari Alkatiri (general secretary), who rejected CNRT's overwhelming domination of the new country's politics. They regarded CNRT as an umbrella organization whose role was irrelevant in the post-independence period, arguing that CNRT was a resistance body and not a government. FRETILIN wanted CNRT to be dissolved so that the political parties could take the lead. The party went further by claiming exclusive rights over the assets of the resistance movement, including the idea of independence, the martyrs of war, the flag of the nation and even independence itself.

At the CNRT Congress in August 2000, one year after independence, FRETILIN was joined by UDT, which had been established in 1975, in demanding that CNRT be dissolved to pave the way for political parties alone to hold political office. The leaders of the opposing groups – that is, CNRT versus FRETILIN/UDT – exchanged harsh words in the local newspapers and in public. Both threatened to 'reveal' what wrongs the other had committed in the past and to mobilize their supporters to overthrow the other (*Suara Timor Lorosae* 2002: 4). Internal conflict within the leadership of FRETILIN and CNRT also became public and appeared in the local media for months (*Suara Timor Lorosae* 2000).

Past 'mistakes' committed during the nationalist struggle became a tool for former members of the resistance turned politician to threaten each other. The aim was to justify their respective positions before the public as competition for political power heightened prior to the Constitutional Assembly election in early 2000 and the general election in 2007. As the 'politically illiterate' population continued to side with their leaders and respective parties, society became divided into different blocks (*Suara Timor Lorosae* 2000). After each election, the sense of difference between these individuals and the bodies they represented intensified. Violent clashes between supporters of different political groups, notably *Conselho Popular pela Defesa da República Democrática de Timor Leste* (CPD-RDTL) and FRETILIN, occurred often in the streets of Dili and in the districts. In the same period, people from the eastern and western parts of Timor were killed in the context of difference over who had fought more in the war against Indonesia.

In sum, attacks on the presence of CNRT/CN in post-independence politics intensified when newly established political groups came into existence. The emergence of new political parties in 1999 aiming to compete for political power intensified as the UN began to facilitate elections for the post-independence period. That in itself, however, does not explain why the contest turned violent. This process will be discussed in the next section.

New divisions and violence

In September 1999, East Timor saw the return of most diaspora politicians.[2] Many had been involved in the conflicts during the period of turbulence in 1974–5. Portuguese colonial rule had come to an end when in April 1974 the new military government in Portugal announced a unilateral withdrawal from its colonial possessions. In East Timor, this led to the formation of several political parties, the major ones being FRETILIN and the UDT.[3] Unable to agree on the succession issue, the parties fought a brief but quite violent civil war in mid-1975. The power struggle was cut short by the Indonesian invasion of East Timor in December 1975. During the subsequent occupation, many of the activists fled the country to take up residence overseas, predominantly in Australia, Portugal, Mozambique and Macau. After separation from Indonesia in 1999, they returned to join the already fragmented political scene to bid for power. Additionally, former guerrilla fighters and political activists who had resisted the Indonesian occupation inside East Timor also joined both old and newly established political parties in the bid for power. Different political parties prepared themselves to contest the upcoming election, which was to be facilitated by the UN.

By this time, FRETILIN, the political party that advocated for independence in 1975, was no longer presenting itself as 'the independence front' but playing the role of a standard political party. Its two first leaders, Lu-Olo and Mari Alkatiri, were veterans of the resistance. During this early period (1999–2003), broad political disagreement split FRETILIN into several groups. The division stemmed not only from ideological differences but also older disputes among the leadership during the war against Indonesia. Five new splinter political parties were born. These included, first, Lu-Olo's and Mari Alkatiri's version of FRETILIN; and second, the *Partido Nacionalista Timorense* (PNT), established a week before the 1999 referendum and headed by a former leader of FRETILIN, Abilio Araújo, who had been dismissed from FRETILIN in the 1980s for accepting reconciliation with Indonesia. The third splinter party was *Associação Social Democrática de Timor* (ASDT); the fourth was the PST, founded by Avelino Coelho, a young East Timorese with strong adherence to Marxist and Leninist ideas. The fifth splinter party was CPD-RDTL, whose objective was to reinstate the proclamation of independence on 28 November 1975 and to reject the proclamation of a new date of independence (*Canberra Times* 2001).

Several factors contributed to this split, but underneath it all was disagreement over who had the right to lead the country. All the groups claimed to be the true representative of the resistance and the competition for post-independence power came to focus on which one was the 'truest' representative of that struggle. The disagreements within FRETILIN and between FRETILIN and CNRT and other political groups were also rooted in long-term political friction that had been further perpetuated by the tragic internal killings that occurred during the resistance against Indonesia.

The split and the emergence of several new parties substantially changed the local political landscape. It divided the East Timorese into factions, which were then transferred from the capital Dili to the villages around the country. During this period (1999–2003), each political group mobilized its supporters and each formed its own security force. CPD-RDTL, like other breakaway groups, was able to bring people to Dili –

often en masse – to attend commemorations of the movement's birthday and other ceremonial events.

As the rift unfolded, mob violence began to occur in Dili and other parts of East Timor, with street fights between members of opposing political groups. The violence involved supporters who did not invoke ideological or party political reasons. Rather, several of the young activists said their anger stemmed from symbolic gestures by their adversaries, such as using their party's attributes, raising their party's flag illegally or even burning it. All political factions treated each other with threats and violence over political symbols. As party supporters repeatedly engaged in acts of defiance, gang fights, killings and sustained political tension followed. Between December 2000 and August 2001, for instance, members of CPD-RDTL raised RDTL's flag in several districts, such as Ainaro, Baucau, Viqueque, Bobonaro and Ermera. This resulted in fights between supporters of this organization and CNRT. CPD-RDTL supporters claimed that CNRT's flag should not be used to represent the resistance's flag because CNRT came to the struggle late in the process, being established only in 1998. A number of conflicts were recorded in different parts of East Timor, particularly in Ossu, a sub-district of Viqueque. In addition, fights occurred between large organized crowds in Dili as well as in the districts of Ainaro, Bobonaro, Baucau and Suai (*Suara Timor Lorosae* 2001: 1–14).

In August 2000, at its first national congress inside the country, CNRT changed its name to CNRT/Congresso Nacional and on 9 June 2001 the original organization was officially dissolved. It was argued that the mission of the CNRT – to fight for independence – had been accomplished. When CNRT was dissolved as the umbrella organization of the resistance, conflict between the two groups scaled down and the leader of CNRT, Xanana Gusmao, was later elected president of East Timor. CPD-RDTL opted to remain outside the new political system, preferring neither to neither collaborate with nor recognize the new government but to operate as a political group – not a political party – outside the system.

Violence after 20 May 2002

Following independence on 20 May 2002, East Timor remained calm. Indeed, during 2003 and 2004 the internal political rift started to heal. New state bodies were established and the new Constitution was approved. The euphoria of the UN 'hand-over' of sovereignty seemed to pave the way for a more democratic process. In August 2001 elections to a constitutional assembly were held. Having written the Constitution, however, the assembly changed its role and declared itself to be the first parliament of East Timor. This act invited criticism from different sections within the Timorese community (UNTAET 2002).

Underneath the calm, old divisions remained. The economic performance of the new government, led by former Prime Minister Mari Alkatiri (2002–6), was poor during the first months. The massive pull-out of UN staff added to the economic downturn (Pires 2009). Discontent with the new Timorese government began to grow and was further exacerbated by its inability to address the issues of the veterans and their sister groups (orphans of war, widows of resistance and disabled groups). As political uncertainty grew, the leaders of the new government resorted to heavy-handed repression when dealing with public protests and dissatisfied groups. For example, in April 2004 police brutally crushed the public protest by a group of veterans led by former war veteran Eli Fohorai Boot (L7) (Radio Australia 2004). The mistreatment of war veterans was regarded by the opposition and by the veterans' organization as a sign of disrespect. Anger over the treatment of war veterans became a national issue and dominated the headlines of the national media for months.

The tensions triggered violence and vandalism in many parts of the country. Heightened political conflict continued unabated, although it did not escalate into large-scale violence until the December 2004 events.

The 4 December 2004 violence: an unresolved issue

In most of 2003 and 2004, the situation remained stable and controlled. Even so, political tensions were high. There were incidental street protests against the government, as well as clashes between martial arts groups and political party supporters and between supporters of different parties, triggered by intensified accusations between political leaders. Issues of the past surfaced occasionally and expressed the reigning political uncertainty. The demonstration that triggered the 4 December violence is viewed by some as the result of contained public anger built up over several months.

Several days prior to 4 December, a brawl between high school students took place in Dili and a couple of students were injured and hospitalized. The protest went on for several days and a number of political elements were believed to have penetrated the crowd and agitated it to turn violent (Silva 2009a). The supposedly peaceful student protest then turned violent as third parties became involved.[4] In the following days, cars and shops were smashed and ransacked while the police, both local and from the UN, were outnumbered and were unable to prevent the violence. On 4 December 2004, the riots peaked as a mob ransacked and set fire to shops and buildings, including a popular store in Dili called 'Hello Mr' (Uma Estorinha 2009) as well as several government buildings and vehicles. The police were unable to control the situation although reinforcements were brought in. As the then-president of the republic, Xanana Gusmão, went to the streets to calm the mobs he was pelted with stones and had to hide behind the trees to avoid injury. When the mobs dispersed in the afternoon half the capital was almost destroyed.

The December 2004 riots should be understood as an act of defiance, caused by the inability of the government to offer a 'truce' that satisfied certain sections of society, first and foremost the veterans of war. No compensation was planned or institutionalized to provide sanctuary for the jobless veterans. Furthermore, unemployment was high and the poor delivery of government goods and services failed to meet public expectations.

A commission of inquiry into the incident was soon established. No results of its work have been released, however. A preliminary report by an investigative forum set up by civil society and based on interviews with several members of the commission hinted at the involvement of a prominent veteran politician, who is now a FRETILIN member of parliament, as having instigated the violence (Silva 2009a). The failure of the state to bring this person to court has set a worrying legal precedent. To date, the public knows very little of what and who were behind the violence that erupted on 4 December 2004 and its antecedents. There were also wider consequences. Failure to prosecute those believed to be guilty sent the message to society that the East Timorese were living a culture of impunity where criminals could roam freely and not be held to account for their actions.

The violence discussed so far occurred against the background of a UN presence in East Timor. After the direct UN administration (United Nations Transitional Administration in East Timor, UNTAET) was terminated in May 2002, the UN assisted independent East Timor through a continued presence of peacekeepers and an international civilian police force. Authorized by the UN Security Council in May 2002 with a three-year mandate, the United Nations Mission of Support in East Timor (UNMISET) had nearly 4,500 peacekeepers, 771 civilian police (CIVPOL) and 465 international civilians. The peacekeepers and CIVPOL were drawn down in 2004 and everyone had departed by the time the mission ended in May 2005. As a result, one common argument later was that the violence which erupted in 2006 showed that the withdrawal had been premature.

The 2006 violence and reference to the past

Most of the violence between 1999 and 2004 consisted of confrontation between civilians and occurred because of political divisions and conflicts between politicians and former activists. Alongside it, however, were occasional confrontations involving members of the national army (FALINTIL, and *Força de Defesa de Timor-Leste* or F-FDTL) and the national police (*Polícia Nacional de Timor-Leste* or PNTL). To some, the two institutions were perceived as representing the eastern and western parts of the country – with the F-FDTL army representing the eastern part and the national police representing the western part. F-FDTL (FALINTIL force) leaders were mostly former guerrilla commanders from the eastern part, while most leaders of the national police were from the western part. Public confrontations between members of the two institutions were based on the east–west dichotomy. This sentiment ran deep between people from the two sides of the country and became the basis for confrontation that spurred further violence. No efforts were made to resolve the situation.

On 9 January 2006, a number of army soldiers submitted a written petition to Brigadier General Taur Matan Ruak, the army chief of staff. The petitioners, who all came from the western part of East Timor, complained about mistreatment by soldiers of eastern origin within the army. Having received no response for several weeks, the petitioners went on strike, refusing to return to the army headquarters. The soldiers complained that they had limited time for leave, sick leave and for travelling to and from the military barracks when taking leave. The trip to their homes in the west could take several days and late reporting to headquarters often resulted in severe physical punishment. The petitioners also alleged the use of abusive language and inappropriate behaviour towards them by their senior commanders, who were of eastern origin. Phrases such as 'westerners did not fight during the resistance against Indonesian occupation and are lazy blokes' were apparently often used to punish soldiers from the west. Such language was alleged to be rampant in army barracks and to have become the order of the day (see coverage in local national newspapers; also United Nations 2006). The use of 'words as punishment' is an indirect reference to the claim that only easterners (and not westerners) fought in the war against Indonesia in the past.

The story of the east–west divide goes back to the resistance years. During the Indonesian occupation, and particularly from 1980 onwards, the resistance operated and resided in the eastern part of East Timor, that is, the region furthest away from the border with Indonesia. During most of the 24-year-long struggle, the war against Indonesia was directed from the east. Some analysts see the decision of the resistance movement to concentrate in the eastern part of the country as merely strategic, reflecting the area's tactical mountainous terrain, which suited guerrilla warfare. The eastern side was consequently made the military operational zone while the western area was designated more as a 'resort' for guerrillas on sick leave (Babo-Soares 2003). It is therefore not surprising that most of the second-generation guerrilla commanders were originally from the eastern part of East Timor.

This does not mean that there was no resistance in the western part of East Timor. In fact, a former FALINTIL commander argued that resistance in the western part of East Timor continued during the occupation, although at a lower level than in the east. Nevertheless, the commonly held view after independence was that the resistance was conducted only in the eastern part of the country. This was also a problem within the armed forces, as we have seen, where it was used to suggest that only people from the eastern part fought during the war, whereas the westerners had little to do with the resistance. It was often also used to make fun of those who came from the western part (Babo-Soares 2003).

In February 2006 the petitioners abandoned their barracks on the grounds that their demands had been ignored. Instead of addressing this issue, barely a month later the army leaders dismissed around 591 petitioners from their military posts. This hasty dismissal was done with little consultation and did not follow proper legal procedures. Critics argued that the decision failed to meet the standard procedures required by the military disciplinary code promulgated by the UNTAET between 1999 and 2002.[5]

In March 2006, President of the Republic Xanana Gusmão, who had been on an overseas trip when the dismissals occurred, returned home and made a speech criticizing the decision. Making reference to the 'east versus west' dichotomy, he argued that the dismissal was a discriminatory act against the soldiers from the western part. The petitioners and their supporters saw the statement as a sign that the president was supportive of their case (United Nations 2006). The petitioners consequently submitted a letter to the general commander of the national police, seeking permission to hold a peaceful demonstration from 24–8 April 2006. After three days of demonstrations, violence erupted on the fourth day. It resulted in the death of two civilians and a couple of serious injuries. In the aftermath of the demonstration, violence occurred sporadically throughout Dili and several parts of East Timor.

The violence was made worse by the involvement of a commander of the military police, who deserted his post, taking with him other military officers, PNTL officers and weapons. The military police deserters, Major Alfredo Reinado Alves and his men,[6] including some of the petitioners, were then joined by other groups. In late April 2006, they launched an attack on the F-FDTL headquarters in Tasitolu, west of Dili, which led to the killing and wounding of some soldiers. In an act of revenge, according to some, the chief of the army singlehandedly and unlawfully distributed weapons to civilians who were originally from the eastern part of the country. The army commander reasoned that these civilian reservists were simply called up to defend the country in a time of crisis (United Nations 2006).

While most of the western soldiers left the army headquarters unarmed, most of the eastern soldiers had remained. These soldiers were called to quell the riots that erupted on the fourth day of the petitioners' demonstration in Dili on 25 April 2006. Alongside them were a group of armed civilians perceived to be armed by the F-FDTL commander. They stormed the PNTL headquarters, perceived to be the fortress of westerners, which resulted in a number of police injuries and deaths. On the same day, a police platoon marching unarmed, waving the flag of the UN and escorted by the UN police (UNPOL),[7] was shot at by alleged members of the F-FDTL and their armed civilian partners (also justified as reservists), killing several police agents and injuring others.

Worse still, Interior Minister Rogerio Lobato, of the then FRETILIN-led government, unilaterally armed two civilian groups from the western side – the Rai Los and Lima Lima groups – with weapons and ammunition belonging to the border patrol unit of the national police. Being from the Liquiça district (western side), it was unclear whether Lobato's aim was to crush the so-called petitioners and the military police who had defected. It was also unclear whether this second arming of civilians was to fight the perceived eastern-dominated army of F-FDTL or its armed civilians. One thing for certain is that the chaotic situation was provoked by armed confrontation, gang fighting and mob attacks on public and private properties. During May and June 2006 sporadic violence poured onto the streets and several districts of East Timor, leading to the destruction of property and killings between the easterners and westerners. Many people – approximately 150,000 – were driven out of their homes and remained internally displaced persons (IDPs) for over two years.

The protest of a group of soldiers on the internal policy of their institution thus turned into a large-scale political-military conflict and aggravated the ensuing violence that led East Timor to the brink of another civil war similar to that of 1974–5.

The attempted assassination of 11 February 2008

The violence, the defection of the commander of the military police (Major Alfredo) and his group, and the new IDP wave aggravated an already chaotic situation. Violence was almost uncontrollable as Major Alfredo and his men were set free to roam, if not control, half the country without interruption for over a year. This occurred despite the deployment of international forces from neighbouring countries to maintain law and order, the wide media coverage of their movements and regular interviews in which Major Alfredo threatened to launch attacks on the capital. The forces from Australia, New Zealand, Malaysia, the Philippines and Portugal, invited under the banner of a UN-authorized international stabilization force (ISF) to calm the situation, failed to persuade the rebels to surrender. The fact that the majority of the population in the western part of the country supported the rebels because they perceived them to be defending the 'western interest' against the 'easterners' exacerbated the situation.[8]

Interestingly, the petitioners and rebels declared a unilateral cease-fire on the eve of the presidential and parliamentary elections in the first semester of 2007. This gesture permitted peaceful elections to take place. A number of incidents were registered during the campaign period, but no armed confrontation between the military and the rebels occurred. The ISF was not mandated in this period to chase and capture the rebel forces, while the government forces confined themselves to Dili and sought to avoid provoking clashes by not participating in security operations. The elections resulted in the former prime minister, José Ramos-Horta, becoming the new president of the republic and the former president, Xanana Gusmão, the new prime minister. While the new leaders embarked on a reconciliatory approach to seek consensus and resolve the stalemate, disagreement and distrust continued to characterize negotiations between these leaders and their followers.

On 11 February 2008, amid intensified threats from renegade soldiers and petitioners, two groups of Major Alfredo's men drove to Dili, the first to the president's house and the second to the prime minister's house. Major Alfredo was with the first group. Upon arriving at the president's residence, the major and one of his men were shot dead by the president's bodyguards. One of Major Alfredo's men shot the president twice and almost killed him, then escaped unharmed into the hills of Dili. At almost the same time, the second group, commanded by Lieutenant Salsinha, ambushed the prime minister, Xanana Gusmão, whose convoy was on its way to work, but no one was killed (*Timor Post* 2007; *Diário* 2007). Some weeks later a Joint Military Operation, co-sponsored by the armed forces (F-FDTL) and the police (PNTL), was formed to capture Major Alfredo's men. It was a sign that relations between the two institutions were on the mend. One by one, Major Alfredo's men were either captured or surrendered to the joint military operation command, and all were tried and sentenced.

The state of imbalance: unresolved issues

The people of East Timor perceive conflict and violence to have arisen from an imbalance between cosmological ideals and worldly practices (the secular setting). Such imbalance is believed to have arisen from the improper handling of the interlinked and parallel issues in each sphere (Babo-Soares 2005). Conflict and violence are hence seen as representing a 'state of imbalance'.

The chronology of events that have given rise to violence in East Timor points to the past. From a Timorese perspective, the evils of the past continue to haunt the peace that was meant to be achieved. Similarly, scholars elsewhere have argued that legacies of war can serve as grounds for new conflict in the period following a war (see Paris 2004). Such legacies reflect not only individual attitudes and interpersonal relations between people who were once national heroes. They also reflect divisions at both the interpersonal and institutional levels that persist during the post-conflict period.

Post-independence East Timor certainly demonstrates the presence of a 'state of imbalance' between past and present, which is characterized by the persistence of conflict and violence. It is a continuity of the same line of history, in spite of the fact that there was an opportunity for major change with the advent of independence in 1999.

Resistance against the Indonesian occupation brought sacrifices and tireless efforts to achieve independence and put an end to the internal conflicts related to the 1975 events and the resistance movement itself. Nevertheless, the political strife during the resistance period had left a legacy because solutions had not been introduced to address such differences in the past. Sources of violence in the post-independence period included two still unresolved conflicts in particular: those among the once nationalist forces, which led to killings among them during the resistance years; and those related to veterans, widows, orphans of war and disabled people, who were all directly affected by the struggle for independence. As regards the conflicts between former nationalists, the symbolic unity forged during the struggle to fight the common enemy crumbled into ashes as new interests emerged during the post-independence period (Babo-Soares 2003: 19–25). When the common enemy (the Indonesian military) disappeared in 1999, new factions and divisions as well as old antagonisms resurfaced.

Post-violence impunity: the absence of justice

Major Alfredo, as mentioned above, was killed in the assassination attempts on the president and the prime minister in February 2007. Several months later his men turned themselves in to the security forces without any shedding of blood; it was a positive step. After this episode of violence and politico-military conflict the situation slowly improved. The government that came to power in 2007 tried to address some of the issues underlying the conflict and its violent manifestations, and the country slowly returned to normality. The government addressed the petitioners' issues by establishing a scheme to provide incentives in cash for former rebels to start businesses and begin a new life. The government also successfully integrated former rebel soldiers into society. Different schemes of economic recovery were introduced to help resolve issues of unemployment and poverty. A new programme was established to use some of the revenue from the oil and gas resources to reward and provide pensions to the elderly and former combatants, including orphans and widows of former combatants. The government also introduced tools to mend differences between different social groups and regions. All this helped to stabilize the situation. Yet the question remains whether this is sufficient to restore peace in East Timor.

Importantly, the issue of impunity remains. Article 160 of the Constitution of the republic states that all the most serious crimes that occurred between 1975 and 1999 are punishable by law.[9] When the Constitution was promulgated in 2002, many believed the rule of law would now be established in a country that had suffered a civil war, foreign occupation, a violent separation from Indonesia and violence in the aftermath of independence as well. An international panel was established to try the crimes committed before and during the events of 1999 and a truth and reconciliation commission was established to help reconciliation among the people of East Timor (Commission for Reception, Truth and Reconciliation, CAVR). The commission's mandate was to compile information about the history of resistance, violence and atrocities from the perspective of the East Timorese. It was also given the mandate to recommend prosecution in cases suspected of constituting crimes against humanity. The commission completed its task two years later. Although no prosecutions had been initiated as at mid-2010, a national wave of reconciliation processes under CAVR was conducted throughout all villages in the country to help former enemies reconcile and reintegrate peacefully in their own society.

In terms of prosecutions, however, all the good intentions of Article 160 of the Constitution have remained unfulfilled. Nothing has been done to execute the Constitution's mandate in this respect. In addition, although the commission's final report was published in 2004 no crimes were prosecuted. No one has been prosecuted for crimes committed during the resistance among the nationalist forces. Not a single investigation has been conducted and no commission to address the issues has been institutionalized.[10] The inability of the new nation's justice system to address this is striking. Why is this so? One of the reasons is that most of the actors who may have been implicated are former combatants and are considered resistance heroes in the war between 1975 and 1999. Their political status seems to place them above the law. It serves even as a political barrier to the implementation of the Constitution's Article 160. As a result, some representatives of victims of violence of 1975 and 1999 are still waiting for justice with respect to the loss of their loved ones.

The commission was only mandated to compile information on individuals and community profiles on the nature of the conflict; it was not a tribunal for prosecuting cases. Although it did recommend that some of the cases be tried in the court system, no prosecution of cases arising between 1975 and 1999 among the resistance forces has resulted. Thus, victims and perpetrators were confronted by the commission only to 'heal the wounds' and not to bring justice in the sense of prosecution. Instead of punishing the perpetrators for what they did, the commission offered to resolve the perpetrated crimes through reconciliation and compensation (CTF Report 2008).

This state of imbalance also extends to the 1999 events, when the Indonesian forces launched a scorched earth policy in East Timor after the country voted for independence. The new justice system has only been able to cover a very small number of cases and has only investigated crimes committed by the Indonesian forces. No attempt has been made to look into the violence committed by and among the East Timorese themselves (CTF Report 2008). There seems to be no political will on the part of either the international community, notably the United Nations, or the Timorese authorities to look into what happened in this period.

Reasoning the nature of violence

This chapter has argued that legacies of war are a significant factor in explaining post-conflict violence in East Timor. After independence in 1999, violence stemmed from interpersonal and inter-group divisions. These divisions were rooted in the period when all East Timorese were fighting for their own homeland against the invading forces, but they persisted after independence and remain unresolved. The East Timorese experience thus suggests that the past will trigger new conflict and violence if its divisive legacy remains unaddressed. While the efforts of the new government which came to power in 2007 were quite encouraging, they did not address the root causes embedded in the unresolved legacies of war.

It requires us, as stated by Lambourne (2009: 28–48),

> To rethink our focus on 'transition' as an interim process that links the past and the future, and to shift it to 'transformation', which implies long-term, sustainable processes embedded in society and adoption of psychosocial, political and economic, as well as legal, perspectives on justice. It also involves identifying, understanding and including, where appropriate, the various cultural approaches to justice that coexist with the dominant western worldview and practice.

Only when the sources of the political divisions discussed above are addressed can violence be minimized. The differences that have emerged since the resistance years therefore should be addressed and the political divisions that have occurred in the post-independence period should be resolved. Otherwise, differences from the past that are aggravated by socio-economic issues such as unemployment and poverty will continue to haunt the state of Timor-Leste. As some Timorese say, unless the past and current issues are resolved the East Timorese will continue to sleep on the mattresses of uncertainty and violence.

Notes

1 For example, abusive graffiti appearing on walls around Dili from August 2007 insulted members of the new government, accusing them of being former collaborators of Indonesia.
2 Until 20 May 2002, the political leadership in East Timor, comprising mostly party leaders, was not democratically elected.
3 These old political parties were FRETILIN (demanded outright independence from Portugal), UDT (demanded independence through a transitional pacification period with Portugal) and APODETI (demanded independence through a transitional pacification period with Indonesia), also two other small parties, KOTA (a local feudally-oriented political party) and Trabalhista (the Labour Party), whose party platforms were unclear.
4 See national dailies in East Timor 5–10 December 2004. The government set up a commission to inquire into the event but did not make its findings public.
5 Discussion with an international observer, Dili, 22 July 2006.
6 Reinado Alves was latter killed while attempting to assassinate the then president of the republic, José Ramos Horta, in February 2007.
7 The crisis in 2006 began in early February when over 600 members of the F-FDTL, mostly from the eastern part of the country, abandoned their headquarters. As the crisis intensified the UN, at the request of the then government of Timor-Leste, sent additional UNPOL personnel to help maintain security. The Security Council then passed resolution 1704 establishing the United Nations Mission in Timor-Leste (UNMIT), which included a contingent of UNPOL to restore security in the country and train the local police.
8 Most of the writers and reports tried to avoid making such a claim, even though the rebel leader and his supporters were able to roam freely in the western districts during 2006 and 2007 (see the Timor dailies during that period).
9 Article 160 of the Constitution states that 'acts committed between 25 April 1974 and 31 December 1999 which are considered as crimes against humanity, genocide or war crimes are punishable under either national or international courts'.
10 Personal communication from a prosecutor, Dili, 8 December 2008.

Bibliography

Babo-Soares, Dionísio (2003) *Branching from the Trunk: East Timorese Nationalism in Transition*, Canberra: RSPAS, Australian National University, unpublished PhD thesis.
Babo-Soares, Dionísio (2005), 'Grassroots reconciliation in East Timor', in Elin Skaar, Siri Gloppen and Astri Suhrke (eds), *Roads to Reconciliation*, Lanham, MD: Lexington Books.
Canberra Times (2001) Australia, 21 September.
CTF Report (2008). Commission of Truth and Friendship, Indonesia – Timor-Leste (2008) *Per Memoriam Ad Spem*, Final Report, Dili and Bali: Ministries of Foreign Affairs of Timor-Leste and Indonesia.

Diário (2009), 16–20 February.

Gusmão, Kay Rala Xanana (1998) *Timor Leste: um povo uma pátria*, Lisbon: Edições Colobri.

Lambourne, Wendy (2009) 'Transitional justice and peacebuilding after mass violence', *International Journal of Transitional Justice*, 3(1): 28–48.

Paris, Roland (2004) *At War's End: Building Peace after Civil Conflict*, Cambridge: Cambridge University Press.

Pires, Emília (2009) *Monitoring the Principles of Good International Engagement in Fragile State and Situations*, Paper presented at the Conference on Development, Dili, 2 March.

Radio Australia (2004) *East Timor: Ex-FALINTIL Guerillas Call for Veterans Affairs Department*, 23 July. Online, available at: www.jsmp.minihub.org.

Silva, Gil da (2009a), *Relatorio Komisaun Inkerito Kazu 04 de Dezembro 2002 Indika Deputado David Diax Ximenes Hanesan Autor*, CJITL, 3 February (Reporter Caetano Atay Alves). Online, available at: http://cjitl.org/index.php?option=com_content&task=view&id=65&Itemid=2>.

Silva, Gil da (2009b) *Maubocy Halo Nabilan Dr. JMF Nia Neon Malahuk*, JND, 19 February. Online, available at: http://forum-haksesuk.blogspot.com/2009/03/klarifikasaun-ba-drjose-manuel.htm.

Suara Timor Lorosae (2000) 15 and 20 November.

Suara Timor Lorosae (2001) 27 January.

Suara Timor Lorosae (2002) April 2002.

Suara Timor Lorosae (2009) 16–20 February.

Timor Leste National Parliament (2004) *Constitution of the Democratic Republic of Timor Leste*, Dili: Timor-Leste.

Timor Post.

United Nations (2006) *Report of the United Nations Independent Special Commission of Inquiry for Timor-Leste*, Geneva.

United Nations Security Council (1999) *Resolution 1272/1999: Security Council Establishes UN Transitional Administration in East Timor for Initial Period until 31 January 2001*, 25 October. Online, available at: www.un.org/News/Press/docs/1999/19991025.sc6745.doc.html.

UNTAET (2002), *Assembly Votes to Transform Itself into Legislature*, Daily Briefing, 31 January. Dili: United Nations Transitional Administration in East Timor.

Part IV
Africa

12 Sexual violence

The case of eastern Congo[1]

Ingrid Samset

Introduction

Sexual violence emerged as a widespread phenomenon in the eastern part of the Democratic Republic of the Congo (DRC) during an internationalized civil war which broke out in 1998. The war grew out of turmoil in the preceding years at both regional, national and local levels; including the 1994 genocide of the Tutsi minority in neighbouring Rwanda and the 'first Congo war' in 1996–7 which resulted in the toppling of the Mobutu regime. It was the successor regime of Laurent Kabila which the governments of Rwanda and Uganda sought to overthrow when they flew troops to western Congo and started advancing towards Kinshasa in August 1998. President Kabila had inherited a weak national army and was only able to stop this advance with the intervention of Angolan armed forces. Zimbabwe, Namibia, Sudan and Chad eventually joined Kabila's side as well. Rwanda and Uganda, in an alliance with Burundi, still succeeded in invading the eastern and northern parts of the country, forging alliances with local armed groups and assuming control of main towns. To fight this coalition on the ground, Kabila mobilized Rwandan Hutus who lived in exile in the Congo as well as local Mai-Mai militias. He also got backing from Hutu rebels in the Burundian civil war (HRW 2002: 15–17; Prunier 2009; Reyntjens 2009).

A 'global and inclusive' agreement signed in Pretoria, South Africa on 17 December 2002 and other peace deals in 2002–3 were followed by the withdrawal of foreign armies, new governance structures and elections. This put an end to the countrywide war, but in eastern DRC armed groups continued to operate and sexual and other violence persisted.

In this chapter I analyse that part of the violence in wartime and postwar eastern Congo which can be called 'sexual' violence. Drawing on Lewis (2009: 3), I define sexual violence as 'any violence carried out through sexual means or by targeting sexuality'. Focusing on South Kivu province[2] and assessing the period from mid-1998 through 2009, I describe the level, evolution, characteristics and main groups of victims and perpetrators of the sexual violence. I then seek to explain why this violence became relatively widespread and persistent. I argue that the violence assumed three main functions for those exerting it: the sexual violence had a strategic function in the armed conflicts; it was of an opportunistic nature; and it served as a bonding mechanism. I further argue that specific structural conditions of eastern DRC, in particular state weakness, deep poverty and significant mineral wealth; facilitated the spread and continuation of sexual violence once it had emerged during the war.

Three questions should be addressed at the outset. To what extent was eastern DRC actually 'post-war' after 2002? And in a book which analyses post-war violence, why include the war period as well in this case study? And why analyse only that violence which assumed a sexual form, and not all the violence?

After the end of the internationalized civil war in 2002, large-scale violence in eastern DRC (i.e. the provinces of Orientale, North and South Kivu, Maniema and Katanga) was concentrated in several zones, mostly within the Kivus and Orientale. These locations shifted over time, and there were also times of relative peace in the most violence-affected areas. So there was not entirely 'peace', but hardly full-blown 'war' either: from 2003 until the end of the decade, the people of the Kivus and Orientale mostly lived in a situation of 'no war, no peace'. There was a sense that the war was over, as foreign-backed rule and division had given way to national reunification, governance changes and elections. My interviews from South Kivu as of 2009 also suggest that violence was less extensive and intensive than it had been during the war. Eastern DRC was thus post-war in a real, though fairly limited sense.

For there was also continuity in the violence. From 2003 through 2009 in eastern Congo, violence continued to be exercised by armed groups and a significant share of it was still sexual violence. This continuity from the war into the post-war phase explain why I find it useful not to limit my analysis to the aftermath of the war, but also to study the war years.

Yet sexual violence was only one type of violence. In post-war South Kivu there was also lynching, political violence, domestic violence, violence related to land conflicts and mining-related violence. Or differently categorized; beyond sexual violence there were mass killings, forced labour, forced recruitment, systematic torture and arbitrary arrests in post-war DRC. The main reason why I have chosen to restrict the focus to one violence type is the complexity of the violence that occurred in the 1998–2009 period in eastern Congo, a time when this huge area was marked by multi-layered conflicts. There is also fairly little research on the post-war violence to draw on in this case.[3] I therefore examine one violence type and picked sexual violence for two main reasons. One was the consensus among those I interviewed in the DRC about the continued incidence of sexual violence in eastern Congo, as opposed to more divergent views on other violence types. I also wished to contribute knowledge on a topic and case which despite growing attention in recent years has been subject to little social science research.[4]

This paucity of research is in large part due to the many difficulties involved in collecting data on sexual violence in contexts of armed strife. Sexual violence is a sensitive phenomenon associated with shame and stigma, and if it is reported at all, such reports come with a number of problems. If the violence is committed in contexts of war and by members of armed groups, victims will often find it hard to identify the perpetrators and what group they belong to. Reporting agencies will have trouble accessing conflict-torn areas for practical and security reasons. And if data collection goes beyond the reporting of incidents, it is not a straight-forward task to interview victims and perpetrators either. Beyond cultural miscommunication, fear, power inequities and linguistic confusion, selective memory and the wish to present events in a way that safeguards one's own interests are likely to come into play.[5]

Yet existing sources take us some way towards an understanding of the phenomenon in the case of eastern Congo during and after the 1998–2002 war. Beyond statistics, advocacy reports and other academic research, in this chapter I draw on 31 interviews conducted in early 2009 as part of my doctoral research (Samset, forthcoming). Most interviews were conducted in South Kivu (27 of 31). Of the 32 interviewees (one interview was with two persons), the majority were Congolese (28 of 32) and male (25 of 32). All Congolese interviewees spoke French and most held leadership positions in a community or organization; they can thus be considered as part of a local elite. Interviewees were selected to enable views of different interest groups to be heard on post-war violence dynamics. I found interviewee narratives varied and well considered, but subject to possible biases, such as an antipathy towards Rwanda. I analyse the interview data critically, keeping such potential bias in mind.

Describing the wartime and post-war sexual violence

It is impossible to know exactly how much sexual violence occurred in eastern Congo during the war from 1998 to 2002 and in the years that followed. Beyond the reasons for uncertainty given above, other reasons are more specific to this case. Eastern Congo is a huge region: its five provinces cover an area corresponding to almost twice the size of France. For many areas within this region and several phases in the 11.5-year period, data on sexual violence is non-existent or of poor quality. Simply put, we know that incidents of sexual violence occurred in much of this region and for much of this time, but we know less about when and where they occurred, by whom and against whom they were committed and how they were organized.

Systematic data collection on sexual violence in eastern DRC began in the mid-2000s. From then on, a growing number of NGOs also started working in this field, responding to the urgent need for assistance to victims. But with the rising external attention and expansion of actors in the field, new obstacles emerged to the collection of reliable data. In political terms, rape accusations became 'a tool of political communication', reportedly used by some local groups to discredit adversaries (Moufflet 2008: 120, 126). Evidence also suggests that rape was 'commercialized' (Eriksson Baaz and Stern 2010: 13) and that rape figures were inflated in order to attract donor money (e.g. Rodriguez 2007: 46). Inconsistencies in registration practices between the various reporting agencies exacerbated the uncertainties about the actual scope of the phenomenon. But on balance, the shame and stigma associated with being sexually violated in eastern Congolese society; the poverty and relative isolation of many of the affected communities; as well as the continued influence of armed groups with an ability to retaliate against those who reported, all suggest that underreporting continued to outweigh factors that might have led to over-estimation. The figures I will now present therefore probably underesti-mate the scope of the phenomenon. They are still useful in giving a rough indication of that scope and of trends over time.

Level and evolution

During the war, at least 2,000 women and girls in South Kivu are said to have been raped each year (HRW 2002: 39). This estimate refers to the period from late 1999 to mid-2001, i.e. the middle of the war. Sexual viol-ence also seems to have increased in scope over time during the war (ibid.: 23, 33). After the war, it continued. Figure 12.1 draws on data from the most extensive data collection effort, conducted by the United Nations Populations Fund (UNFPA) in partnership with a number of NGOs. It depicts the level and evolution of reported rapes in the Kivus in some of the post-war years.[6]

As the figure shows, the overall post-war trend is downward. For the Kivu provinces, the sum of reported rapes declined from approximately 11,000 in 2004 to around 8,000 in 2008. In South Kivu only, reported rapes dropped from around 5,500 in 2004 to less than 3,000 in 2008. Yet this downward trend was combined with a high level in the first post-war years. If the above-mentioned estimate is correct, of 2,000 women and girls raped annually during the war in South Kivu; then the rape rate actually increased in years one and two after the war. The trend of an early post-war increase and a later decrease in sexual violence is also detected in another study, which analyses South Kivu only and draws on other data (HHI and Oxfam 2010: 17–18).

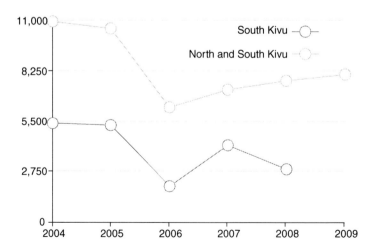

Figure 12.1 Rape trends in eastern Congo, 2004–9 (sources: UNFPA-RDC 2007: 28, 2008: 13; HRW 2009a: 14; UN News Service 2010).

Characteristics

Sexual violence in eastern Congo during and after the 1998–2002 war went far beyond one-on-one rapes in the private sphere. Much of the sexual violence had a public and collective nature, and was physically and psychologically devastating for the victims.

It is reported that as well as rape, sexual torture and sexual mutilation took place during the war. Incidents occurred in the victims' homes, in villages, along roads, in the fields, or in situations where victims had been abducted by armed men (HRW 2002: 25, 39). The perpetrator-to-victim ratio was one-to-one or many-to-one, as in gang rapes (ibid.: 25, 35, 39). In some cases there were no spectators to the incidents, but in others members of the family or community were forced to watch (ibid.: 35, 39). While 'ordinary' rapes seem to have been most common, in some rapes objects were forcibly inserted into the victim's vagina (ibid.: 39, 54). Wartime rape was also sometimes combined with other violence, such as beating or whipping; the mutilation of the sexual organs of the victim; or the killing of the victim (ibid.).

Little changed in the character of sexual violence from 2003 onwards. Rape, sexual torture and sexual mutilation continued and many of the rapes were gang rapes (Moufflet 2008: 121). Some women 'were preyed upon by armed combatants in the fields, along the roads or in their homesteads … [and were] abducted and taken as hostages to the combatants' bases in the forest' (Longombe *et al.* 2008: 139). Rape was still sometimes combined with other violence, such as forcibly inserting objects into the victim's body and/or killing her (ibid.: 133; Wakabi 2008: 15). Another continuity from war to post-war was that sexual violence still took place 'in full, deliberate and enforced view of husbands and family members' (Longombe *et al.* 2008: 133; Taback *et al.* 2008: 653). In addition, family and community members were sometimes forced to conduct rapes themselves (Wakabi 2008: 15; Moufflet 2008: 121). In sum, if the level of sexual violence dropped over time in the post-war years, the violence does not seem to have turned less brutal.

Victims and perpetrators

Both during and after the war, victims of sexual violence were overwhelmingly civilians and most were women and girls. The reported share of male rape victims in the post-war Kivu and Orientale provinces varies from 1 per cent to 10 per cent (UNFPA-RDC 2007: 39; Eriksson Baaz and Stern 2010: 44). But given the particular stigma associated with being sexually violated as a man, underreporting may have been more common for male than for female victims (Eriksson Baaz and Stern 2010: 44).

Both during and after the war, the perpetrators of sexual violence in eastern Congo were almost invariably men. For the period 2004–6, for instance, UNFPA-RDC (2007: 45) finds that less than 1 per cent of the perpetrators were women. The large majority of perpetrators belonged to an armed group, but there is also evidence of sexual violence by the police

(Taback *et al.* 2008: 654; Longombe *et al.* 2008: 133), and by civilians (HRW 2002: 26). After the war, the share of civilians among the alleged rapists increased (Rodriguez 2007: 45; HHI and Oxfam 2010: 2; Moufflet 2008: 128). By one account, in 2004–6, 4 per cent of rapists in South Kivu were civilians, a share that rose to 27 per cent in 2007 (UNFPA-RDC 2007: 46; 2008: 25).

Yet most of the sexual violence continued to be committed by men in military attire. There is evidence of sexual violence by members of virtually all the armed groups – whether foreign or local, state or non-state. While probably not exhaustive, the following list includes some of reported perpetrator groups. During the war, in South Kivu sexual violence was reportedly committed, on the side of the ruling coalition, by the local RCD (Congolese Rally for Democracy), the Rwandan army and the Burundian army, and, on the other, by the local Mai-Mai militias; Rwandan Hutus, many of whom were organized in the Democratic Forces for the Liberation of Rwanda (FDLR); and Burundians in the Forces for the Defence of Democracy (FDD) and the National Forces of Liberation (FNL) (HRW 2002: 23, 25, 27, 45, 47). After the war, sexual violence in both the Kivus and Orientale was reportedly committed by members of the new Congolese army, the Armed Forces of the Democratic Republic of the Congo (FARDC), by the National Congress for the Defence of the People armed group (CNDP) and by the Mai-Mai; and among armed groups with a non-Congolese membership, by the FDLR in the Kivus and the LRA (Lord's Resistance Army) in Orientale (Rodriguez 2007: 45; Wakabi 2008: 15; Taback *et al.* 2008: 654; HRW 2009b, 2010). Finally, there are reports of sexual exploitation and abuse by UN peacekeepers in the United Nations Mission in the Democratic Republic of the Congo peace operation (MONUC)[7] (Kent 2007: 47; Notar 2006).

Explaining the wartime and post-war sexual violence

The vastness of eastern Congo, the poor quality of much of the data on sexual violence and the complexity and sensitivity of the phenomenon makes it a daunting task to explain the sexual violence that took place from mid-1998 through 2009. The chapter format indeed only allows for exploring some causal dynamics. I have chosen to focus on the question of *incidence*, addressing why sexual violence became fairly widespread and persistent in eastern Congo during the war from 1998 to 2002 and in the first seven post-war years. Another set of questions relates to variation: why, for instance, did sexual violence vary over time during and after the war; across space within the DRC; and between different armed groups? While this also must be studied to reach a deeper understanding of the phenomenon, given the paucity of research it is necessary first to identify the conditions under which sexual violence emerged and became widespread in this case. This work can in turn facilitate future research on variation in sexual violence within the structural conditions that applied in wartime and post-war DRC.

To identify the structural conditions which facilitated the emergence and continuation of sexual violence, I draw on the emerging theoretical literature on sexual violence in armed conflicts as well as the empirical literature on the DRC. From the theoretical literature, I deduce three explanatory accounts which I apply to evidence from the eastern Congo, finally I bring the narratives together and contextualize them.

Strategic sexual violence

The first theoretical account holds that sexual violence is deliberately used by armed groups because it helps them conquer and control populations and the land they live on. The sexual violence is exerted during conquest or under occupation, then sometimes as punishment of subjects for not having shown enough 'loyalty' (Wood 2006: 331). This account departs from ideas and roles that are commonly associated with gender in patriarchal societies. Women have traditionally been associated with reproduction, nurturing and community, and men with protection and toughness (e.g. Moser and Clark 2001: 8; Alison 2007: 80; Skjelsbæk 2001: 220). Seifert (1996: 39) remarks that the female body 'in many cultures ... embodies the nation as a whole'. If people adhere to such beliefs about gender, then an external sexual attack on women becomes a devastating assault on the entire community. The attack will traumatize the victimized women and reduce their ability to play their (perceived) gender role within reproduction and nurturing. It will also humiliate the men, since the fact that the attack happens reflects a failure on their part to protect. Sexual violence thus demoralizes the entire targeted population, drains it of energy and reduces its ability to resist conquest and occupation (Gottschall 2004: 131; Wood 2006: 327–8).

In the case of eastern Congo, my interview data and other studies (e.g. HRW 2002; Longombe *et al.* 2008) do suggest that sexual violence reached high levels in part because it helped armed groups conquer and control territory. Sexual violence worked as a 'weapon of war', I will argue, because it terrorized communities into submission. Submission – rather than effective resistance – was the result because the violence was shocking and humiliating, because it recurred over a long period and because the targeted communities had few resources to muster in order to resist effectively.

To grasp how sexual violence could produce this effect, we should first note that according to my interview data, in eastern Congo prior to the war sexual violence had mostly been restricted to one-on-one acts in private and to rapes by young men of young women which often resulted in out-of-court settlements. According to RFDA *et al.* (2005: 27), rape was seen as deeply humiliating: 'although rape has always existed in the traditional society of South Kivu, it has been regarded as a deeply reprehensible act and an extreme humiliation for the victim and her family, especially her husband'. So when armed groups from 1998 onwards entered villages and took women by force, in public, and often in brutal ways, this came as a shock. Sexual violence of this nature was something most locals had not seen before,[8] and one reason it had hardly happened was that these rapes made it more difficult to uphold the customary gender roles. In traditional eastern Congolese society, women were the child-raisers, the cooks and the cultivators of the soil and thus symbolized the lifeblood of society. Male identity was tied to the ability to provide for the women, children and the collectivity – such an ability proved a man worthy of being an authority and decision-maker, in the wider polity as well (Eriksson Baaz and Stern 2009: 507). The humiliating effect of sexual violence was probably amplified by the way in which this violence made it harder for both men and women to play their prescribed roles. Sexual violence against women constituted a symbolic attack of the community's source of continued life, as the physical and psychological effects would reduce the women's ability to reproduce and nurture. And if intruders succeeded in hurting women and children in devastating ways, then the men had utterly failed too in protecting. The shame that would result for men is illustrated in this interview extract:

> A: If in a family, someone comes around and rapes your wife, you don't have the force to defend your wife. And the wife of someone, really, that's his precious good that he has to protect. So when someone comes around to attack, he comes to your home, he rapes your wife and your children before your eyes … you'll go mad.
> Q: And the greater the brutality, the greater the humiliation?
> A: Yes.
>
> (Interview 13)

It is conceivable, though, that sexual violence by armed groups may not terrorize a population into submission, but rather provoke their resistance. If sexual violence persisted in eastern Congo, was this perhaps in part because communities refused to give in and their attempts at resistance were 'punished' with more violence?

There is evidence of some popular resistance against the sexual violence in eastern Congo (e.g. Gottschall 2004: 132), but in general, reports have little or no information about popular attempts to resist the rapes. And though a number of NGOs emerged to assist victims of sexual violence, I found no evidence of any movement initiated by the victims themselves to promote their interests, the lack of which was deplored by several of my interviewees. One probable reason for this lack is the trauma inflicted by repeated exposure to degrading and physically devastating sexual violence. As one interviewee remarked, referring to an area where rapes had occurred recently and it was unclear who was responsible: 'given that people are already traumatized, they don't ask questions anymore' (Interview 25).

Beyond trauma, the apparent lack of organized resistance by victims was probably also linked to limited resources. Due to the poverty and relative isolation of most eastern Congolese communities, they were not in a favourable position to build an effective international network for their cause once they were exposed to sexual violence from the late 1990s onwards. Given this vulnerability, armed groups could reduce or break initial resistance by repeating the sexual violence over time. And while rapes were sometimes resisted in less organized ways (as my interviews suggest), such spontaneous resistance does not seem to have helped curb the violence. Instead, more rapes could result, in line with the 'revenge' mechanism.

Sexual violence thus seems to have worked as a 'weapon of war' because initial resistance was broken and new resistance proved surmountable. A harder question is how it can be 'proven' that sexual violence was deliberately used by armed groups in order to conquer and control territory. Evidence that commanders of armed groups ordered combatants to rape was not found in the eastern Congolese case. But there is strong evidence to suggest that commanders condoned sexually violent behaviour – that they knew that the rank-and-file were committing sexual violence, yet did not tell them to refrain from it (e.g. Eriksson Baaz and Stern 2010: 15–16, HRW 2009a). Only in recent years, after a new law on sexual violence came into force (Government of the DRC 2006) and external pressure increased, have the Congolese authorities begun to signal more clearly that sexual violence should not take place (HRW 2009a: 35–6). But had sexual violence proved counterproductive in military terms, it is likely that commanders would have taken earlier initiatives to stop it. Evidence of public statements to this effect from the war or the first post-war years was not found.

In sum, one reason sexual violence became widespread in eastern Congo during and after the war was its tragic effectiveness as a means of conquest and control in this resource-rich, patriarchal and institutionally weak area:

> It [sexual violence] is also a practice of survival, a means to access the riches. You have to pass via traumatization, be nasty, and show that you're not easy. And once they fear you, they will leave you with space and then you can have fun with the women. It's a theory of occupation. If you want to occupy a given population and subdue the men there, you pass directly by the women.
>
> (Interview 25)

Opportunistic sexual violence

In the second theoretical account, war becomes an opportunity for fighters to take shortcuts to satisfy certain needs (Goldstein 2001: 364–5; Wood 2006: 321–3). Shortcuts are taken because situations of war tend to weaken the influence of state institutions such as the judiciary and the police and of social control more broadly. Combatants will therefore be less deterred from engaging in behaviour they might have refrained from as civilians and under 'normal' circumstances. This account further suggests that the reasons why persons at war may want to use the war-induced 'opportunities' for sexual violence are of both a sexual and social nature. Sexual violence in war is driven by a sexual urge and can satisfy the perpetrator sexually, but this effect is accentuated under conditions of patriarchy. If the pre-war society is dominated by males and 'the masculine', with females and 'the feminine' occupying a subordinate position, then wartime rape becomes a way for men to enforce these unequal gender roles (Wood 2006: 325).

Sexual violence takes place in war not only because combatants *can* commit it, in other words, but also because they may *want* to. Broader opportunities certainly do not imply that all soldiers will rape, but as Wood (2006: 322) argues, 'with an increase in opportunity, men with a propensity to rape will do so more frequently or ... more men (but not necessarily all) will rape'.

In the case of eastern Congo, the theory of opportunistic sexual violence does elucidate some of the sexual violence which took place during and after the 1998–2002 war. But if we consider the war and post-war period as a whole, sexual violence with a strategic function seems to have predated and preconditioned opportunistic violence. Because sexual violence was used from early on to conquer and control territory, the moral barrier that had existed against rape in public and against gang rape started to erode. And with the thresholds lowered, more men eventually used the 'opportunity' to rape that the war and post-war situation offered.

A crucial reason why many men did so was the entrenchment of patriarchal norms. The following interview extract from South Kivu gives a glimpse of the nature of this patriarchy:

> During the war the woman was ... considered as a thing. The woman was commodified. They found that they could play whenever, in whatever way with the woman. But according to our custom ... Before, if a boy liked you and wanted to marry you and you didn't like him, the boy ... would take you by force ... And later the family of the boy would come ... to say sorry, and they would discuss the dowry. But ... what we saw during the war was that if they took you by force, if they would play with you, then afterwards they would just chase you back to where you came from, to make you go home after they had played with you. And no one will talk about you.... That's why the women have said, 'no, we are not considered as persons' [any more].
>
> (Interview 15)

This account suggests that rape went from constituting an act with consequences in pre-war society to an act with no clearly adverse consequences for the rapist during the war. The war appears to have enabled men to rape without being expected to make up for it. The fact that some armed men would now rape without making up for it and also, as the following quote suggests, without suffering adverse consequences in terms of combat capacity, may have lowered the threshold for other fighters as well:

> The men at war were in the bush, with their practices. They would say that when you are at war, you cannot touch a woman ... because ... if you touch a woman, you will die during the war. The majority of these guys did not touch a woman. [But then] there were people who tried to touch the women. When the woman went to the field, he would rape her, and ... he goes back to war, and he is not killed. He says that it's normal, he tells his friends, 'look, I tried it, and it worked'. So people got involved like that.
>
> (Interview 15)

Opportunities for sexual violence thus opened up and thresholds were lowered during the war. And after the war, perpetrators in eastern Congo were still unlikely to face any visibly adverse consequences. A new law against sexual violence came into force in 2006, involving prison sentences of up to 20 years for instances of such violence (Government of the DRC 2006, Art. 168). Anecdotes from my interview data suggest that in cases where rapists had been brought to justice and this became known in local communities, individuals who might have considered raping would refrain from it. Yet such indications were patchy and the Congolese justice system remained under-resourced and marked by corruption in the first post-war years (ILAC and IBA HRI 2009; Vircoulon 2009). Most crimes remained unpunished and the probability was still small that rapists would be held to account. As one interviewee said, sexual violence continued 'because no one prevents them from doing that' (Interview 8). There is therefore little doubt that some of the sexual violence in eastern Congo can be attributed to the opportunities for such violence that the war and post-war situation offered, combined with entrenched patriarchal norms in eastern Congolese society.

Sexual violence as a bonding mechanism

In the third theoretical account, sexual violence happens because it con-tributes to build cohesion within military units in the stressful, high-risk situation of war (Cockburn 2001: 22; Goldstein 2001: 365, Cohen 2010). In a parallel to the narrative on strategic sexual violence, in this account too the violence is allowed to happen because it performs certain func-tions that are useful for the perpetrators as a group. The presumed useful effects include solidarity or bonding between combatants, unit cohesion and loyalty to the war effort. Sexual violence can produce these effects through the intermediary of identity, since the use of sexual violence departs from and shapes the identity of the perpetrator as a 'fighter'. This happens in several ways. The most straightforward mechanism is that a combatant who sexually violates a person shows that he (or she) is able and willing to commit violence against someone; an ability and willingness which is required to be a 'good fighter'. The use of sexual and not another type of violence also carries the message that the soldier can transgress rules that apply in 'normal' society; it is a sign of 'toughness'. The sexual violence can thus help confirm the perpetrator's loyalty to his or her unit and the war effort. A more specific argument along these lines is that for armed groups where members have been forcibly recruited, building a coherent fighting force is particularly challenging. Given the bonding functions of sexual violence, such violence is likely to be more commonly used by armed groups whose members are forcibly recruited (Cohen 2010). Soldiers who are reluctant to rape might do so, moreover, in order not to undermine group cohesion: 'Men who would not rape individually do so as part of a display within the male group, to avoid becoming an outcast' (Goldstein 2001: 365).

Some of the sexual violence in eastern Congo clearly seems to have had bonding and identity-confirmation functions. To examine this more closely, I will draw on a set of studies on the sexual violence of a key armed group which emerged after the war, namely the new Congolese army (Eriksson Baaz and Stern 2008, 2009, 2010). This army, the FARDC, comprises former members of various armed groups, many of whom had fought each other during the war. In the east of the DRC, the FARDC is estimated to have been responsible for a significant share of the post-war rapes: from 2006–8 some 24– 70 per cent (Eriksson Baaz and Stern 2010: 8, fn. 7). Eriksson Baaz and Stern's (2009) study of the soldiers' own narratives of sexual violence suggests that one function of the rapes indeed was to reconstitute the 'masculinity' and fighter identity of each combatant. Expanding on this study, I will argue that this also worked at a collective level, as rapes confirmed each soldier's belonging to the 'community of fighters' and thus helped to forge cohesion within the disparate army organization.

Army soldiers interviewed for the Eriksson Baaz and Stern (2009) study referred to the lengthy absences from their regular sex partners and their lack of pay to justify or 'normalize' the rapes of local women. A central premise of this reasoning was the idea that men in general, and men at war in particular, need regular sex (i.e. heterosexual intercourse): 'brave fighting necessitated … sexual relief' (ibid.: 506). And if the soldiers could not get consensual sex or buy it, then what they constructed as their non-negotiable need for sex would 'dictate' that they take a woman by force (ibid.: 508–10). What the soldiers called 'lust rapes' occurred, in other words, 'because a man must release sexual tension' (ibid.: 209).[9] In Eriksson Baaz and Stern's (2009: 510) interpretation, the soldiers here

> Recast that which in 'normal' circumstances is 'abnormal' (i.e. sex by force) as 'normalized' in the military setting through discourses of disempowerment and unfulfilled masculinity … It is through this normalizing reasoning that rape becomes a possible performative act of masculinity.

Eriksson Baaz and Stern (2009) do not explicitly discuss how these dynamics played out in interactions between soldiers. But their study points to how, in the interview situation, soldiers would reinforce each others' narratives in a way which comes across as adding weight and social legitimacy to the idea of 'lust rape' as something that was 'necessary' for them, given the circumstances. The function such rapes assumed for the army soldiers of 'reconstituting masculinity' (ibid.: 514) thus seems to have operated not only at the individual level, but also in a collective dynamic reinforced through peer pressure and mutual expectations. Given the way 'manhood' was constructed by the soldiers, rape appears to have performed a role of manifesting both identity and belonging within the social sphere of the armed group.

It is also useful to consider Cohen's (2010) theory on rape as a socialization mechanism in armed groups where combatants are forcibly recruited in order to explain FARDC sexual violence. In theory, army recruitment was voluntary: after the war ended, armed group members were given a choice of whether to join the new army or go back to civilian life. However, many opted for army integration not because they were particularly motivated to do so, but due to the scarcity of other economic opportunities and to pressure. Eriksson Baaz and Stern (2010: 26) report that the majority of the army soldiers they interviewed 'described the choice of integration (rather than demobilization) as being made because they saw no other option – they had nothing to go back to. Also, many who wished to demobilize were hindered by their commanders, who needed them in order to maintain the position of being in command of many men and in order to advance their importance and position within the army'. They conclude that 'a large part of the army consists of soldiers who perceive themselves as having been more or less forced to enlist' (ibid.).

In practice therefore, the degree of voluntarism in army recruitment was much lower than it might seem. At the same time, the army faced a daunting challenge of integration, given that many soldiers had recently fought each other during the war. It was this army much of the post-war sexual violence was attributed to – largely in line with what the combatant socialization theory would predict. The use of sexual violence by many army soldiers can thus be partly explained by how this violence served the urgent priority of building cohesion in military units and the army more broadly, which in the early post-war years remained a highly disparate organization.

The broader context

Though they do not capture all causes of sexual violence in wartime and post-war eastern DRC, the three theoretical accounts I have presented shed light on important dynamics. Available evidence does not allow us to determine the relative importance of each explanation, but it is clear that sexual violence in wartime and post-war eastern DRC had at least three different functions. This complexity helps explain why the sexual violence phenomenon became so widespread and persistent over time.

The extension and protracted period of sexual violence is best understood, however, in a broader perspective. For wartime and post-war insecurity, patriarchy and institutional weakness combined with other conditions in eastern DRC from the late 1990s on which also facilitated the emergence and continuation of sexual violence. One such condition was state weakness. Even prior to the outbreak of the war in 1998, state institutions in this huge country were on the verge of collapse. Eastern Congo was also marked by widespread and deep poverty, and has significant deposits of valuable minerals. Combined with regional turmoil, porous borders and the location of the East on the periphery of the Congolese state, this shaped a context where incentives for violence grew and constraints upon its use weakened.

These contextual factors also shaped the sexual violence patterns. For once the war had broken out in 1998 and some armed groups had adopted the rape tactic, widespread poverty and institutional decay made effective resistance against the rapes very difficult. The effectiveness of sexual violence as a weapon of war was thus enhanced. The prior weakness of institutions also expanded the war-induced 'window of opportunity' for sexual and social gratification through violence. Joblessness and poverty, combined with the mineral riches that could be gained by armed men organized in a group, also made it tempting not only to join armed groups but also to remain loyal to them by not shying away from the 'toughness test' of rape. A broad range of structural conditions thus combined in eastern Congo at this juncture in ways that made the area, once it found itself embroiled in a major war and for many years to come, particularly prone to the emergence and multiplication of actors who were ready to break the social taboos associated with sexual violence.

Conclusions

When the topic is sexual violence during and after war, and the case is a large part of Africa's third-largest state over a period of more than a decade marked by armed conflicts, we are faced with major challenges of 'knowing'. Writing this chapter has implied identifying questions on which the available data could shed light. This has meant ignoring a possibly huge 'hinterland', likely to include – beyond the question of variation – local and global drivers of sexual violence, interactions between local, national, regional and global levels, and deeper historical causes. What remains certain is that the emergence and continuation of sexual violence in wartime and post-war eastern DRC cannot be reduced to one or a few factors alone.

This chapter has argued that the strategic, opportunistic and bonding functions of sexual violence, combined with the particular conditions of eastern DRC from the late 1990s onwards, together facilitated the emergence of sexual violence during the 1998–2002 war and its continuation after the war ended. Sexual violence helped armed groups subdue the population so that they could conquer and control their land. Combatants took advantage of the war-induced weakening of institutions to satisfy certain needs, and sexually violent behaviour was condoned since this built cohesion within military units and helped reassert a fighter identity. Sexual violence thus assumed several significant functions, which were amplified by political and economic circumstances. Deep poverty, isolation and a weak state complicated resistance against the rapes and facilitated armed groups' use of sexual violence as a 'weapon of war'. Dysfunctional and hollow institutions made it hard to close the 'window of opportunity' for sexual violence that the war had opened. And mineral wealth and the militarization of extraction, combined with poverty and unemployment, made it attractive to join armed groups and adhere to their rules, including the use of rape as a mechanism of bonding and identity confirmation.

Reports of new mass rapes continue to come out of eastern Congo (e.g. Stearns 2010) and efforts to curb this violence remain urgent. But as North *et al.* (2009: 13) remind us, 'no society solves the problem of violence by eliminating violence; at best, it can be contained and managed'. A key question for societies emerging from war is thus how to reduce the violence to a level considered 'normal' or acceptable. Yet as the introductory chapter to this book suggests, it is not entirely clear what this 'norm' or acceptable level of violence should be in post-war societies.

In the case of eastern Congo, and of the South Kivu province in particular, post-war violence was so extensive that it made 'peace' ephemeral at best and elusive for most. But if the task is to 'contain and manage' the violence, the question remains how this can best be done, given that the DRC still has weak state institutions and has already hosted the world's largest UN peacekeeping mission for many years. If much of the post-war violence – that which assumed a sexual form – had strategic, opportunistic and bonding functions, and was amplified by poverty, institutional weaknesses and mineral wealth, then security sector reform (SSR), a stronger justice system, civilian job creation, poverty reduction and improved resource governance all seem crucial. So too does the transformation of gender relations, as this Congolese interviewee suggested:

> There is not entirely peace. I can say that there is peace because I sleep at home, there is no gunfire, no bullet fire. But some way or another, peace has not yet arrived in our territory, because we women, we live in insecurity. If we go to the field, to draw water from the well, or to the markets far from the centre of town, we are always raped, looted. We are attacked by armed gangs, by men in uniform, but they are never identified by the brigades in the area.
>
> (Interview 15)

As long as women live in insecurity, the interviewee says, 'there is not entirely peace'. It may be a paradox then that also in societies considered to be 'at peace', many people – both women and men – live in insecurity or in fear of violence on a daily basis, whether domestically or in other settings. Though sexual violence in post-war eastern Congo was more extensive than that occurring in 'peaceful' societies, the case also calls for further exploration of the boundaries between 'war' and 'peace' – and of the conditions under which different groups in a post-war society will experience the situation as one of 'entirely peace'.

Notes

1 For very helpful comments on previous versions of this chapter, I wish to thank Mats Berdal, Michael Boyle, Trine Eide, Martin Kimani, Owen J. Logan, Randi Solhjell, Jason Stearns, Åstri Suhrke and participants in the post-conflict violence project workshop at the Chr. Michelsen Institute in Bergen, Norway on 30/31 March 2009. I am also deeply grateful to my interviewees in the Democratic Republic of the Congo (DRC) for generously sharing of their time and insights during my fieldwork in February and March 2009. For purposes of confidentiality and the security of the interviewees, their names are withheld. Interview quotes in this chapter are all from my transcripts of these DRC interviews. Translations from the French original of the interview transcripts, as well as from other French sources, are all by the author.

2 According to the DRC's 2005 Constitution, by early 2009 the number of provinces should have increased from 11 to 26. By late 2009 the change had not yet been effected, however. In this chapter I therefore refer to the old provincial configuration and the corresponding territorial entities.

3 Beyond research on single types of violence (sexual violence, mining-related violence etc.), scholarly studies of post-war violence in eastern DRC include Autesserre (2010), Beneduce *et al.* (2006) and Eriksson Baaz and Stern (2008).

4 Carlsen (2009), Eriksson Baaz and Stern (2009) and Moufflet (2008) are among the few social science studies on sexual violence in wartime and/or post-war eastern Congo that have been published in international, peer-reviewed journals.

5 See Cohen (2010: 53–67) for an in-depth discussion of the potentials and pitfalls of interviewing victims and perpetrators of sexual violence in conflict and post-conflict contexts for purposes of social science research on this topic.

6 The figures for 2006 are based on statistics for the first nine months, extrapolated for the whole year. The UNFPA reports from 2007 and 2008 cover the periods 2004–6 and 2007 respectively, while the two latter sources refer to UNFPA studies which cover 2008 and 2009 respectively. The conceptualization of rape changed over time, however. The 2007 report analyses simply 'cases of rape' (UNFPA-RDC 2007: 11), irrespective of the gender of perpetrator and victim, but without explicitly stating whether rape by many perpetrators of one victim (gang rape), or rape by one perpetrator of many victims (mass rape), would count as one or several cases of rape. The 2008 report, by contrast, analyses only rapes where the victims were female, counting how many rapes each female victim had experienced in a year (UNFPA-RDC 2008: 12). The same logic seems to have applied for the 2008 data, but the 2009 figure refers to the female victims of rape and no longer to the number or rapes per female victim. The changes over time, uncertainties about how mass and gang rapes were counted and the eventual exclusion of male victims imply that these data must be read critically, and that the identified trends only represent a rough approximation.

7 On 1 July 2010, the name of the UN peacekeeping mission in the DRC was changed to United Nations Stabilization Mission in the Democratic Republic of the Congo (MONUSCO).

8 For the area we today know as eastern DRC, little suggests that sexual violence was widespread in wars prior to the 1990s (Hochschild 1998; Chretien 2003; Nzongola-Ntalaja 2002; Reid 2007). The scarcity of evidence may be due to underreporting, or it may signify that widespread sexual violence in war is in fact relatively new to this zone. Though sexual violence reportedly took place in armed conflicts in North Kivu in the early 1990s and in the war of 1996–7, both my interview data and other studies (e.g. HRW 2002) suggest that enduring sexual violence on the large scale and of the nature seen from 1998 onwards had no known precedents in earlier decades.

9 Eriksson Baaz and Stern (2009) identify two types of rape in the soldiers' accounts: the 'lust' rapes I have outlined here, as well as 'evil' rapes. 'Evil' rapes 'are the particularly brutal acts of sexual violence, involving mutilations and sometimes the subsequent killing of victims' (ibid.: 510). The soldiers presented these rapes as motivated by a wish to destroy and humiliate, stemming 'from a sense of moral disengagement that accompanies the climate of warring and violence' (ibid.). Soldiers also related the commission of 'evil' rapes to anger coming from the feeling of being ignored by their superiors and of being unable to play the 'provider' role vis-à-vis their wives and families. I focus on the 'lust' rapes here since the soldiers' tendency to ascribe greater acceptability to these rapes than to the 'evil' ones are likely to have made the 'lust' rapes more powerful as bonding mechanisms within the army.

Bibliography

Alison, M. (2007) 'Wartime sexual violence: women's human rights and questions of masculinity', *Review of International Studies*, 33: 75–90.

Autesserre, S. (2010) *The Trouble with the Congo: Local Violence and the Failure of International Peacebuilding*, New York: Cambridge University Press.

Beneduce, R., Jourdan, L., Raeymaekers, T. and Vlassenroot, K. (2006) 'Violence with a purpose: exploring the functions and meaning of violence in the Democratic Republic of Congo', *Intervention*, 4: 32–46.

Carlsen, E. (2009) 'Ra/pe and war in the Democratic Republic of the Congo', *Peace Review: A Journal of Social Justice*, 21: 474–83.

Chretien, J.-P. (2003) *The Great Lakes of Africa: Two Thousand Years of History*, trans. S. Straus, New York: Zone Books.

Cockburn, C. (2001) 'The gendered dynamics of armed conflict and political violence', in C.O.N. Moser and F.N. Clark (eds) *Victims, Perpetrators or Actors? Gender, Armed Conflict and Political Violence*, London: Zed Books.

Cohen, D.K. (2010) 'Explaining sexual violence during civil war', unpublished thesis, Stanford University.

Eriksson Baaz, M. and Stern, M. (2008) 'Making sense of violence: voices of soldiers in the Congo (DRC)', *Journal of Modern African Studies*, 46: 57–86.

Eriksson Baaz, M. and Stern, M. (2009) 'Why do soldiers rape? Masculinity, violence, and sexuality in the armed forces in the Congo (DRC)', *International Studies Quarterly*, 53: 495–518.

Eriksson Baaz, M. and Stern, M. (2010) *The Complexity of Violence: A Critical Analysis of Sexual Violence in the Democratic Republic of Congo*, Sida Working Paper on Gender Based Violence, Stockholm and Uppsala: Swedish International Development Cooperation Agency in cooperation with The Nordic Africa Institute. Online, available at: http://nai.diva-portal.org/smash/record.jsf?searchId=1& pid=diva2:319527 (accessed 31 August 2010).

Goldstein, J.S. (2001) *War and Gender: How Gender Shapes the War System and Vice Versa*, Cambridge and New York: Cambridge University Press.

Gottschall, J. (2004) 'Explaining wartime rape', *Journal of Sex Research*, 41: 129–36.

Government of the DRC (2006) 'Loi no 06/018 du 20 juillet 2006 modifiant et completant le décret du 30 janvier 1940 portant code pénale congolais', *Journal Officiel*, 15 (1 August).

HHI and Oxfam (2010) *'Now, the World is Without Me': An Investigation of Sexual Violence in Eastern Democratic Republic of Congo*, Cambridge, MA: Harvard Humanitarian Initiative, with support from Oxfam America. Online, available at: http:// hhi.harvard.edu/images/resources/reports/hhi-oxfam%20drc%20gbv%20 report.pdf (accessed 31 August 2010).

Hochschild, A. (1998) *King Leopold's Ghost: A Story of Greed, Terror, and Heroism in Colonial Africa*, Boston and New York: Houghton Mifflin.

HRW (2002) *The War within the War: Sexual Violence against Women and Girls in Eastern Congo*, New York: Human Rights Watch. Online, available at: www.hrw. org/en/reports/2002/06/20/war-within-war (accessed 31 August 2010).

HRW (2009a) *Soldiers Who Rape, Commanders Who Condone: Sexual Violence and Military Reform in the Democratic Republic of Congo*, New York: Human Rights Watch. Online, available at: www.hrw.org/en/reports/2009/07/16/soldiers-who-rape-commanders-who-condone-0 (accessed 31 August 2010).

HRW (2009b) *The Christmas Massacres: LRA Attacks on Civilians in Northern Congo*,

New York: Human Rights Watch. Online, available at: www.hrw.org/en/reports/2009/02/16/christmas-massacres-0 (accessed 31 August 2010).

HRW (2010) *Trail of Death: LRA Atrocities in Northeastern Congo*, New York: Human Rights Watch. Online, available at: www.hrw.org/en/reports/2010/03/29/trail-death-0 (accessed 31 August 2010).

ILAC and IBA HRI (2009) *Rebuilding Courts and Trust: An Assessment of the Needs of the Justice System in the Democratic Republic of Congo*, International Legal Assistance Consortium and the International Bar Association Human Rights Institute. Online, available at: www.ibanet.org/Search/Default.aspx?q=rebuilding%20courts%20and%20trust (accessed 31 August 2010).

Kent, V. (2007) 'Protecting civilians from UN peacekeepers and humanitarian workers: sexual exploitation and abuse', in C. Aoi, C. de Coning and R. Thakur (eds) *Unintended Consequences of Peacekeeping Operations*, Tokyo, New York and Paris: United Nations University Press.

Lewis, D.A. (2009) 'Unrecognized victims: sexual violence against men in conflict settings under international law', *Wisconsin International Law Journal*, 27: 1–49.

Longombe, A.O., Claude, K.M. and Ruminjo, J. (2008) 'Fistula and traumatic genital injury from sexual violence in a conflict setting in eastern Congo: case studies', *Reproductive Health Matters*, 16: 132–41.

Moser, C.O.N. and Clark, F.C. (2001) 'Introduction', in C.O.N. Moser and F.C. Clark (eds), *Victims, Perpetrators or Actors? Gender, Armed Conflict and Political Violence*, London: Zed Books.

Moufflet, V. (2008) 'Le paradigme du viol comme arme de guerre à l'Est de la République démocratique du Congo', *Afrique Contemporaine*: 119–33.

North, D.C., Wallis, J.J. and Weingast, B.R. (2009) *Violence and Social Orders: A Conceptual Framework for Interpreting Recorded Human History*, New York: Cambridge University Press.

Notar, S.A. (2006) 'Peacekeepers as perpetrators: sexual exploitation and abuse of women and children in the Democratic Republic of Congo', *American University Journal for Gender, Social Policy and Law*, 14: 413–29.

Nzongola-Ntalaja, G. (2002) *The Congo from Leopold to Kabila: A People's History*, London and New York: Zed Books.

Prunier, G. (2009) *Africa's World War: Congo, The Rwandan Genocide, and the Making of a Continental Catastrophe*, Oxford and New York: Oxford University Press.

Reid, R. (2007) *War in Pre-Colonial Eastern Africa: The Patterns and Meanings of State-Level Conflict in the 19th Century*, London and Nairobi: James Currey, Fountain Publishers, Ohio University Press and Eastern African Educational Publishers.

Reyntjens, F. (2009) *The Great African War: Congo and Regional Geopolitics, 1996–2006*, Cambridge and New York: Cambridge University Press.

RFDA, RFDDP and IA (2005) *Women's Bodies as a Battleground: Sexual Violence against Women and Girls during the War in the Democratic Republic of Congo, South Kivu (1996–2003)*, Réseau des Femmes pour un Développement Associatif, Réseau des Femmes pour la Défense des Droits et la Paix and International Alert. Online, available at: www.international-alert.org/pdf/sexual_violence_congo_english.pdf (accessed 31 August 2010).

Rodriguez, C. (2007) 'Sexual violence in South Kivu, Congo', *Forced Migration Review*, 27: 45–6.

Samset, I. (forthcoming) 'Explaining variation in violence after civil war: Angola and DR Congo compared', unpublished thesis, University of Bergen.

Seifert, R. (1996) 'The second front: the logic of sexual violence in wars', *Women's Studies International Forum*, 19: 35–43.

Skjelsbæk, I. (2001) 'Sexual violence and war: mapping out a complex relationship', *European Journal of International Relations*, 7: 211–37.

Stearns, J. (2010) 'Mass rape in Walikale: what happened?', *Congo Siasa*, 24 August. Online, available at: http://congosiasa.blogspot.com/2010/08/mass-rape-in-walikale-what-happened.html (accessed 31 August 2010).

Taback, N., Painter, R. and King, B. (2008) 'Sexual violence in the Democratic Republic of Congo', *Journal of the American Medical Association*, 300: 653–4.

UNFPA-RDC (2007) *Les violences sexuelles en République Démocratique du Congo: Rapport d'enquête sur l'ampleur du phenomène, le profil des victimes et des auteurs, et la prise en charge des victimes*, Kinshasa: Fonds des Nations Unies pour la Population (UNFPA), République Démocratique du Congo.

UNFPA-RDC (2008) *Rapport des cas incidents de violences sexuelles en RDC: statistiques des cas incidents de violences sexuelles rapportées en 2007*, Kinshasa: Fonds des Nations Unies pour la Population (UNFPA), République Démocratique du Congo.

UN News Service (2010) *More than 8,000 Women Raped Last Year by Fighters in Eastern DR Congo – UN*, 8 February. Online, available at: www.un.org/apps/news/story.a sp?NewsID=33703&Cr=democratic&Cr1=congo&Kw1=drc&Kw2=&Kw3= (accessed 31 August 2010).

Vircoulon, T. (2009) 'Réforme de la justice: réalisations, limites et questionnements', in T. Trefon (ed.) *Réforme au Congo (RDC): attentes et désillusions*, Paris: L'Harmattan.

Wakabi, W. (2008) 'Sexual violence increasing in Democratic Republic of Congo', *Lancet*, 371: 15–16.

Wood, E.J. (2006) 'Variation in sexual violence during war', *Politics and Society*, 34: 307–41.

13 The political economies of violence in post-war Liberia

Torunn Wimpelmann Chaudhary

Liberia emerged out of a brutal war in 2003 and has since taken significant steps towards stability, although violence has not altogether ceased and security remains a concern, as indicated by the continued presence of UN peacekeepers. Post-war Liberia has experienced violent protests in connection with disarmament, vigilante and mob violence, several clashes over land and natural resources and a violent crime wave. Young ex-combatants are commonly said to be behind this violence and have been the focus of programmatic intervention and academic enquiry alike. This is in line with a general paradigm about the dangers of restive ex-combatants and the threat they pose to post-war countries, especially in what is described as 'youth crisis' settings such as Liberia. What Jennings (2008) has termed the securitization of the ex-combatant is part of a broader explanatory framework for contemporary wars which sees marginalized youth as a major cause of conflict and – in a post-war setting – emphasizes the need to engage with, co-opt or contain this youth, now hardened by their experience of war, to stop them from taking up arms again.

This chapter critically examines this view with respect to Liberia. Liberia's post-war violence, it is argued, can only be properly understood – and by implication dealt with – in relation to the political economy from which it arises, a perspective that cannot be accommodated through a sole focus on ex-combatants or youth. The analysis below seeks to demonstrate that the main forms of violence in the post-2003 period are inseparable from a given political and economic context, which in turn is shaped by Liberia's particular history of state formation and a rent-based political economy.

The youth crisis narrative

The 'youth crisis' narrative emerged out of broader debates on the causes of conflicts from the 1990s onwards. With the end of the Cold War, and superpower rivalry gone or at least suspended, the explanatory frameworks that presented conflicts in the developing world as proxy wars or ideological struggles between communist and capitalist models no longer applied. Questions were raised as to why in the post-colonial world – which had been the actual battlefield of the Cold War – some conflicts continued and several new wars broke out. The West African regional theatre of war, which in the 1990s engulfed Liberia, Sierra Leone, Côte d'Ivoire and Guinea, had a prominent role in these debates.

There were several attempts to identify the causes of the 'new' wars of the post-Cold War world. These attempts were often characterized by the pursuit of a single explanatory factor (for critical overviews see Cramer 2006; Bøås and Dunn 2007). One influential hypothesis claimed that the new conflicts were mainly undertaken for material gain, in particular the capture of valuable resources such as diamonds, timber and opium (Keen 1998; Collier 2000). Concerned with the policy implications of such claims, which made wars akin to crime, and invoked law enforcement-like responses, a counterclaim arose. The latter argued that these conflicts in fact had important political dimensions. Although not fought under the banner of a recognisable political ideology, the conflicts originated in poverty, marginalization and in the associated failure of the state. In the West African case in particular, the two perspectives eventually formed a metamorphosis of a kind. A 'youth crisis' narrative established itself as an influential perspective, based on the argument that the disintegration of the postcolonial state had thwarted the economic and social aspirations of youth, who took up arms in frustration (Richards 1996; Utas 2003; Richards *et al.* 2004). Fighting, in turn, was sustained by the presence of valuable natural resources, which offered an alternative route towards economic and social mobility.

The 'youth crisis' narrative and the focus on ex-combatants have also influenced the practice of peacebuilding. It is commonly assumed that if young ex-combatants, hardened by their experiences as fighters, again are excluded from economic opportunities and lack productive ways of spending their time, it will be only a matter of time before they once more take up arms (Human Rights Watch 2005). As Jennings has shown in her analysis of the DDR (disarmament, demobilization and reintegration) process in Liberia, such discourses of 'aimless, unemployed and angry' ex-combatants (McGovern 2008: 344) has underpinned many policy interventions in the post-war period. A number of other aid programmes and policy strategies have been premised on the same 'youth/ex-combatant' logic.[1]

On the surface it seems obvious that ex-combatants and the larger social group of poor and marginalized youth to which they often belong play a role in post-war violence and crime. Yet an exclusive focus on ex-combatants and their characteristics is problematic and can only take us so far in accounting for and addressing Liberia's post-war violence. It risks pathologizing ex-combatants by abstracting them and any violence in which they might take part from the specific historical context of these events. This in turn might lead to superficial and misplaced policy interventions, which, rather than addressing underlying political and economic relations, target youth or ex-combatants *as a problem in itself* (Bøås and Dunn 2007: 25). The starting point of this chapter, therefore, is that the violence in post-war Liberia only makes sense when analysed as part of specific economic and political dynamics. In particular, I attempt to sketch out how multiple layers of contested claims to the country's resources and an extraction-based political economy (Bayart 1993) serve as a useful set of parameters for understanding post-war violence in Liberia.

Historical background

Modern Liberia was founded in 1847 by a group of freed slaves who had been repatriated from America. The Americo-Liberian settlers progressively expanded from the coast and established their power over the hinterland. Settler domination of the indigenous population was established through measures that resembled colonial indirect rule and revolts were often put down using violence (Clegg 2004; Ellis 2007). Liberia's political system, like that of many other African states, bestowed differentiated political and civic status on its inhabitants. Those who were descendants of settlers or otherwise attached to the political elite were granted 'civilized status'. Civilized status amounted to full citizenship – a status which entailed political rights and enabled its holder to acquire land and property through statutory law. In contrast, the indigenous population was seen as aliens, 'subject to the terms of treaties and customary law entered into and recognized by their kings and the Liberian government' (Levitt 2005: 91).

Power was furthermore highly personalized and concentrated in the hands of a narrow business elite of Americo-Liberians in the capital Monrovia, whose income was based on the export of Liberia's rich natural resources, such as iron and rubber. By the late 1970s, this hegemony had begun to crack (Harris 2008). The oligarchy's strategy of incorporating a limited number of 'country people' into their networks proved unsustainable as the number of aspiring hinterland people grew, whereas the patronage available dwindled due to the fluctuating prices of the country's export trade in primary commodities (Clapham 1989). A new generation of more radical politicians from within both the Americo-Liberians and the indigenous population called for reform, accompanied by a series of popular protests. This was followed by a bloody coup in 1980, led by Master Sergeant Samuel Doe, a young man of indigenous origin. In a prelude to the violent years to come, most of the cabinet were executed. Unable to manoeuvre the elite politics of Monrovia, Doe relied increasingly on his fellow Krahns and the minority Mandingo (a common term for Muslim traders of Sahelian or Guinean descent throughout the West African region) group to stay in power, pursuing a strategy of politicizing 'tribal' divisions, although many members of the pre-coup elite also retained their positions. After a coup attempt in 1985 Doe's regime became increasingly repressive and his main patron, the United States, gradually distanced itself from his government.

War broke out in December 1989 when Charles Taylor, an Americo-Liberian and a former member of the Doe government, launched an armed uprising from Nimba county. With support from the governments of Burkina Faso, Côte d'Ivoire and Libya, Taylor's National Patriotic Front of Liberia (NPFL) was able to mobilize widely amongst the population groups that had been at the receiving end of Doe's ethnic persecution, above all the Gios and Manos. The first phase of the war thus took the form of a popular uprising, partly in reaction to the Doe army's brutal counterinsurgency. A number of Gio and Mano youth in Nimba county joined the rebel NPFL force, often encouraged by their parents and armed with simple weapons. Attempts to protect family members and self from the violence inflicted by Doe's armed groups are thought to have been a major reason why people joined the war (Pugel 2007; Bøås and Hatloy 2008). All faction leaders claimed to be fighting on behalf of the interests of one ethnic group, although factional membership could cut across ethnic lines. Factional politics was also linked to established patronage politics in Liberia, where members of groups and alliances commonly seek to place their leader in a position where benefits can be garnered and distributed. Few fighters received any pay and shifting from faction to faction was quite common.

The result was also splits within the NPFL. As new factions emerged, violence became more predatory, with combatants engaging in widespread looting. Supported by international businessmen and governments, factional leaders or warlords sought to establish control over areas rich in natural resources (notably timber, diamonds and rubber) (Atkinson 1997). Charles Taylor became particularly notorious for his establishment of a 'Greater Liberia' in 1992–3, when he controlled large parts of the country's timber resources, which were shipped out through connections with international companies.

After several attempts at settlement, a temporary and relative peace was achieved in August 1996 following the Abuja II agreement, which provided for a ceasefire, disarmament and elections. In July 1997, Charles Taylor won the presidential elections with an overwhelming majority and the country was relatively stable for about two years. Nevertheless, human rights violations by the state security agencies (now loyal to Taylor) were widespread, including raids and violence against opponents, executions and 'disappearances'. There was also much crime, particularly in Monrovia, which was sanctioned by the state security apparatus (Utas 2003). In the countryside, sporadic clashes continued.[2] The personalized system of government was taken to new extremes: Taylor abolished the treasury, channelled all state income into his personal coffers, and made public servants work directly for him for a salary.

In 1999, war started again when another armed movement, Liberians United for Reconciliation and Democracy (LURD) emerged, supported by Guinea and the United States, the latter thus reversing its earlier support for Taylor. By 2002, LURD controlled 80 per cent of Liberia. Taylor also faced increased international opposition as his role in the conflict in neighbouring Sierra Leone became obvious.[3]

In the summer of 2003, LURD and its offshoot group Movement for Democracy in Liberia (MODEL), closed in on Monrovia. Fighting continued for another two months until a peace deal was reached in August 2003, brokered by the Economic Community of West African States (ECOWAS). Under the 2003 Accra agreement, Taylor went into exile in Nigeria and a transitional government (National Transitional Government of Liberia, NTGL) consisting of the three parties was formed: the government until recently headed by Taylor and the two rebel movements, LURD and MODEL, were to govern until presidential elections in 2005. Ministerial posts and state agencies were divided between the three parties by the agreement, which also provided for standard peacebuilding procedures (security sector reform, SSR; and the disarmament, demobilization and reintegration of combatants, DDR) and a UN peacekeeping force. Before long, the transitional government found itself the target of international scrutiny for large-scale corruption. Keen to avoid a repeat of the situation in neighbouring Sierra Leone, where government corruption was emerging as a significant political issue, the international aid community imposed a system of 'economic peacekeeping' on Liberia. Known as the Governance and Economic Management Assistance Program (GEMAP), the programme placed international auditors with co-signing authority in key government institutions to control Liberian state spending. The elected president Ellen Johnson Sirleaf inherited GEMAP when she took office in 2006.

The war had been enormously destructive, although estimates vary widely. By the time the war formally ended in August 2003, between 60,000 and 200,000 people out of a population of around 3 million were dead (Hoffman 2004).[4] More than 800,000 people had been displaced and the infrastructure was in a shambles. The mode of fighting was widely regarded as extraordinarily horrific: 'tortures and atrocities committed by factions on countless occasions were sometimes brutal almost beyond belief' (Ellis 2007: 146). Civilians were targeted by all factions and often killed on suspicion of being collaborators, sometimes based on ethnic targeting, i.e. of belonging to the 'enemy ethnic group' (Utas 2003).[5] Numerous women were raped and many children, both male and female, were forcibly recruited as combatants (Pugel 2007).

Post-war violence

Compared to the war period, it seems safe to conclude that post-war violence in Liberia has been relatively limited. In particular, the country has experienced little overt political violence in the form of activities explicitly challenging the authority of the government or the peace settlement. The political landscape following Taylor's departure has been remarkable for its wide-ranging accommodation of wartime leaders, a fact that helps explain the absence of organized and explicitly political violence. The 2003 peace agreement included all the main armed factions and gave them significant rewards for accepting the settlement, and the effect was the disintegration of the armed groups as cohesive organizations. None of the factions transformed into political parties, as is common with post conflict elections. As Harris points out, the 2005 elections were noteworthy for the 'the almost unprecedented and virtually complete disappearance of the rebel forces in the political process' (Harris 2008). Yet with regards to the actual actors in power, continuities from the war could be observed. Many 'war time notables' (Reno 2009: 54), various commanders and faction leaders were elected to the Liberian legislature as senators (Sawyer 2008). Following her election victory, President Ellen Johnson Sirleaf sought to include a wide range of political actors in her administration and most of the opposition gained a vested interest in government.

There were more fundamental structural continuities as well. Like other resource-rich African countries, Liberia's *political economy of extraversion* (Bayart 1993), more specifically its insertion into the world economy in a mode of dependence, has generated a number of rents which have been exploited by dominant social groups (Bayart *et al.* 1999: xvi).[6] These rents have in turn shaped the process of state formation and the county's system of politics. As Bayart *et al.* (1999) show, such rents were in earlier times obtained from the control of exports such as gold, ivory and slaves, from collaboration with colonial governments, and in the post-colonial period from military and diplomatic alliances, trade and exports of various raw materials, as well as the management of aid and other external financing. These rents have given rise to a system of political and economic patronage where, in the absence of industrialization and economic alternatives, those in a position to control such rents have been able to command loyalty from those less fortunate.

In Liberia, this rent/patronage system developed in a more extreme and pure form than in most other African countries (Clapham 1989). During the rule of the Americo-Liberian oligarchy, the economy was 'heavily based on the extraction of minerals and rubber through multinational companies' (Clapham 1989: 107). Few attempts were made to invest in agriculture, let alone industrialization. By and large, the system was reproduced during the Doe era and the succeeding war and the post-war orders. I argue that these historically specific economic and political relations, and their intersections with the legacy of wartime cleavages, provide useful parameters for a discussion of the various forms of post-war violence that Liberia has experienced. In the following, I flesh out this argument through an investigation of the main forms of violence in the post-war period.

Land conflicts

Land conflicts are a common source of violence in post-war societies. The return of refugees and displaced people to land that in their absence has been used or claimed by others, sometimes 'enemies', can lead to violent contestations. Disputes over unclear or multiple claims to ownership may be exacerbated by wartime destruction of land registries, especially if state structures more generally have disintegrated. In post-war Liberia land has emerged as a significant political issue and several of the most serious incidents of post-war violence are linked to conflicts over land. Yet land conflicts in Liberia have deep historical roots that precede the war. Only by unpacking these multiple layers of land contestation and examining how they interact with more recent war-related cleavages and disruptions can this form of 'post-war' violence be properly understood.

One such layer of conflict is autochthony, a social and typically informal practice common in Sub-Saharan Africa. Autochthony bestows land rights on 'sons of the soil' (i.e. communities who claim first arrival status). This makes the land rights of newcomers, often established through their alliances with local leaders, more tenuous. In Liberia such 'stranger status' has historically been most pronounced for the Mandingo population, a group which also constituted a key constituency of LURD (Bøås 2009).

A second layer of land conflict originates in the arrival of freed slaves in the nineteenth century. The America-Liberian settlers established a dual land tenure system which has remained in place since. For descendants of settlers and others who have acquired 'civilized status' there is a system of private land ownership sanctioned by statutory law. For the non-settler Liberians, land rights are communal and guarded by chiefs. However, whereas most African land laws recognize that statutory law applies to urban land and customary law applies to rural community land, in Liberia statutory law can also apply to communal land (World Bank 2008). All communal land is considered 'public land' by the state, which means that such land can be disposed of and regulated by the state. This has formed the basis of a discriminatory system where communal land has been progressively taken over by the America-Liberian elite. Those with civilized status can obtain private ownership of communal land at a set price through statutory law, given the local chief's permission. Those without civilized status have generally been unable to acquire land through statutory law. The legislation supporting these arrangements was still in place in 2009.

A third layer of land conflict relates to the large concessions acquired by private commercial companies to exploit natural resources such as timber, rubber and palm oil. These concessions have been granted under statutory law, but they have normally included areas where indigenous Liberians reside. Over the years, profuse uncertainty has developed with regard to user rights and the boundaries of these concessions, whether they exclude the use of the area by local communities for other purposes, and exactly what surface areas are included under the concessions.

Severe administrative disarray has added to the confusion over land. There is no central land registry in Liberia. Documentation is often lost and sometimes deliberately destroyed. Boundary demarcations are unclear. Land has often been sold many times over by persons taking advantage of the unclear situation. There is little state capacity to deal with disputes, which after the war were estimated to represent 75–90 per cent of the cases in the official court system (Unruh 2009).

It is against this backdrop that post-war land disputes have played out. Pre-existing land disputes have combined with the legacy of war – displacement, politicization of group cleavages and militarization – to produce several violent incidents in the post-war period. One event in October 2004 illustrates the dynamic in such cases. At this point Monrovia was brought to a standstill by an outbreak of violence which, unusually for Liberia, seemed to have a religious dimension. Mosques and churches were torched, and crowds looted and attacked Muslims and Christians respectively, leading to the death of 16 people and a curfew lasting several days (Amnesty International 2005). It later emerged that the violence had started over a dispute concerning land that involved the brother of a leader of the erstwhile LURD rebels. Former LURD fighters had beaten up a man for challenging the brother's claim to a piece of land. The victim retaliated by mobilizing attacks against the Mandingos – the community most associated with LURD – in the area (IRIN 2004b). As the Mandingos are a Muslim religious minority in Liberia, the violence took on a religious dimension as well. As the violence spread, the government announced that former fighters wanting to delay the disarmament processes had joined the disturbances.

Whenever there is a land dispute where one party is Mandingo, the conflict typically takes on a larger significance as 'ethnic conflict' defined around the status of Mandingos. The Mandingos have often been perceived as *strangers* in Liberia, having arrived originally from Guinea. As traders, they have typically settled in towns and set up businesses through accommodations with local leaders (Bøås 2009). With their access to capital and role as moneylenders, the Mandingos have sometimes faced resentment. During the war, Mandingos were first allied with the Doe government and later constituted the backbone of the LURD faction. In the two counties where much of the fighting took place, Nimba and Lofa, the Mandingos fought the Gios and the Manos, groups who consider themselves sons of the soil vis-à-vis the Mandingo population.

Under the system of autochthony, the Mandingos' claims to land use have historically been insecure due to their status as 'strangers' or newcomers. This is particularly the case in Nimba county, where Mandingos only arrived in the 1960s (International Crisis Group 2004). When Mandingos fled during the war, their land and buildings were often seized by Manos and Gios, some of whom claimed that the land and properties belonged to them anyway. After the war, many Mandingos have been unable to return. In May 2006, rumours circulated in the Nimba town of Ganta that ethnic Mandingos were about to launch an attack on the city to reclaim their land. Hundreds of Gio and Mano youth armed with machetes took to the streets. Intervention by local authorities and United Nations Mission in Liberia (UNMIL) forces prevented matters from escalating. Nonetheless, this show of force seemed successful in discouraging the Mandingos from returning and many continue to live in Guinea as refugees (Bøås, unpublished paper).

The government established an ad hoc commission to look into this issue,[7] but by 2008 the situation in Ganta remained unsolved with Mandingo politicians accusing commission members of helping fellow Manos and Gios to hold on to the land. At the centre of the dispute were the shop buildings on Ganta's main road. Whoever controls these buildings is in a strong position to control the important trade route to and from Guinea. The refusal of Gios and Manos to return these buildings might therefore be perceived as an effort to break what they regard as a Mandingo trade monopoly in the area (Bøås, unpublished paper).[8]

The interplay between wartime processes and earlier entrenched tensions over land were similarly evident in a brutal and widely reported episode that took place in June 2008 and left up to 19 people dead.[9] The victims were attacked when attempting to clear a disputed area for cultivation. The area was claimed by two politicians and long-time rivals who had belonged to different factions during the war and had since competed for a seat in the Senate. The method of killing and the fact that all the casualties were from one side suggested an outright massacre. The media noted that many of the victims had been *tarbayed* – a wartime practice of arms tied behind the back for execution.

While the media and UN staff explained the case as one of personal rivalry between the two politicians, the two protagonists themselves described the event as a tribal matter between the Bassa and Kpelle, two local ethnic groups. The latter version prevailed in the courts when, as predicted, no evidence was produced to implicate the politician whose fellow tribesmen had attacked the clearing party. Yet the case reveals multiple dynamics. The insecurity of land rights in Liberia had made it easier to mobilize individuals to go on the attack, but so had hostilities sharpened by the war. The personal rivalry between the two politicians was mirrored in animosity between the two ethnic groups they belonged to and had been representing, and which had fought on different sides during the war. Prior to the massacre, rumours were circulating amongst the Kpelle people in the area that should any 'outsiders' come to take away the land, there would be retaliation. Anxieties were further heightened by rumours that one of the two politicians, a former LURD member, would bring in ex-combatants to take over the land.[10] The spectre of ex-combatants was clearly raised to invoke fear, but they were nevertheless only one factor in a dispute that involved a more complex set of issues.

The rubber economy

A much publicized feature of the post-war landscape in Liberia has been the occupation by former fighters of a number of rubber plantations. Yet, whilst often presented as a problem of renegade ex-combatants, the violence linked to the rubber sector has involved a number of other interested parties as well.

Liberia's rubber plantations are vast, covering up to 10 per cent of the country.[11] Before the war, rubber constituted Liberia's second largest total export earner[12] and directly supported some 20 per cent of the Liberian population (Atkinson 1997). The plantations were either under long-term concessions granted to international corporations or owned by the government and managed by private companies (UNMIL 2006). During the war, some rubber holdings were abandoned, whereas on others tapping continued both legally and illegally (ibid.).

In 2000, one of the major rubber plantations, the Guthrie plantation, owned by the government and managed by a Malaysian company, was occupied by LURD and turned into a key military base (UNMIL 2006). Some 500 ex-combatants continued to control it until August 2006. Attempts by security firms contracted by the legal managers to enter the plantation resulted in the murder of staff and death threats to managers. During the time when ex-fighters were occupying the Guthrie plantation, residents in the local area complained about insecurity, accusing ex-combatants of murder and rape (GoL/UNMIL 2006). LURD leaders, for their part, claimed that the occupants of Guthrie were renegade soldiers over whom they had no control.

After preparing the ground through dialogue with the ex-combatants on Guthrie, UNMIL eventually repossessed the plantation on behalf of the government. It then emerged that some of the lower level plantation workers had been exploited by their former commanders and were only too happy to see the UN intervene. According to UNMIL, most continued to work on the plantation after it reverted to the government.

Violence has also occurred on other rubber plantations. The violence was partly related to opposition from local communities to what they saw as outside encroachment on their land and resources. This dynamic was evident at the Sinoe plantation in the southeast. The Sinoe plantation was occupied by ex-LURD and MODEL fighters after 2003. Whereas the occupiers of Guthrie had been outsiders, the ex-combatants occupying the Sinoe plantation had ties with the local community[13] and the occupation was linked to local claims to ownership presented to the external management who represented the previous concession holders, a prominent Monrovia-based settler family. Both the occupiers and the local community were unwilling to return the plantation to the government owing to the possibility that the latter might transfer the plantation to the previous concession holders. While encouraged by the government to intervene, the UN was reluctant to play a role until the question of ownership had been settled, not wishing to been seen taking sides in a conflict that was framed in settler–indigenous terms.

Other incidents suggested similar conflicts between local communities and external concession holders. In November 2007, the manager of the Dutch-owned LAC plantation was shot dead whilst inspecting an area earmarked for expansion. The expansion, although signed by the government, was known to be opposed by the local community. Another incident took place in March 2008 in Bong county. In an apparent bid to challenge the expansion plans of a smaller rubber plantation, local villagers carried out a series of arson attacks. When the plantation owner travelled from Monrovia to investigate, he was taken hostage by the villagers. Stumbling upon the hostage situation by accident, UNMIL secured his release and a deal was later negotiated through which the local villages would be guaranteed 500 acres of land from the 2,000-acre concession.[14]

Fuelling the occupations and rubber theft more generally was the fact that Liberia's rubber processing facilities – until recently solely under foreign control – were operating with surplus capacity (Jordan 2008).[15] Following the war, all the processing facilities bought unprocessed rubber from the occupied plantations (as well as rubber stolen from their competitors), thereby sustaining both illicit tapping and the occupations.[16] This is a continuation of wartime practices, when the rubber companies purchased from the various military factions. Moreover, reports suggest that local government authorities have been collecting significant informal taxes on rubber from 'occupied' plantations before the rubber reaches the buying stations.[17] With a temporary sharp rise in rubber prices, the lucrative rubber business thus spread the benefits of occupation and theft to actors well beyond the ex-combatants.

Human rights abuses on plantations under recognized management have been a separate source of plantation-linked violence in the post-war period. At the Firestone plantation alone, there were some 700 security guards in 2008,[18] operating without much oversight or accountability to the government or the local communities. Reportedly, private security companies at the rubber plantations have severely beaten persons caught thieving, sometimes with management endorsement. They have also illegally detained persons without the knowledge of the Liberian police and without handing detainees over to the police (UNMIL 2006).

Amidst predictions that land disputes will cause Liberia's next war (Truth and Reconciliation Commission 2008), the Liberian government slowly started to look into the matter. An act establishing a five-year land commission was passed into law in 2009. Ultimately, however, the 'land issue' is tied up with complex political issues related to the dual system of citizenship, which historically had made land tenure for indigenous people insecure and benefited Monrovia-based elites.

Contested DDR and SSR

The Accra Comprehensive Peace Agreement of 2003 contained provisions for DDR[19] and for the restructuring of the security apparatus (SSR). Whilst DDR and SSR have become standard components in international peace operations, they have proved to be anything but straightforward in the Liberian case. A complication at the outset was the lack of a clear-cut transition from war to peace. When the peace deal was reached in August 2003, armed factions were still positioned all over the countryside and sporadic clashes between the parties continued after the agreement was signed.[20]

Much of the violence after the Accra agreement, however, seems to have comprised uncoordinated acts by fighters adjusting to a new situation. Following the peace deal, many ex-combatants were without means to maintain themselves, having been more or less abandoned by their leaders in Monrovia. There were reports of LURD, MODEL and government forces harassing and beating up civilians for money and food. Ex-combatants would occasionally set up roadblocks, particularly at border crossings, for extortion purposes, as well as attacking villages to get food and livestock. Sometimes ex-combatants used forced labour, making civilians cook or carry goods for them. As the UN blue helmets deployed more widely across the country, such reports subsided.

Following the full deployment of UNMIL forces, a DDR process was started in December 2003. Initially, only one site was opened on the outskirts of Monrovia (Paes 2005). Fighters were required to hand in one firearm in order to register. They would then spend three weeks in cantonment and receive various forms of counselling and a cash payment of $150 when discharged. On the opening day, four times as many fighters as the UN expected turned up, many wrongly expecting immediate cash payments. Ex-combatants took over the camp and then returned to Monrovia, where two days of rioting ensued, resulting in the death of nine Taylor militia members. After this chaotic opening, UNMIL suspended the programme for four months and redesigned the process (Paes 2005).

Entry criteria were reduced to 150 rounds of ammunition. The programme was also opened to dependents – women and children associated with the fighters – who were not required to hand in weapons or ammunition.[21]

At the start of the programme UNMIL had estimated the number of participants to be 38,000. The eventual number of participants proved to be over 100,000 (Jennings 2008). There were numerous reports that commanders or others with access to weapons had distributed weapons to civilian followers, sharing the cash payment. In many cases actual combatants were unable to qualify for the programme because commanders had taken their weapons. The inflated numbers led to a significant shortfall of funds, which undermined the reintegration part of the programme. Disarmament was completed in December 2004, but by January 2007 around 40,000 of the ex-combatants had yet to be processed for reintegration. There were numerous protests and attacks on NGOs and the UN as ex-combatants claimed they had been cheated or the process unduly delayed (IRIN 2004a, 2004b, 2005; Amnesty International 2005). To promote their demands, some of the ex-combatants formed well-organized interest groups[22] and eventually succeeded in having reintegration benefits distributed to the remaining 40,000 ex-combatants.

The most efficient mobilization came from former army personnel in relation to SSR. SSR involving structural reform of the military, police, intelligence and other security agencies has become a common element in post-conflict operations. In neighbouring Sierra Leone, the United Kingdom took the lead in funding and overseeing a programme for the recruitment and training of a new army and police. The Accra Comprehensive Peace Agreement suggested a similar role for the United States in Liberia. As it turned out, however, SSR in Liberia has been slow and controversial and contributed to post-war violence involving soldiers and ex-soldiers.

Part of the problem was the deep-rooted politicization of the security forces. With the 1980 coup, the army (Armed Forces of Liberia, AFL) became associated with groups allied to Samuel Doe, especially the Krahn people. Thus, when Charles Taylor came to power in 1997 he was deeply distrustful of the AFL and proceeded to establish a competing network of security agencies and militias headed by his trusted allies (Malan 2008). The AFL was left unpaid and its barracks scattered all over the country (International Crisis Group 2009).

The peace agreement called for all non-statutory armed factions to be disbanded, including LURD, MODEL and the government militias that had been loyal to Taylor. The AFL was to be restructured. In December 2004, however, the total disbandment of the AFL was announced as a precondition for US support for rebuilding the army. Soldiers from the pre-2003 AFL would receive severance pay but would have to apply for positions in the new army on an equal basis with everyone else. The decision proved controversial and delays in the disbursement of the severance pay further added to the resentment of the dismissed soldiers, who protested violently on several occasions. The most serious incident occurred in April 2006, when about 100 ex-soldiers from the AFL who claimed that they had not received their promised payment of salary arrears brought the capital to a standstill for two days, throwing stones and setting up roadblocks. The former soldiers proved skilful at mobilization and remained an organized group for many years.[23] According to one spokesman they were still able to mobilize up to 15,000 people five years after the war.[24] In May 2008, 350 ex-soldiers marched on the national legislature to present a petition calling for the impeachment of the president, claiming that the dissolution of the army had been in breach of the Constitution. The move was unsuccessful, but indicated high levels of political skill.

In retrospect, it seems that expectations of DDR benefits generated an economy of demands, in which ex-combatants took advantage of practices that paid off fighters for their wartime activities. The large number of total claimants, furthermore, makes it probable that not all were bona fide combatants. If so, these 'fake' fighters took action that was quite rational in a context where the majority of the population live on less than $1 per day, the formal employment rate is 15 per cent and access to resources often depends on the ability to position oneself as the rightful beneficiary of a well-endowed patron (in this case the international community). A similar dynamic seems to have applied to the demonstrations organized by former army members, although the army protestors were at times accused of being manipulated by the opposition to undermine the credibility of the government. In any case, it seemed by 2009 that the legacy of war did not include a highly organized structure of predatory security forces and/or ex-combatants of the type that has, for instance, plagued the post-war peace in Guatemala. While groups of ex-combatants exist on the local level, most agreed that at the national level few organized structures remain (UNMIL 2007; International Crisis Group 2009). The violent demonstrations are therefore perhaps best understood as attempts to exhaust resources available through former combatants,[25] rather than as the emergence of a permanent power bloc of ex-fighters.

Crime and vigilante action

Reports of a post-war crime wave in the form of armed robberies have become a widespread concern in post-war Liberia, particularly since the latter half of 2006. Numerous media reports emerged of gangs roving the capital armed with cutlasses, knives and guns and attacking houses at night. Accusations pointed towards ex-combatants, the majority of whom had settled in Monrovia. Yet there was little to suggest the presence of an organized ex-combatant crime structure. Robberies appeared small-scale compared to the profits associated with higher-level crime such as taxation of rubber exports, kickbacks on concessions, and various other schemes (*Africa Confidential* 2008). Typically, robbers targeted poorer neighbourhoods that had no private security guards, entering houses at night armed with cutlasses, machetes and guns.[26]

Aggregate crime rates for post-war Liberia are difficult to ascertain: the Liberian National Police (LNP) and the UN police force started issuing crime reports in 2005, but figures are unreliable and any increase or decrease could also be due to changes in reporting patterns (Mbadlanyana and Onuoha 2009). From January to September 2008, the police recorded 70 armed robberies in Monrovia, which in a city of one million people does not seem to suggest crime spiralling out of control, and overall crime rates compare favourably with other countries in the region (Mbadlanyana and Onuoha 2009).

Armed robberies mostly appeared as opportunistic acts rooted in widespread unemployment and poverty. They were facilitated by Monrovia's weak police force. Underpaid, underequipped and in most cases unarmed, the LNP were often unable to respond to calls and in some cases allegedly collaborated with the robbers (Mbadlanyana and Onuoha 2009). In the face of a public outcry the Justice Ministry in 2006 controversially called for the formation of vigilante groups, citing 'police inability to decisively deal with this upsurge in criminal activities'. Embarrassed by the admission of such impotence in the midst of a major UN mission, UNMIL quickly emphasized that it did not approve of vigilantism and preferred the term 'neighbourhood watch groups'. Whatever the term, such groups have proliferated in post-war Monrovia. A common trajectory seems to be that one community member is robbed, and shaken by his experience, takes the initiative to establish a watch group.[27] These groups could also be a way for aspiring local community leaders to demonstrate their proactivity in defending the community against robbers who, strangely, sometimes appear considerate enough to distribute letters announcing their arrival. More sinister, such groups sometimes become a predatory force themselves. Mandatory fees payable by each household, roadblocks and control over night-time movements might easily become tools of misuse.[28] Such groups are required to register with the police, but both parties reported varying levels of cooperation.[29]

There have also been several instances of what appear as spontaneous mob justice, where alleged criminals have been killed. In some cases, crowds have stormed police stations and seized detained suspects in a bid to inflict their own punishment (Mbadlanyana and Onuoha 2009). Such incidents have in several cases led to the death of the suspect. Overall, the disarray of the formal justice system in Liberia presents a serious obstacle to addressing the situation of crime and rough justice. It is estimated that only 3 per cent of prison inmates have been tried and judicial institutions are widely held to be corrupt and inefficient. One police officer suggested that such distrust is fuelled by the common belief that anyone summoned to court was automatically guilty. Acquittal could therefore only be explained by corruption.[30]

Conclusion

Much has been made of the dangerous young ex-combatants in Liberia, an image that some of the persons concerned have only been too happy to cultivate. While this chapter shows that ex-combatants are indeed involved in post-war violence, it demonstrates that such violence cannot be explained merely with reference to their existence alone. Rather, it is argued that the specific economic and political relations of Liberia offer a more useful way of understanding post-war violence. The main forms of violence described in this chapter – land conflicts, crime, plantation 'occupations', unrest linked to demobilization – are far more multifaceted than a mere product of the frustrations or aspirations of 'idle young men'. The violence is rooted in complex social relations and must be approached as such. Importantly, a singular focus on ex-combatants obscures economic and political structures that historically have benefited certain groups in Liberia. Post-war, these elites seem to have sought to revert to an economic and political system that has benefited themselves much more than the demonized 'ex-combatants', a system that the international peacebuilding intervention to some extent appeared to have reproduced.

More generally, the case of Liberia defies general and common-sense assumptions that wars necessarily produce a legacy of continued violence. Such assumptions, often espoused in claims that war creates a 'culture of violence' that somehow sticks in the post-war period (Steenkamp 2005), suggest an automatic relationship between war and subsequent waves of violence. Yet, despite a brutal and prolonged war, the overall levels of violence in post-war Liberia have been relatively limited. Thus, we must look beyond universal and mechanical relationships and towards an analysis of post-war violence that sees it as the result of specific agents operating in specific situations and within the logic of certain social relations. Such analysis necessitates a historical perspective of the kind that has been attempted here.

Notes

1 See for instance, the youth component of Sierra Leone's UN peacebuilding strategy. The Liberia security strategy argues: 'Since the end of the war, most Liberian youths have been unemployed. This is a major challenge to the Government and society, with compelling security implications' (National Security Strategy of the Republic of Liberia 2008).

2 Up to 1,000 people are estimated to have been killed in a single confrontation with the ULIMO leader in September 1998.

3 Following investigations by its panel of experts, the United Nations imposed a travel ban on senior government officials, grounded Liberian-registered aircraft and put in place sanctions on diamonds exported from Liberia, which were believed to be fuelling the insurgency in Sierra Leone.

4 The lower estimate is from Ellis (2007) and, as Hoffman (2004) points out, the higher estimate of 200,000 has appeared without attribution in various media reports, in particular towards the last phase of the conflict.

5 However in the last phase of the conflict, the 'new' faction LURD is reported to have sought to limit atrocities against civilians by using disciplinary measures against those attacking civilians, albeit with varying success. The International Crisis Group (ICG) claims that LURD had learnt from the Sierra Leonean Revolutionary United Front (RUF), who lost popular support as a consequence of massive and indiscriminate violence against civilians (International Crisis Group 2002).

6 One can subscribe to this narrative without necessarily agreeing with the authors' description of this transaction as a relatively equal exchange between local power holders and external profiteers.

7 Presidential Commission on the Nimba Inter-ethnic Disputes.

8 Offers to build a second high street with shop buildings were reportedly turned down by all parties (interview, Monrovia, September 2008).

9 In September 2008, 14 bodies were retrieved whereas another five people remained missing.

10 Interviews, Kakata, September 2008.

11 Rubber plantations are large in size, often having a population (workers and families) of 5,000 or more.

12 The largest was iron.

13 Interview with UNMIL official, Monrovia, September 2008.

14 Interview with aid official, Monrovia, September 2008.

15 Despite this, sizeable quantities of unprocessed rubber were also being exported from Liberia.

16 Joint Government of Liberia – United Nations Rubber Plantation Task Force Report, May 2006.

17 Interviews with UNMIL official, Monrovia, 2008.

18 Number from UNMIL HR official.

19 The DDR process in Liberia was officially called disarmament, demobilization, rehabilitation and reintegration. However, since DDR is the common way of referring to such processes, it is used here.

20 For instance, fighting between pro-Taylor militias and MODEL in the River Cess caused many civilians to flee. In Monrovia in December 2003 there were clashes between pro-Taylor forces and LURD, as LURD attempted to enter Monrovia with a number of vehicles and in breach of the Accra conditions. There were also reports of LURD fighters attacking and in some cases executing civilians perceived to anti-LURD.

21 The decision to include dependents appeared to be based on the experience of the DDR programme in Sierra Leone, which had been criticized for excluding 'bush wives', e.g. women attached to the fighters, often recruited against their will.

22 Leaders of one ex-combatant association in Monrovia explained how they had representatives at local educational institutions such as vocational schools and colleges. The representatives would map ex-combatants enrolled at each institution for the purpose of mobilizing them as a pressure group (interview with ex-combatant representatives, Monrovia, September 2008).

23 Some suggested that the current government's endorsement of the AFL's disbandment was also comprehensible in terms of old enmities, with some present power holders having been at the receiving end of violence by soldiers during the Doe regime (interview with government official, Monrovia, September 2008).

24 Personal communication with NGO official, Monrovia, September 2008.

25 Or in the words of Hoffman, 'what Bayart alludes to in his theorization of a "politics of the belly" – a frantic, almost gluttonous effort to capitalize on a palpably narrow window of opportunity to benefit from one's position' (Hoffman 2004: 211–26).

26 According to Monrovia residents, in a group of armed robbers one person would normally carry a gun, whereas the others might have cutlasses or machetes, the latter a standard agricultural tool in tropical countries.

27 Interview with government official, Monrovia, September 2008.

28 One leader described how his groups cooperated with five other groups to set up a password each night preventing any 'strangers' from passing though their communities, which together amounted to a large area. These passwords, however, were only known to the members of the groups themselves, in practice giving them control over movements in the area, including those of local residents. The leader also said that they had assembled road blocks, but had been told by UNMIL to discontinue this practice.

29 In meetings, some leaders argued that they had a direct line to the police and that they would always show up. One leader, however, argued that the police never bothered to respond to distress calls and if they did come it was invariably the next morning (interviews with neighbourhood watch group leaders, Paynesville and Mamba Point, Monrovia, September 2008).
30 Interview with senior police official, Monrovia, September 2008.

Bibliography

Amnesty International (2005) *Liberia: Violence, Discrimination and Impunity*. Report, 18 September 2005.

Atkinson, P. (1997) *The War Economy in Liberia: A Political Analysis*, Relief and Rehabilitation Network Paper, 22, London: Overseas Development Institute.

Bayart, J.-F. (1993) *The State in Africa: The Politics of the Belly*, London and New York: Longman.

Bayart, J.-F., Ellis, S. and Hibou, B. (1999) *The Criminalization of the State in Africa*, Oxford: James Currey.

Bøås, M. (2008) 'A funeral for a friend: contested citizenship in the Liberian civil war', Presented at: BISA Annual Conference 2008, University of Exeter 15–17 December, unpublished.

Bøås, M. (2009) ' "New" nationalism and autochthony – tales of origin as political cleavage', *Africa Spectrum*, 44(1): 19–38.

Bøås, M. and Dunn, K.C. (2007) 'Introduction', in M. Bøås and K.C. Dunn, *African Guerillas Raging Against the Machine*, Boulder, London: Lynne Rienner.

Bøås, M. and Hatloy, A. (2008) ' "Getting in, getting out": militia membership and prospects for re-integration in post-war Liberia', *Journal for Modern African Studies*, 46(1): 33–55.

Clapham, Christopher (1989) 'Liberia' in Donal B. Cruise O'Brien, John Dunn, Richard Rothbone (eds) *Contemporary West African States,* Cambridge: Cambridge University Press (99–111).

Clegg, C.A. (2004) *The Price of Liberty: African Americans and the Making of Liberia*, Chapel Hill: University of North Carolina Press.

Collier, P. (2000) *Economic Causes of War and Their Implications for Policy*, Washington, DC: World Bank.

Cramer, C. (2006) *Civil War is not a Stupid Thing: Accounting for Violence in Developing Countries*, London: Hurst & Co.

Ellis, S. (2007) *The Mask of Anarchy: The Destruction of Liberia and the Religious Dimension of an African Civil War*, New York: New York University Press.

GoL/UNMIL (2006) *Final Report May 2006,* Joint Government of Liberia–United Nations Rubber Plantations Task Force,

Harris, D. (2008) *Post-Conflict Elections or Post-Elections Conflict in Sierra Leone and Liberia*, Unpublished thesis, London: School of Oriental and African Studies, University of London.

Hoffman, D. (2004) 'The civilian target in Sierra Leone and Liberia: political power, military strategy and humanitarian intervention', *African Affairs*, 103(411): 211–26.

Human Rights Watch (2005) *Youth, Poverty and Blood: The Legal Legacy of West Africa's Regional Warriors*, New York: Human Rights Watch.

International Crisis Group (2002) *Liberia: The Key to Ending Regional Instability*, Africa Report, 43, 24 April.

International Crisis Group (2004), *Liberia and Sierra Leone: Rebuilding Failed States*, Africa Report, 87, 8 December.

International Crisis Group (2009), *Liberia: Uneven Progress in Security Sector Reform*, Africa Report, 148, 13 January.

IRIN (2004a) 'Liberia: disarmed fighters riot to demand cash payment', Monrovia: IRIN.

IRIN (2004b) 'Liberia: religious riots erupt in Monrovia, curfew imposed', Monrovia: IRIN.

IRIN (2005) 'Liberia: UN admits funding shortage for rehabilitation after ex combatants riot', Monrovia: IRIN.

Jennings, K.M. (2008) 'Securitising the economy of reintegration in Liberia: whose peace?', in M.C. Pugh, N. Cooper and M. Turner, *Critical Perspectives on Political Economy in Peacebuilding*, Basingstoke: Palgrave Macmillan.

Jordan, M.L. (2008) *Joint Ministry of Agriculture/UNMIL Study on Rubber Theft: Final Report*, Ministry of Agriculture/UNMIL.

Keen, D. (1998) *The Economic Functions of Violence in Civil Wars*. London: Oxford University Press.

Levitt, J.L. (2005) *The Evolution of Deadly Conflict in Liberia: From 'Paternaltarianism' to State Collapse*, Durham, NC: Carolina Academic Press.

'Liberia: graft never really went away' (2008) *Africa Confidential*, 49.

McGovern, M. (2008) *Liberia: The Risks of Rebuilding a Shadow State. Building States to Build Peace*, C. Call, V.H. Wyeth and International Peace Academy, Boulder, CO: Lynne Rienner.

Malan, M. (2008) *Security Sector Reform in Liberia; Mixed Results from Humble Beginnings*, London: Strategic Studies Institute.

Mbadlanyana, T. and Onuoha F.C. (2009) *Peacekeeping and Post-Conflict Criminality: Challenges to the (Re-)Establishment of Rule of Law in Liberia*, ISS Paper 190, Institute for Security Studies, South Africa.

National Security Strategy of the Republic of Liberia (2008) Monrovia: January

Paes, W.-C. (2005) 'The challenges of disarmament, demobilization and reintegration in Liberia', *International Peacekeeping*, 12(2): 253–61.

Pugel, J. (2007) *What the Fighters Say: A Survey of Ex-Combatants in Liberia, February–March 2006*, A UNDP-funded empirical study conducted in partnership with African Network for the Prevention and Protection against Child Abuse and Neglect (ANPPCAN), UNDP Liberia.

Reno, W. (2009) 'Understanding criminality in West African conflicts', *International Peacekeeping*, 16(1): 47–61.

Richards, P. (1996) *Fighting for the Rain Forest: War, Youth and Resources in Sierra Leone*, London: International African Institute in association with James Currey.

Richards, P., Bah, K., Vincent, J. (2004) *Social Capital and Survival: Prospects for Community-Driven Development in Post-Conflict Sierra Leone*, Social Development Papers: Community Driven Development/Conflict Prevention and Reconstruction, Washington, DC: World Bank.

Sawyer, A. (2008) 'Emerging patterns in Liberia's post-conflict politics: observations from the 2005 elections', *African Affairs*, 107(427):177–99.

Steenkamp, C. (2005) 'The legacy of war: conceptualizing a "culture of violence" to explain violence after peace accords', *Round Table*, 94(379): 253–67.

Truth and Reconciliation Commission (2008), *National Conflict Mapping Survey*.

UNMIL (2006) *Human Rights in Liberia's Rubber Plantations: Tapping into the Future*, Monrovia: UNMIL HQ.

UNMIL (2007) *Unpublished Intelligence Report.*

Unruh, J.D. (2009) 'Land rights in postwar Liberia: the volatile part of the peace process', *Land Use Policy*, 26(2): 425–33.

Utas, M. (2003) *Sweet Battlefields: Youth and the Liberian Civil War*, Uppsala: Dissertations in Cultural Anthropology, Uppsala University.

World Bank (2008) *Liberia: Insecurity of Land Tenure, Land Law and Land Registration in Liberia*, Environmental and Natural Resources (AFTEN), Africa Region.

14 Violence, denial and fear in post-genocide Rwanda

Trine Eide

Rwanda has a history of extraordinary mass violence. State-sponsored massacres (1959–63) civil war (1990–4) and genocide (1994) are important keywords in the historical contextualization of a violent past. Another important keyword is ethnicity – the dominant prism through which violence is interpreted. Without revisiting the entire debate on the origin of ethnicity in Rwanda, the main point here is to foster an understanding of so-called ethnic violence that moves beyond the primordialism versus constructionism debate. Fruitful contributions in this regard come from approaches that focus on the spirals of violence and the images and the memories thereof as essential dynamics that structure ethnic communities of fear (Chrétien and Bangeas 2008). These approaches may be extended to facilitate an analysis of three central characteristics of the 'victor's peace' that took shape in post-genocide Rwanda: denial of state-sponsored violence despite its massive scale, 'victor's justice' and the politics of fear. Apart from a growing revisionist literature (Braeckman 1994; Lanotte 2006; Ruzibiza 2005; Pean 2005), there has been a tendency to under-communicate violence committed in the aftermath of the 1994 genocide. Although this chapter focuses primarily on post-genocide violence, it should be read not as support for revisionist claims in general, but rather as an addition to the conventional analysis.

This chapter is divided into two main parts. The first part outlines a genealogy of state-sponsored violence in post-genocide Rwanda. This provides a context for illustrating how the politics of fear and impunity structure feelings of ethnic belonging. These are discussed in the second part, which draws heavily on six months of anthropological fieldwork conducted in 2006–7. The fieldwork was multi-sited and included one genocide court, *Gacaca*, one prison, one rural community and one larger city located in the South Province of Rwanda. The data collected were products of everyday participant observation, semi-structured interviews with rural farmers and university students, and more formal interviews with prisoners.

'Victor's peace' and the denial of state-sponsored violence

The genocide – which claimed the lives of an estimated 800 000 persons – was ended in July 1994 by the Rwandan Patriotic Front (RPF), the rebel group dominated by Tutsi exiles, who had invaded from Uganda in 1990 and sparked a four-year-long civil war. The victory of the RPF in 1994 simultaneously meant the total defeat of the former regime, whose supporters and approximately two million Hutu fled across the borders to Zaire and, to a lesser extent, Tanzania. By officially ending the genocide, the RPF also won the initial moral support of the international community, drawing on a deep-felt sense of international guilt for having stood aside during the massacres. The regime's active use of an 'official discourse of denial' (Cohen 2001: 101) also served to obscure and thus facilitate the continuation of violence in the aftermath of the genocide.

We can distinguish three main waves that make up the *genealogy of violence* of the post-genocide state.

The Kibeho massacre (April 1995)

Apart from the violence of the genocide itself, the massacres led to a large number of internally and externally displaced people. The main internally displaced people's (IDP) camp was Kibeho, where some 80,000 persons, mostly Hutu civilians, had gathered (Prunier 1997: 321, Pottier 2002). On 18 April 1995, RPF soldiers surrounded the camp and cut off the water and food supply, followed four days later by opening fire on the camp population while UN peacekeepers and aid agencies watched from the sidelines. International observers started a body count that reached 4,700 before they were abruptly stopped by RPF soldiers. The government – again in the logic of denial – maintained that only 338 had been killed and that its forces had responded to fire from 'criminal elements' hiding in the camp. The Kibeho massacre consequently constitutes a significant event in the genealogy of violence. It also marked the beginning of the end of the 'government of national unity' composed of both Hutu and Tutsi, which had been formed in accordance with the Arusha Peace Accords of August 1993, when the prominent Hutu politician, Prime Minister Faustin Twagiramungu, resigned (Prunier 2009b: 30).

Continuation of the civil war on foreign territory: Zaire (1996–7)

The next wave of post-war violence took place across the border within (then) Zaire. It was, in effect, a continuation of the civil war, just on a smaller scale and on foreign territory. In September 2006, parts of Kagame's RPF army – now called the Rwandan Patriotic Army (RPA) – crossed the border in order to dismantle refugee camps and disarm the former Rwandan army (ex-FAR) and the infamous Hutu militias (*Interahamwe*), the principal agents of violence during the genocide. Most of the camp population were Hutu civilians, but with military and militias mixed in. The Rwandan government identified the targets as 'genocide perpetrators' who used refugee camps as bases from which to launch attacks against Rwanda.

Joined by anti-Mobutu armed factions, RPA forces started attacking the main camps in mid-October 1996. The attacks generated a massive exodus of refugees to other camps, which in turn, became sites of subsequent attacks. The violence thus had a domino effect, causing more than one million refugees to flee in several directions (Emizet 2000: 174, Prunier 2009b: 143).

By 4 February 1997, when the last main camps had fallen, it became evident that the strikes had taken a huge toll. While the precise figures of missing or killed refugees remain controversial, careful estimates suggest around 220 000 'disappeared refugees' (Emizet 2000: 178, Prunier 2009a: 148). The Special Rapporteur for Zaire commissioned by the UN high commissioner for human rights (UNHCR), Roberto Garreton, raised another question:

> One cannot of course ignore the presence of persons guilty of geno-
> cide, soldiers and militia members among refugees ... It is neverthe-
> less unacceptable to claim that more than a million people, including
> large numbers of children, could be collectively designated as persons
> guilty of genocide and liable to execution without trial ... Very often
> the targets were neither *Interahamwe* combatants nor soldiers of the
> former FAR. They were women, children, the wounded, the sick, the
> dying and the elderly and the attacks seem to have had no precise mil-
> itary objective.
>
> (Cited in Prunier 2009a: 147–8)

A subsequent UN investigation categorized the violence against refugees as 'an abhorrent crime against humanity', but kept open whether nor not it was genocide (United Nations 1998: para. 96).

The Rwandan government, for its part, rejected the charges, claiming that the targets had been the former army and militia, in other words 'genocide perpetrators' who constituted a security threat. It also rejected the legal framework used by the UN investigation by arguing that the target of the intervention had been genocide perpetrators, thus concealing the fact that women, children and the elderly were also among the victims.

De facto war and disappearances in northwestern Rwanda (1996–8)

The third wave of post-war violence took place within Rwanda, in its in northwestern region. While significant, the violence was on a much smaller scale than the genocide and the violence in Zaire/DRC. The struc-ture may be described as a widening spiral in which the numbers of victims increased following incursions by 'armed groupings' (the ex-FAR and the genocide militia), which conducted cross-border raids from their bases in Zaire and clashed with RPA soldiers. Reports by Amnesty International (AI 1996a, 1996b, 1997a, 1997b, 1998) reveal additional patterns of violence: indiscriminate targeting of unarmed civilians by both parties and extra-judicial executions and 'disappearances' by the state forces. In the main, these killings followed ethnic lines, but not exclusively so.

Before 1997, the ex-FAR and genocide militia were presumed to target primarily symbols of Tutsi power with the long-term objective of destabilizing the region and overthrowing the government (AI 1996b: 8). Although the high proportion of Tutsi victims (who included the elderly, children and infants) suggest an ethnic logic, this was probably not the sole motive of the later attacks. Other potential targets were 'traitors' (Hutu seen as cooperating with the RPF/A) and genocide witnesses (Hutu and Tutsi who could testify in trials against participants in the genocide), as well as opportunistic aspects and disputes tied to land. With land being quite scarce in Rwanda, murder for personal gain is a not uncommon crime in peacetime, and land shortages increased with the return of Tutsi refugees (Pottier 2006).

Mounting attacks by the armed opposition led in turn to an increase in government 'cordon and search operations' in communities presumed to have Hutu sympathizers who aided the ex-FAR and genocide militia. The deaths reported after these operations largely exceeded the deaths attributed to the armed opposition (AI 1996, 1997a, 1997b, 1998). 'Disappearances' also increased significantly and by 1998 had

> Become so routine that many Rwandese seemed resigned to this violence as an inevitable part of their lives ... many families no longer made the effort to notify the authorities or international organizations about the 'disappearance' of their relatives, either for fear of their own lives or in the knowledge that little or no effective action would be taken to investigate them.
>
> (AI 1998:1)

The government responded as it did after the killings in Zaire and Kibeho, that is, admitting 'raw facts' (i.e. 'civilians were caught in cross-fire') or shifting the responsibility to the armed opposition whilst denying the victimhood of children and elderly ('genocide perpetrators, criminal elements and their sympathizers were the targets'). The disappearances were in themselves an important dimension of official denial. The phenomenon of disappearances, as Cohen writes, 'takes its very form from the government's ability to deny that it happened. The victim has no legal corpus, or a physical body; there is no evidence to prosecute, not even a sign of crime' (Cohen 2001: 105).

The killings and disappearances associated with the state forces do not suggest a genocidal strategy. Rather, the violence can be understood as an attempt to establish political control through terror (Verwimp 2003: 442, Prunier 2009a: 19–24). Combined with official denial, the violence seemed to send a clear message. The denial of state-sponsored violence in Rwanda and Zaire/DRC not only showed what RPA soldiers were capable of doing, but also that they could get away with it. Impunity hence manifests itself as another central characteristic of the Rwandan 'victor's peace'.

The successive waves of post-genocide violence and the official denial of Hutu victimhood have created fear, distrust and bitterness among those who regard themselves as victims of state-sponsored post-genocide violence. The matter is talked about in private among rural Rwandans, but there is no public discussion. Rather, we find closed, discursive communities where memories of violence and experiences of injustice in relation to genocide trials structure feelings of ethnic belonging.

Impunity and fear in post-genocide Rwanda

By the end of 1998, the RPA had mostly neutralized armed opposition groups and reports of civilian deaths within Rwanda decreased (Human Rights Watch 2001, 2003). Yet while physical violence declined, fear, intimidation and repression did not. The adoption of two new laws – the law on divisionism (2001) and the creation of Gacaca courts (2001) – helped improve the government's image internationally, but, also consolidated its power and impunity for its actions. Both laws and their implications have been central in the structuring of feelings of ethnic belonging in post-genocide Rwanda.

The winner takes all: the 2003 election, divisionism and victor's justice

The master narrative promoted by the post-genocide state depicts ethnicity as a colonial invention, and as the root of past evils: bad governance, conflicts, violence and genocide. Pre-colonial Rwanda, by contrast, is presented as a 'true' nation populated by one people (Rwandans, not ethnic groups), who spoke the same language and shared a national culture of unity. In this narrative, the invention of ethnicity shattered unity and led to the development of a culture of divisionism and impunity that encouraged violence against Tutsi.

The post-genocide government has adopted several mechanisms to constrain the curse of ethnicity and impunity: the law on divisionism (criminalization of ethnic identification) which became a central tool in the run up to the 2003 elections and Gacaca jurisdictions (transitional justice courts) which served to further conceal violence committed by the RPF/A.

The law on divisionism defines division as being 'when the author makes use of any speech, written statement or action that causes conflict that causes an uprising that may degenerate into strife among people' (Law no. 47/2001 of 18/12/2001 Art. 3). With this open definition, accusations of 'divisionism' became a central tool to discredit or imprison journalists, human rights workers and members of the political opposition in the run-up to the 2003 presidential and parliamentary elections. In 2003, the only political party powerful enough to challenge the RPF, the Democratic Republican Movement, was effectively dissolved, which, combined with arrests, flights and disappearances, decisively affected the pre-election climate. The result was an overwhelming political victory for RPF. Paul Kagame was elected president with 95 per cent of the votes and the RPF coalition received 78 per cent of the votes for the Chamber of Deputies (Samset and Dalby 2003: 54–9).

Yet the election victory did not soften the government's stance. By 2004, the campaign against divisionism was broadened to include 'genocide ideology', an elusive concept that covered political support for non-RPF political candidates and associated RPF with war crimes (HRW 2008: 34). The government thus ensured national impunity for crimes committed by RPF soldiers in two ways. First, the mere mention of possible war crimes was prohibited. Second, state agents had the power to remove war crimes from Gacaca jurisdiction (Kirkby 2006). The official rationale for the establishment of Gacaca courts was to overcome structural constraints of the legal system (lack of personnel and court buildings, overcrowded prisons etc.) and promote a vision of reconciliation. Gacaca courts were designed as an 'updated' traditional justice mechanism (Karekezi *et al.* 2004) that truth-telling, punishment – which varied from 5–30 years in prison – and forgiveness would facilitate a process of national reconciliation. In contrast to the International Criminal Tribunal for Rwanda (ICTR) in Arusha and national courts, Gacaca courts were presented as both a participatory and a traditional way of coping with the legacy of violence committed by Hutu perpetrators against Tutsi in 1994.

The international community did nothing to challenge the impunity for possible RPF war crimes committed in the same period. In fact, the UN had much earlier suppressed a report by a UNHCR consultant (Robert Gresony) just after the genocide which concluded that RPF forces had killed 25,000–45,000 persons, mostly Hutu, from April to mid-September 1994 (Des Forges 1999: 701–28).

Initial efforts by the ICTR to open a special investigation of war crimes allegedly committed by RPF soldiers in 1994 likewise stalled, apparently on the behest of the United States (Del Ponte 2009: 231–41).

By 2003, the dominant axis of political discourse had been established by the government's instrumental use of law and electoral intimidation to reconfigure social categories. Rwandans once again became divided in two opposing official categories: genocide perpetrators (with a subtext of 'Hutu') and genocide survivors with a subtext of 'Tutsi'). While officially denied, ethnic identity thus was indirectly reintroduced and established an ethnic hierarchy which legitimized RPF rule and post-genocide violence.

Ethnification of guilt and suffering and memories of violence

The prism of ethnicity likewise structures common perceptions. The subtle recategorization of 'perpetrators and survivors', the effective ban on any expressions of this issue, and the lack of accountability or even recognition of violence perpetrated by RPF/A soldiers in the context have sown seeds of bitterness, suspicion and fear and even further violence. These seeds have been nurtured by the weekly Gacaca meetings where Hutu generally feel they have to admit collective guilt, while Tutsi feel they have to express collective forgiveness.

Spending six months in Rwanda from 2006–7, living and speaking with rural farmers and university students,[1] I was struck by how most of them altered the presentation of their views on the political and everyday life situations as I came to know them. For instance, persons who had openly welcomed the Gacaca at one point were highly critical of it two months later. When I confronted my informants with these issues, the usual reply was that after realizing that my interpreters and I were probably not spies, they felt freer to engage in conversations that under current laws could be considered illegal.[2] Another striking aspect was the recurrence of themes that illustrated discrepancy between state ideologies (peace, justice, reconciliation etc.) and experienced local realities. Among the most frequent were the experiences of injustice and the fear of the 'ethnic other'. Both themes must be seen in the context of the subtle recategorization of ethnic identities and its institutionalization in Gacaca courts, which organized feelings of ethnic belonging despite the official master narrative that denies ethnicity and emphasizes justice as a principal element of 'never again'.

Most Rwandans who contest the official discourse of justice do not object to the punishment of genocide perpetrators. Their main concern is the recasting of ethnic groups and the experienced demand that all Hutu must admit collective guilt, whilst all Tutsi must display collective forgiveness. In general, most of those who criticized the Gacaca proceedings (both Hutu and Tutsi) feared that the experiences of injustice would fuel large-scale conflicts in the future. As one Rwandan told me, 'to fight impunity is a good idea in theory, but if it only concerns one side of people, Gacaca will not reach its objectives'.

The objectives of the Gacaca proceedings were envisioned as a four-step process: truth (as told by witnesses and confessing perpetrators), justice (punishment), forgiveness and finally reconciliation. Both Hutu and Tutsi whom I came to know challenged these steps, but sometimes on different grounds. The notion of truth was contested by Hutu, whose stories, memories and experiences of suffering and loss have been silenced in the Gacaca structure. The institutionalization of silence has created resentment against the proceedings among those who regard themselves as victims of violence but are not officially recognized as such. In response, some Gacaca attendants engage in 'silent protests', i.e. they do not testify or attend the proceedings (Waldorf 2006). This in turn has fuelled bitterness and anger among some of those who are officially categorized 'survivors', who interpret Hutu silence as another form of victimization. Some Tutsi also contest the motives for what is said during the proceedings, given that confessions and apologies may reduce sentences. This view is illustrated by the transcript of a conversation between Therese (a 38-year-old agriculturalist) and myself:

THERESE: It [Gacaca] does not work because some perpetrators lie. They hide the truth. They say: 'it was not me; it was the [killer] group that did it' ... Gacaca makes me sad. It makes me sad to see the faces of my family's killers and to remember our sufferings and then to see that the one who did it gets his sentence reduced ... One man asked my forgiveness, this was in the information gathering period. I told him: 'I have no right to forgive you. It is the government's job to forgive you'. It made me sad because he was apologizing *after* the meeting was held. If he truly meant it, he would have come to my house instead and apologized in other ways. But he did not. This apology was meaningless to me. In Gacaca they asked for forgiveness to get a reduced sentence. I know this for a fact because before the trial they were not confessing willingly.

Therese and many other Rwandans I met who referred to themselves as 'genocide survivors' questioned the demand for collective forgiveness in return for what they perceived as false confessions. The demands appear in two forms. Some prisoners claim that since the government has forgiven them, so must the survivors (Buckley-Zistel 2006: 13). More generally, the official religious–moral discourse of reconciliation invites a fusion of the government with the image of the Christian God, who (here in the words of Therese) 'commands forgiveness'. This may help explain why Therese emphasizes that it is the government's 'job' to forgive, not hers. Therese, moreover, is the sole survivor of the family and as such is expected to express collective forgiveness on behalf of her dead family members. This, she feels, she has no right to do and at any rate not on the basis of what she perceives to be meaningless confessions unwillingly presented.

Presidential decrees have permitted the temporary release to prisoners who confess during the period of investigation, but several imprisoned genocide suspects are reluctant to provide what some call 'survivor apologies'. Talking to prisoners, I found that some who had given testimonies and confessions while in prison were nevertheless disinclined to apologize or testify to the community prior to their trial if given the opportunity. Their reluctance reflected fears that 'the survivors' or others with whom they had a conflict would use the information to make new and false accusations against them that would result in a maximum penalty. Possibly the prisoners were disingenuous, using 'fear' of new accusations as an excuse not to confess and hoping for a lesser punishment Yet false accusations and testimonies in Gacaca trials have not been uncommon. Gacaca courts have in many ways become an arena through which non-genocide-related disputes linked to poverty, scarce land recourses, polygamy, dowry etc. play themselves out (Waldorf 2006). Like the Truth and Reconciliation Commission in South Africa, Gacaca may be an institution that facilitates 'procedural pragmatism', that is, some individuals become involved not to promote 'the ideology of reconciliation' but for personal benefits (Wilson 2001). Several Rwandans with whom I spoke had come to see Gacaca as an institution that was riddled with lies, which 'fuels hatred', as one woman said. This 'hatred', she emphasized, does not necessarily run along ethnic lines: both Hutu and Tutsi can make accusations of genocide participation. However, the official discourse on peacebuilding, which criminalizes any reference to ethnicity, constructs two opposing roles in the genocide: perpetrator and survivor. This of course implies that only Hutu will be accused of genocide participation. Consequently, individuals who previously held Hutu identity cards feared that they or family members could be (falsely) denounced as perpetrators.

Given contestations over the notion of Gacaca truth, it follows that 'justice' is contested as well. One critical viewpoint on Gacaca justice sees it as 'RPF justice' (or the 'high people's justice'),[3] that is, as justice dictated by the RPF. One point of discontent in this connection is that Gacaca does not have jurisdiction to try rape cases. Numerous Tutsi women – some estimate half a million – were raped in the genocide period from April to June 1994, and several were infected with HIV/AIDS and impregnated. Living with the trauma, the stigma of being HIV positive and as a mother of a 'fatherless child', or 'a child of the enemy', several women thus found the Gacaca proceedings, created by the government, unjust.[4] Another point of discontent was advanced by several Hutu, who viewed the political discourse of the RPF on justice as 'empty talk'. Two conversations between Damascene (a 41-year-old agriculturalist and former journalist) and Carine (a 32-year-old agriculturalist) and myself are illustrative:

DAMASCENE Gacaca is about collective blame of Hutu and victor's justice; that's all. If it was not, then the RPF [soldiers] would also sit on the perpetrator's bench during trial. But you have never seen any one of them there, have you?

CARINE: Some people died. The RPF killed them. I know this for a fact. My elder sister, her husband, their children, her neighbours and their children were killed by the RPF. There have been no trials, no justice. There is no way this will be taken to any court. If it were taken to court, look, they are the ones in power. It will not happen. Since the power is in its own hands, it will not punish itself. ... We are forced to forget our relatives that we lost during the war. People are obliged, forced to keep quiet. There is nowhere to ask, there are no doors to knock on.

As an institution that asserts 'victor's justice', the Gacaca courts are also an arena in which the official narrative of Rwanda's violent past is affirmed. Within this narrative, Hutu and Tutsi are cast as ethnic ideal types of perpetrator and victim, while the role of hero is bestowed upon the RPF, the ones who ended the genocide and hence brought 'peace' and 'justice' to Rwanda. Objections to this narrative – from which the genealogy of post-genocide violence is excluded – are not voiced in the public sphere. The official silence and fears among people of criticizing persons not deemed trustworthy constitute a significant aspect of the Rwandan 'victor's peace'. In the words of Carine:

CARINE: There are jails here in Rwanda. If you criticize the government, if you mention ... the RPF [killings] and it is heard by the wrong ears then you are accused of divisionism and that [jail] is where they send you [or] you disappear. No; you better shut up if you want to live in peace, otherwise you will regret it so much.

Persons deemed to be trustworthy tend to belong to the same ethnic category. As a result, articulated memories and histories connected to the genealogy of post-genocide violence are shared among discursive ethnic communities in a state where ethnicity officially does not exist. In a society with strong oral traditions of storytelling, private histories run alongside and compete with the rewritten official history of the violent past. Freddy (a university student) reflected on these issues:

FREDDY: The government has silenced the noise, but ethnicity is still important, it is talked about in all Rwandan homes … We still know where we belong. The children come to know it as well. You see, family history is talked about. If a child hears that his grandparents fled to Uganda, he knows he is Tutsi. If he is told that he lost many relatives in the genocide he also knows he is Tutsi. But if his father is in jail he knows that he is probably Hutu.

Rwandans who are extremely critical of Gacaca make the connections between Tutsi and the RPF explicit, claiming that Gacaca justice is 'survivor's justice'. These claims, articulated particularly by prisoners as well as Hutu non-prisoners, tend to be embedded in narratives that emphasize 'revenge' and are structured through a prism of ethnicity that accentuates in-group solidarity and out-group hatred. The mechanism whereby violence inflicted along ethnic lines tends to harden ethnic divisions between groups imagined as internally homogeneous is illustrated by a conversation between Karikezi (a 57-year-old agriculturalist) and myself. Karikezi lost his son and daughter-in-law during the attacks on one of the refugee camps in Zaire. Talking about his loss, he engaged in a narrative of revenge in which he explains that the RPF/A killed Hutu owing to the genocide of Tutsi. The Gacaca proceedings he sees as an additional 'form of revenge':

KARIKEZI: I give you one example: two persons are fighting on the ground. One of them is a superpower and he sits upon the weak one, beating him. Imagine, then, that for some reason the one who is down gets on the top: that their positions switch. The one who was weak is now the most powerful, he must perform better, and he must beat harder. But he must also be cleverer; there are several ways to beat people, keeping people in jail for 30 years and destroying families is one of them.

Karikezi here makes an implicit connection between the RPF/A and local Tutsi. The plot of his narrative is simple: under the rule of former Hutu presidents, Tutsis suffered as they were excluded from political life and subjected to violence. Now that the RPF are in power, *the* Tutsi have become powerful as they may use Gacaca proceedings to make *the* Hutu suffer (e.g. by presenting false accusations and testimonies). Karikezi's narrative is not unique. Rwandans engaged in 'narratives of revenge' tend to depict Gacaca variously as 'a trick to imprison Hutu and make Hutu children suffer', and/or as a 'price that all Hutu have to pay for the suffering of the Tutsi'.

To an outsider, narratives of these sorts may appear exaggerated. Nevertheless, as Linstroth (2009) argues, the social importance of such representation should not be dismissed on the basis of a Western positivistic notion of 'truth'. In his study of Maya cognition, memory and trauma from the Guatemalan civil war, Linstroth powerfully shows how episodic memories of trauma cease to be individual when turned into oral histories among members of a victimized group. Linstroth's findings resonate with Malkki's (1995) writings on the construction of memories of violence during the 1972 Burundian genocide that occurred in Hutu refugee camps in Tanzania. Linstroth's notion of exaggeration thus bears some similarity to Malkki's notions of mythico-history:

> [It] is not meant to imply that it was mythical in the sense of being false or made up ... What made the refugee narrative mythical ... was not its truth or falsity but the fact that it was concerned with order in a fundamental cosmological sense. ... It was concerned with the ordering and reordering of social and political categories, with the defining of self in distinction to other, with good and evil.
>
> (Malkki 1995: 237)

By targeting Hutu in particular, the post-genocide violence produced experiences of ethnically based victimization that structured and strengthened feelings of group belonging. Local narratives that emphasize revenge are centred around the violence in Zaire/DRC, where massive and indiscriminative violence against refugees during the RPA intervention led to the disappearance of over 200,000 Hutu in 1996–7. Other violence perpetrated by RPA soldiers (the massacres in Kibeho and the undeclared war in the northwest) tend to be seen as additional events in a narrative where the justice process of Gacaca is but another form of 'survivors' revenge'.

Histories, rumours, memories and experiences of 'what is done to the collective by outside forces' become a central part of a 'we experience', whether or not these atrocities are autobiographically experienced (Linstroth 2009: 153–4). Narratives of revenge against the Hutu in Rwanda may be understood as narratives of selected memories that are (re)produced within particular discursive ethnic communities, whose members experience them as real in a 'we' sense and which contribute to the construction of the ethnic and/or political consciousness of an 'us'. Narratives that emphasize the revenge of *the* Tutsi place the suffering of *the* Hutu in the centre of an alternative account which conflicts with a RPF master narrative of the violent past that denies Hutu victimhood. These accounts are also a response to the master narrative that is played out in the Gacaca courts throughout the country on a weekly basis. The court process serves as an institutional reminder of the violence and suffering experienced and lived by Tutsi, but excludes histories of violence and suffering experienced by Hutu. The government's master narrative is not restricted to the Gacaca process, but evident in the rewriting of official history and in the politicized landscape of genocide memorials and signposts which, in government media usage, emphasize truth, justice, reconciliation and 'never again'. This 'socially controlled memory' (Cohen 2001: 240) serves to legitimize the normative political reordering of ethnic categories and thus to enhance government control.

To generalize: two significantly different narratives of the violent past which run along ethnic lines coexist in Rwanda. The relatively peaceful coexistence from the late 1990s and onwards has been explained with reference to 'pragmatism' and a 'lack of choice' (Buckley-Zistel 2006: 138, 144–6). Living in one of the most densely populated countries in the world, rural Rwandans are mutually dependent in many aspects of every-day life: in cultivating fields with traditional tools, fetching water, partici-pating in funerals and births, bringing people to hospital, etc. This makes collaboration across perceived ethnic boundaries necessary. In everyday encounters it may be crucial to 'remember to forget' past agonies and viol-ence that have run, or are perceived to have run, along ethnic lines, as Buckley-Zistel argues (2006: 131). Yet although these memories are silenced in the public sphere, they are not forgotten. Rather, they are socially (re)produced in private ethnicized spheres as collective experi-ences that reinforce the structuring of discursive communities of fear.

Revenge and reprisals: fearing the 'ethnic other'

In late 2006, official accounts and rumours of renewed attacks, harass-ments, beatings and killings of Tutsi, Gacaca judges and witnesses reached the area in southern Rwanda where I was conducting fieldwork. Most of my informants usually called this 'revenge killing', while the government-controlled mass media explained the violence as being the result of 'geno-cide mentality' fostered by the politics of previous Rwandan regimes. Renewed attacks against individuals related to the Gacaca proceedings were a much discussed subject among my Hutu and Tutsi informants, who generally condemned these acts of violence. Although these events took place at some distance from where I was conducting my fieldwork, rumours and official accounts of violence clearly created fear among Tutsi, who incorporated the events into collective narratives of past terror inflicted by Hutu. Yet uncertainty was also created among Hutu. Some feared that being a witness in Gacaca courts would incur revenge from Hutu neighbours; others feared that the attacks against 'survivors' would incur revenge from Tutsi and/or agents of the state against Hutu as a col-lective body. The reactions were shaped by rumours and official media accounts of two particular episodes of post-genocide civilian violence in Mugatwa village in eastern Rwanda. These episodes, to be elaborated below, were those most referred to by my Hutu and Tutsi informants alike, who incorporated them as a central reference in narratives that emphas-ized revenge.

In general, several informants who identified themselves as survivors saw the renewed attacks, harassments, beatings and killings of Tutsi as a consequence of failed Gacaca courts. As a result, they feared attending the institutions of justice which the RPF, heavily supported by international donors, had created in their name. As Therese emphasized in one of our conversations:

THERESE: During the Gacaca process the situation is not good. Usually we survivors who are neighbours in the Imidugudu [village settlement created for returnees and survivors] go together to the trial. When we walk in front of the others they whisper 'look at them – those are the people who took us to court and those are the people we will face tomorrow'.

TRINE: Who is whispering those things?

THERESE: It is the perpetrators and the families of the perpetrators, and those people who have their family members in jail. We survivors do not even go to bars any more. And if we do, we go home together before it gets dark.

TRINE: Is there any particular reason for that?

THERESE: I tell you this. I seldom go anywhere except to the church, the market and to the trials. Here in the village it is not like in the cities, here everyone knows who is Muhutu [Hutu] and who is Mututsi [Tutsi]. We survivors do not go out after dark, simply because our lives may be in danger. But for us it is an obligation to attend Gacaca; we fear, but still we must go. We must go because the government commands unity and reconciliation and Gacaca is supposed to be for that.

TRINE: Do you think that Gacaca helps what the government calls 'reconciliation?

THERESE: No, no it does not. Gacaca does not work the way the government says.

TRINE: In which ways does Gacaca not work like the government says?

THERESE: It does not work because [of the] lies. The perpetrator who lies, he will not change his bad heart; he will be free and kill again. I know this. Recently there was a man here who came out from prison. This man, he got to know that while he was away someone had stolen bananas from his tree. The man told the thief in these words: 'Are you going to be punished because you stole some bananas? I will rather be punished for cutting those filthy Batutsi [Tutsi].' That is what he said. Also people say it on the radio all the time.

TRINE: What is said in the radio?

THERESE: That those perpetrators who are free from jail go and kill again. I hear this all the time. It is because of Gacaca. There has just been another killing in an eastern province of a young Mututsi [Tutsi] who witnessed in a trial. The perpetrator was freed and he killed the other!

The event Therese refers to in our conversation is the murder of F. Murasira, the nephew of a Gacaca judge in Mugwata village in eastern Rwanda. One of the government-owned newspapers, the *New Times*, covered this episode with particular frenzy, arguing that more protection for 'genocide survivors', witnesses and Gacaca judges was necessary. According to the *New Times*, Murasira was 'hacked to death by I. Habninshuti, a genocide perpetrator who was waiting for his upcoming Gacaca trial to be held by Murasira's uncle' (20 November 2006). In the context of the massive media attention devoted to killings of Gacaca witnesses, judges and genocide survivors, it is understandable that Therese and the people she includes in her categorization of 'we survivors' (Tutsi) fear attending Gacaca trials because doing so means a potential lethal encounter with 'the others' (Hutu), who she believes will never 'change their genocide mentalities'. In response to previous experiences of violence, rumours of renewed violence and official accounts thereof, Therese thus says that it is safer to walk in company with other Tutsi and to avoid single encounters with the ethnic other, particularly after dark, an act which in turn reinforces local ethnic divisions in the community.

The attacks on Gacaca judges and witnesses also created uncertainty and fear among Hutu witnesses. A conversation with one witness whom I came to know expresses these concerns:

PIERRE: I [have] asked for protection [in the Gacaca trial] because I was worried about the family of suspect [name withheld]. That man [the suspect], he spat in my face once and told me that I would suffer seriously if I told anything [pause]. Sometimes I think that the survivors are more willing to understand and forgive than some of the others in this community. Family members of perpetrators are usually angry when there is a trial and the names of their families are mentioned. They say that their family is put away because of people who denounce them. They take it as hatred.

Pierre, like Therese, feared attending Gacaca courts. These fears were reinforced by rumours and accounts of civilian violence elsewhere in the country and partly explain the silence in Gacaca courts. Several Gacaca participants have 'kept their mouths shut', because not doing so may lead to social exclusion or have potentially lethal consequences, which in turn reinforce the experience of victimization among Tutsi. Another noticeable similarity between the conversation of Therese and Pierre concerns the experienced behaviours of family members related to individuals suspected of genocide participation. This apparent resentment must be seen in the context of fear attached to perceived false accusations and experiences of injustice and also of insecurity tied to the emotional and economic burden of having a family member imprisoned. Rwanda continues to be one of the poorest counties in the world, with 67 per cent of its inhabitants living in extreme poverty. The long-term imprisonment of family members, and particularly adult males, strains already poor households, which lose one income yet have to feed the family member in jail. The economic consequences of imprisonment reinforce emotional experiences of a collectivization of guilt, which, in turn, aid the construction of narratives depicting Gacaca as a form of 'revenge' and structure social encounters with the ethnic other before, during and after these proceedings, as described above. Rumours of post-genocide violence perpetrated by Tutsi civilians against Hutu, but officially denied, add a powerful conceptual force to narratives which centre on revenge.

The murder of the genocide survivor Murasira in Mugwata village received massive media attention, but the government-owned media did not cover the violent reactions of residents identified as survivors in Mugwata against Hutu residents in a neighbouring village. Human Rights Watch reported that several houses were burned and looted and eight Hutu (five of them children under the age of 18) were murdered (HRW 2007a). Only some of the persons involved in the killings and lootings had been taken into custody, thus rendering little hope for justice for victims who did not fall under the official category 'genocide survivors'. Two months after this episode, the government-friendly newspaper, the *New Times*, commented on the events, but only to echo criticism of the Human Rights Watch report made by the Rwandan National Human Rights Commission:

> HRW's report was based upon last November's murder of eight people, who were killed after a genocide survivor schoolboy F. Murasira was gruesomely sliced to pieces by one genocide suspect I. Habninshuti in broad daylight. Scores of Genocide survivors and Gacaca witnesses and judges have been in recent past killed, mainly by genocide perpetrators, suspects or their sympathizers.
>
> (*New Times* 7 February 2007: 1–2)

None of the following articles in the *New Times* (or the printed readers' letters) mentioned the alleged murders, beatings, burnings of houses or lootings. Hutu victimhood is, in other words, concealed in these articles in a similar manner to the official discourse of denial from 1995–9. Further, by emphasizing the 'segregationist logic' of Human Rights Watch, the *New Times* relied upon a recognizable discursive strategy of implicatory denial, namely 'condemning the condemners' (Cohen 2001: 112). As after the Kibeho killings, witnesses' accounts used in the report are dismissed as speculative and based upon hearsay.[5] The representation reproduced a view of ethnicity that kept the fear of 'the ethnic other' alive.

In this connection, consider the following conversation between Ernest, a 55-year-old prisoner convicted of genocide participation, and myself:

ERNEST: Being in prison, it is the survivors' revenge, they seek the revenge because they have suffered much. I made them suffer, and for that I have confessed, and I have asked for forgiveness. I deserve this revenge, I am not like some of the other extremists here in prison who hope for people [the *Interahamwe* and ex-FAR] to come from Congo and set them free. But I want to ask you, what do you think will happen if someone shoots Kagame tomorrow?

TRINE: I don't know – you tell me.

ERNEST: It will be a new genocide. The survivors will shoot him themselves and blame it on us. The powerful will kill the weakest. The one with the gun will kill. The survivors will have their revenge killing and they will get away with it like they did in Mugwata. Mugwata is the proof. They slaughtered at least eight people there, even women and children. Innocent people, just like the Batutsi at that time – beaten, cut, killed. And what happened? The killers got away with it because they are the collages of Ibuka, the police, the local authorities and the government. This is God's true punishment. If the president dies – they will kill us. I can feel it. If he dies, the matter of a new genocide is open.

Ernest makes an explicit connection between vengeance-seeking state agents and Tutsi in the community, perceived to be empowered by the new regime. Moreover, to him the civilian violence against Hutu in Mugwata constitutes 'proof' that a future genocide by Tutsi against Hutu will occur under certain circumstances. His fears may appear exaggerated, yet the structural conditions of his daily life must be taken into account here. Surrounded by others who have been convicted, or who await their upcoming Gacaca trial, Ernest partakes in an environment where narratives and rumours about revenge by the ethnic other and false accusations circulate. At the time, several prisoners I talked to recounted and reproduced rumours that a group of Tutsi was planning to kill all the prisoners.

Incidents occur that give credence to such rumours. A total of 14 prisoners accused of attacking Tutsi and others involved in the Gacaca process were reportedly killed by the police and soldiers between April 2006 and May 2007, according to Human Rights Watch (HRW 2007b). The official reporting of killings of individuals suspected of genocide crimes follows the pattern of a discourse of denial. The suspect is shot while trying to escape or in a struggle with the police; his death is thus 'necessary' and also morally justified, which one official response to Human Rights Watch illustrates: 'it should be noted that the suspects [shot by the police] were of extreme criminal character ready to die for their genocide ideology. They are terrorists in nature and don't care about their own lives leave alone others' (HRW 2007b: 37). The justification of extrajudicial executions of this kind sends powerful messages to the effect that Hutu refigured as collective evil may continue to be killed with impunity. This in turn fuels local rumours of state reprisals that are incorporated into local narratives that emphasize revenge.

It is from such rumours and narratives that ethnic communities of fear are constructed. Rumours of violence, anthropologists have found, are significant both to the experience and expression of terror and in the politicization of ethnicity (Kirsh 2002; Stewart and Strathern 2004; Skidmore 2003). Like the imagined narratives of violence discussed above, the social (re)production of rumours involves the narration of a collective 'we' experience, whether or not it is autobiographically experienced. Apart from carrying information and terror, rumours carry emotion that often confirms 'the worst fears' (Skidmore 2003), reinforcing images of self and other, particularly when rumours are traded within closed discursive ethnic communities. Silence and secrecy prevail between these discursive communities, while narratives and rumours of violence circulate within, driving a wedge of insecurity and mistrust between them.

Trust, as Skidmore writes, 'is a precious commodity that is easily lost but hard indeed to take root'(2003: 16). During and in the aftermath of violence, the antonym of trust, mistrust of the other, reigns. Yet in Rwanda, rural farmers are not the only 'insecurity entrepreneurs' (Prunier in Chrétien and Bangeas 2008: 180). The state-owned media fuels narratives of terror as experienced by Tutsi and Hutu alike. For Tutsi, the media serves as a reminder, not only about the violent past but also of the constant threat to survivors who are surrounded by people who harbour elusive, hidden 'genocide mentalities'. For Hutu, the media sends powerful messages of what agents of the state and communal Tutsi are capable of doing against Hutu with impunity. By thus routinizing and inflicting terror on its citizens, the Rwandan regime has, in the words of Taussig (1992:11), succeeded in 'stringing the nation's nervous system one way towards hysteria, the other way towards numbing and apparent acceptance'.

Conclusions

The massive violence unleashed by the new Rwandan state in the aftermath of the genocide was made possible not only because the RPF was superbly organized and had inflicted a decisive military victory on the previous regime, but, importantly, because the international community mostly stood aside, paralysed by its own failure to prevent the genocide itself. The subsequent more sporadic killings were reported by international human rights organizations, although met with an official and total discourse of denial. By 1997–8, the remaining military threat from the enemy had been decisively broken and the government used other instruments to establish social control, create a new political order and destroy the evil genie of genocidal violence by officially denying ethnicity whilst creating special genocide courts. The process and instruments of establishing this new order, however, had contradictory effects by helping to create communities of fear and mutual distrust that followed ethnic lines. As I observed during fieldwork in the country, the law on divisionism and the Gacaca courts, although officially represented and internationally supported as instruments of reconciliation, justice and peacebuilding, also had contradictory effects. The overall result, it seems, was a striking juxtaposition of political order with social conflict: the government exercised cohesive political control over a large part of the rural Hutu and Tutsi population, who, however, lived their everyday lives in fear and distrust as mutual victims of the 'victor's peace'.

Notes

1 Locations and identities have not been revealed in order to protect the local participants. Personal names that appear in this section are fictitious.
2 I employed three interpreters of different gender and ethnic backgrounds in order to gain trust.
3 Term used for persons possessing positions of prestige, for example politicians.
4 The ICTR has, however, recognized that under international law rape can be prosecuted as an act of genocide (*Prosecutor* v. *Akayesu, Case No. ICTR-96-4-T* (Trial Chamber), 2 September 1998).
5 Such announcements were made in the *New Times* (8 February 2007) as well as on the government-controlled radio.

Bibliography

Agamben, G. (1998) *Homo Sacer: Sovereign Power and Bare Life*, Stanford, CA: Stanford University Press.
Amnesty International (1996a) *The Return Home: Rumors and Realities*, AI Index AFR/02/01/96.20, February. Online, available at: www.amnesty.org/en/library/info/AFR/02/01/96 (accessed 2 May 2008).

Amnesty International (1996b) *Rwanda: Alarming Resurgence of Killings*, AI Index: AFR/47/13/96 12 August. Online, available at: www.amnesty.org/en/library/info/AFR47/013/1996 (accessed 7 July 2009).

Amnesty International (1997a) *Rwanda: Ending the Silence*, AI Index: AFR 47/032/1997, 24 September. Online, available at: www.amnesty.org/en/library/info/AFR47/032/1997 (accessed 7 July 2009).

Amnesty International (1997b) *Rwanda: Civilians Trapped in Armed Conflict: 'The Dead can no Longer be Counted'*, AI Index: AFR 47/43/97, December. Online, available at: repository.forcedmigration.org/pdf/?pid=fmo:3977 (accessed 7 July 2009).

Amnesty International (1998) *Rwanda: The Hidden Violence: 'Disappearances and Killings Continue'*, AI Index: AFR/47/203/1998. 22 June. Online, available at: www.amnesty.org/en/library/info/AFR47/023/1998 (accessed 7 July 2009).

Bangeas, R. (2008) 'Introduction: rethinking the Great Lake Crisis, war, violence and political recomposition in Africa', in J-P. Chrétien and R. Bangeas (eds) *The Recurring Great Lakes Crisis: Identity, Violence and Power*, London: Hurst, pp. 1–26.

Braeckman, C. (1994) *Rwanda: historie d'un genocide*, Paris: Fayard.

Brubaker, R. (2004) *Ethnicity without Groups*, Cambridge, MA: Harvard University Press.

Buckley-Zistel, S. (2006) 'Remembering to forget: chosen amnesia as a strategy for local coexistence in post-genocide Rwanda', *Africa*, 79: 131–50.

Chatterji, R. and Metha, D. (2007) *Living with Violence: An Anthropology of Events and Everyday Life*, London: Routledge.

Chrétien, J-P. and Bangeas, R. (2008) *The Recurring Great Lakes Crisis: Identity, Violence and Power*, London: Hurst.

Cohen, S. (2001) *States of Denial: Knowing about Atrocities and Suffering*, Cambridge: Polity.

Del Ponte, C. (1999) *Leave No One to Tell the Story. Genocide in Rwanda*, Human Rights Watch, 1 March. Online, available at: www.grandslacs.net/doc/1317.pdf (accessed 17 December 2009).

Del Ponte, C. with C. Sudetic, (2009) *Madame Prosecutor: Confrontations with Humanity's Worst Criminals and the Culture of Impunity: A Memoir*, New York: Other Press.

Des Forges, Alison (1999) *Leave None To Tell The Story: Genocide in Rwanda*, Paris and New York: Human Rights Watch and International Federation of Human Rights.

Eide, T. (2007) *Pretending Peace: Discourses of Unity and Reconciliation in Rwanda*, unpublished thesis, University of Bergen.

Emizet, K. (2000) 'The massacre of refugees in Congo: a case of UN peacekeeping failure and international law', *Journal of Modern African Studies*, 38(3), 2000: 163–202.

Front Line Rwanda (2005) *Disappearances, Arrests, Threats, Intimidation and Co-option of Human Rights Defenders, 2001–2004*, Ireland, March 2005. Online, available at http://frontl.org/files/en/FrontLineRwandaReport.pdf (accessed 23 November 2009).

Gagnon, V.P. (2004) *The Myth of Ethnic War: Serbia and Croatia in the 1990s*, Ithaca, N.Y.: Cornell University Press.

Green, L. (1995) 'Living in a state of fear', in C. Nordstrom and A.C.G.M. Robben (eds), *Fieldwork under Fire: Contemporary Studies of Violence and Survival*, Berkeley: University of California Press, pp. 105–27.

Human Rights Watch (2001) *Rwanda: Observing the Rules of War?*, 20 December. Online, available at: www.hrw.org/node/78533 (accessed 2 February 2009).

Human Rights Watch (2003) *Preparing for Elections. Tightening Control in the Name of Unity*, 8 May. Online, available at: www.hrw.org/en/node/77843 (accessed 2 February 2009).

Human Rights Watch (2004) *Struggling to Survive: Barriers to Justice for Rape Victims in Rwanda*, 29 September. Online, available at: www.hrw.org/en/node/11975/section/1 (accessed 6 February 2009).

Human Rights Watch (2007a) *Killings in Eastern Rwanda*, 22 January. Online, available at: www.hrw.org/en/reports/2007/01/22/killings-eastern-rwanda (accessed 6 February 2009).

Human Rights Watch (2007b) *'There Will be no Trial': Police Killings of Detainees and the Imposition of Collective Punishments*, 24 July. Online, available at: www.hrw.org/en/reports/2007/07/23/there-will-be-no-trial (accessed 6 February 2009).

Human Rights Watch (2008) *Law and Reality: Progress in Judicial Reforms in Rwanda*, New York: Human Rights Watch, 25 July.

Kapferer, B. and Bertelsen, B.E. (2009) *Crisis of the State: War and Social Upheaval*, New York: Berghan.

Karekezi, U.A. Nishimiyimana and Mutamba, B. (2004) 'Localizing justice: Gacaca courts in post genocide Rwanda', in E. Stover and H.M. Weinstein (eds) *My Neighbour, My Enemy: Justice and Community in the Aftermath of Mass Atrocity*, Cambridge: Cambridge University Press.

Kirby, C. (2006) 'Rwanda's Gacaca courts: a preliminary critique', *Journal of African Law*, 22(1), 2006: 94–117.

Kirsh, S. (2002) 'Rumour and other narratives of political violence in West Papua' *Critique of Anthropology*, 22(1): 53–79.

Lanotte, O. (2006) *La France face aux conflits rwandais, 1990–1994*, Louvain: Université Catholique de Louvain.

Linstroth, J.P. (2009) 'Mayan cognition, memory and trauma', *History and Anthropology*, 20(2): 139–82.

Longman, T.P (1998) *Proxy Targets: Civilians in the War in Burundi*, New York: Human Rights Watch.

Longman, T.P (2001) 'Church politics and the genocide in Rwanda', *Journal of Religion in Africa*, 31(2): 163–86.

Malkki, L.H. (1995) *Purity and Exile: Violence, Memory and National Cosmology among Hutu Refugees in Tanzania*, Chicago: University of Chicago Press.

New Times (2007) 'Rights body blasts over HRW report', 7 February.

New Times (2007) 'Human Rights Watch Report always biased', 8 February.

Pean, P. (2006) *Noires fureurs, blancs menteurs*, Paris: Mille et Une Nuits.

Pottier, J. (2002) *Re-imagining Rwanda: Conflict, Survival and Disinformation in the Late Twentieth Century*, Cambridge: Cambridge University Press.

Pottier, J. (2006) 'Land reform for peace? Rwanda's 2005 Land Law in context', *Journal of Agrarian Change*, 6(4): 509–37.

Prunier, G. (1997) *The Rwanda Crisis: History of a Genocide*, London: Hurst.

Prunier, G. (2008) 'The "ethnic" conflict in the Inturi District: overlapping of local and international in Congo-Kinshasa', in J-P. Chrétien and R. Bangeas (eds) *The Recurring Great Lakes Crisis: Identity, Violence and Power*, London: Hurst, pp. 180–205.

Prunier, G. (2009a) *Africa's World War: Congo, the Rwandan Genocide and the Making of a Continental Catastrophe*, Oxford: Oxford University Press.

Prunier, G. (2009b) *From Genocide to Continental War: The 'Congolese' Conflict and the Crisis of Contemporary Africa*, London: Hurst.

Rittner, C., Roth, J.K. and Whitworth, W. (2004) *Genocide in Rwanda: Complicity of the Churches*, St Paul: Paragon House.

Ruzibiza, A.J. (2005) *Rwanda: l'histoire secrète*, Paris: Editions du Panama.

Samset, I. and Dalby, O. (2003) *Rwanda: Presidential and Parliamentary Elections 2003*, NORDEM Report no 12/2003, Oslo: Norwegian Centre for Human Rights.

Scheper Hughes, N. (1997) 'Peace time crimes', *Social Identities*, 3(3): 471.

Seaton, J. and Allen, T. (1999) *The Media of Conflict: War Reporting and Representations of Ethnic Violence*, London: Zed Books.

Skidmore, M. (2003) 'Darker than midnight: fear, vulnerability and terror making in urban Burma (Myanmar), *American Ethnologist*, 30(1): 5–21.

Sleigman, C.G. (1930) *Races of Africa*, London: Butterworth.

Stewart, P.J. and Strathern, A. (2004) *Witchcraft, Sorcery, Rumours and Gossip*, New York: Cambridge University Press.

Stewart, P.J. and Strathern, A. (2008) 'Rwanda's security trap and participation in the 1994 genocide', in J-P. Chrétien and R. Bangeas (eds) *The Recurring Great Lakes Crisis: Identity, Violence and Power*, London: Hurst, pp. 168–80.

Taussig, M. (1992) *The Nervous System*, New York: Routledge.

United Nations (1998) *Report of the Secretary General's Investigative Team Charged with Investigating Serious Violations of Human Rights and International Humanitarian Law in the Democratic Republic of Congo*.

Verwimp, P. (2003) 'Testing the double-genocide thesis for central and southern Rwanda', *Journal of Conflict Resolution*, 47(4): 423–42.

Waldorf, L. (2006) 'Mass justice for mass atrocity: rethinking local justice as transitional justice', *Temple Law Review*, 79(1): 1–88.

Warren, K.B. (1993) *The Violence Within: Cultural and Political Opposition in Divided Nations*, Boulder, CO: Westview Press.

Wilson, R. (2001) *The Politics of Truth and Reconciliation in South Africa: Legitimizing the Post Apartheid State*, London: Cambridge University Press.

Part V

Latin America

15 The multiple forms of violence in post-war Guatemala[1]

John-Andrew McNeish and Oscar López Rivera

Introduction

With the signing of the Peace Accords in 1996 Guatemala's credentials of democratic governance were re-established, but as media reports and the international community have observed the killing and crimes of the civil war have continued. With thoughts of the apparent contradictions of continued violence in a time of peace, this chapter aims to characterize and identify the causes of this violence. We propose that whilst carrying some validity, current academic, media and political explanations largely fail to capture the extent and significance of the violence in Guatemala. We argue that this is because of their general tendency to disarticulate certain forms of violence from each other and their failure to place these acts of violence collectively in a wider socio-political context that stretches beyond Guatemala and between historical periods of peace and war. Aiming to better understand the span and kind of violence in Guatemala, we propose here a rough typology that qualitatively maps out the indices, locations and different acts of physical violence in the country. In an effort to understand better the comprehensive nature of violence in post-conflict Guatemala, the typology also seeks to trace many of the interconnections and intertwined relationships that exist between the physical and broader analytical understandings of violence i.e. structural, symbolic, socialization and natural. These linkages not only reveal a more nuanced picture of violence in post-conflict Guatemala, but also help to highlight the close relationship that violence today has both with recent war and with persisting historical social conflicts, divisions and prejudices in the country. The typology produced here then aims to highlight the contextual outcomes of a continuum of violence in Guatemala 'that ranges from the interpersonal and delinquent to the self-consciously political and purposeful' (Bourgois 2005: 428).

Rates of violence in Guatemala

Comparative studies of violence in Latin America have identified Guatemala as a country with one of the highest levels of homicide in the region. In the mid-1990s a survey of the levels of homicide worldwide demonstrated that the annual median was 10.7 for each 100,000 inhabitants. In this same survey Latin America was registered at a level of 22.9 per 100,000 inhabitants, and Guatemala, El Salvador, Colombia and Jamaica as exceeding this regional median (Buvinic *et al.* 2000). More specifically, according to a report produced in 2007 by the national office of the United Nations Development Programme (UNDP) in Guatemala:

> In the last seven years the levels of homicides have increased by over 120 per cent, exceeding 2,665 homicides in 1999 and 5,885 in 2006. This growth is equivalent to a growth of 12 per cent per year since 1999, and is greater than the 2.6 per cent annual growth of the population. In 2006 the country showed a level of 47 homicides per 100 inhabitants nationally and 108 in Guatemala City. These statistics position Guatemala as one of the most violent peacetime countries in the world.
>
> (UNDP 2007: 9)

Perhaps the most surprising conclusion based on the available figures is that there has been a higher rate of killings overall in the time of peace than during the time of war (Briceño 2002). This conclusion is supported by a comparison of figures produced by the ombudsman and an earlier report of the Commission for Historic Clarification[2] (*Comisión para el Esclarecimiento Histórico*, CEH) (see Table 15. 1).

Current explanations for violence

As the number of homicides has risen in Guatemala there has been a growing effort by both the government and the international community to explain and develop suitable responses to this clearly increasingly unstable situation. Most explanations for the high levels of violence in the post-accord period are limited to different aspects of recent social development and/or the legacy of the civil war (Moser and McIlwaine 2000, 2001; Keen 2003; Cleary 2002; Peacock and Beltrán 2003).

With 80 per cent of homicide victims under the age of 30, it has been particularly easy for the Guatemalan government to make a case for blaming the majority of the violence on the existence and steady expansion of youth gangs, or *maras*. The *mara* (a name originally drawn from an analogy with the Amazonian *marabunta* or army ant, known for its destruc-

Figure 15.1 Extra-judicial killings

	No. of dead	
Extra-judicial killings during the war	23,371	Commission for Historic Clarification (CEH)
Annual average for violent deaths	649	
Violent deaths (January–July 2005)	3,051	Report to the United Nations Ombudsman for Extra-judicial Killings
Violent deaths (January–July 2006)	3,455	
Annual average for violent deaths	3,255	

tive behaviour) appeared as a serious social problem in Guatemala and a number of Central American countries in the course of the 1990s. The *maras* were formed in the 1980s, when immigrants (many of whom were demobilized army soldiers or guerrillas) fleeing the brutal civil war in Central America settled in Los Angeles and San Diego. To protect themselves from already established street gangs, these immigrants banded together and formed their own. They began flooding back to Central America in 1996, when the United States began to deport immigrants convicted of various petty and serious crimes. Many of the *maras* continue to carry the names of, and be connected with, the gangs to which they belonged in the United States, (such as Salvatrucha, MS-13 and Mara 18). They are described in social terms as representing a sector of the population that is young (female and male), commonly unemployed and lacking opportunities for economic improvement in the period of peace and reconstruction since the war.

The *maras* are known to be well organized, with linkages throughout the Americas, and with time they have equipped themselves with more sophisticated weaponry, moving from knives and machetes to the now more common use of small automatic weapons, acquired through the large black market in weaponry in Guatemala. As the press and Guatemalan authorities have warned, the *maras* are no longer just an urban phenomenon, but have increasingly spread into rural, local society. The populations controlled by the *maras* live in an environment of constant fear, where nearly all aspects of public life are affected by these groups' practices of selling and enforcing 'security'. It is now common for bus drivers, schoolchildren and everyday commuters in Guatemala City to have to pay a toll to the *maras* when passing through the areas controlled by them (*zonas rojas*). Those who refuse to pay are assaulted and sometimes killed. Shop owners in gang-controlled parts of the city must also pay a regular fee to the *maras* for security, any failure to comply meaning that their property and even their own survival are put at risk. The *maras* have also been known to levy 'rape taxes' on the parents of young neighbourhood girls, intended to ensure their daughters are not attacked.

Despite the widely recognized terror caused by the *maras* in Guatemalan society, no official investigations have been undertaken to confirm, or refute, the extent of their culpability for the totality of violence in the country. Indeed, a number of human rights organizations and academics now point to the problem of the government's heavy-handed militarized tactics (*mano dura*) and its over-emphasis on the *mara* as the only security issue. These analysts argue that the *maras* should be understood not as the perpetrators of violence but as victims of the same. Academics have also stressed that gang members do not join a *mara* out of a desire to engage in violence. They value the friendship, protection, unity and solidarity that membership brings in communities where families have broken down and state institutions have failed (Levenson 2003; Winton 2004). There is also recognition that cases of mistaken identity often occur. 'For the police, the youths' appearance – baggy pants and T-shirts, tattoos – is enough to signal that they are gang members and therefore subject to arrest, despite there being no law to justify this' (Mejía 2007: 27). The *maras* are also directly on the receiving end of the institutional violence applied by the police, military and paramilitary forces, aimed at both their incarceration and their elimination.

Indeed, critics of the state's handling of the problem of violence argue that the government itself and the weakness of state legal institutions are responsible for the creation of the climate of impunity in which the *maras* are able to operate efficiently. This climate of impunity is demonstrated by Guatemala's one-digit conviction rate (1.4 per cent) for murder in general and the even more dramatic failure to convict in cases related to the killing of women in recent years. The implications of these findings are, as the UN Special Rapporteur on extrajudicial, summary or arbitrary executions, Philip Alston, has commented, that 'Guatemala is a good place to commit murder, because you will almost certainly get away with it' (Alston 2006: 17).

Gendered violence

Since 2001 over 2,200 women and girls have been murdered in Guatemala and the rate of murders is on the increase. Between 1 January and 5 May 2006, according to police statistics, 229 women and girls were killed.[3] Although a small percentage of total killings (90 per cent of those killed are men), what is striking about these killings is the frequent involvement of extreme acts of cruelty before the murder takes place. In these cases it is common for the bodies of murdered women to appear in a public space after a disappearance of several days bearing the signs of rape, bodily mutilation, dismemberment and other forms of torture. According to research carried out by the Human Rights Ombudsman's Office (*Procuradoría de Derechos Humanos*, PDH), in the majority (80 per cent) of murders of men firearms are used, with no intimate physical contact occurring between the victim and the perpetrator. In the case of women, however, firearms are used in 69 per cent of the murders and in 31 per cent of cases the attackers use direct physical violence (knives, blunt objects, strangulation). Many victims are raped, tortured or mutilated before being killed. According to the PDH, 'the difference is that in the case of women they are made to suffer more before being killed'.

The alarming number of female killings has caught the attention of the international community and prompted demonstrations across Latin America and hearings in the European Parliament and the US Congress. Many international and national human rights groups and country analysts have been shocked at the lack of interest on the part of the Guatemalan state and its reluctance to investigate the circumstances of these deaths properly, despite the level of international concern. The response by the police authorities to reports of missing women or girls, including cases where there are witnesses to their abduction, continues to be inadequate. Amnesty International has received many reports of cases where the police failed in their duty to take urgent action to prevent injury to women and girls believed to be at immediate risk. The failure of the authorities to identify, detain and bring to justice those responsible for killing women and girls sends the message to perpetrators that they will not be held accountable for their actions. To further illustrate this, it should be noted that whilst 2,781 women were killed in this manner in the period 2000–8, only 16 sentences related to this kind of crime were issued by the Guatemalan courts.[4] In addition, cases have been identified where one or more of the perpetrators were agents of the national police.

The climate of impunity produced by the inaction of the legal apparatus is held by human rights organizations and other analysts as representative of the much greater failure of the state to work as it should have done to implement the Peace Accords. In a recent paper Handy (2004: 534–5) writes:

> The Peace Accords signed in December 1996 did not pave the road to peace and an end to violence and social dislocation, and the presence of lots of guns led to accelerating rates of criminal violence and decreasing levels of confidence in the police and judiciary.

The state's responsibility for the increasing levels of violence is clearly stated in the UNHCR's report for 2006. The report is explicit in stating that this has stemmed not only from the failure of successive governments to enforce agreements on cultural, economic and social rights, but also from the active continuation of a logic of counter-insurgency and the direct connection of powerful sectors of the military, police and government with organized crime in the country. Indeed, the brutality of the violence (often involving torture, rape and humiliation) – common techniques of terror in the civil war – are highlighted by some analysts as telling of the continuation of a 'moral and social' re-education or cleansing project started during the civil war. Rape was also used as a systematic means of terrorizing indigenous and peasant communities in the civil war.

Social cleansing and hidden powers

In recent years there has been a series of killings that many analysts now see as being politically motivated. Indeed, questions are asked as to whether the state's lack of response to the general context of violence is an intentional means of covering the tracks of more purposive acts of political violence. 'While many acts of violence appear to be common crime, the number and patterns of the cases point to a systematic targeting of civil society actors and others involved in "anti-impunity" initiatives' (Peacock and Beltrán 2003). Lists of these targeted killings are updated by the various human rights and public research centres in the country. Further reports of politically motivated killings also appeared during the 2007 national election campaign in Guatemala. Around 50 people, most of them running for the National Unity for Hope Party and Rigoberta Menchu's 'Encounter for Guatemala' Party, were killed in the course of local campaigning before the elections. According to some reports these killings significantly helped to prepare the ground for the former army general, Otto Peréz Molina. However, despite the support this violence might have given Molina, it was the social democrat, Álvaro Colom Caballeros, running on a platform of reducing violence by tackling poverty, who eventually won the 2007 election with 52.7 per cent of the vote. Since winning the presidency Colom has launched a government-backed programme to ensure that the Peace Accords are finally put into practice. This has not, however, reduced the violent trend.

Academics and human rights organizations in the country, such as the Association for Crime Prevention (APREDE), claim that organized and secretive groups, possibly elements of the pre-accord paramilitary patrol groups (*patrullas de auto-defensa civil*, PAC), are performing a social cleansing scheme that involves the murdering of supposed delinquents (gang members as well as political leaders) and the targeting of those leading non-conformist lifestyles (homosexuals, transvestites, prostitutes and so on). During the civil war PAC were formed as a paramilitary force to help the Guatemalan army in its counter-insurgency efforts. Government collusion in these acts is seen to be signalled by the fact that the police and military have made little effort to follow up the well-founded suspicions that the PAC carried out similar acts of state-sanctioned violence during the civil war, and that although officially disbanded and discredited for their role in earlier human right violations these organizations' members continue to receive a state pension.

Peacock and Beltrán (2003) also discuss the evidence for the existence of a series of upper-level 'hidden' and parallel political powers that through informal linkages also influence the official workings of the police, military and government. Operating under a series of pseudonyms (e.g. El Sindicato, La Cofradia, the Moreno Network) these hidden powers are described as 'networks of powerful individuals who use their positions and contacts in public and private sectors to enrich themselves from illegal activities (organized crime, drug trafficking, skimming, bribery, kickbacks and other forms of corruption) and to protect themselves from prosecution' (Peacock and Beltrán 2003: 6). An Amnesty International report (2002) claims that there is an 'unholy' alliance between traditional sectors of the oligarchy, some 'new entrepreneurs', the police and military and common criminals. In addition to reaping huge profits, the hidden powers in Guatemala use their connections with political actors and with the military and police to intimidate and eliminate those that get in their way, know too much, offer competition, or try to investigate their activities. Many victims are targeted because they seek to investigate and prosecute current or retired government and military officials for human rights abuses committed during the war (Peacock and Beltrán 2003: 6).

In addition to connections with organized crime, Schirmer's (1999) and Keen's (2003) research also draws attention to the continuing dominance of structures of counter-insurgency in the Guatemalan police and military. The peacetime enemies are defined as criminals and subversives, 'a transition that is in some ways smoother than it might appear, since the rebels were also referred to as criminals and subversives' (Schirmer 1999: 92–107). Although promises were made in the Peace Accord process of a change in the logic, financing and techniques of the country's security apparatus, recent studies demonstrate that little change has occurred apart from the introduction of new rhetoric. Whilst efforts were made to meet the targets of demobilization through a reduction of the armed forces from 46,900 to 31,423 soldiers and a reduction in the number of officers, the budget for the armed forces has not been reduced. Indeed, a peace analyst quoted by Keen states: 'The army is supposed to have been reduced by 33 per cent since the end of the war, but the budget is still growing' (2003: 8). In addition to this continuation of high levels of financing, no real change has been made in the geographical deployment of the military. As a result the military continues with a deployment oriented towards internal counter-insurgency and not for the defence of Guatemala's maritime and territorial jurisdiction and airspace (Keen 1998: 9).

Security sector reform (SSR) intentions after the Peace Accords further included the abolition of existing police forces and the creation of a new expanded National Civil Police (PNC). The PNC was meant to give substance to a new way of policing in tune with the building of democratic governance and effective law enforcement. However, despite the efforts to create, finance and equip this new police force, there are many indications from existing command structures and financing that police institutions remain subordinate to central government bodies and militarized to varying degrees. In addition, reports from the Guatemalan media of police involvement in different forms of illegal activity ranging from drug smuggling to murder appear to indicate that they continue to share with the military links to organized crime.

Echoes of the civil war

With the characteristics described above the violence being carried out in present-day Guatemala is clearly linked to the legacy of the civil war. This was a civil war that stands out in the history of the region for its length and brutality. Guatemala suffered the longest internal armed conflict in Central America. Over 200,000 people were brutally killed during the civil war that began with a US-backed coup in 1954 against the democratically elected government of President Jacobo Arbenz. At the height of the counter-insurgency campaign led by the ruling military government in the 1970s and early 1980s, approximately 1 million people were internally displaced and hundreds of thousands fled the country from a population numbering a little over 8 million at the time.

Large-scale repression did not begin until the 1960s, but directly after the takeover the army began gathering the names of those who had been active under the socialist administration. In association with the CIA they put together a list of some 70,000 people that would become a much-used reference source once the killing began. Throughout the 1960s political violence increased, focused not only on the organized guerrilla force in the eastern highlands but on all political opponents, intellectuals and left-wing sympathizers. Between 1966 and 1977 some 10,000 combatants were killed in a bid to destroy a guerrilla force that at that time numbered no more than 500. In the capital the campaign to eradicate 'traitors to the fatherland' gave birth to paramilitary death squads, such as the *Mano Blanco* (white hand), who took part in a process to eradicate unionists, left-wing and centrist politicians and students. Victims were usually abducted by men in unmarked cars and later their mutilated bodies were found, dumped in public places by the roadside.

Although with different cycles of intensity and geographical focus, this kind of violence continued throughout the period of the civil war. Driven by a desire to escape this violence, drawing inspiration from Catholic liberation theology and receiving some Cuban military assistance, the guerrilla movement grew and became increasingly well established as a counterweight to the military. Four main guerrilla organizations were created: the Guatemala Workers' Party (PGT), which operated in Guatemala City and on the Pacific coast; the Rebel Armed Forces (*Fuerzas Armadas Rebeldes*, FAR), which fought in the lowland jungle of the Petén; the Guerrilla Army of the Poor (EGP), which had several fronts in northern Quiché; and the Organization of People in Arms (ORPA), which functioned in San Marcos and Atitlán. The last two of these organizations were the most open to the entry into their ranks of the country's majority indigenous population, who would bear the brunt of military oppression in the course of the 1980s. Important grassroots organizations, such as the Committee for Peasant Unity (CUC), were also formed at this time. However, while some were involved in efforts of active resistance other members of indigenous populations were forced to participate in the PAC, in the process themselves becoming part of the system of repression and responsibility for the intimidation, murder and abductions of the period.

By 1988, two years after the return to civilian rule, the level of violence had not decreased, but rather had increased sharply. Many of the people's worst fears were confirmed when 22 bodies were found in a shallow grave near a village in the department of Chimaltenango. The killings continued throughout President Cerezo's term in office and there was no real effort either to find the bodies of the disappeared or to bring the guilty to trial. In 1990 Cerezo handed power to President Serrano but the human rights situation in the country remained bleak under the Guatemalan governments of the early 1990s, with daily abductions, torture, intimidation and extrajudicial execution still commonplace. According to a number of US human rights groups, 500 Guatemalans either 'disappeared' or were killed in extrajudicial executions in 1992 alone. The persistent failure of the civilian government to control the military, together with a rising international interest in human and indigenous rights and development policy, celebrations of the quincentenary of the 'discovery' of the Americas and the award in 1992 of the Nobel Peace Prize to the female indigenous activist, Rigoberta Menchu, helped, however, to focus increased international attention on the ongoing violence and the plight of Guatemala's indigenous population. New international pressure (accompanied by financing) was brought to bear on the Guatemalan government and the then dominant guerrilla group, the Guatemalan National Guerrilla Unity (URNG), to continue peace talks started in the late 1980s and to reach a peace agreement.

In 1995 the Indigenous Rights Accords were signed as a part of these new peace talks, and as a means of ending the oppression and marginalization of the indigenous population through the legal security of the ILO Convention 169's stipulations regarding participation and prior consultation. This agreement was to form the start of a series of accords that were designed ostensibly to defend and realize social, political and economic rights under the banner of the 1996 Peace Accords. A truth commission, overseen by the UN Verification Mission to Guatemala (MINUGUA), was also established to investigate human rights abuses committed during the war. In all, 2,928 URNG combatants were demobilized and issued with temporary identification cards, and 535,102 weapons and rounds of ammunition were handed over to MINUGUA. However, despite these successes and setting the scene for tackling the post-war climate of impunity described above, the commission lacked legal teeth and was short-lived (January to May 1997), and the legal stipulation that only abuses 'linked to the armed conflict' should be investigated meant that its powers were limited from the outset and no names were named. Despite this, MINUGUA did manage to conclude that 93 per cent of the violent killings during the civil war were carried out by the army, civil patrols, the police and death squads commanded or defended by the government.

Other efforts to attribute blame also ended in similar frustration and disappointment. The Catholic Church-backed research team *Proyecto Interdiocesano de Recuperación de la Memoria Histórica* (REMHI) painstakingly documented the civil war atrocities over a period of three years, proving that government military forces were responsible for 90 per cent of the killings between 1980 and 1993, and the guerrillas for the remainder. Two days after the report was presented, Bishop Juan Geradi, the leader of the REMHI project, was found beaten to death at his home in Guatemala City. The assassination outraged the nation and provoked widespread demonstrations, but the investigation was allowed by the government to drag on for three years before charges were finally made against three military chiefs and a priest. The Geradi case confirmed the weakness of the nation's justice system and the threat of political violence that remains in the post-war period.

It is evident from the above that war is far more than a memory in Guatemala. Indeed, it is suggested here that in many respects the Peace Accords failed to end little more than the formalities of war. Although no simple connections of cause and effect are made today, an awareness of the past highlights the linkages between present-day violence and the relations and violations of the past. The existence of clandestine groups and criminal organizations in present-day Guatemala is clearly linked to arrangements for political loyalty and counter-insurgency in the war. Indeed, many of the techniques employed and much of the extremity of violence seen today (i.e. kidnapping, rape, torture, bodily dismemberment, lynching) have their inspiration in the terror tactics used by the military during the civil war.

As a result of the longevity of the war and what many see as the failures of disarmament and demobilization, and with it the joint conditions of a lot of guns and little work, these kinds of violence have also remained a part of Guatemalan society. Indeed, they have become socialized mechanisms that express meaning and needs at different levels of life. In this way they represent *everyday* violence in the sense expressed by Nancy Scheper-Hughes (1992) as experiences that normalize petty brutalities and terror at the community level and create a common sense or acceptance of violence.

> The normalization of internecine violence in the broader context of political violence makes sense if the extent of the pain and terror that political repression causes is fully appreciated as a 'pressure cooker' generating everyday violence through the systematic distortion of social relations and sensibilities.
>
> (Bourgois in Scheper-Hughes and Bourgois 2004: 431)

At another level these gruesome acts also represent *symbolic* violence, or the internalized humiliations and legitimation of inequality and hierarchy that Bourdieu sees as being 'exercised through cognition and misrecognition, knowledge and sentiment, with the unwitting consent of the dominated' (1997: 162). However, in verifying these connections to a legacy of violence we think it is also important to question whether the civil war is sufficient explanation for the extent and severity of continuing violence in Guatemala. Recognizing that the kinds of violence described above are only a partial picture of the total panorama of violence, it is pertinent to question whether another interpretation of events can be created when, as in the following pages, other facets and types of violence are revealed. Indeed, in the course of highlighting this wider panorama it is also worth considering whether it is possible to escape the dangers of the largely static portrayal of the role and occurrence of violence in Guatemalan society in existing 'continuity of violence' explanations.

A culture and environment of violence

In Guatemala, and in Latin America more generally, there has been a tendency, as evident in many of the great literary works, to over-mythologize the embodiment of violence, to the extent that it has become a static metaphor for the nature not only of individuals and their culture, but also of the nation itself. In the process of disputing and attempting to transform understandings of society in the region, connections have been built between mutually sustaining relationships of *cultures of violence* and the *violence of the natural environment*. The result has been that political instability is connected to the extremes (mountains, volcanoes, earthquakes, floods and hurricanes) of the Latin American landscape in an effort to form an alternative nationalism that is both naturally brutal and entirely naturalized by the population. The problem with this characterization of Latin American nature is that it cuts both ways:

> While it unveils the criminal acts of government that seem to exist merely to serve the interests of a blessed minority, it also has the

danger of portraying Latin Americans as children of Cain, unable to erase their father's mark and unable to escape a land where brutality is bred in the primal bone.

(Grandin 2004: 172)

The Guatemalan sociologist Edelberto Torres-Rivas states, for example, that during the 1970s and 1980s Latin America

Passed through one of those authoritarian cycles, to which the region appears to be fated, in its oscillating path between democracy and dictatorship. Dictatorships have been a recurrent element in the region, and up until now there is no evidence to suggest that ... we shall not see them in the future.

(Torres-Rivas 1999)

In Guatemala, observers describe victims of the civil war's genocide both as descendants of Cain and as children of Abel, incapable of escaping the temptation and weight of centuries and centuries of violence (e.g. Green 1999). By not disaggregating or historicizing Cold War repression, these scholars naturalize it, evoking an image close to Walter Benjamin's famous aphorism of a 'state of emergency' that is not the exception but the rule (Grandin 2004: 172), or Agamben's thesis of a 'state of exception' (Agamben 2005).

A closer look at the changing nature and spread of violence in Guatemala indicates a socialization of violence that is not locked into an essentialized or easily recognizable culture of violence, but where history and political processes in the *longue durée* continue to have clear importance.

In the last few years new kinds of violence have developed alongside those apparently embedded in Guatemalan society. In the last few years, apparently embedded violence has also taken on a more intense character. The *maras* are part of this changing complex of violence that at once reminds the observer of the past and the present. However, so too are other types of violence – that is, land invasions and evictions, political protests, drug-related crime, the abuse and smuggling of children and women for prostitution, kidnappings, hangings and vigilantism. These acts of violence are embedded in the country's history of war, but are also part of a new political economy of violence produced by much more recent and ongoing processes of international trade liberalization, multicultural and other internationally inspired development reforms, urbanization and international migration. Acknowledgement of this not only makes us realize that violence in Guatemala is more than the civil war, but that to identify the perpetrators of this violence it is necessary to look beyond poor street youth and the links between organized crime and the state, to national business elites and the too easily ignored collusion and vagaries of the international community.

History as an ongoing process forces an appreciation of the catalytic power of political reaction to breed accelerating rhythms of frustration, fear and extremism. Indeed, it shows that violence in Guatemala is the product not only of a national past but of different time frames that are further compounded by global political and economic processes, from the Cold War to the present. Indeed, external forces have as great a role to play in the character of violence in Guatemala as internal historical memories and structures. After all, many of the brutal techniques of violence seen in Guatemala today did not originate there. The Guatemalan military forces were taught the use of torture and rape as tactics of terror by members of the CIA, sent by the Reagan Administration to assist efforts of anti-communist insurgency in Guatemala during the civil war (Culluther 2004). In the same way present-day structures of violence in Guatemala are not just the product of internal historical processes but rather the outcome of their combination with external political and economic pressures. In recent years the most important of these external pressures has been the arrival of neoliberalism and national adaptation to it.

A wider panorama of violence

Bourdieu has argued that

> The violence exerted in families, workshops, banks, offices, police station, prisons and even hospitals and schools ... is, in the last analysis, the product of 'inert violence' of economic structures and social mechanisms relayed by the active violence of people.
>
> (1997: 233)

Whilst we agree with Bourdieu's emphasis on economic structures and social mechanisms, the argument we make here aims to emphasize that these structures and mechanisms are not 'inert' but are actively violent in their own right. Whilst some social structures and mechanisms remain present, their character and therefore role in either the direct application or indirect formation of spaces of violence are seen to change. In the case of Guatemala, a further key example of this is the development and transformative role played by changes in the country's economy.

Burdened with a growing debt and at the behest of the World Bank, its principal lender, Guatemala shifted course and began implementing neoliberal development policies in the 1980s. In line with other Latin American states, this shift ended a trend in national import-substituting industrialization and opened the doors to international trade liberalization and the scaling down of the national government bureaucracy. Following the signing of the Peace Accords neoliberalism became further established in the country through a new discourse of development formed with the assistance of the international community in which human rights are balanced by decentralization, the creation of new free trade zones and assistance to the poor through policies aimed at privatization of land and their connection to the formal international market. For the elites and traditional landowning oligarchy neoliberalism opened up new opportunities and channels for the reorganization of their previously stagnating economic interests and the opportunity for some to diversify into new forms of production and business. Neoliberalism allowed sectors of the Guatemalan oligarchy to become transnational, moving beyond national borders in both their investment interests and residential patterns.

However, for the country's majority poor the shift to neoliberalism failed to generate improvement in their lives and further increased the already enormous gap between the upper and lower echelons of society, and between ethnic groups. While the richest segment of the population saw their share of national GDP grow from 62.7 per cent in 1989 to 64.0 per cent in 2002, the poorest sector of the population saw their share decrease from 2.7 per cent to 1.7 per cent (UNDP 2002). According to the National Institute of Statistics (INE), from 1989 to 2004 the general level of poverty decreased (from 62 per cent to 57 per cent). However, according to UNDP (2004) these improving figures must be nuanced by recognition that almost three-quarters of the indigenous population remain poor.

Although neoliberalism has enabled the conditions for national economic growth, the form of these new economic activities – that is, industrialized agriculture and *maquila* industries (sweatshops) aimed at North American markets – and their placement on the boundary between the formal and informal sectors have furthermore resulted in few benefits for a society still predominantly reliant on communal or familial *minifundia* (small-scale agricultural production). Here the systemic violence of capitalism cannot be reduced to the 'evil' intentions of individuals, but to frequently objective, often uncanny and anonymous acts (Žižek 2009: 11). By setting the context for new forms of economic exploitation (no ownership of the means of production, low wages and poor labour conditions), neoliberalism can be seen to have contributed further to the existing structural conditions for violence, and not only at the macro-level. A series of very real links can be made between new forms of economic production, the smuggling and mixing of legal products with illegal products and the violence of those responsible for keeping this illegal trade unchecked by border controls or the curious.

The changing geography of violence

Although a process started in the 1960s, the changing nature of the economy has also led to the speeding up of migration from rural areas to the cities, or beyond the borders of the country. Guatemala is a major recipient of migrant worker remittances, registering $2.6 billion in 2004 and $3.6 billion in 2006 – that is, more than the total channelled to the region by overseas development assistance.[5] A fall in coffee prices and the changing land usage connected to the development of agro-industry have left people without jobs or land. Added to this, the new *maquila* industries in urban centres and their attraction in terms of work, urban services and lifestyles, have tempted people away from their land and into ever growing urban slums. However, rather than finding connection with the benefits of globalization through this process many find themselves expelled from the formal economy. As Davis argues,

Rather than being the 'engines of growth' ... cities are rapidly becoming 'dumping grounds' for those who are excluded from globalizing and increasingly technological and informational production processes, with slums emerging as a fully franchised solution to the problem of warehousing the twenty-first century's surplus humanity.

(2004: 28)

Today's slum dwellers are seen to serve no purpose for the dominating groups in society, who feel no qualms in engaging in increasingly violent ways to keep them out of their lives (Rodgers 2007). In Guatemala City, as in other Latin American cities, urban morphologies now demonstrate a form of 'splintered urbanism' that underlines social, racial and class divisions. Cities are now built to reinforce class differences and to divide the poor physically from the rich through the construction of walled and gated communities, high-rise office buildings, life-zones (*zonas vivas*) and shopping malls (Caldeira 2000). The access to and safety of these fortified non-spaces are supervised by private security companies and externally strengthened by heightened public security measures in the poor and frequently physically isolated areas of the city.

Whereas urbanization is easily connected with violence, care must be taken in characterizing the role and identity of citizens in its expression. Contrary to common perceptions, no easy connections can be made between poor urban neighbourhoods and acts of violence. In Guatemala, the available statistics demonstrate that 33 per cent of the hangings and 40 per cent of the *femicidios* (killings of women) have taken place in the capital. The UNDP reports that 'the poorest municipalities, where over 25 per cent of the population live in conditions of poverty, are not the places where concentration of ... homicide takes place' (2007: 29). It is therefore not possible to establish a positive correlation between poverty and violence. Whilst there are clearly high rates of violence in poor urban neighbourhoods, some kinds of violence (such as drug-related violence) also occur with high frequency in the playground life-zones of the rich and wealthy communities outside the city (such as Escuintla).

As Rodgers (2007) underlines, through the process of urbanization political and social violence have become joined together. Using urbanization as a point of departure, Rodgers nuances the picture of the *mara* created by earlier writers by arguing that the gangs provide 'micro-regimes of order as well as communal forms of belonging to definite, albeit bounded, collective entities, in a wider context of chronic insecurity and social breakdown' (2007: 10). In many ways, he argues, they correspond to forms of 'insurgent citizenship' (Holsten 1999: 158), attempting the violent construction of new spaces for 'possible alternative futures'. This underlines the importance of the turmoil and the opportunities gang structures create, but also the repeated failure to challenge the system as a whole. In their drive towards self-sufficiency and turf-war survival the gangs, just as peasant rebels before them, fail to question the basis of the existing larger social order.

Recent economic changes and globalization have also had violent unforeseen consequences for the projects and actions of the middle classes and the previously powerful. In Guatemala, as elsewhere in the Americas, middle-class people 'lament the limited "popular" enthusiasm for human rights and often act, through politics, churches, charities, NGO and citizens groups, to build a more caring society' (Gledhill 2006). Yet they also contradict these values on a daily basis through actions in defence of class interests, for example in questions of urban development. Everyday violence is expressed here as an enforcement of the right to accumulate. It is, however, also possible to link this everyday violence further with more organized expressions of crime and violence rooted in a sectoral sense of betrayal. Whilst some elites have managed to capitalize on the transformation of the national economy, others less well suited to the qualifications of the time have felt betrayed by the failure of reality to meet their expectations of and aspirations to new prosperity. This is particularly the case amongst military elites. In an era of thawing Cold War tensions, where human rights and investment climate concerns take precedence over earlier paradigmatic struggles, the Guatemalan private sector and the United States have tended to retreat from their earlier unquestioning support of the army. For some elites this left a sense of betrayal and marginalization, and may help to explain further the deviation of some of the upper echelons of the military into criminal activities and an apparent symbiosis with organized crime (Keen 2003).

Conclusion

The pages above have sketched out the extent of the violence with which post-war Guatemala continues to struggle. As we have demonstrated, this violence is expressed in a variety of physical forms and impacts; but have little meaning or explanation without having regard to their interconnections, intertwined relationships and their setting in a larger social history and political economy. It is through connection with this larger picture that it is possible to identify connections between present-day violence and the impact of Guatemala's civil war. These connections suggest that present-day violence may to some extent represent an extension of the war's conflict into a more domestic setting, a symbolic, socialized and everyday violence. However, they also help to underline that present-day violence is not only the historical product of recent war but the result of much longer processes of structural violence that stretch from the distant past of conquest to the economic neoliberalism of the present. This structural violence is not abstracted from physical acts of violence, in that they are sustained not only by political and economic forces but by persisting social structures, natural forces, prejudices and the premeditated actions of individuals operating at different levels within its whole.

Notes

1 A version of this chapter was first published as an article in *Forum for Redevelopment Studies*, 35(1): 2009.
2 Also see Guatemalan Commission for Historical Clarification report. Online, available at: http://shr.aaas.org/guatemala/ceh/report/english/toc.html.
3 See Amnesty International website. Online, available at: www.amnesty.org/en/library/info/AMR34/019/2006/en.
4 Report to the UN ombudsman for extrajudicial killings, Guatemala, 2006.
5 See multilateral investment fund website. Online, available at: www.iadb.org/mif/remesas_map.cfm?language=English.

Bibliography

Agamben, G. (2005) *State of Exception*, Chicago and London: University of Chicago Press.
Alston, P. (2006) 'Los Derechos Civiles y Politicos, en Particular las cuestiones relacionados con las desapariciones', UN Report to the General Assembly A/HRC/4/20/Add.2.
Arriaga, I. and Godoy, L. (2000) 'Diagnóstico de la seguridad cuidadania y de la violencia en América Latina', *Revista de CEPAL*, 70, April.
Bourdieu, P. (1977) *Outline of a Theory of Practice*, Cambridge: Cambridge University Press.
Bourdieu, P. (1997) *Pascalian Meditations*, Stanford, CT: Stanford University Press.
Bourgois, P. (2005) 'The continuum of violence in war and peace: post-cold war lessons from El Salvador', in N. Scheper-Hughes and P. Bourgois (eds) *Violence in War and Peace: An Anthology*, Oxford: Blackwell Publishing.
Briceño, Leon R. (2002) 'La nueva violencia urbana de América Latina. DOSSIE: Sociologiás', Year 4, No. 8, Porte Alegre, Brazil.
Buvinic, M., Morrison, A. and Shifter, M. (eds) (2000) *La Violencia en América Latina y el Caribe: un marco de referencia para la acción*, Washington: BID.
Caldeira, T.P.R. (2000) *City of Walls: Crime, Segregation and Citizenship in Sao Paulo*, Berkeley: University of California Press.
Carey, D. (2004) 'Maya perspectives on the 1999 referendum in Guatemala', *Latin American Perspectives*, 139, 31(6), November: 69–95.
Comaroff, J. and Comaroff, J. (2000) 'Millennium capitalism: first thoughts on a second coming', *Public Culture*, 31: 34–53.
Cojtí Cuxil, D. (2002) 'Educational reform in Guatemala: lessons from negotiations between indigenous civil society and the state', in Sieder (ed.) *Multiculturalism in Latin America: Indigenous Rights, Diversity and Democracy*, London: ILAS/Palgrave Macmillan.
Culluther, N. (2004) *CIA: Guatemala Operación PBSuccess*, Guatemala: Tipografia Nacional.
Davis, M. (2006) *Planet of Slums*, London: Verso.
Figueroa Ibarra, C. (2004) *Protesta popular y cooptación de masas en Guatemala*, Mexico: Universidad Autónoma de Puebla.
Fischer, T. and Benson, P. (2006) *Broccoli and Desire: Global Connections and Maya Struggle in Postwar Guatemala*, Stanford, CT: Stanford University Press.
Gaviria, A. and Pages, C. (1999) *Patterns of Crime and Victimisation in Latin America*, IDB Working Paper No. 408.
Gledhill, J. (2006) 'Resisting the global slum: politics, religion and consumption in

the remaking of life worlds in the 21st century', *Bulletin of Latin American Research*, 25(3): 322–39.

Goldstein, D. (2004) *The Spectacular City: Violence and Performance in Urban Bolivia*, Durham: Duke University Press.

Grandin, G. (2004) *The Last Colonial Massacre: Latin America in the Cold War*, Chicago, IL: Chicago University Press.

Green, L. (1999) *Fear as a Way of Life: Mayan Widows in Rural Guatemala*, New York: Colombia University Press.

Hale, C (2002) 'Does multi-culturalism menace? Governance, cultural rights and the politics of identity in Guatemala', *Journal of Latin American Studies*, 34: 485–524.

Hale, C and Millimán, R. (2004) 'Rethinking indigenous politics in the era of the "indio permitido"', *NACLA Report on the Americas*, September/October, New York.

Handy, J. (2004) 'Chicken thieves, witches and judges: vigilante justice and customary law in Guatemala', *Journal of Latin American Studies*, 36: 533–61.

Kapferer, B. (1997) *The Feast of the Sorcerer: Practices of Consciousness and Power*, Chicago, IL: University of Chicago Press.

Keen, D. (1998) 'The economic functions of the violence in civil wars', Adelphi Paper 320, London/Oxford: International Institute for Strategic Studies/Oxford University Press.

Keen, D. (2003) 'Demobilising Guatemala', Working Paper 37, Crisis States Working Papers, Series 1, London School of Economics.

Levenson, B. (2004) 'The life that makes us die/the death that makes us live', *Radical History Review*.

Londoño, J.L. and Guerrero, R. (1999) 'Violencia en America Latina: epedemiologia y costos', IDB Working Paper R-375.

Mejía, T. (2007) 'In Tegucigalpa the iron fist fails', *NACLA Report on the Americas*, 40(4), July/August, New York.

Moser, C. and McIlwaine, C. (2000) 'Violence in Colombia and Guatemala: Community Perceptions of Interrelationships with Social Capital', unpublished paper, Crime and Violence Conference, Colombia.

Moser, C. and McIlwaine, C. (2001) 'Violence in a post-conflict context: urban perceptions from Guatemala', Washington: World Bank/Sida.

Nordstrom, C. (2004) 'The violence of tomorrow', in N. Whitehead (ed.) *Violence*, School of American Research Advanced Seminar Series, Santa Fe and Oxford: School of American Research Press/James Currey.

Nordstrom, C. and Robben, A. (1995) *Fieldwork under Fire: Contemporary Studies of Violence and Survival*, Berkeley: University of California Press.

Peacock, S.C. and Beltrán, A. (2003) *Hidden Powers in Post-conflict Guatemala: Illegal Armed Groups and the Forces Behind them*, Washington: Washington Office on Latin America.

Rodgers, D. (2007) 'Slum wars of the 21st century: the new geography of conflict in Central America', Working Paper 10, Crisis States Working Papers, Series 2, London School of Economics.

Rose, N. (1999) *Powers of Freedom: Reframing Political Thought*, Cambridge: Cambridge University Press.

Scheper-Hughes, N. (1992) *Death without Weeping: The Violence of Everyday Life in Brazil*, Berkeley: University of California Press.

Scheper-Hughes, N. and Bourgois, P. (2004) *Violence in War and Peace: An Anthology*, Malden and Oxford: Blackwell Publishing.

Schirmer, J. (1999) 'The Guatemalan politico-military project: legacies for a violent peace?', *Latin American Perspectives*, 26(2): 92–107.

Schmidt, B. and Schröder, I. (eds) (2001) The *Anthropology of Violence and Conflict*, London: Routledge.

Taussig, M. (1983) *The Devil and Commodity Fetishism in South America*, Pembroke, NC: University of North Carolina Press.

Taussig, M. (1997) *The Magic of the State*, London and New York: Routledge.

Torres-Rivas, E. (1999) 'Epilogue: Notes on Terror, Violence, Fear and Democracy', in K. Koonings and D. Kruijit (eds) *Societies of Fear: The Legacy of Civil War, Violence and Terror in Latin America*, London: Zed Books.

Torres-Rivas, E. (2005), unpublished paper presented at conference on 'New Violence in Central America', University of Utrecht, Holland.

UNDP (2000) Special Rapporteur on the Sale of Children, Child Prostitution and Child Pornography, *Report on the Mission to Guatemala*, United Nations Development Programme.

UNDP (2004) *Diversidad Etnico-Cultural: la cuidadanía en un estado plural*, Informe Nacional de Desarrollo Humano, Guatemala.

UNDP (2007) *Informe Estadístico de la Violencia en Guatemala*, Guatemala City: Programa de Seguridad Cuidadana y Prevención de la Violencia del PNUD, Guatemala.

Whitehead, N. (ed.) (2004) *Violence*, School of American Research Advanced Seminar Series, Santa Fe and Oxford: School of American Research Press/James Currey.

Winton, A. (2004) 'Young people's view on how to tackle gang-violence in "post-conflict" Guatemala', *Environment and Urbanization*, 16(2): 83–99.

Wolf, E.R (1969) *Peasant Wars of the 20th Century*, Norman: University of Oklahoma Press.

Part VI

Conclusions

16 Reflections on post-war violence and peacebuilding

Mats Berdal

Introduction: general findings

The book began with the observation that societies emerging from war to peace often exhibit high and persistent levels of violence following the formal end of hostilities, and that attempts by legally constituted authorities and external actors to mitigate and reduce such violence have met with decidedly mixed results. The cases covered here – diverse not only in terms of geographical scope but also in terms of their historical, cultural and political context – confirm the truth of this *general* observation: the end of wars very rarely, if ever, marks a definitive break with past patterns of violence. This holds true even when, as in the present volume, the focus of enquiry is confined primarily to acts of deliberate *physical* harm inflicted on people and property.[1]

The case material brought together in the book also makes it clear that to conceive of such violence as little more than the burning embers of a dying conflict, perpetrated, to borrow Donald Rumsfeld's infelicitous phrase, by 'pockets of dead-enders' imperfectly reconciled to a new order, fails to capture its scope as well as its complexity.[2] Post-war violence is frequently widespread, intense and bloody, not just residual and isolated. In Iraq, the death and destruction witnessed *during* the US-led invasion pales against the scale of violence in the years that followed. Indeed, as Toby Dodge notes, by whatever definition of civil war one chooses to adopt, Iraq was by 2005 undeniably in the midst of one (this volume, Chapter 7). As of late 2010, some 107,000 civilians are estimated to have died in Iraq since May 2003, a figure that exceeds the number of people killed – both military and civilians – during the Bosnian war from 1992 to 1995. In Guatemala too, available figures point to a rate of extra-judicial killings in peacetime that is higher than during the civil war and which, worryingly, has only *increased* over the past decade (McNeish and Rivera: this volume, Chapter 15). Even in those cases where the political dispensation at war's end is comparatively clear-cut, the post-war period is often marked by recurring cycles of deadly violence, as Dionísio Babo-Soares' study of the years following East Timor's achievement of full independence in 2002 so clearly illustrates (this volume, Chapter 11).

Post-war violence can also last for a long time. In Cambodia, government forces and troops loyal to Prince Norodom Ranariddh's royalist party fought remnants of the Khmer Rouge until early 1999, some eight years after the formal signing of the Paris Peace Agreements. In the case of Spain, Michael Richards speaks of an 'extended period of violent conflict' lasting from the outbreak of civil war in 1936 until 1948, even though General Franco formally declared an end to the war on 1 April 1939 (this volume, Chapter 2). The violence of both post-bellum Spain and the American South in the Reconstruction era (1865–77) also shows that the blurring of the distinction between war and peace, while it is often seen as a distinguishing characteristic of contemporary armed conflict, is far from unique to the post-Cold War era. Indeed, as Tony Judt has persuasively argued elsewhere, 'violence became part of daily life' in much of Europe in the early years following the end of the Second World War (2007: 37). Nor, it should be added, can forms of post-war violence that have received special attention in recent years and are covered in some detail here – most notably criminal, economic and sexual violence – be said to be a phenomenon of the post-Cold War period alone (Ruff 2001).

For individuals affected by and caught up in post-war violence, its consequences are direct, personal and catastrophic. For societies as a whole, seeking to lay the foundations for lasting peace, the effects of continuing violence of the kind explored in this book are invariably destabilizing and inimical to post-war recovery. Post-war violence breeds fear and a deep sense of insecurity about the future. Failure to bring it under control encourages further violence and typically sets in motion a vicious circle. Crime, initially perhaps largely opportunistic in character, assumes increasingly sophisticated and organized forms, faith in the rule of law is undermined and efforts to nurture the legitimacy and trust vital for effectual peace-building – whether by national authorities, outsiders or both – are weakened, sometimes fatally. As violence begets further violence, the legitimacy of nascent governing structures and institutions seeps away. Middle and professional classes leave the country (if in a position to do so), while vigilantism, mob-violence and various forms of self-policing and 'popular justice', including lynching and the use of 'people's courts', can assume endemic proportions.

The book as a whole, then, offers further evidence showing that post-war societies are prone to violence; that such violence can be extensive and long lasting; and that its effects are always to leave behind deep human and societal scars. While largely confirmatory in nature, these findings are still significant and noteworthy, based as they are on in-depth case studies and qualitative research. By themselves, however, they do not amount to a particularly striking or surprising set of conclusions. Of far greater academic and policy interest is the evidence pointing to large *variations* in the intensity, types and scope of post-war violence across different cases. Indeed, while the aforementioned figures from Iraq and Guatemala offer stark and extreme examples of the scale that such violence can assume, other cases provide a more mixed picture. Of Cambodia, Sorpong Peou notes that new, specifically economic, forms of violence have increased over the past decade but he also stresses that political violence has declined and, strikingly, that 'serious' ethnic violence has virtually disappeared. Viewed against the backdrop of Cambodia's turbulent and bloody recent past, his *overall* conclusion is that developments since the signing of the Paris Peace Accords in 1991 'have been generally far more positive than negative' (Peou: this volume, Chapter 10). Similarly, in respect of Liberia, Torunn Wimpelmann Chaudhary concludes that the overall level of post-war violence has been 'relatively limited', in spite of the brutality and longevity of the war itself (this volume, Chapter 13). And in Bosnia, while certainly not spared of violence, developments since 1995 provide, all in all, a picture of residual violence and instability that compares favourably to many other cases.

The fact that post-war violence, while ubiquitous, is also diverse and of variable intensity, suggests that policy interventions can influence, for better or worse, its trajectory. While escaping post-war violence is, on the evidence presented here, plainly very difficult, it is equally true that such violence does not spring from a simple primordial source but needs to be differentiated and contextualized. It is a finding of obvious importance to policy-makers and external actors engaged in peacebuilding, many of whom have been inclined, not only to confront the challenges of post-war recovery in terms of ready-made templates and off-the-shelf solutions, but to do so on the basis of crude and simplistic readings of the drivers of post-war violence. The reality is that outsiders have on the whole failed to appreciate the complex and multi-faceted character of much post-war violence. Through their actions and policies they have often displayed a disturbing ignorance – sometimes wilful, sometimes not – of the multiple sources and functions of violence, its primary and secondary causes, as well as its local and often highly context-specific roots. Indeed, the very use of 'anarchic', 'collapsed', 'senseless' or 'chaotic' as shorthand descriptions of post-war environments is indicative of this undifferentiated approach. This, indeed, constitutes a further general finding to emerge from the book.

Against these considerations, this concluding chapter is concerned with the policy relevance, broadly conceived, of the case study material brought together in the present volume. It does not attempt to provide a grand synthesis of findings, something that would at any rate not be possible. It seeks instead, through selected examples and drawing on different cases, to demonstrate how and why empirically informed and critical analyses, making judicious and intelligent use of theory and conceptual tools, are indispensible to sound policy-making. To this end, the discussion proceeds in two parts.

Part one briefly revisits three of the general theories or 'approaches' to explaining post-war violence that were reviewed in the introductory chapter of this volume (Suhrke: this volume, Chapter 1): socio-cultural factors, specifically the notion of cultures of violence; faltering institutions and weak states; and the effects of violent and predatory political economies on post-war stability. It notes how each of them requires qualifications in light of the findings provided by the qualitative case studies. As far as the question of policy-relevance is concerned, the case being made is, at least in the abstract, relatively straightforward: effectual peacebuilding demands of policy-makers that they attempt to unpack and engage analytically with the varieties and multiple sources of violence. This requires not only an appreciation of the historical context, socio-economic backdrop and local roots and dynamics of violence, but also of how different forms of violence overlap and interact in post-war settings. Without this, policy interventions aimed at tackling post-war violence are certain to prove, in the words of Wimpelmann Chaudhary, both 'superficial and misplaced'. Crucially, they are also likely to feed into renewed violence.

Applying the findings from the case material in a more concrete fashion, the second part of the conclusion explores the role of international actors engaged in a peacebuilding capacity and is specifically concerned with the impact of their presence on the levels and intensity of post-war violence. While the effectiveness of an international military-cum-civilian presence in terms of controlling violence has typically been treated as a function of its size and 'footprint', underpinned by 'adequate' resources and political commitment, this is only part of the story. The effects of an outside force are often ambiguous and contradictory, especially on levels of violence. It is a further contribution of the present book to show precisely why this is so.

Explaining the varieties of post-war violence

It was noted at the outset that the 'variations in post-war violence suggest that there is no such thing as a generic post-war environment' (Suhrke: this volume, Chapter 1). The basic truth of that observation is amply confirmed by the cases. All of them, without fail, show that the form and intensity assumed by post-war violence in any given case *must* be understood against the backdrop of a historical context, a set of socio-economic realities and a balance of external influences – both regional and global – bearing on the post-war environment, which remains, in important respects, unique to the case in question. At the same time post-war environments do display common features and this has naturally stimulated work on more general studies or 'approaches' aimed at explaining post-war violence. While these have undeniably provided valuable insights, bringing to the fore new and potentially significant points of analytical emphasis, the case material collected here makes it clear that the heuristic value of such general theories is often limited and problematic. Certainly, on their own, each of the approaches discussed below is incomplete, offering at best a partial explanation of post-war violence and, as such, run the risk of missing out on key dimensions of violence in any given case.

Socio-cultural factors: cultures of violence?

Explanations that privilege socio-cultural factors have all tended to emphasize the disruptive effects of protracted war and violence on the social fabric of society, on the bonds of civility, solidarity and trust that underpin relations between individuals and groups. Wars serve to weaken peacetime norms of social behaviour and in so doing 'tend to legitimize the general use of violence within domestic society' (Archer and Gartner 1976: 958). The result is a culture of violence, that is, a 'socially permissive environment within which the use of violence continues, even though violent politics has officially ended' (Steenkamp 2005: 54). Central to this is the idea that violence becomes routinized within the private and public sphere through the lived experience of war and the sanctioned lifting of peacetime prohibitions and taboos, notably on killing. Such cultures, it has reasonably been argued, are particularly likely to emerge where the violence perpetrated during war has been especially brutal, intimate and pervasive, where whole societies have been caught up in conflict and where atrocities and outrages have inordinately targeted civilians and their communities. These are all, of course, features typically associated with civil wars; an association well supported by the evidence collected in the book.

Several of the cases assembled here lend *general* support to the view that protracted wartime violence habituates societies to renewed bouts of violence after the formal end of hostilities. The findings of John Andrew-McNeish and Oscar López Rivera echo other studies of Guatemala and El Salvador that have emphasized the degree to which the 'routinization of terror and the socialisation of violence' during war can leave lasting and pernicious legacies of post-war terror and violence (Preti 2002: 112). In a similar vein, the ease with which large-scale collective violence was mobilized in Iraq after 2003 can be traced in part to 'societal trauma' but also to the fact that violence in Iraq was already deeply ingrained as a 'common currency in both politics and crime' (Dodge: this volume, Chapter 7). The state of near-continuous violence in eastern Congo since the late 1990s, largely unaffected by the supposed end in 2002 of what Gerard Prunier termed 'Africa's world war', has likewise, and not implausibly, been linked to the crystallization of a culture of violence. Specifically, seeking to explain why sexual violence has assumed such extensive and sustained proportions in eastern Congo, Ingrid Samset notes in her important contribution to the volume how the Rwandan genocide of 1994 'introduced large-scale sexual violence into the repertoire of violence of some of the Rwandan Hutus who fled to eastern Congo'. This, she continues, 'probably led to a degree of "normalization" of such violence and a lower collective and individual threshold against reverting to such violence' when armed conflict erupted later in the decade (Samset: this volume, Chapter 12). While causal connections are notoriously hard, if not impossible, to establish in this area, this seems plausible, especially with regard to the role played by the Hutu-led *Forces démocratiques pour la liberation du Rwanda* (FDLR), a movement with a 'powerful core membership' of *genocidaires* from the Rwanda that has been deeply involved in horrific and large-scale sexual violence in the DRC (Spittaels and Hilgert 2008: 8).[3]

And yet other cases show there is no simple or automatic relationship between even very high and protracted levels of atrocious violence and its persistence into the post-war period. Particularly striking in this respect is the case of Lebanon where post-civil war violence has remained low in spite of the fact that the war itself, lasting some 15 years, was distinguished by great brutality and numerous atrocities, including massacres of civilians (Knudsen and Yassin: this volume, Chapter 6). While sectarian tensions are still high and no reconciliation process took place after the war, either formally or informally, 'people did not take justice into their own hands and retributive killings were rare' (ibid.). Especially notable is the fact that little or no retributive violence appears to have occurred in South Lebanon against either the SLA or 'collaborators' after the Israeli withdrawal in 2000.[4] War weariness and the pacifying effects of *Pax Syriana* no doubt provide part of the explanation for this. Moreover, as Knudsen and Yassin explain, politically targeted violence has remained a distinctive feature of the post-war landscape, suggesting perhaps an element of sublimation of wartime violence into more discriminate and instrumental forms. Yet, the case of Lebanon is not an isolated one. Liberia, another instance where wartime violence was intimate, widespread and notoriously horrific, also 'defies general and common-sense assumptions that wars necessarily produce a legacy of continued violence' (Wimpelmann Chaudhary: this volume, Chapter 13).

State weakness and faltering institutions

Given the importance that the international organizations and leading donor countries have attached to 'state-building' as the route to effectual peacebuilding, the subject of state weakness and its relationship to the generation of post-conflict violence is of obvious relevance to any discussion of policy implications.[5] Although the state-building literature is now voluminous, the crux of the argument is easily enough summarized: postwar violence is critically linked to the absence of effective state institutions that can regulate and control the lawful exercise of force, that can provide security and a measure of predictability for its citizens, along with a minimum of basic, life-supporting services. No matter how state weakness or collapse comes about – whether it is through a long drawn-out process of hollowing out from within, as in Liberia and Sierra Leone in the 1970s and 1980s, or it is the result of a sudden, external shock as in Iraq in 2003–4 – unless state capacity and public authority is re-constituted, so the argument runs, violence will remain a contingent liability, while the legitimacy of still functioning institutions will continue to be undermined.

The links between state weakness, or fragility, on the one hand, and post-war violence on the other, is indeed a central theme to emerge from the book. Of particular interest is the light shed by the cases on the *mechanisms* whereby, and the circumstances under which, state weakness is transmuted into violence. As in the discussion of how cultures of violence may give rise to post-war violence, those mechanisms are complex and far from automatic. Three, partly overlapping, sets of conclusions merit special attention. The first concerns the ways in which uncertainty and insecurity result in violence; the second relates to the challenges of disarmament, demobilization and reintegration (DDR) and security sector reform (SSR) in the transitions from war to peace; and the third on how 'strong', as well as weak, states can be a source of post-war violence.

State collapse and violence. Where the salient feature of state weakness is the inability of legally constituted authorities to provide physical security, owing to the loss of its monopoly of armed force, the resulting security vacuum creates conditions for violence of different kinds – political, economic, criminal, identity-driven – to flourish. These will overlap, interact and, inevitably, become increasingly difficult to separate on the ground. But, as Michael Richards reminds us, it is when 'public authority [is] placed fundamentally into question' that violence becomes 'possible' in the first place (this volume, Chapter 2). That is also the moment – though it will necessarily vary in length from case to case depending on circumstances – when 'previously "fuzzy" or secondary identity traits' (Dodge: this volume, Chapter 7) harden and become politicized, when 'us-and-them boundaries' (Richards: this volume, Chapter 2) are activated with violence as result. A striking example of such violence-generating and disintegrative processes at work is provided by the case of Iraq, whose post-conflict phase following the US-led invasion of 2003 was cut short and rapidly overtaken by the effects of a comprehensive collapse of state capacity and authority, so graphically symbolized by the spate of uncontrolled looting in April 2003. The wider relevance of this admittedly extreme case lies in what it tells us about the response of communities and individuals to the loss of the state's coercive capacity, radical uncertainty and escalating violence. Faced with such a situation, populations will, unsurprisingly, try to reduce uncertainty and insecurity in their localities; a process that in Iraq's case involved turning to 'whatever grouping, militia or identity offers them the best chance of survival' (Dodge: this volume, Chapter 7). The effect of state collapse was thus to usher in 'an unpredictable fracturing of the polity':

> This unstable and violent process will be shaped by path dependencies built up before the collapse of the state and political entrepreneurs active afterwards. Local, sub-state and ethnic identities will emerge from the wreckage to provide channels for mobilisation and the immediate basis for political organisation.
>
> (Dodge: this volume, Chapter 7)

None of this is to suggest that ethno-sectarian politics, criminality and even cultures of violence cannot become, in Iraq as elsewhere, sources and significant drivers of post-war violence, but these cannot be understood in isolation; they are secondary to the disintegration of the state's coercive capacity, or to the manifest unwillingness of those who still wield coercive authority to provide security to the community *as a whole* (Dodge: this volume, Chapter 7). It was uncertainty and insecurity of the latter kind that provided the backdrop to Bosnia's most concentrated burst of post-war violence, sparked by the exodus of Serb civilians from parts of Sarajevo in 1996. The proliferation of militias and armed groups in eastern Congo over the past decade is also partly driven by the search for security and survival at the local level in conditions of state collapse. An important policy-implication here is that 'there is nothing inevitable about the unfolding ... process' of escalating violence (Dodge: this volume, Chapter

7). An external force – properly resourced, appropriately deployed and one that, additionally, enjoys legitimacy in the eyes of local actors (all, of course, big 'ifs') – can serve as a stabilizing factor and reduce levels of post-war violence.

State weakness and DDR. The second conclusion to emerge from the case material relates to those situations where the state has not dissolved entirely (as arguably it did in the extreme case of Iraq in 2003) but nonetheless remains contested and weak, retaining only 'a broken or at best partial monopoly on force' (Beaton: this volume, Chapter 3). In these circumstances, specifically when institutional weakness combines with a lack of legitimacy on the part of still-functioning or nascent institutions and a 'divided peace', the result is likely to be a violent competition for power and control of the coercive apparatus of the state. As Antonio Giustozzi stresses with reference to Afghanistan after 2001, the 'absence of a central monopoly of armed force' meant that political competition became 'distorted', allowing 'specialists in violence', strongmen and their militias, to capture state institutions, notably the Ministry of Defence and the Interior at the centre (always, unsurprisingly, a battleground in post-war conditions of divided peace) (Giustozzi: this volume, Chapter 8). It is because so many post-war environments share the aforementioned characteristics – contested legitimacy, a partial monopoly on force and weak institutions – that the management, design and implementation of DDR and, especially, SSR programmes become a critical 'point of vulnerability' in transitions from war to peace.

Again, the value of the case studies assembled is not simply to reaffirm this uncontested point. It is rather to show how existing knowledge on the subject among policy-makers may, in some respects, require modification in light of empirical evidence, while in others, it may be deepened by the addition of more nuanced and concrete detail. Two broad lessons in relation to DDR/SSR emerge from the cases and serve to illustrate the point.

First, where the process and arrangements for demobilizing and reintegrating regular and irregular soldiers have been fragmentary, incomplete and poorly conceived, the release of a large number of former combatants within a short space of time – typically young men, often with limited skills, ill-prepared for civilian life but sometimes expecting 'rewards' for hardships endured – has resulted in dramatic rises political and criminal violence. As Babo-Soares stresses in the case of East Timor, it was the treatment of veterans and failure of the government to meet their expectations that resulted in widespread violence and riots in December 2004. The examples of El Salvador in 1993 and, even more strikingly, Iraq in 2003–4, illustrate further how poorly sequenced, ill-advised and rapid demobilization can be catastrophic to immediate post-war stability and lead to spikes of violence.[6] In all these cases, it was the combination of mass and speed of demobilization in post-conflict settings that has proved so destabilizing: too often the ability of society and of local economies to absorb surplus soldiers has simply been overwhelmed by the speed with which a large number of men were released from military controls and discipline.

But this also means that one should not automatically assume that young, unemployed ex-soldiers are necessarily, almost as if by definition, prone to violence and *ipso facto* a source of post-war instability; a view that Wimpelmann Chaudhary dismisses as part of an unhelpful 'youth crisis narrative'. The problem with such a narrative, she persuasively argues, drawing on post-war Liberia where unemployment at war's end was estimated at 85 per cent, is that 'it risks pathologizing ex-combatants by abstracting them and any violence in which they might take part from the specific historical context' (Wimpelmann Chaudhary: this volume, Chapter 13). The policy implication is clear: there is no simple causal connection between levels of unemployment on the one hand, and violence and instability on the other. Unemployment per se – like poverty per se, as McNeish and López Rivera point out with reference to urban poverty and 'acts of violence' in Guatemala (this volume, Chapter 15) – is not a trigger for violence; if that were the case one would expect greater levels of violence than witnessed in many cases. This is not, of course, to suggest that tackling unemployment and poverty are not critical to the wider, long-term effort to build peace, only that a simplistic understanding of the relationship between primary and secondary drivers of violence can distract from an understanding of the sources of violence in the short to medium term.[7]

Second, threats to post-war stability come, above all, from formations and units associated with the security and military intelligence apparatuses of former belligerents. These come in many guises: special militias, 'self-defence' groups and paramilitary forces, customs bodies and border guards, police units and intelligence outfits of various kinds. In wartime their ranks swell and their influence grows, just as other law-enforcement bodies – judicial and correctional services – are likely to have become politicized, corrupted and unaccountable. Because members of the security sector have previously enjoyed a privileged status and, crucially, have had access to instruments of coercion, knowledge and economic resources, they have proved critically important to post-conflict stability. These formerly privileged groups and/or individuals, as examples from Guatemala, Afghanistan, Iraq and the DRC show, are critical for another reason: their members often assume a dominant role in organized crime in post-conflict states, though their motives for doing so are always difficult to distinguish from more overtly political agendas. Of the case studies assembled here Guatemala offers perhaps the clearest example of a post-war environment where the 'nature of peace' is indubitably marked by the survival of war-time repressive structures, with the 'continuing dominance of structures of counter-insurgency in the Guatemalan police and military' a continuing source of post-war violence (McNeish and Rivera: this volume, Chapter 15).

Strong states and post-war violence. As the previous discussion suggests, state weakness is not a function of capacity alone and indeed a major problem with much of the state-building literature is precisely its tendency to focus overwhelmingly on 'low capacity'. While state capacity is critical, it is how that capacity is reconstituted and what form the 'state' takes that has the more direct bearing on the prospects for post-war violence. In Spain, as Richards notes, 'the "purge" of society began instantly as a central element in the construction of the new authority', suggesting that a 'strong' state can also be a major source of post-war violence. As this and the much more recent violence accompanying the end of Sri Lanka's civil war make clear, the enforced stability of a 'victor's peace' can come at very high price in terms of violence and human suffering. The aforementioned considerations also suggest that 'state failure' should not be treated as some kind of mechanical process; treating failed states 'like broken machines, [which] can be repaired by good mechanics' or rather by social engineers (Ellis 2005: 6). This, of course, is also the fundamental insight offered by political economy approaches to violence and armed conflict.

Political economy of post-war violence

Those who search for the roots of post-war violence in the political economy approach to armed conflict are fundamentally concerned with the ways in which actors in conflict develop, over time, a vested interest and see functional utility in the continuation of violence. It is a perspective that focuses, not on 'state failure' per se, but on alternative, often highly local-ized, political and economic orders that emerge in response to the disinteg-ration and weakness of formal institutions (Berdal and Keen 1997: 797). Its starting point is the recognition, and demonstrable fact, that individuals and communities are not passive in the face of conflict but find ways of adapting to and coping with the realities of socio-economic dislocation, violence and uncertainty. The result of these adaptations by local and external actors is a distinctive political economy that persists into the post-war period. As in eastern Congo today, these are often underpinned by highly resilient war economies at the heart of which is often a 'perniciously symbiotic relationship between the economic activity and violence' (Jackson 2002: 527). In short, while new 'orders' emerge to fill the space vacated by the erosion of formal and properly functioning institutions, these are often illiberal, predatory and rest on incentive structures that reward violent behaviour. While political economies are dynamic and mutate in response to external and local pressures and influences, they cannot be abstracted from what is usually a distinctive historical context. In the case of Liberia, the political economy of transition needs to be under-stood against the country's 'particular history of state formation and a rent-based political economy' (Wimpelmann Chaudhary: this volume, Chapter 13). Likewise, post-civil war violence in Guatemala is *both* 'embedded in the country's history of war, but [is] also part of a new political economy of violence' (McNeish and Rivera: this volume, Chapter 15).

Stated in these terms, there is an obvious, almost matter-of-fact, quality to the assertion that confronting the sources of post-war violence requires an understanding of the political economy underpinning conflict. As Wimpelmann Chaudhary notes of Liberia, 'the main forms' of post-war violence 'are inseparable from a given political and economic context' (this volume, Chapter 15). It is an observation that holds true for all of the cases covered in the volume.

Several of those cases, however, also remind us that an emphasis on the economic agendas and motivations of actors can sometimes lead to a neglect of *politics* and *ideas* in the perpetuation of violence.[8] There are two aspects to this. First, in many cases ideology and political convictions are in fact the primary sources of violence, even though economic motives, social conflict, criminal and private agendas add fuel to the flames of violence. 'The litany of violence that accompanied the Redemption' in the American South, Beaton notes, was 'at every turn a political one, coloured by social and economic feuds, and fuelled by racial and ideological hatreds' (this volume, Chapter 3). And, while 'there was an important level of "privatization" of violence in Spain', Richards stresses that 'the rebels' ideological imperative, stated often enough before the rebellion took place and which informed the military modus operandi, should not be doubted' (this volume, Chapter 2).

Second, even in those cases were economic agendas do play an important role and help explain the dynamics of violence, as motive forces they may still be secondary to ideological and political drivers. A contemporary example of particular interest in this respect is provided by Kristian Berg Harpviken's careful study of the political trajectories of three warlords hailing from the Pashtun southeast in Afghanistan: Mullah Rocketi, Qari Baba and Haqqani Jalaluddin. None of these, he notes, was 'driven by economic concerns' as 'economic resources were only a means to an end' (this volume, Chapter 9). Indeed, 'ideologically, the differences among the three are marked', with Jalaluddin Haqqani – at the heart of the so-called Haqqani network – 'so ideologically committed that he challenges the conventional concept of the warlord as a non-ideological leader' (ibid.).

What are the wider policy implications of such findings? The focus on economic motives and drivers of violent behaviour has proved attractive to the policy community in part because it serves to simplify the complexity of conflict. The ongoing violence in eastern Congo now tends to be reported and discussed almost entirely in terms of the economic agendas that underpin it. One can see why this happens. To the policy community, the reduction of a conflict to a struggle over economic resources also reduces, at least in theory, the policy challenge. Subjective and elusive drivers of violence such as ethnicity, religion, ideas and a historical sense of grievance, are all by definition hard to address and do not provide obvious entry points for policy intervention. As the aforementioned examples illustrate, however, to ignore those factors also means that critical dimensions of relevance to the understanding of violence are neglected.

Policy-making for peacebuilding: the use of theory and importance of analysis

The limitations to the general approaches identified above are not meant to imply that comparing individual cases, employing analytical categories and making use of 'ideal' types amount to an exercise in futility. On the contrary, while the qualitative studies presented here make it clear that general or all-embracing explanations should always be treated sceptically, the examples underscore the central importance – also for those concerned with the making of policy – of trying to distinguish analytically between categories and motivations, and of looking both at the 'legacies of war' and the 'nature of peace'.

The point is well illustrated by the Michael Boyle's study of 'post-conflict' violence in Kosovo in the period between 1999 and 2001, that is, in the wake of NATO's bombing campaign against Yugoslavia and the subsequent establishment of UNMIK (UN Mission in Kosovo) in June 1999. In analysing two distinct waves of violence perpetrated by the Kosovo Liberation Army (UCK, *Ushtria Çlirimtare e Kosovës*) against Serbs and Roma in Kosovo, Boyle draws an analytical distinction between 'revenge' and 'reprisal' violence. The former is fundamentally motivated by emotions such grief and anger and is defined by Boyle as 'acts of expressive violence against a member of a targeted group with the intention of punishing them for a previous act of violence' (this volume, Chapter 5). By contrast, reprisal violence is politically driven and instrumental. It is an act of strategic violence designed, through the use of force, terror and intimidation, to alter 'the balance of power and resources' within a disputed piece of territory. It is the element of 'ruthless calculation of strategic advantage' involved that makes reprisal violence conceptually distinct from expressive or retributive forms of violence (Knudsen and Yassin: this volume, Chapter 6). The aim of such violence may be to consolidate territorial control, secure electoral advantage by 'cleansing' a territory of unwanted inhabitants or to secure economic benefits by looting assets, perhaps by obtaining control of natural resources, or by forcefully acquiring control of lucrative criminal franchises. The categories thus help us to unpack and differentiate the sources and dynamics of violence, not just in Kosovo but elsewhere. Samset's study of eastern Congo, for example, found that 'sexual violence reached high levels in part because it helped armed groups conquer and control territory'. It 'worked', she argues, 'as a "weapon of war" ... terrorizing communities into submission', all the while making it easier to control populations and engage in ruthless economic exploitation of acquired territory (Samset: this volume, Chapter 12). Similarly, much of the post-war violence in Bosnia between 1995 and 1997 – the targeting of returning refugees, attacks on religious symbols and monuments, violence and harassments at check-points – had a fundamental strategic objective.

Boyle is careful to add that these are *ideal* types and that violent acts in reality often fall between these categories (this volume, Chapter 5). This, however, is indeed partly the point: 'Recognizing these two types, even as heuristics for interpretation rather than as airtight conceptual categories, is essential for unpacking what is commonly called "revenge" in post-conflict states' (this volume, Chapter 5). This is of direct relevance to the way external actors – governments, influential politicians and peace builders on the ground – approach or seek to understand the sources of post-war violence; an 'understanding' that can feed into renewed or further violence if it is rigidly based on 'fixed notions about who is the victim and perpetrator and about what is natural following wartime atrocities' (Boyle: this volume, Chapter 5).

By presenting revenge attacks to the outside world as an 'understandable', partly inevitable or uncontrollable, response to past wrongs, local political entrepreneurs and violent actors in post-conflict settings will use the language of revenge (or what Boyle calls the 'metaphor of revenge') as a cover to mask more instrumental and strategic violence. This is what happened in Kosovo between 1999 and 2001 when the Kosovo Liberation Army 'rode the wave of revenge violence', enabling it to mask 'reprisal attacks within the real expressive violence at low cost and risk' (Boyle: this volume, Chapter 5).

The example suggests that the understanding of violence by outsiders as driven entirely by revenge – for whatever reason, including a sense of guilt for failure to confront the consequences of conflict earlier but also for more narrow calculations of interest – can end up encouraging further violence. And, indeed, the analytical differentiation drawn between strategic and reprisal violence is clearly relevant to the case of Rwanda and the state-sponsored violence that *followed* the genocide of 1994. As Trine Eide makes clear, the sense of guilt induced by the international community's passivity in the face of the genocide enabled the victorious Rwandan Patriotic Front (RPF) regime under Paul Kagame later to deflect attention away from acts of extreme violence against targets that included Hutu communities and individuals that could not plausibly be categorized as former *genocidaires* or as remnants of the *Interahamwe* (this volume, Chapter 14). The report by the UN high commissioner for human rights released in 2010 detailing the scale of post-genocide violence against Hutu groups in eastern Congo between 1994 and 2003, though challenged on details and not unproblematic, suggests that the scale of violence was very high.[9]

International context: outside intervention and post-war violence

The discussion thus far has sought to demonstrate how and why case studies of the kind brought together in the present volume offer important and policy-relevant insights to decision-makers concerned with peace-building. At the same time, it has stressed that specific findings will often only be applicable under a restrictive set of conditions and, therefore, general theories of post-war violence should always be treated with caution. Against this, it worth asking the basic question of whether and under what circumstances an international military and civilian peace-building presence – its size, mandate, composition – can make a difference to the effective regulation of post-war violence.

In February 2003, on the eve of the US-led invasion of Iraq, the then US Army Chief of Staff, Eric Shinseki, told congressional lawmakers that 'something on the order of several hundred thousand soldiers' would be needed to provide security in post-war Iraq. Angrily dismissed by Paul Wolfowitz at the time as an estimate that was 'wildly off the mark', it soon became clear that Shinseki had been prescient in his warnings about the need for a substantial footprint to deal with the likely challenges of post-invasion Iraq. There is little doubt that the rapid growth of criminal, insurgent and militia violence after the invasion in 2003 was linked to the fact that the US 'lacked the troop numbers to control the situation' (Dodge: this volume, Chapter 7).

The importance of adequate numbers to fill the security vacuum that is frequently a feature of post-war situations is reinforced by other cases covered in the present volume. As Beaton notes of post-bellum American South, the US Army frequently found itself 'overstretched and outnumbered' after 1865 and as a result was usually unable to prevent violence, looting and riots from occurring, even when there was the political commitment to do so. In the case of post-Dayton Bosnia – where General Shinseki at one stage served as commander of NATO's Stabilisation Force – the sheer scale of the outside military and civilian presence, some 60,000 soldiers aided by 2,000 police, deployed to implement Dayton plainly did contribute to controlling overt levels of violence. In Kosovo, Kosovo Force (KFOR) troop numbers reached nearly 50,000; a major force given the small size of the territory covered. Likewise, in Liberia, the international presence since 2003, with the UN Mission in Liberia (UNMIL) numbering close to 15,000, has been comparatively large given the size of the country and its population.

In all these cases, the size and deployment pattern of the outside force determine whether or not three sets of tasks can or cannot effectively be accomplished: providing basic security where local authority and governance structures lack the capacity and/or legitimacy to do so; providing psychological reassurance by signalling a long-term and credible commitment to the stabilization of a post-conflict environment; and, finally, preventing a 'climate of impunity' from taking hold.

But this is only part of the story and it would be entirely wrong to deduce from the case material assembled here that limiting post-war violence is simply a function of numbers. There are three major and intertwined reasons for this.

First, and most obviously, size and capability have to be matched by a mandate that enables force to be used effectively, along with the evident political willingness to do so. In 2001, KFOR, despite its considerable resources, failed to prevent a series of attacks against Serbian Orthodox churches and cemeteries in Kosovo by remnants of the Kosovo Liberation Army who were able, for a period, to 'operate with impunity', orchestrating violence to encourage cleansing of territory (Boyle: this volume, Chapter 5). Widespread riots and violence in the city of Mitrovica in March 2004 again showed that there is no automatic relationship between size and capabilities on paper and the ability to respond effectively to violence.[10] IFOR in Bosnia, notwithstanding the large number of highly trained and capable troops and police at its disposal, failed utterly to respond to the wave of inter-ethnic violence that accompanied the transfer of Sarajevo suburbs to federation control in 1996 (the irony of which was not lost on UN officials who for three years, with a far more exposed and a much less capable force than IFOR, had been charged with peacekeeping in the midst of an ongoing war). In both cases, a restrictive interpretation of the force's mandate, driven above all by a concern with protecting one's own force, limited the ability of outsiders to act decisively and, when required, *proactively* to fill the security gap. Even in the American South in the aftermath of the Civil War, where as noted above the US army presence was thin on the ground, rising violence was also a function of 'a *waning appetite* in the North to provide Federal enforcement for the Reconstruction project' (Beaton: this volume, Chapter 3 – my emphasis).

Second, strategic decisions taken by outsiders may themselves, and often have, served to fuel tensions and further expose fault-lines among former belligerents and conflict actors. In particular, attempts to impose solutions, especially if these run against the grain of local balances of power, often provoke a violent reaction or set the stage for renewed violence. Iraq again provides an extreme though illustrative example, with the initial effects of the US-led invasion on the state capacity profoundly exacerbated by an ill-conceived demobilization programme and far-reaching de-Ba'athification process. Elsewhere, as Suhrke perceptively notes of Afghanistan's 'divided peace' between 2001 and 2005, inconclusive political bargains at war's end combined with a weak yet contested central state fought over by actors with an undiminished 'capacity for armed action', all make for an inherently unstable peace. Uncertainty relating to the political end-state in post-war settings, in many cases aggravated by divisions *among* sponsors and contributors to a peacebuilding force, explains why even comparatively robust and well-equipped forces – notably KFOR in Kosovo – have struggled to control post-war violence. The wider point here is that in all of these, admittedly very different cases, one-sided focus on the need for 'adequate' numbers and resources to be deployed (which is often how debate is framed in troop-contributing countries) can unhelpfully distract attention away from what are more fundamental political problems at the root of post-war violence.[11]

The third reason why the presence of an outside force, its size and deployment pattern, may confound efforts to control post-war violence is one that, for a long time, was largely absent from Western policy discussions about *local* perceptions and effects of liberal interventionism. This is the tendency for any large and intrusive foreign presence, however well-intentioned, to stimulate nationalisms and fuel various forms of local resistance. Historical memories, suspicions about ulterior motives and a sense of humiliation and impotence can all combine to produce complex and contradictory reactions among locals to the peacebuilding efforts by outsiders. Western military involvement has amounted to more than just to 'prod the nerve of nationalism', and, many would argue, with predictable consequences (Orwell 1994: 315). Indeed, as Anatol Lieven (2009) has argued with characteristic forcefulness, in respect of Afghanistan given the 'history of Pashtun resistance to outside military conquest over the past 150 years, it would be nothing short of astonishing if a massive insurgency had not occurred'.[12] But even in those cases where local support for the initial intervention and the early peacebuilding activities is overwhelming, indigenous reactions and responses to foreign intervention can be highly ambivalent beneath the surface, especially when interventions turn out to be protracted and fail to deliver on public pronouncements. One example from the cases covered here is East Timor. Although international intervention under UN auspices in 1999 was critical to securing independence and freedom after 25 years of oppressive colonial rule by Indonesia, it did not take long before the Timorese began to 'view the UN as a second "occupier"' (Power 2008: 323).

The wider point here is not whether the nationalism provoked by outside intrusion is constructed or is appealing to a fictitious and mythical past. The key question as far as the post-war violence is concerned is whether those with a vested interest in continued violence succeed in appropriating and harnessing the power and symbols of nationalism to serve their own purposes. Their ability to do so depends in part on the actions of outsiders and the ability of the latter to satisfy, or rather manage, expectations for a 'peace dividend' – another 'point of vulnerability' in war to peace transitions flagged in the introduction to the book.

Concluding thoughts

There is final, broader consideration here, relating to the relationship between academic research on the one hand, and the making of policy and 'policy-relevance' on the other. The emphasis placed on the need for policy-makers to engage critically with post-war violence as a complex and multi-faceted phenomenon is not meant to imply that the process itself will necessarily result in clear-cut and obvious policy choices. The aim of the process, as the contributions to this volume illustrate so clearly, is just as much to highlight the risks, possible unintended consequences and unavoidable dilemmas, including of a moral kind, that face outsiders engaged in peace-building. The fact that this ought to induce caution and humility when contemplating involvement in post-war settings is, judging from the record of the recent past, not a bad thing. It also underscores the wider importance of the distinction that Jeremy Black (2004: 242), concerned specifically with the uses of history, draws between 'providing history as answers' and 'history as questions offered by scholars alive to the difficulties and dangers of predicting outcomes'.

Notes

1 This does not, of course, mean that any of the cases covered are unconcerned with what is elsewhere, though often loosely and without much precision, referred to as 'structural' violence. In some chapters, notably the study of Guatemala by John-Andrew McNeish and Oscar López Rivera, the connections between overt physical violence and its underlying structural causes are treated in more explicit fashion than in others. These connections are nonetheless an obvious and central concern throughout the book as whole.

2 'Rumsfeld blames Iraq problems on "pockets of dead-enders"' (2003) *USA Today*, 18 June. Online, available at: www.usatoday.com/news/world/iraq/2003–06–18-rumsfeld_x.htm (accessed 31 October 2010).

3 'Rwandan rebel arrested for Congo rapes' (2010) Reuters, 11 October. Online, available at: www.reuters.com/article/idUSTRE69A32R20101011.

4 This point was made to me separately by Yezid Sayigh.

5 For thoughtful contributions on the subject of the relationship between state-building and peacebuilding, see Charles T. Call and V. Wyeth (eds) (2008) *Building States to Build Peace*, Boulder, CO: Lynne Rienner.

6 On 23 May 2003, 'CPA Order Number 2' disbanded the Iraq Army with imme-
diate effect and without pay. See 'CPA Order No. 2, Dissolution of Entities', 23
May 2003. Online, available at: www.cpa-iraq.org/regulations/20030823_
CPAORD_2_Dissolution_of_Entities_with_Annex_A.pdf.

7 It is worth noting in this context that at least one detailed survey of ex-
combatants in Liberia found that their decisions to take up arms and join militias were more likely to have been motivated by security concerns than 'idleness
and poverty'. See Morten Bøås and Anne Hatløy (2008) 'Getting in, getting
out: militia membership and prospects for re-integration in post-war Liberia',
Journal of Modern African Studies, 46(1): 34.

8 That, of course, was one of the major problems with the 'greed thesis' of rebellion originally advanced by Paul Collier, to which the more subtle political
economy analysis was a response. See Mats Berdal and David Malone (eds.)
(2000) *Greed and Grievance: Economic Agendas in Civil War*, Boulder, CO: Lynne
Rienner; and Karen Ballentine and Jake Sherman (eds) (2003) *The Political
Economy of Armed Conflict: Beyond Greed and Grievance*, Boulder, CO: Lynne
Rienner.

9 'Leaked UN report accuses Rwanda of possible genocide in Congo' (2010)
Guardian, 26 August. Online, available at: www.guardian.co.uk/world/2010/
aug/26/un-report-rwanda-congo-hutus (accessed 2 November 2010).

10 On this occasion, NATO contingents, though they eventually quelled violence,
were initially too passive in response to Kosovo Albanian instigated violence.

11 There is a certain parallel here to the way in which counter-insurgency doctrine and thinking has recently been re-discovered and is now treated, in some
circles at any rate, as the solution to the challenges facing outsiders in
Afghanistan.

12 Lieven cites one activist of the anti-Taleban Awami National Party: 'The
problem is that most Pashtuns feel that to resist foreign occupation is part of
what it is to follow the Pashtun Way.'

Bibliography

Archer, Dana and Rosemary Gartner (1976) 'Violent acts and violent times: a comparative approach to post-war homicide rates', *American Sociological Review*, 41,
December.

Berdal, Mats and David Keen (1997) 'Violence and economic agendas in civil wars:
some policy implications', *Millennium: Journal of International Studies*, 26(3).

Black, Jeremy (2004) *Rethinking Military History*, London: Routledge.

Ellis, Stephen (2005) 'How to rebuild Africa', *Foreign Affairs*, September/October.

Jackson, Stephen (2002) 'Making a killing: criminality and coping in the Kivu war
economy', *African Review of Political Economy*, 29(93/94).

Judt, Tony (2007) *Postwar: A History of Europe since 1945*, London: Pimlico.

Lieven, Anatol (2009) 'The war in Afghanistan: its background and future prospects', *Conflict, Security and Development*, 9(3), October.

Orwell, George (1994) 'Notes on nationalism', in *The Penguin Essays of George
Orwell*, London: Penguin.

Power, Samantha (2008) *Chasing the Flame: Sergio Vieira de Mello and the Fight to Save
the World*, London: Penguin Books.

Preti, Alessandro (2002) 'Guatemala: violence in peacetime – a critical analysis of
the armed conflict and the peace process', *Disasters*, 26(2).

Ruff, Julius R. (2001) *Violence in Early Modern Europe, 1500–1800*, Cambridge: Cambridge University Press.

Spittaels, Steven and Filip Hilgert (2008) 'Mapping conflict motives: Eastern DRC', International Peace Information Service (IPIS), Antwerp: IPIS, 4 March. Online, available at: www.ipisresearch.be/maps/Oost-Congo/20080506_Mapping_ Eastern_DRC.pdf.

Steenkamp, Chrissie (2005) 'The Legacy of war: conceptualizing a 'culture of violence' to explain violence after peace accords', *Round Table*, 94(379), April.

Index

Lightning Source UK Ltd.
Milton Keynes UK
UKOW050630070712

195618UK00001B/130/P